Additional Praise for *The Catalysts*

"A riveting wake-up call for anyone who still thinks the global financial system is stable. With the clarity of a prosecutor and the urgency of a frontline witness, Amanda Wick unpacks how political chaos, technological disruption, and eroding trust are rewriting the rules of money and power. *The Catalysts* isn't just a book about finance—it's a roadmap to understanding the forces reshaping our world."

—THE HONORABLE STEPHANIE MURPHY, former US Representative from Florida

"As economic centers of gravity shift and global trust in institutions wavers, the US dollar faces new pressures on all sides. Amanda Wick offers a sharp analysis of these converging trends, exploring what's at stake for the dollar's dominance and the broader economic and political order. *The Catalysts* is essential reading for policymakers, investors, and anyone trying to make sense of a world in flux."

—DANTE DISPARTE, chief strategy officer and head of global policy, Circle

"Few people have seen the levers of financial and political power up close like Amanda Wick. In *The Catalysts*, she delivers a sober assessment of what ails the global financial system and the social and technological forces hastening its decline. A must-read for policymakers and students alike."

—CHRIS BRUMMER, Agnes Williams sesquicentennial professor of financial technology, Georgetown University Law Center

"An insightful book for our tumultuous times. Amanda Wick takes readers on a fascinating journey through the shifting landscape of global finance meets policy and technology with a storyteller's flair."

—SANDRA RO, CEO, Global Blockchain Business Council

"Look into the abyss of global financial and political threats today, and it's easy to be pessimistic about the future. Yet, despite ostensibly insurmountable challenges, *The Catalysts* offers solutions and a call to action: Not only *can* we embrace innovation while building a safer, more transparent, and more resilient financial system, we *must*."

—ARI REDBORD, **former federal prosecutor, US Treasury official, and global head of policy at TRM Labs**

"In *The Catalysts*, Amanda Wick tackles the complex interplay of technology, power, and economics with remarkable clarity. This book is a must-read for anyone seeking to comprehend the forces driving the new world financial order."

—HOCK LAI CHIA, **cochairman, Global Fintech Institute**

"*The Catalysts* rips the bandage off and exposes the wounds of Washington and the US financial system. Wick spares no one—Republicans, Democrats, Donald Trump, Big Tech—from blame. In the chaos lies a significant opportunity for policymakers, regulators, and politicians to fill the void of US leadership."

—BRODY MULLINS, **Pulitzer Prize–winning journalist and coauthor of** *The Wolves of K Street*

"Amanda Wick has written the right book at the right moment. Amidst seismic shifts in money, technology, culture, crime, and government, she helps us think ahead."

—JO ANN BAREFOOT, **founder and CEO, Alliance for Innovative Regulation**

"Regardless of your political conviction, Wick provides a unique, illuminating perspective on the perils and opportunities in the impending world financial order. Policymakers, finance leaders, and citizens who fail to read *The Catalysts* will be woefully unprepared for the massive changes rapidly approaching."

—RALF KUBLI, **independent board member, investor, executive**

"National borders and governments no longer constrain the movement of money. Against this backdrop, Wick has penned a comprehensive primer on creating a new, more secure world financial order—one that reinforces inclusivity, personal security, and access to essential services. If you want to shape the future of global finance for good, while securing our collective economic security, read *The Catalysts* now."

—**AMIT SHARMA, former US Treasury Department, CEO and founder, FinClusive**

"Blockchain technology has created global network effects that are connecting people with finance at levels never reached before. Malevolent actors are inevitable, and Amanda Wick brings her unique investigative skills to this threat. *The Catalysts* is a clarion call to arm law enforcement with the tools to protect users' property rights so the technology can continue to thrive among law-abiding users."

—**CAITLIN LONG, founder and CEO of Custodia Bank**

"Amanda Wick's call for principle-based policies and her refreshing restatement of the issues we face are both thought-provoking and inspiring. *The Catalysts* will move you."

—**DAVID G. W. BIRCH, author, advisor, and commentator on digital financial services**

THE CATALYSTS

THE CATALYSTS

THE ACCELERATING FORCES FORGING THE NEW WORLD FINANCIAL ORDER

AMANDA WICK

RACKET

Gilbert, AZ

Copyrighted Material

The Catalysts: The Accelerating Forces Forging the New World Financial Order

Copyright © 2025 by Amanda Wick. All rights reserved.

No part of this publication may be reproduced, stored in a retrieval system, or transmitted, in any form or by any means—electronic, mechanical, photocopying, recording, or otherwise—without prior written permission from the publisher, except for the inclusion of brief quotations in a review.

A human being wrote this book, not artificial intelligence. The author expressly prohibits any entity from using this publication to train AI technologies in text generation, including technologies capable of generating works in the same style or genre as this publication. The author reserves all rights to license uses of this work for generative AI training development of machine learning language mode.

For information about this title or to order other books or electronic media, contact the publisher:

Racket Publishing | www.racketpublishing.com

Hardcover ISBN: 9798990924222

Paperback ISBN: 9798990924208

ebook ISBN: 9798985814798

Audiobook ISBN: 9798990924215

Printed in the United States of America

Cover design: Jessica Angerstein

To my family and friends.
You are everything.

"The forest was shrinking but the trees kept voting for the axe,
for the axe was clever and convinced the trees that
because his handle was made of wood, he was one of them."
—*Proverb of Unknown Origin*

"Nothing in life is to be feared, it is only to be understood.
Now is the time to understand more, so that we may fear less."
—*Marie Curie*

CONTENTS

List of Figures and Tables xiv

PART I
HOW THE CURRENT WORLD FINANCIAL ORDER CAME TO BE

Introduction: America's Day of Reckoning 3
The Many Roles of Money 4
Shocking, but Not Surprising 4
Unprecedented Times and Events 4
A Unique Opportunity 6
Working for the Committee 8
Two Paths, One Destination 14
Why I Wrote This Book 16

Chapter 1: Money Matters 19
The Many Roles of Money 21
Money, Utility, and Value 25
Our Shaky Knowledge of Money 30
Threats to Money 32

Chapter 2: Money in Motion 37
Critical Concepts 41
Breaking Down Banks 43
Regulations and Regulatory Bodies 47
International Trade, Banking, and Payments 51
The Technologies: The Banking Rails in Brief 53

Chapter 3: US Financial Hegemony 57
Building the Weapon 61
Modernizing the World Financial System 64
Dollarization and US Dominance 69

Chapter 4: Constrained Capitalism 77
Antitrust Law 101 80
Examining America's Relationship With Antitrust Law 82
The Courts 89

PART II
THE CATALYSTS

Chapter 5: US Political and Economic Dysfunction 99
Unprecedented Political Dysfunction 104
The Erosion of the American Middle Class..105
The Clock Is Ticking on America's Economic Dominance 111

Chapter 6: The Rise of the Tech Nation-State 123
Public No More: The Privatization of Government Responsibilities 125
Causes, Considerations, and Accelerants 134
Consequences 139

Chapter 7: Financial Disintermediation.. 147
Assumptions and a Disclaimer 149
Blockchain and Distributed Ledger Technologies 150
Cryptocurrencies Enter the Mainstream 158
Asset Tokenization 161
Types of Tokens 163

Chapter 8: The Erosion of Institutional Trust and Democracy 169
Trust and Democracy..170
How We Got to Now..174
Ramifications..187

Chapter 9: The Contagion of Neo-Nationalism 191
Not Just England: Hypernationalism in Action 193
Economics 101 and the Benefits of Globalism...197
Understanding the Sudden Reemergence of Nationalism...........................200
The Ramifications of Neo-Nationalism...205

Chapter 10: New Innovation Hubs Bloom 211
The Changing Nature of Global Innovation 212
Why Innovation Hubs Are Emerging in New Locales................................218
How New Innovation Hubs Are Changing the Game................................229

Chapter 11: The War Over Transparency... 235
Transparency and Traditional Finance: A Quick Overview........................237
The Powerful Forces Opposing Financial Transparency.............................245
Where We Are Now..252

Chapter 12: Social Engineering 261
Modern Social Engineering Explained 263
Why Social Engineering Works So Well Today 267
Ramifications 278

PART III
THE NEW WORLD FINANCIAL ORDER

Chapter 13: The Catalysts Collide 289
Authoritarian Capitalism Overtakes Liberal Democracy 290
What Comes After Democratic Rule 290
The US Dollar Loses Dominance 294
The Global Financial System Forks 300
Dangerous Criminals Operate Freely at Home and Abroad 305
The Flight to Safety, Sanity, and Quality of Life 309

Chapter 14: Principles and Policies 313
Taking a Step Back 314
The Freedom of Speech 318
Crime, Enforcement, and the Right to Privacy 322
Government, Politics, and International Relations 326
Economics and Cautious Capitalism 332
Finally Crossing the Gender Chasm 340

Afterword: A Citizen's Call to Action 347
Knowledge Combats Fear 348
You're Not Alone 349
Together We Can Act 349

Thank-You 351
Bulk Purchases 359
About the Author 361
Bibliography 363
Endnotes 367
Index 405

List of Figures and Tables

Figure 1.1: Number of Credit Cards Per Person by Country as of 2022

Figure 1.2: The Diamond-Water Paradox

Figure 1.3: Consumer Surplus: A Transportation Example

Figure 1.4: Percentage of Adults Who Are Financially Literate as of 2014

Table 2.1: Partial List of Attendees at the NY Federal Reserve Meeting on September 12, 2008

Figure 2.1: Largest Banks in the World by Market Capitalization

Figure 2.2: Centralized Ledgers Make Third-Party Trust Essential

Figure 2.3: World Poverty Rate: Percentage of People Living on Less Than $5.50 USD Per Day

Figure 3.1: Number of Active Economic Sanctions as of April 2024

Figure 3.2: Groups That Iranians Hold Most Responsible for Sanctions

Figure 3.3: US Dollar Dominance as of March 8, 2025

Figure 3.4: Currency Composition of Official Foreign Exchange Reserves

Figure 3.5: New Additions to OFAC Sanctions Lists by Year

Table 4.1: Summary of Previous World Financial Order

Table 5.1: Partial Timeline of Donald Trump's Pandemic-Related Behavior

Figure 5.1: Satisfaction With Federal Response to COVID-19 From Feb. 25, 2020 to Apr. 1, 2020

Figure 5.2: Increases in Selected US Consumer Goods and Services From 2000 to 2023

Figure 5.3: US National Debt in Billions of Dollars (Rounded)

Figure 5.4: Total US Public Debt as Percent of Gross Domestic Product

Figure 5.5: Tweet From House Speaker Kevin McCarthy

Figure 6.1 US Post-Tax Corporate Profits in Trillions of USD

Figure 7.1: Bitcoin P2P Decentralized Digital Ledger

Figure 8.1: Perceptions of Competency and Ethics for Government vs. Business

Figure 8.2: Government Incompetence in Regulating Emerging Innovations

Figure 9.1: Voting Percentage for Past Two French Presidential Elections

Figure 9.2: World Gross Domestic Product From 1960 to 2022

Figure 10.1: Changes in the Venture Capital Landscape

Figure 10.2: Global Startup Ecosystem Ranking—Summary of Top Thirty by Region

Figure 10.3: Singapore Foreign Direct Investment From 1970 to 2023 (Billions, USD)

Figure 10.4: Top Unicorns in Singapore as of 2024 (Billions, USD)

Figure 11.1: Growth of Private Equity

Figure 11.2: Annual Number of Ransomware Attempts Worldwide From 2017 to 2023

Table 12.1: Partial Results of 2022 YouPoll Survey

Table 13.1: Summary of New World Financial Order

PART I

HOW THE CURRENT WORLD FINANCIAL ORDER CAME TO BE

INTRODUCTION
AMERICA'S DAY OF RECKONING

> "Look back over the past, with its changing empires that rose and fell, and you can foresee the future, too."
>
> —*Marcus Aurelius*

In the early afternoon of January 6, 2021, I was speaking to some professional colleagues on a routine Zoom call. Suddenly, my phone started blowing up. I briefly diverted my attention to read a series of scary text messages. "Please stay in your house." "Are you safe?" I was perplexed, at least until I read a particularly ominous one. "Capitol overthrown."

Flabbergasted, I turned on the television but couldn't believe what I was seeing. Hundreds of enraged Donald Trump supporters were storming the US Capitol building in Washington, DC.

THE CATALYSTS

Shocking, but Not Surprising

American politics in the months preceding the 2020 election was nothing short of surreal. Case in point: On August 17, 2020, Trump said, "The only way we're going to lose this election is if the election is rigged."[1] Since his November defeat, he had dangerously doubled down and repeatedly made erroneous and public claims of massive voter fraud.

Trump's claims weren't falling on deaf ears. Instead, his deluge of misinformation and lies managed to convince one-third of the country that the Democrats had stolen the safest election in American history.[2] Die-hard Trump supporters flooded social media with terrifying memes, such as "By Bullet or Ballot, Restoration of the Republic Is Coming." (Ultimately, Facebook, Twitter, and YouTube would suspend or temporarily ban the soon-to-be ex-president from their platforms.[3])

Trump's behavior had also become perceptibly more erratic. For example, on November 17 that year, he tweeted that he'd fired Chris Krebs, chief of the Cybersecurity and Infrastructure Security Agency (CISA). CISA and several other agencies responsible for election safety contradicted Trump's claims. In their words, the 2020 election was the "most secure" in US history.[4]

Unprecedented Times and Events

As January 6 approached, Trump upped the ante. His claims intensified, and his team bombarded supporters with as many as twenty-five emails per day.[5] Remarkably, three of his four biggest fundraising days took place after he *lost*.[6] Trump and his team quickly realized that perpetuating the stolen election narrative was their most profitable fundraising technique. Between the election and January 6, Trump supporters donated more than a quarter of a billion dollars to an "Official Election Defense Fund" that didn't even exist.[7] While raking in roughly $250 million,[8] the world watched in shock as the head of the most powerful democracy was hell-bent on remaining in office, election results, the will of the people, facts, and the law be damned. Something had to give.

4

Anything but Normal

Until that moment in American history, the transfer of power from one administration to another had been peaceful. The results may have involved litigation, but once decided, the start of the next administration had always been a fait accompli.[9]

Vice President Mike Pence only needed to certify the election results—something that every one of his forty-four predecessors did without incident. Instead, a mere seven blocks from my apartment, an irate mob of American citizens was determined to prevent Pence from carrying out these duties.

On that fateful January afternoon, I excused myself from the call and quickly turned on my television. Like millions of Americans, I watched with horror as rioters climbed the gates and scaffolding surrounding the Capitol. Their attack quickly overwhelmed the small cadre of Capitol police officers. Subsequent videos showed the attackers horrifyingly chanting, "Hang Mike Pence."[10] Even worse, later reports confirmed that these self-anointed patriots roamed the halls planning to capture and kill politicians. Ultimately, five people died in the rampage.[11] Any reasonable historian would be hard-pressed to find a lower point in American history.

The Wake-Up Call That Wasn't

In the weeks following that horrific and historic day, I remained hopeful that the US would learn an invaluable lesson. After all, Albert Einstein reportedly said, "In the midst of every crisis, lies great opportunity." Surely, these unprecedented events would serve as the wake-up call America and its leaders so sorely needed. The country's current path was both figuratively and *literally* leading to its destruction. If January 6 didn't crystallize American fissures and spur profound changes, what would?

Unfortunately, a surprising thing happened in the months that followed. Far-right American politicians, institutions, and media outlets downplayed the attack. The same folks who routinely screamed "Blue Lives Matter"*

---

* Launched in 2014 as a countermovement to Black Lives Matter.

conveniently ignored Brian Sicknick, the US Capitol police officer who died from riot-induced injuries.[12] Far too many leaders and citizens merely wanted to pretend that the insurrection didn't even happen, never mind ask why it did. Perhaps most appallingly, a bevy of prominent Republican politicians tried to whitewash it or rebrand January 6 as a "righteous protest."[13] Sadly, many of their constituents accepted their shameful rationalizations. As a nation, America had reached rock bottom.

A Unique Opportunity

My life then took an unexpected turn. A friend asked if I would advise the House Select Committee Investigating the January 6th Attack on the US Capitol on how to investigate whether cryptocurrency had funded the incident. I agreed, but during the call, Chief Investigative Counsel Tim Heaphy unexpectedly asked if I'd be willing to quit my current job and lead the entire financial investigation. In this role, I'd serve as senior investigative counsel, examining all financial aspects of the incident, including the funding of the protest and subsequent attack, Trump's fundraising off the stolen election claims, and even the funding patterns of the right-wing extremist groups involved in planning the insurrection. If I accepted it, I'd play a much greater role in the aftermath than I could have possibly imagined.

Why me?

By way of background, I'd spent most of my career as a civil servant at the US Department of Justice (DOJ). Most recently as a line prosecutor,* I investigated money laundering and other financial crimes. Since 2012, my cases had involved cryptocurrencies in addition to traditional financial instruments, such as cash and wire transfers. As it turned out, the committee strongly suspected that the insurrectionists had received funding

---

* The term *line prosecutor* traditionally refers to those in the office who charge and try cases. Contrast them with *lead prosecutors*: those who may set the overall goals of the office or oversee the work of line prosecutors to ensure their discretion furthers their offices' policies. See https://tinyurl.com/the-cat-lp for more information.

from sources outside of the traditional finance system. Its leadership needed someone with essential experience and expertise.[14]

Only a handful of people in the country possessed the skills to conduct the requisite investigation. I'd worked with most of them and knew they couldn't afford the pay cut that came with working for the House of Representatives.[15]

Although I was on the fence about joining the committee, I decided to proceed with the interview process.

Interviews and Politics

During my unexpected, impromptu interview, the committee's staff director told us that the hiring process was deliberately nonpartisan; he didn't even want to know our party affiliations, if any. Our mission required us to follow the facts *wherever* they led.

These claims left me skeptical, though. I knew from experience that *everything* was political on Capitol Hill. The post-insurrection words and actions of Republican leadership and right-wing media did nothing to disabuse me of that notion. If anything, they only confirmed my deepest fears. Politicians on both sides were exacerbating the situation, and the mood in Washington was becoming even more toxic.

As a career prosecutor* who identified as an Independent voter, I was unaccustomed to working in a highly politicized environment; my role at the DOJ was nonpartisan by design and by law.[16]

I'd always respected and observed those strictures. In a word, I was torn. The committee's staff director demanded a decision in thirty-two hours, and time was quickly running out.

A Fateful Decision

I called one of my mentors, a former high-profile political appointee. I explained my situation and asked her point-blank: Should I take the job?

---

* The term *career* usually refers to government employees hired through a competitive process—not appointed based on political affiliation.

Her response was illuminating: "Whether you've ever chosen a political party or not, this job will effectively choose one for you." Sage words, to be sure, but as an Independent, I was still conflicted. Republicans alone weren't responsible for America's sad events. Democrats also shouldered their fair share of the burden. (Chapter 5 delves deeper into the profound state of American political dysfunction and its ramifications.)

Ultimately, I thought about the prime movers that have driven my career: my twin passions for public service and justice. Much to my father's dismay, those passions have always won out over my pragmatism and desire for a comfortable retirement. I accepted the job with the committee and started my new position in October 2021.

Working for the Committee

I began my new position optimistic about what the committee and I could do. Together, we could pull America back from the edge of the abyss. After all, the US had rallied together after 9/11. We're the only country to have landed a human being on the moon. We'd faced—and overcome—great challenges before. That trait has arguably defined the United States of America since its inception. During his inaugural address on January 20, 1993, Bill Clinton famously said, "There is nothing wrong with America that cannot be cured by what is right with America." In my new role, I'd play an active part in helping the US to course-correct.

What If We Could Fix America?

During my time on the committee, I worked closely with Jamie Raskin, a Democratic representative from Maryland's eighth congressional district since 2017. Before holding public office, he served as a brilliant law professor at American University for a quarter-century. He still serves on its faculty as a professor emeritus today.

As an elected official, Raskin is above reproach. It's no overstatement to call him the epitome of what the founding fathers envisioned when they created the concept of a representative democracy led by the people. In other words, he's the embodiment of the word *statesman*, truly believing in improving the system. Working with him on the committee reaffirmed my faith in America's imperfect union.

On the beautiful Tuesday morning of September 27, 2022, Rep. Raskin and I were in his office furiously drafting a new script for the committee's ninth hearing. Along with the rest of the members and many staff, we'd held a dress rehearsal the previous day. Neither Raskin nor I had written that version of the script, however.

That job fell to Liz Cheney, a powerful Republican Wyoming congresswoman from 2017 to 2023. (At one point, she held the third-highest position in the House Republican leadership.) About a month before I joined the committee, Democrats had appointed her the vice chairwoman of the January 6 panel.[17] Her presence and the aegis of bipartisanship would preempt—or at least minimize—right-wing claims that the committee's work was nothing more than a political witch hunt. In fact, under her de facto leadership, they were anything but.

Rep. Cheney didn't so much as edit the script's first draft; she napalmed it. She ripped the guts out of it, replacing our new content with a boring, anodyne, and repetitive facsimile. She cut anything that shifted too much attention or blame away from Trump.

Her priority had become clear over the course of the hearings: Blame Trump while limiting alienation of her voter base when she ran for future office as a true Conservative Republican. (I may be politically independent, but I'm not naive.)

During the dress rehearsal, I watched the faces of key committee members and read the room: Someone would need to burn the midnight oil. Our previous eight hearings had yielded plenty of revelations. We needed to keep the momentum going and build on our previous successes. All committee members and staff knew the consequences of a flop. No one needed to remind us that we were working under an intense political microscope and, more importantly, that our actions impacted the fate of a nation.

THE CATALYSTS

We needed to rewrite Cheney's script to prevent a trainwreck. That fell to Congressman Raskin and me, and we sat together in his office the next day to revise the hearing script. We couldn't leave until we sent the proposed final version to the committee's leadership for final review and approval.

Raskin and I spent several hours adding evidence back into the script that Rep. Cheney had previously left on the cutting-room floor. First, Raskin was—and remains to this day—passionate about disclosing the rise in violent right-wing extremism, white Christian nationalism, and the clear and present danger they present to America. (Chapter 8 covers how a new wave of nationalism is impacting countries, their economies, and the world financial order.)

Second, social media and tech companies were complicit in the events of January 6. What's more, they present an ongoing weapon for disaffected citizens to coordinate future attacks. A few examples will illustrate this point.

Facebook didn't remove the inflammatory content from the notorious "Stop the Steal" group until a full sixty-nine days *after* the November election.[18] For its part, customer relationship management titan Salesforce knowingly allowed the Trump team to send millions of emails to its subscribers to condone violence and spread election misinformation. The company ignored numerous external complaints and internal policy violations until a brave employee unilaterally shut it all down when the attack started. After January 6, the company finally took credit for the employee's action,[19] but it was too little, too late. Against the advice of its internal "Abuse Desk,"* Salesforce had already given Trump's team the tools it needed to send "red meat" messages† that would encourage violence and defraud millions of donors.[20] (Chapter 6 discusses the considerable risks that largely unregulated tech companies present. For now, suffice it to say that they collect massive amounts of personal data that bad actors and governments can use and access to manipulate people with impunity.)

---

* This was Salesforce's moniker for its internal privacy and abuse management team. It worked to prevent customers from using its platform to commit fraud and abuse.

† Politicians often use these messages to whip their audiences into a frenzy.

Whistleblowers had bravely come forward when their employers failed to sound the alarm. Time and time again, these employees had flagged violent rhetoric indicating that something dangerous would happen on January 6. Rep. Raskin was certainly willing to discuss the blame Donald Trump rightly deserved, but the former's role obligated him to go deeper. Raskin recognized the need to broach massive and systemic problems that Trump and his minions exploited when they summoned his followers to the Capitol and then marched on it.

Why Our Hands Were Tied

Raskin's commitment to the truth was inspiring and unwavering. He made it easier for me to do my job: in this case, to write the script and contribute pertinent facts and evidence. We needed to tell the story of what really led up to and caused the attack on January 6. It was far too important to ignore. At the same time, though, I began to realize that we were fighting an uphill battle. Our time finalizing that draft was ultimately an exercise in futility.

The messy politics of the situation would ultimately yield little fruit. Cheney's *formal* title on the committee was vice chair. In practice, though, she ran it. Cheney made many of the critical decisions, sometimes unilaterally, and was more involved than any other member. Pelosi had clearly struck some type of Faustian deal with Cheney for her participation: The committee and its report could assign blame to the former president—and no one else on the right. In Cheney's overly simplified view of things, Donald Trump—and Donald Trump alone—singlehandedly caused the January 6 attack. End of story.

But let's be clear about two undeniable facts. First, without Cheney's time, attention, and sometimes dictatorial leadership, we wouldn't have had the success we did in the limited time we had. Her stewardship often combated staggering mismanagement. Consequently, my feelings toward her will always remain torn among immense gratitude, frustration, and anger.

THE CATALYSTS

Second, the attack wouldn't have happened without Donald Trump.* However, he was by no means the *only* cause. Put differently, his actions were necessary but insufficient for the insurrection to take place. More broadly, our investigation found that he was the symptom of a larger disease that had been metastasizing for *decades*.

America: Myth vs. Reality

Before that final hearing was to occur on September 28, I was exhausted. I'd been constantly answering the incessant pings on my phone. Everyone was asking for the final script's status. We were working as fast as we could. Rep. Raskin had so many ideas, each of which needed accurate yet delicate words to flesh out. As the clock ticked away, our team's television producers complained about the time needed to load the script into the teleprompter and how close we were cutting it. My boss continued to deluge my phone with a near-constant stream of messages.

Suddenly, the messages stopped. Rep. Raskin received a text and looked down to read it.

"Bennie† just postponed the hearing," he said. "They're calling it because of the hurricane."

Was this a joke? I laughed out loud. My parents lived directly in the path of Hurricane Ian, and we'd been anxiously tracking it for days. Florida had been calling for evacuations because of the anticipated damage. Between the hearing and worrying about my folks, I'd bitten every nail off my fingers. Oddly, no one except Rep. Stephanie Murphy, a House Democrat from Florida's Seventh District,‡ had cared about Ian before. Things suddenly changed, though, when it became abundantly clear that massive

---

* Lawyers often refer to this as a *but-for cause*. Cornell University's Law School sums it up as follows: It's "sometimes used interchangeably with actual cause, is a necessary element for both liability in civil cases and a guilty verdict under much of criminal law." For more information, see https://tinyurl.com/the-cat-cu.

† Bennie was shorthand for the Chairman of the Committee, Bennie G. Thompson, a Missouri Democrat.

‡ Representative Murphy's district included Orlando and other parts of central Florida; given the capricious path of hurricanes, she'd been monitoring the storm's path closely.

damage would consume a media cycle far more than a congressional hearing presenting a paucity of new evidence.

I asked Rep. Raskin about the new hearing date, but he couldn't provide an answer. He hoped that it would take place in a few days, yet given the likely fallout from the hurricane, no one could say. Maybe sometime in October? Raskin asked if I could stay on until the hearing was rescheduled. I paused and thought before carefully responding.

> Mr. Raskin, I have been building a nonprofit in my spare time for over a year. When I was hired, we were told this would be finished by Labor Day, and I planned my life around that. Thanks to delays at the Ethics Committee,* I had to invest several thousand dollars of my own money to launch the association with three events that are scheduled next week in San Jose, DC, and New York. But if you tell me that you're going to march down the hall, demand to speak to Pelosi, and fight the fight needed to override Liz's veto and get all this evidence we just spent seven hours writing about back into the hearing script, then I will postpone everything in my life to stay on and do this hearing with you. Are you telling me that's what will happen?

He didn't immediately answer the question, but his demeanor said everything. I'll never forget what happened next. He looked me directly in the eyes and earnestly said, "You call me if you *ever* need help with that nonprofit." I don't recall if he hugged me afterward, though given his warmth, I'd be shocked if he didn't. I do remember walking out of his office, returning to mine, and wrapping everything up by the end of that week.

I've never had a more enlightening conversation with anyone in my life. It shined a light on one of the most broken aspects of the American political system. At that time, Rep. Raskin was running to become the top Democrat on the House Committee on Oversight and Reform. To be sure, he had

---

* Because I qualified as senior staff, House rules significantly hampered my ability to raise money to start a nonprofit without obtaining a solicitation waiver from the Committee on Ethics. Delays in that office meant that I couldn't obtain it in time.

strong feelings about what needed to be in our committee hearings. Sadly, they couldn't outweigh his stronger needs:

- To "go along to get along" with party politics in Washington, DC.
- To remain in the good graces of his party's leadership.

No one can credibly blame Raskin for that troubling aspect of US democracy. It's a feature of contemporary America, not a bug. As H. L. Mencken said, "The cure for the evils of democracy is more democracy."

The ninth hearing was held on October 13, 2022. On December 22, the committee released its final report. Although I'd guessed what would—and what *would not*—be inside, I still had to read it. As expected, it omitted some of our most important findings. I was sad, horrified, and unsurprised.

Two Paths, One Destination

In the following year, I healed by seeing my nonprofit come to life. The Association for Women in Cryptocurrency seeks to build a global network of supportive professionals in the cryptocurrency, blockchain, and web3 industries who advocate for women's equal inclusion in the future of digital finance and related technology. Simultaneously, I traveled extensively around the globe, speaking at fintech* conferences on dynamic topics, including:

- The future of digital assets.
- The interplay between government regulation and innovation.
- The ramifications if those two forces collide, as opposed to complementing each other.

At first, I considered my year on the committee an unrelated tangent—a year of government service that was necessary but irrelevant. As it turns out, I couldn't have been more wrong. Ironically, I can thank the unlikeliest of

---

* *Fintech* is shorthand for *financial technology*, an industry that fuses modern technology with financial services.

sources for that epiphany: a former White House communications director whom I'll decline to name here.

In May 2023, I was sitting in the audience of Blockchain Ireland, a fantastic conference showcasing the amazing work people are doing there. It brings thought leaders from around the world to collaborate and discuss the future of blockchain technology.

The speaker addressed the audience virtually via Zoom. He discussed his optimism for how America would continue to lead the nascent digital asset industry. (Yes, you read that correctly.)

Upon finishing, he took a few questions from the audience. Importantly, he could hear us but not see us. I raised my hand and asked a question that went something like this:

> In America, we have a major regulator who would rather enforce the industry out of existence than admit he doesn't have the vision to regulate it responsibly. We have a senator whose self-interest led her to hypocritically create an "army" against the very technology that could achieve her self-proclaimed goal of democratizing finance. We have a dollar that loses more and more dominance every day, and political divisiveness and extremism on both sides are literally destroying us from within. Given the lack of regulatory clarity in America, which shows no signs of improvement anytime soon, what is it that gives you your optimism that America will be a leader in digital assets? Besides unbridled, unmerited American exceptionalism, what gives you that much hope? Because I could really use whatever you're seeing that I'm not.

I finished the question, and you could hear a pin drop in the auditorium. He could tell from my accent that I was American. His circuitous, tangential answer baffled and horrified the mostly Irish audience. For five meandering minutes, he politely mansplained the history of the US national debt and how to eliminate it in a mere ten to fifteen years. (Oddly, he was sanguine that the US could do it sooner.)

As he rambled, he also name-dropped. He assured everyone that he still frequently spoke with then-US House Speaker Kevin McCarthy and some of the most important individuals in the Republican party (all of whom are now gone). It wasn't clear *what* he was discussing with them—other than some type of vague debt-reduction strategy. Rest assured, though, he was talking to all the right people.

And at that moment, everyone in the room singularly understood one thing: The days of the US empire were coming to an end. It was only a question of when.

Why I Wrote This Book

People have penned entire lengthy tomes on specific problems with American politics:

- Politicians' extensive and alarming levels of self-interest and self-dealing.
- The failure of its campaign finance laws to prevent the wholesale purchase of our issues and politicians.
- The significant decline in the intelligence and intellect of its elected officials.

Each issue in and of itself is both formidable and scary. I sat watching a former White House communications director reduce America's profound problems to *debt* while providing unhelpful advice on how to address even that single issue. At that point, the gravity of the situation quickly came into focus. What's worse, he's no lone duck. I fear that a dangerously high percentage of US policymakers, regulators, and politicians—especially Democrats—lack a cogent plan for remaining globally competitive in a rapidly changing world of digital finance, decentralization, and loss of dollar dominance.

America Is Broken

After many of my talks, fellow Americans have told me that I'm being pessimistic. They point to our country's storied history. They say that the US has *always* recovered from a wide array of crises; it routinely meets adversity head-on and gets up off the mat. But I know from personal experience that it doesn't. The attack on January 6 and its fallout represent something much bigger: America has fallen, and it can't get up.

Unfortunately, many, if not most, Americans and America's leaders are in a deep state of denial. Their rose-colored viewpoint includes the misguided beliefs that:

- The country will magically get its act together.
- It will fix its broken legislative and executive branches led by two even more broken political parties.
- Our politics will suddenly become less toxic and tribal.
- We'll make the essential repairs America needs to have a chance at remaining competitive and possibly saving its democracy.

Absent a horrible crisis on par with 9/11, none of these scenarios will happen. And, like it or not, that bodes well for policy leaders in other nations looking to capitalize on America's decline in a multipolar world.

What to Expect

The Catalysts is no *cri de coeur* about fixing America; plenty of excellent, unfollowed road maps are already on the shelves. Rather, it's an ambitious yet realistic text about the powerful, inexorable forces that are changing the world as we know it, including America's decline. They include the ascension and popularity of cryptocurrencies, decentralized finance, the decline in institutional trust, the rise of nationalism, the consequences of Big Tech gone wild, and the birth of innovation hubs. (Part II delves into each of them.) Together, they're forging a new, vastly different world financial order.

The Catalysts answers audacious questions such as these:

- What will this new, uncertain financial system look like?
- What are the rules?
- Where are the minefields and opportunities?
- What are the most intelligent policies to effect?
- How can a nation, its elected officials, a nongovernmental organization, or a think tank navigate this frequently chaotic milieu?

In the following pages, you'll find dozens of examples, case studies, and visuals that coalesce into a single, unifying thesis. This book connects the dots, especially with what first might appear to be discrete trends and unrelated topics. I've included plenty of analysis, synthesis, and, yes, some predictions on how these key trends play out.

Intended (and Unintended) Audiences

International policymakers and advisors will benefit from the knowledge dispensed in this book. Ditto for policy wonks at international corporations, non-governmental organizations (NGOs), and think tanks. Although I've primarily written *The Catalysts* for policymakers, it benefits people who feel a sense of impending dread that they can't quite articulate. They're right: Massive change is coming quickly—and from unseen forces.

I don't profess to have a crystal ball. No one does. With so many moving parts, I won't be able to predict the future tomorrow, much less a decade down the road. Instead, *The Catalysts* sheds light on the world's financial stage and how seemingly separate forces act in concert. It analyzes what's really happening, why, and what policy professionals can do to best position their constituents for the vastly different world that lies ahead.

Let's get started.

CHAPTER 1

MONEY MATTERS

OUR WORLD HAS LONG REVOLVED AROUND A MADE-UP
MECHANISM UNBACKED BY HARD ASSETS.

> "Money often costs too much."
> —*Ralph Waldo Emerson*

In June 2012, the London-based British Museum opened a new and decidedly commercial exhibit. You might even call it unique. Any expecting to see the works of Francis Bacon or William Hogarth would be disappointed.

No, this gallery celebrated the vibrant, four-millennia history of money. From the museum's website:

> The history of money can be traced back more than 4,000 years.
>
> During this time, money has taken many different forms, from coins to banknotes, shells to mobile phone payments.

THE CATALYSTS

This gallery displays the history of money around the world. From the earliest evidence to the latest developments in digital technology, money has been an important part of human societies. Looking at the history of money gives us a way to understand the history of the world.[1]

Here are a few of the display's most notable highlights, presented in ascending chronological order:

- An electrum stater, otherwise known as an ancient Greek coin.
- Arabian and African cowrie shells.
- A fourteenth-century Chinese Ming banknote.
- A 1903 UK penny etched with the words *Votes for Women*. That's no accident. In the early twentieth century, protestors intentionally defaced pennies to promote the suffragette cause. (As we'll see throughout this book, money has often reflected and influenced policies and politics.)*

The British Museum visually demonstrated two essential facts about money. First, money is fundamentally an imaginary construct. In the preface of his 2014 book *Money: The True Story of a Made-Up Thing*, Jacob Goldstein calls it a *shared fiction*. He's not wrong.

Second, money always changes. That is, it's nothing if not dynamic. Remarkably, depending upon where you lived and when at each point over the past four millennia, each of these trinkets on display—and plenty more not included in the exhibit—would have allowed you to purchase valuable goods and services at different points in history.

Put differently, the appearance and underpinnings of money have morphed considerably over time—a trend that won't abate anytime soon. Make no mistake: Money and how we interact with it are changing as I write these words. A few diverse examples will illustrate my point.

---

* See https://tinyurl.com/the-cat-money-museum to view highlights of the exhibit online.

Citing declining use, low purchasing power, and high production costs, governments around the world are ceasing the production of low-denomination coins. The Bahamas halted production of 1 cent in 2020.[2] In 1990, Finland stopped making 1, 5, and 20 *penniä*.[3] Expect more countries to follow suit in the coming years.

The halcyon days of the physical check have long passed. What used to be "the most widely used noncash payment method in the United States"[4] is disappearing. Think about it. Have you ever seen a teenager take out a checkbook?

In Brazil in May 2022, Mastercard launched a retail biometrics pilot program. Rather than taking out their phones or twisting their wrists to reveal their watches at the counter, some Brazilians now use their faces and even their veins to authenticate themselves.[5]

Merchants are increasingly refusing to accept customers' cash at the time of checkout.[6] For this reason, people are having to find reverse automated teller machines (ATMs) or cash-to-card kiosks to complete their purchases. These contraptions allow individuals to convert their bills, coins, and credit or debit card funds into prepaid, digital cards. (And, yes, they charge transaction fees for the privilege.)

This chapter examines money. In so doing, it also looks at several adjacent concepts, including payments, commerce, inflation, and value.

The Many Roles of Money

Money's form has changed significantly over time. Regardless of time and location, however, certain precepts have remained remarkably constant. Any economics and finance textbook worth its salt should describe the main functions of money. Let's briefly cover them.

Store of Value

First and arguably most importantly, money serves as a store of value. Whether you cash your paycheck or put it in the bank, it lets you pay your mortgage, car loan, student debt loan, or credit card bill. Thanks to money, you can fulfill your current needs and save for future ones.

Prior to the advent of money, barter ruled the day. Farmer A sought to trade his bushel of corn for Farmer B's bag of rice. A shoe shiner might offer his services to a barber.

To state the obvious, the practice wasn't terribly efficient. (Interestingly, the rise of collaborative consumption has resurrected the practice in recent years, especially among environmentally conscious millennials.) By serving as a commonly accepted medium of exchange, money has obviated bartering. Because of it, we no longer need to swap rice for corn, vintage cars for new computers, and compact discs for sneakers. At a higher level, nations can operate their economies more efficiently and raise the standard of living for future generations. Everybody wins.

Unit of Account

Money also solves a related problem by providing a unit of account, a common denominator to value disparate goods and services. We may *value* items differently, but money lets us easily compare apples and oranges. We can measure the value of myriad purchasing decisions and make ones that are theoretically in our best interests. (More on value later in this chapter.)

Without a proper and legitimate unit of account, each of the following would be far more difficult, if not impossible:

- Conducting international trade.
- Buying and selling stocks in a publicly traded company.
- Any company generating accurate and legally binding reports from accounting systems, including profit-and-loss (P&L) statements and trial balances.

In short, if money didn't serve as a widely accepted unit of account, our current world would look very different.

MONEY MATTERS

Form of Payment

Next, in many countries, money serves as a legally recognized form of payment. Legally speaking, it settles an outstanding debt for goods and services. Say that you treat yourself and your significant other to a delicious six-course meal at La Tour d'Argent, arguably Paris's most luxurious restaurant. The bill is €800, which means you now legally owe the restaurant that amount of money. You can pay in cash or via credit card, but that's not all. If the manager is willing to accept a flattering Instagram post in lieu of proper payment, that will suffice. Legally speaking, you're now free of your financial obligation.

The Evolving Nature of Payment Methods

Admittedly, the credit card may not represent a perfect proxy for hard currency,* although brick-and-mortar establishments have long let customers pay their bills with Visa cards and cash.

Still, *how* we pay resembles the physical manifestation of money; both have evolved considerably over time. Stater, shells, and other ancient forms of money are typically confined to museums these days. Along these lines, credit cards offer a stark reminder of our evolving preferences at the register.

Prior to 1950, people typically paid for goods and services with checks, cash, or promissory notes. That year, the first credit card—a Diners Club card—debuted.[7] Cut to today. These modes of payment continue to drive a mind-boggling share of commerce. In 2022, global payment card transaction volume surpassed a whopping $40 trillion.[8] That number, however, masks the variation of their use within countries. Some people are far more enamored with plastic than others. Figure 1.1 displays the popularity of credit cards in the US, Canada, and a few other nations.

---

* In strict accounting terms, the two couldn't be more different: The former is an asset; the latter creates a liability.

THE CATALYSTS

Figure 1.1: Number of Credit Cards Per Person by Country as of 2022

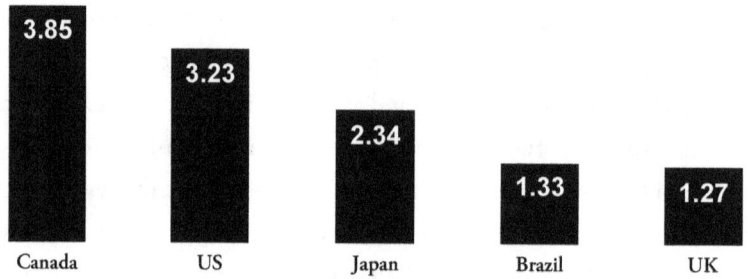

Source: PaymentsJournal | https://tinyurl.com/the-cat-cc

Much like money, expect payments to continue evolving in ways that challenge economic orthodoxy.

The $700 Million Pizza

On May 22, 2010, a Florida programmer named Laszlo Hanyecz was hungry, tech-savvy, and curious. A few days earlier, he had set out to buy two large pizzas with Bitcoin.[9] Until then, no one had ever purchased anything with the inchoate digital currency.

Hanyecz couldn't find a pizza joint that would accept direct payment in the cryptocurrency. Undeterred, he got creative and found an intermediary. Hanyecz ultimately engineered a trade with nineteen-year-old Jeremy Sturdivant, whom he met on the online forum bitcointalk.org. The deal: 10,000 bitcoin* for two Papa Johns pizzas. For his part, Sturdivant had procured the pies through a far more conventional payment mechanism.

Call it a novelty or a proof of concept, but it worked, and Hanyecz enjoyed his slices.

Of course, hindsight is 20/20. Do a little math, and you'll realize that Hanyecz's meal turned out to be the most expensive in history. Writing for CoinDesk in 2022, Benedict George notes that, "If Hanyecz had

---

* In this book, I'll follow industry practice as follows. The term *bitcoin* with a lowercase *b* refers specifically to a currency—aka, *BTC*. *Bitcoin* with a capital *B* describes the protocol and payment network and the ecosystem as a whole.

hypothetically sold his entire stash at bitcoin's all-time high of $68,990.* he could have made around $690 million—enough to buy 46 million large Papa Johns pizzas at $15 apiece."[10] Bitcoin subsequently hit a high of $108,000 in December 2024, making those pizzas even more expensive in hindsight.

For this very reason, crypto enthusiasts annually celebrate May 22 as Bitcoin Pizza Day.

Interestingly, Hanyecz doesn't fret his purchase. In fact, he's proud of it and believes he represents the start of a proper movement.

These days, you may not need to find a third party to make a purchase with digital currencies. In June 2022, Chipotle began accepting cryptocurrency payments in US locations.[11] These new digital currencies are gaining acceptance among tech-savvy merchants eager to court a younger demographic.

Money, Utility, and Value

Adam Smith published his magnum opus in 1776: *An Inquiry into the Nature and Causes of the Wealth of Nations*. His thoughts on value are particularly relevant for our purposes:

> The word value, it is to be observed, has two different meanings, and sometimes expresses the utility of some particular object, and sometimes the power of purchasing other goods which the possession of that object conveys. The one may be called "value in use;" the other, "value in exchange." The things which have the greatest value in use have frequently little or no value in exchange; on the contrary, those which have the greatest value in exchange have frequently little or no value in use. Nothing is more useful than water: but it will purchase scarcely anything; scarcely anything can be had in exchange for it. A diamond, on the contrary, has scarcely any use-value; but a very great quantity of other goods may frequently be had in exchange for it.[12]

---

* It has since eclipsed that number.

Economists today often refer to Smith's astute observation as the *diamond-water paradox* (also known as the *paradox of value*), represented visually in Figure 1.2.

Figure 1.2: The Diamond-Water Paradox

In his 1848 book *Principles of Political Economy,* John Stuart Mill delineated between two types of value: use and exchange. The former represents the amount you're prepared to pay for something; the latter equates to what someone else would pay for it. If you think that there's usually a difference between the two, you're right.

To be sure, sometimes the relationship among money, utility, and value makes perfect sense. Case in point: In 2020, the average preinsurance cost of a heart transplant in the US exceeded $1.6 million.[13] Other times, as is the case with diamonds and water, there's no correlation at all. (Fun fact: The expression "worth its weight in gold" first appeared in English in the 1300s. Its etymology, though, dates to Roman times.[14])

MONEY MATTERS

Horses, Uber, and Consumer Surplus

The notion of *value* has never been absolute or objective. Philosophers have debated intrinsic vs. extrinsic values since the dawn of Western philosophy in ancient Greece. We'll leave that heady discussion alone.*

Today, the *Oxford English Dictionary* defines *value* as "the *relative* worth, usefulness, or importance of a thing or (occasionally) a person."[15] (Emphasis mine.) The value that two people ascribe to a good or service often differs dramatically. Techies and early adopters often pony up beaucoup bucks for the latest iPhone or Google Pixel. Others are fine with keeping their relics until they become virtually unusable.

We've arrived at a key concept in contemporary economics: consumer surplus. Definitions abound, but a decent one is "the difference between the consumers' willingness to pay for a commodity and the actual price paid by them, or the equilibrium price."[16]

If consumer surplus seems a tad boring or abstract, consider traditional taxicabs for a moment. "The first black taxi in London was the hackney coach in the 17th Century. The name comes from *hacquenée*, the French term for a general-purpose horse."[17]

At the turn of the twentieth century, gas-powered vehicles replaced these stallions. Despite the change, the underlying business model remained constant: Patrons would stand on corners attempting to hail cabs, sometimes for longer periods of time. Once they did, they typically paid a *fixed* fee to get in, additional per-mile charges, tolls, and other surcharges. Passengers would then pay with cash and, eventually, via credit cards if their wallets were light. Compared to today, that quaint process wasn't exactly the acme of efficiency but represented the best we could do at the time.

Enter the Apps

Fast-forward to 2009. Smartphones and apps had already allowed new business models to envision things previously thought impossible. That very

---

* Visit https://tinyurl.com/the-cat-value if you're curious.

same year, Garrett Camp, Travis Kalanick, and Oscar Salazar founded the ridesharing company Uber. Soon, Lyft, Ola, Didi, and others built better mousetraps. Summoning a driver via your phone proved to be immensely popular and convenient. As Mike Isaac details in his book *Super Pumped: The Battle for Uber*, the genius of Uber involved dynamic pricing: the idea that people would pay different (read: higher) prices based on specific conditions. These conditions included time, date, weather, current and desired location, and other variables.

For example, paying even $5 for someone to drive you one mile to work on a pristine spring morning might offend your sensibilities. If, however, your critical presentation starts in ten minutes and it's been snowing for a few hours, you'd happily fork over $20 for the privilege. In this scenario, that $5 is a veritable bargain. In effect, you've *saved* $15. The price you paid falls far short of the value you assign to it.

Fuse together dynamic pricing, consumer surplus, and a convenient transportation option, and you wind up with Figure 1.3.

Figure 1.3: Consumer Surplus: A Transportation Example

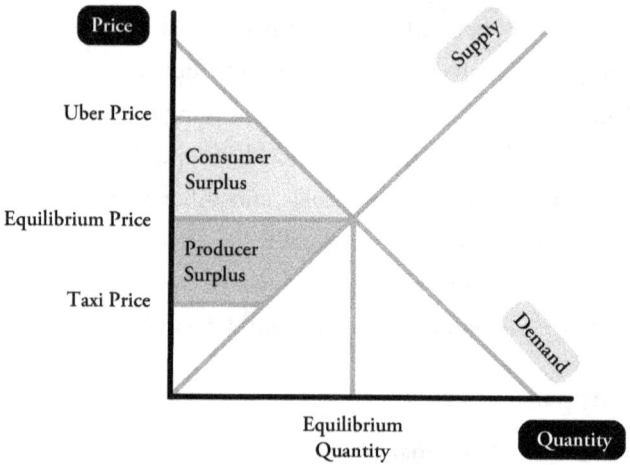

Uber methodically recruited a cadre of independent contractors willing to work without employment benefits. Management even used its sophisticated technology and powerful, ever-improving algorithm as cudgels, sometimes playing psychological games with its drivers.[18] Against that backdrop, the company built an impressive network. The virtuous cycle worked as follows:

- More customers requested and used Uber.
- This increase in demand allowed them to offer drivers more money to sign up.
- More did, allowing Uber to increase its coverage and popularity.
- Even more people used Uber.
- And so on.

Creating this extensive network was no small feat. Once it did, however, Uber was in the driver's seat (pun intended). It could now efficiently and *automatically* adjust prices to extract every penny of value from each customer. As of June 11, 2024, Wall Street valued Uber at a cool $140 billion,[19] despite needing a full five years as a publicly traded company to turn a proper profit.[20]

Not surprisingly, Uber's rapid ascent pummeled Yellow Cab and other storied taxi outfits. Their revenues plummeted. Ditto for the *value* of taxi medallions in major cities. In effect, Uber killed the taxi industry.[21]

Lessons From Uber

The tale of Uber and ridesharing is instructive for our purposes. First, a trip is ultimately worth whatever an individual is willing to pay for it at the time. In the same vein, so is *any* product or service.

As we'll see in Chapter 9, the same concepts of *relative* value are currently playing out in many arenas, including non-fungible tokens (NFTs). You may find it absurd to pay any amount of money for a digital image of a cartoon ape, yet someone else might gleefully pay millions for that NFT.

THE CATALYSTS

Second, new technologies have upended centuries-old norms, products, and services. Pre-Uber and Airbnb, would any sane person consider hopping a ride with a stranger or staying in a random cottage or apartment?

If you think that nothing can disrupt traditional money, think again. Banks and traditional payment methods are clinging to antiquated tech and processes. As we'll see in Part II of this book, rapid change is coming to the financial system, and it's impossible to overstate its consequences.

Our Shaky Knowledge of Money

The means by which we spend money has changed, but that's a moot point, right? Don't all people know the basics of money, and isn't just about every adult financially literate today?

Not even close.

In 2014, the Global Financial Literacy Excellence Center conducted its S&P Global FinLit Survey. Barely half—52 percent—of adults in the European Union are financially literate. As expected, though, there's a great deal of variation among countries. Norway, Denmark, and Sweden cracked the 70 percent barrier, but many other nations didn't fare so well:

> In Greece and Spain, literacy rates are 45 percent and 49 percent, respectively. Italy and Portugal have some of the lowest literacy rates in the south. Financial literacy rates are also low among the countries that joined the EU in 2004 and after. In Bulgaria and Cyprus, 35 percent of adults are financially literate. Romania, with 22 percent financial literacy, has the lowest rate in the European Union.[22]

Outside of the EU, wide variation exists among nations. Figure 1.4 displays the financial literacy rate for a few countries.

Figure 1.4: Percentage of Adults Who Are Financially Literate as of 2014

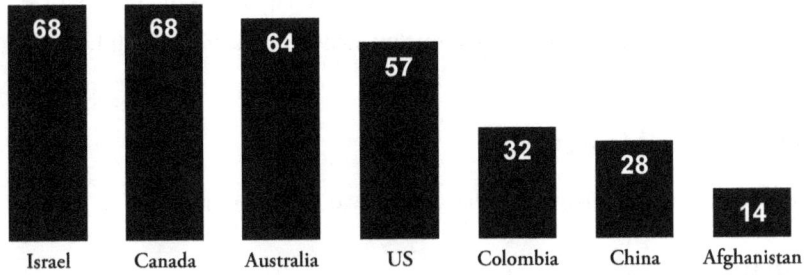

Source: Global Financial Literacy Excellence Center

In many cases, adults are financially illiterate because no one compels them to be otherwise. As a case in point, consider the state of Wisconsin. In 2023, Republican legislators:

> floated a plan to require high school students to complete a full credit of financial literacy in order to receive their diploma. It would have gone into effect for the 2022–23 school year. But the tight timeline and cost to school districts to implement the classes caused the measure to fail.[23]

At least in part due to these legislative failures, many people fail to fully grasp the foundational concepts of managing their money. A 2017 survey of more than 2,000 US adults found that nearly one-quarter of them erroneously believe that purchase activity on debit cards affects their credit scores.[24]

Is it any wonder, then, that the importance of compounding interest, managing their debt, and diversifying their investments is lost on them? Regardless of why, the current situation profoundly affects the lives of billions of people and their immediate families.

While we're on the subject of financial literacy, let's delineate between *money* and *currency*. People often mistakenly conflate these terms, but technically speaking, an important distinction exists between the two. *Money* is an inherently intangible concept. Currencies are physical or tangible representations of money. Think of *currency* as paper bills or coins. Currency also comes in non-money forms, but we needn't review them all here.

Threats to Money

Let's wrap up this chapter by discussing two threats to money.

Inflation

Ideally, and as we've already seen in this chapter, money serves as a stable store of value, but what if it becomes less stable over time? That is, what if the same money tomorrow yields less purchasing power than it does today?

Yes, it's time to talk about inflation. Increases in the price of goods and services erode the purchasing power of dollars, pesos, and yen.

COVID-19

Put mildly, COVID-19 disrupted the global supply chain. Reports of individuals hoarding hand sanitizers and price gouging surfaced.[25] Predictably, consumers often vented their sticker shock on social media and posted pictures of grocery stores' empty shelves.

Most industrialized countries saw the annualized rate of inflation jump 200 or even 300 percent. The cost of many household staples spiked. For instance, in the US the price of eggs soared 60 percent in a single year.[26] Though inconvenient and often frustrating, a little perspective is in order. Those twenty-first-century price increases pale in comparison to what took place in Germany a century before.

Post-WWI Germany

In the aftermath of World War I, the Allies imposed war reparations on the country. As Erin Blakemore writes, "The Treaty of Versailles didn't just blame Germany for the war—it demanded financial restitution for the whole thing, to the tune of 132 billion gold marks, or more than $500 billion today."[27] (As an aside, Germany's debt from World War I took a remarkable 92 years to pay off.)

Workers' wages couldn't keep up with inflation. Many went on strike. Stuck between a rock and a hard place, the German government simply printed more money. Unfortunately, that practice exacerbated the problem and resulted in hyperinflation. A vicious cycle ensued: The more money the government printed, the more prices rose. Consider the following astonishing facts:

- A loaf of bread cost 250 marks in January 1923. A mere ten months later, it cost 200,000 million marks.
- By the fall of 1923, printing a note cost the Weimar Republic more than the note itself was worth.
- During the crisis, companies often paid workers twice per day. Prices rose so fast that their wages were virtually worthless by lunchtime.[28]

Not surprisingly, these economic conditions spurred widespread public resentment—and ultimately, the rise of a dangerous demagogue. The rest, of course, is history.

For obvious reasons, central banks, policymakers, and elected officials take drastic measures to keep inflation at bay. Here's a harrowing thought, though: What if citizens distrust the very people making these macroeconomic decisions?

A Decline in Trust

Money has always included a social element—one perhaps best articulated by the influential German sociologist and philosopher Georg Simmel. As Nigel Dodd of the London School of Economics and author of *The Social Life of Money* writes:

> Simmel once described money as a claim upon society. By doing so, he captured the sense in which the monetary system must be

underpinned by trust, not merely between particular individuals but also across society as a whole.*

Simmel is right. Money—and any national monetary system, for that matter—requires a covenant between the citizenry and its government. Preserving *the idea behind money* is paramount. Returning to Goldstein's book for a moment:

> Money is a made-up thing, a shared fiction. Money is fundamentally, unalterably social. The social part of money—the "shared" in "shared fiction"—is exactly what makes it money. Otherwise, it's just a chunk of metal, or a piece of paper, or, in the case of most money today, just a number stored on a bank's computers.[29]

As we'll see throughout this book, this simple yet powerful relationship explains a great deal about how the world works. If we (correctly) view money through this social lens, we understand why industrialized nations have long tracked down and apprehended counterfeiters—and continue to do so.

In July 2023, Australia warned its citizens about the burgeoning number of counterfeit notes circulating throughout the country.[30] Three months later, in a separate case, UK authorities arrested three men on suspicion of manufacturing bogus currency in Greater Manchester and Cheshire.[31]

Catching the bad guys preserves the trust behind money—the social contract between the government and its citizens. But what happens if that essential trust is breached—and not just via the actions of a few rogue actors? What if a significant minority or majority of citizens lack trust in their elected officials and financial institutions?

It's a scary thought—and one that's playing out as we speak. Part II dives deeper into this subject. For now, suffice it to say that the future of Bitcoin is rooted in "reasonable paranoia."[32]

---

* Nigel Dodd, Response to HAU Book Symposium on *The Social Life of Money*, Princeton University Press, 2014.

We now know more about money, but we've ignored one key question: How does it move? Let that serve as the starting point for the next chapter.

Key Points

- Money has always evolved. Today, it serves key functions that allow our current world to function effectively.
- Value is an amorphous and inherently subjective concept.
- How we spend our money changes over time.
- A significant percentage of adults in the world are financially illiterate.
- Increases in the price of goods and services erode the purchasing power of dollars, pesos, and yen.

CHAPTER 2
MONEY IN MOTION

ITS UNFETTERED MOVEMENT MAKES THE GLOBAL FINANCIAL SYSTEM POSSIBLE.

"Capital is like water: If it does not flow, it stagnates."
—*Thomas Babington Macaulay*

In 1844, a man by the name of Henry Lehman immigrated to the United States from Rimpar, Germany. He ultimately settled in Montgomery, Alabama, the state's soon-to-be capital. Not long after, he opened a general store specializing in dry goods.[1] His brothers Emanuel and Mayer joined Henry a few years later. The troika formed a financial enterprise eponymously called Lehman Brothers. In the ensuing decades, it became a storied global financial services behemoth on par with any in the world.

Fast-forward to February 2007. Remarkably, Lehman Brothers was still standing. To Wall Street, it was even humming along better than ever. In that month, its stock hit an all-time high of $86 per share, giving the company a staggering market capitalization of nearly $60 billion.²

In the prior decade, though, Lehman had planted seeds that would soon threaten its very existence. The firm had adopted risky strategies designed to supercharge its growth. In 2004, Lehman's *leverage ratio*—a common Wall Street measure that divides a firm's debt by its assets or equity—was an eyebrow-raising 20:1. A mere three years later, that metric had more than doubled, to 44:1.³ In simple terms, for every $1 on its books, the firm owed $44.* The source of its burgeoning debt: an array of sophisticated financial products related to home mortgages, including credit default swaps and collateralized debt obligations.

Like many of its contemporaries, Lehman aggressively targeted borrowers with poor credit histories—people whose backgrounds required them to pay higher interest rates for home loans. Yes, these subprime borrowers† *were* theoretically more likely to default en masse, but Lehman's ultra-aggressive powers-that-be decided that the risk was worth it.⁴

A little more than eighteen months later, though, that theoretical black-swan‡ threat had become a stark reality. Mortgage default rates were skyrocketing in the US and abroad. The chickens were coming home to roost, and Lehman's viability as a standalone entity was suddenly in dire straits. At least its CEO at the time, Richard Fuld, could take solace in the fact that he was hardly alone.

The year 2008 was turning out to be a historically abysmal one for American banks. By September 12 of that year, eleven had already failed. Most notably, the storied investment and securities institution Bear Stearns went belly-up that March. By way of comparison, only ten banks had fallen in the prior five years *combined*. In total, more than two dozen US banks would ultimately collapse in 2008.⁵

---

* Do the math, and you'll realize that a mere 2.3 percent drop in Lehman's assets would wipe out all its equity.
† By contrast, prime borrowers pay significantly lower interest rates because their risk of default is much lower.
‡ To borrow a term from Nassim Nicholas Taleb's book of the same name.

US officials and policymakers weren't oblivious to recent events. Far from it. They'd declared a code red. On that September evening, New York Federal Reserve President Timothy Geithner summoned the head honchos of many of the most powerful financial institutions in the world to Manhattan for a sit-down. The goal: a last-ditch attempt to save the reeling Lehman Brothers.

Table 2.1 displays the attendee list—a veritable who's who of contemporary American banking and finance at the time.

Table 2.1: Partial List of Attendees at the NY Federal Reserve Meeting on September 12, 2008

Name	Role and Organization
Hank Paulson	Secretary, US Treasury
Christopher Cox	Chairman, US Securities and Exchange Commission
Lloyd Blankfein	CEO, Goldman Sachs
John Mack	CEO, Morgan Stanley
Jamie Dimon	CEO, JPMorganChase
Vikram Pandit	CEO, Citigroup
John Thain	CEO, Merrill Lynch

Representatives from the Royal Bank of Scotland and the Bank of New York Mellon also attended the meeting.

Why would the Federal Reserve require the CEOs of the largest banks in the country to discuss saving one of their main competitors? After all, isn't the whole point of capitalism to defeat your competition?

As Eric Dash of *The New York Times* reported at the time:

> Mr. Geithner told the participants that an industry solution was needed, no matter what, and that it was not about any individual bank, according to two people briefed on the meeting but who did not attend. They said he told them that if the industry failed to solve the problem their individual banks might be next.[6]

In other words, the contagion was about to spread, and every major financial institution in the country was at risk.

THE CATALYSTS

The CEOs knew that Geithner wasn't just blowing smoke. For months, the current economic environment had been hammering their companies' stock prices and the market in general. For instance, Morgan Stanley saw its market capitalization plunge more than 80 percent between 2007 and 2008.[7] (The firm survived by the skin of its teeth.)

The group's best efforts, however, bore no fruit. Lehman Brothers filed for bankruptcy three days after the historic meeting. Global markets justifiably panicked, and a massive sell-off ensued. A full-blown global financial crisis was underway.

On October 3, 2008, President George W. Bush signed into law the Emergency Economic Stabilization Act. A full recap of the intricate legislation isn't necessary here, but it created the Troubled Asset Relief Program (TARP). The new initiative allowed the Federal Reserve to take the necessary steps to slow the contagion. In the words of Chair Ben Bernanke, the Federal Reserve could "provide liquidity to the financial system and thus promote the extension of credit to households and businesses."[8] TARP ultimately disbursed roughly $443.5 billion[9] in large part because banks had become too big to fail. (Andrew Ross Sorkin's lengthy 2010 book by the same name is worth the read.)

We'll see in Part II how the decision to bail out the banks caused unintended consequences, but for now we'll stick to the matter at hand.

The key word in Bernanke's statement for our purposes is *liquidity*.[*] Banks that lack sufficient liquidity can't fulfill one of their main functions: lending money to individuals and other businesses. A doom loop ensues. Absent the ability to borrow, enterprises scale back investment and hiring. Pinched consumers purchase fewer goods and services. The economy contracts. Mass unemployment and social unrest result. And so on.

---

[*] A bank's *liquidity* measures its available cash and other assets "to quickly pay bills and meet short-term business and financial obligations." For more on this subject, see https://tinyurl.com/the-cat-liq.

More succinctly, for our global financial system to function efficiently, money needs to be able to freely and quickly move. And that, in a nutshell, is the subject of this chapter.

Critical Concepts

The overarching goals of the global financial system may seem simple. Its execution, however, is anything but. As we'll see in the forthcoming pages, the global financial system is an incalculably complex beast—a vast network of interconnected entities. At a high level, it seeks to efficiently allocate money, capital,* and investments to different countries, regions, corporations, and even individuals. Such a massive and ongoing undertaking could never occur naturally. It requires a slew of interwoven financial institutions, regulatory frameworks, and technologies.

Custodians

All banks serve as legal custodians for their clients and their assets. The *Oxford English Dictionary* defines a legal custodian as "a person who or organization which has custody or guardianship of something or someone; a guardian."[10]

Of course, not all custodians are created equally. In her 2023 book *Broken Money*, Lyn Alden describes the different ways in which financial institutions act as custodians for their clients and profit while doing so:

> The most basic type of bank serves as a 100% asset-backed custodian. People deposit gold or another monetary asset, and the custodian bank issues paper claims against it; the bank doesn't do anything else with it other than keep it safe. Custodians generally charge fees for the services they provide.

---

* Some people conflate the terms *money* and *capital*. The latter, however, typically connotes cash being used explicitly for productive or investment purposes.

Related examples today include holding physical gold in a vault, where you'll usually have to pay a recurring vaulting fee. The same is true for a safe deposit box.

If you hold an exchange-traded fund filled with stocks, the fund charges an administrative fee. These are various types of full reserve custodial and administrative services. Rather than making money from lending out your assets (and thus risking the possibility that they won't get them back), they mostly just hold them and charge you a fee to cover their overhead and make a profit.[11]

In a vastly simplified world, banks would keep all their clients' funds on hand. A financial institution that adheres to *full-reserve banking* would be able to return every dollar owed to each of its clients at any given time, even if they all showed up at the door and demanded to immediately cash out.

Fractional Reserves

In practice, however, no bank today engages in this dated practice; it's been antiquated for a long time. Again, to quote Alden's book:

> Eventually throughout the world, improvements in banking… reduced the need for coins, and improved gold's limited divisibility. People could deposit their gold into banks and receive paper credit representing redeemable claims on that gold. Banks, knowing that not everyone would redeem their gold at once, went ahead and issued more claims than the gold they held, beginning the practice of fractional reserve banking.[12]

Banks are only legally required to hold a percentage of their customers' deposits as reserves. They lend the rest of their funds to borrowers. This process allows them to do the following:

- Create credit and fuel economic growth.
- Expand the money supply: the total amount of money available in an economy for spending.

While these are admirable goals, the practice of fractional reserves can subject banks to liquidity risks and, in the extreme, solvency ones. Generally speaking, though, the advantages of fractional-reserve banking exceed their disadvantages. As a result, it remains a fundamental precept of the global financial system.

Breaking Down Banks

Up until now, I've described banks in a general, even monolithic way. It's now time to explore them in earnest.

To be sure, the very idea of a bank has evolved considerably over the centuries. In this way, banking parallels its cousin from the previous chapter: money. (Interestingly, the etymology of the word *banker* is Italian. *Banchieri* roughly translates to *bench sitters*: "venetian men who gave loans on the benches over the Grand Canal centuries ago."[13])

Although the thought of proper bankers handing over money to customers on public benches seems quaint today, remember this: As Lehmann Brothers showed us earlier, loaning available funds to interested individuals remains a core bank function.

Commercial Banks

Every business day, employees at the Bank of Ireland's roughly 169 branches[14] sign papers authorizing loans to new and existing clients. As of 2023, it held €155.71 billion in assets, making it the country's largest commercial bank.[15]

The Bank of Ireland is hardly unique in this regard. All commercial banks make loans, but that's hardly their only purpose. They also accept their clients' cash deposits, cash their checks, and safeguard their assets in government-protected savings and checking accounts. Commercial banks have historically also facilitated international transactions. For example, these institutions have typically charged customers approximately $35 to process a wire transfer from Person X in one country to Person Y in another.

THE CATALYSTS

Investment Banks

The aforementioned Morgan Stanley, Bank of America, Merrill Lynch, Citigroup, Goldman Sachs, and their brethren handle complicated and high-profile mergers and acquisitions (M&A) transactions for their clients. They issue securities and arrange financing for large-scale business projects.

Universal Banks

Admittedly, there's often considerable overlap between these two types of financial institutions. Depending on where you live, you may have heard the term *universal bank*—an entity that "can offer the entire range of financial services within the bank or through subsidiaries."[16] Figure 2.1 shows the largest banks in the world by market capitalization. Clearly, money mavens recognize the massive financial gains to be realized by serving a diverse group of clients.

Figure 2.1: Largest Banks in the World by Market Capitalization

JPMorgan Chase	Bank of America	Wells Fargo & Co.	HSBC Holdings	Royal Bank of Canada
533.7	270.4	197	148.6	136.5

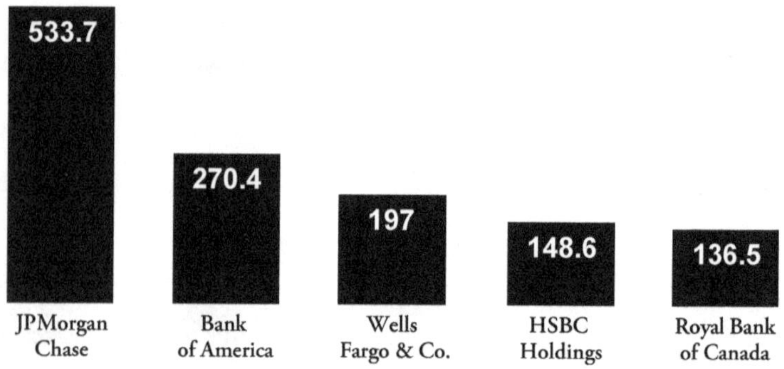

Data as of March 2024, Billions (USD)
Source: Insider Monkey | https://tinyurl.com/the-cat.im

Central Banks

As we've seen throughout history, crises occur when private banks go rogue. Sadly, the subprime crisis of 2008 served as just the latest example in the long, disturbing pattern of banks behaving badly.

Unlike the previous three types described so far, a country's central banks don't seek to maximize profits or serve as custodians for their clients. On the contrary, they perform the following functions for a nation:

- Set its monetary policy.
- Regulate its money supply.
- Control inflation.
- Maintain the stability of its financial system—or at least attempt to do so.
- Oversee its banking system.
- Act as lenders of last resort during financial crises. (The story at the start of this chapter aptly illustrated this key role.)
- Decide which banks enter the banking system.

As the following sidebar illustrates, central banks' core functions can evoke controversy.

Custodia Clashes With the Fed

Based in the sleepy town of Cheyenne, Wisconsin, Custodia isn't your typical mom-and-pop local bank. Rather, it's "a special purpose depository institution (SPDI) founded under Wyoming law to cover cryptocurrency and other digital assets."[17]

The company first completed the extensive process of obtaining a state banking charter. It then dutifully filed an application with the US Federal Reserve to obtain a master account. Banks and depository institutions that receive one can "directly access the Federal Reserve, rather than require them to go through intermediary banks."[18] If direct access to the Fed sounds like a big deal, it is.

The Fed ultimately denied the bank's request. Custodia's top brass was understandably displeased and took the Fed to court. In June 2024, Wyoming US District Court Judge Scott Skavdahl ruled that

THE CATALYSTS

> the Federal Reserve Banks can legally deny master accounts, even to state-chartered banks.
>
> Custodia is currently appealing the ruling.

A Common Denominator

Before wrapping up this section, it's essential to make one final point. Each of these financial institutions has operated—and continues to operate—in a structured or, if you like, *centralized* fashion. That is, "centralized authorities control financial assets and the flow of money. They set the rules and standards for how assets are managed and transacted."[19] Figure 2.2 displays the relationship between central and private banks and the need to trust third parties.

Figure 2.2: Centralized Ledgers Make Third-Party Trust Essential

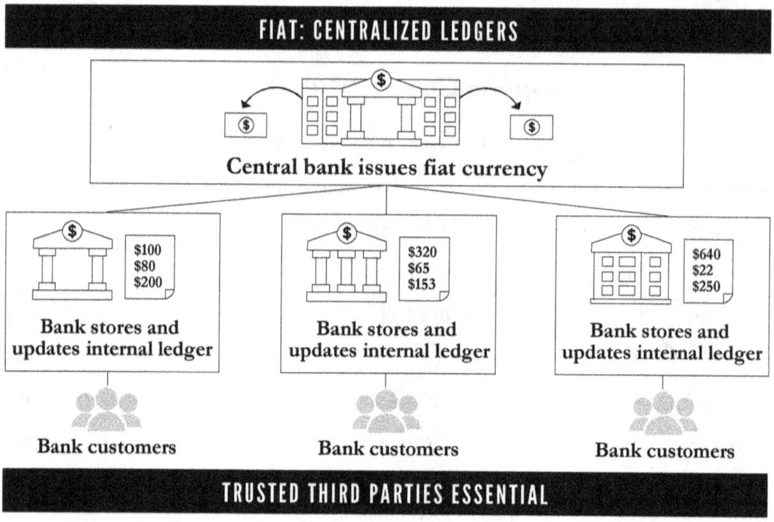

FIAT: CENTRALIZED LEDGERS

Central bank issues fiat currency

Bank stores and updates internal ledger	Bank stores and updates internal ledger	Bank stores and updates internal ledger
$100 $80 $200	$320 $65 $153	$640 $22 $250
Bank customers	Bank customers	Bank customers

TRUSTED THIRD PARTIES ESSENTIAL

Historically, individuals and institutions that disapproved of their banks' terms of engagement possessed little recourse beyond trying to find a competitor or heading to court. (As Chapter 9 will amply demonstrate, that ship is finally starting to sail. *Decentralized* financial alternatives are becoming more and more viable.)

Regulations and Regulatory Bodies

We've known about the butterfly effect since the early 1970s. Mathematician and meteorologist Edward Norton Lorenz popularized the notion that "small, seemingly trivial events may ultimately result in something with much larger consequences—in other words, they have non-linear impacts on very complex systems."[20] More recently, American political commentator Thomas Friedman released his book *The World Is Flat: A Brief History of the Twenty-First Century* in 2005. Since that time, can anyone credibly argue that the world has only become *less* flat?

Case in point: In 2008, the US was hardly the only nation dealing with major financial issues. Iceland, Portugal, Italy, Ireland, Greece, and Spain faced similar problems. In other words, ours is a connected world. The internet, World Wide Web, smartphones, social media, and other relatively recent technological advances have only intensified this trend.

Against this backdrop, only a die-hard libertarian or anarchist would argue that banks—and banking, for that matter—should operate autonomously. Scrutiny and international cooperation are imperative. It's time to discuss the organizations that attempt to minimize chaos in the global financial system.

International Financial Institutions

Let's begin at the highest level: organizations that attempt to coordinate the actions of individual countries.

THE CATALYSTS

International Monetary Fund

Founded in July 1944 after WWII, the IMF:

> works to achieve sustainable growth and prosperity for all of its 190 member countries. It does so by supporting economic policies that promote financial stability and monetary cooperation, which are essential to increase productivity, job creation, and economic well-being. The IMF is governed by and accountable to its member countries.[21]

From its website, its three critical missions include:

- Furthering international monetary cooperation.
- Encouraging the expansion of trade and economic growth.
- Discouraging policies that would harm prosperity.

The 190 IMF member countries work with each other and with the other international bodies included in this section. For example, in 1982, the IMF worked closely with Latin American nations to mitigate the region's debt crisis.*

The World Bank

Founded the same year, this 187-country international development organization attempts to "reduce poverty by lending money to the governments of its poorer members to improve their economies and to improve the standard of living of their people."[22]

Many reasons beyond the scope of this book explain the reduction in extreme poverty in recent decades. At least some of the credit, though, undoubtedly goes to the World Bank's extensive efforts to combat the epidemic; they've certainly borne fruit. Figure 2.3 shows the drop in the world poverty rate since 1980.

---

* See https://tinyurl.com/the-cat-imf for an interactive IMF timeline of historic events.

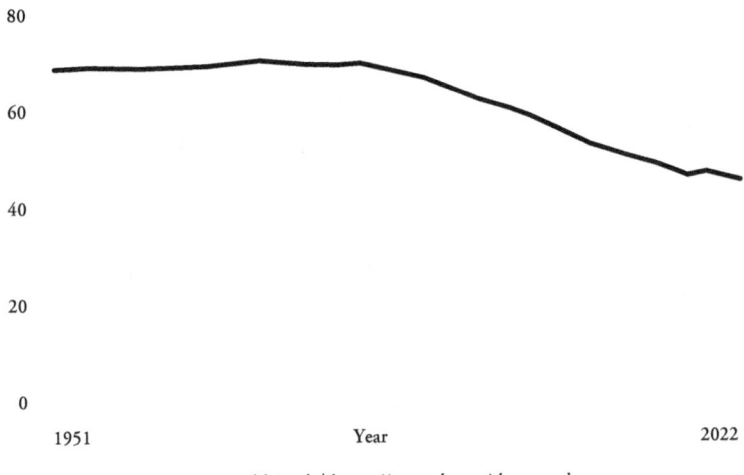

Figure 2.3: World Poverty Rate: Percentage of People Living on Less Than $5.50 USD Per Day

Source: World Bank | https://tinyurl.com/the-cat-stl

The World Bank also conducts extensive primary research on economic development. Its specialized departments "use this knowledge to advise countries in areas like health, education, nutrition, finance, justice, law, and the environment."[23]

For financing, the organization relies upon member contributions, bond flotations, and trust funds to operate and then uses these funds to help nations in need. For instance, in 1961, the World Bank granted Honduras a $9 million credit to enhance the country's transportation infrastructure.[24]

Bank for International Settlements

Founded in 1930, the BIS tries to "promote global monetary and financial stability through international cooperation."[25] The arrows in its quiver include providing economic assistance to member countries and conducting primary research.

A recent example of the latter is its cross-country analysis of the burgeoning buy now, pay later (BNPL) trend.[26] These reports ideally will help countries educate their citizens about crucial financial matters.

(Remember from Chapter 1 that a considerable percentage of the world's population is financially illiterate.)

National Regulatory Authorities

To varying extents, each country authorizes its regulatory bodies to avoid national financial crises, such as the one in 2008. To this end, these regulators do their best to oversee financial markets, protect investors, and prevent illegal financial activities such as money laundering and terrorist financing.

In the US, because of a patchwork of regulations, multiple agencies maintain responsibility. The primary ones include:

- The Financial Crimes Enforcement Network (FinCEN).
- The Securities and Exchange Commission (SEC).
- The Commodity Futures Trading Commission (CFTC).

Other countries delegate these functions more efficiently. In the UK, it's the Prudential Regulation Authority (PRA) and the Financial Conduct Authority (FCA). Japan's integrated regulator is its Financial Services Agency (FSA).

To be sure, these agencies *attempt* to accomplish the same high-level goals. In practice, structural differences and political will can result in starkly different outcomes. Without interagency turf wars over who regulates what, countries that have consolidated their regulators around financial services operate at a distinct advantage over sprawling bureaucracies.

Domestic Financial Regulations

Earlier in this chapter, I discussed the concept of *liquidity*. Banks need to maintain some funds on hand to operate. A completely illiquid bank wouldn't last long. Imagine a kind grandmother who wanted to withdraw $100 to give to her grandson but couldn't because the bank lacked the cash. A *bank* run would soon follow; all hell would break loose.

But liquidity isn't a binary; there's a happy medium between complete and zero liquidity. The obvious question becomes: Who decides the right level or, more technically, *the liquidity ratio*?

A country's regulators make these determinations, among many others. These agencies and individuals also mandate:

- The amount of capital that each financial institution must maintain. (Whether they do and pass subsequent stress tests to verify those levels, however, are entirely different matters altogether.)
- Frameworks that govern collateralization practices.
- Measures to combat financial crimes. Money laundering and terrorist financing quickly come to mind.

Failure to comply with these regulations results in severe financial penalties. Offenders even face potential incarceration. At least, that's the theory. Despite nearly bringing the world economy to a halt in 2008, only a single American banker spent any time in jail.[27]

International Trade, Banking, and Payments

Money movement isn't confined to a single state, province, or territory. Money needs to move across borders, and we need to understand how this happens.

Correspondent Banking

Many of the financial institutions in Figure 2.1 also qualify as *correspondent banks*. That is, these institutions provide reciprocal services to one another, especially when one of them primarily operates in another country.

For instance, say that Brazil's Banco Itaú Unibanco S.A. has established a correspondent banking relationship with Banco de la Nación Argentina. The two banks can use each other's services to process transactions in their non-native currencies as needed. In this way, each bank serves as an intermediary to perform core bank functions discussed earlier in this chapter.

As for the downside, the practice isn't always above board. It can facilitate money laundering among unscrupulous types. In January 2023, the Southern District of New York sentenced Copenhagen-based Danske Bank to three years of probation and forfeiture of more than $2.059 billion. The bank processed "several hundred billion in suspicious transactions ... at the bank's former Estonian branch."[28]

Trade Finance

International trade doesn't magically occur. It requires myriad importers and exporters. Ideally, these two groups can conduct business with as little friction as possible. How can governments facilitate international trade?

The answer largely hinges upon *trade finance*—a concept that describes different strategies and instruments. Popular trade finance techniques include letters of credit, forfeiting, factoring, export finance, and trade credit insurance.[29]

Cross-Border Payments

Money movement isn't confined to a single nation, province, or territory. No, money needs to move across borders, which brings us to the subject of cross-border payments (CBPs). Banks and other financial institutions have long facilitated the two main types of CBPs.

Wholesale payments involve large transactions between banks or institutions, typically for businesses or governments. For instance, the US remits billions in aid to Ukraine. For their part, retail CBPs differ in both size and audience, but they're often orders of magnitude smaller than their wholesale counterparts. Individuals make purchases via small businesses outside of their home countries or send some money to a distant relative.

All told, CBPs are big business. In August 2020, Boston Consulting Group estimated that the total value of these payments would explode from $150 trillion in 2017 to more than $250 trillion by 2027.[30] As for why, the Bank of England posits the following four reasons:

- Manufacturers continue to expand their supply chains across borders.

- Cross-border asset management and global investments have increased.
- International trade and e-commerce drive revenue expansion.
- Migrants send money via international remittances.[31]

I'll add an obvious fifth: inflation. Absent massive change, one would expect these numbers to increase because a peso or euro today is worth more than one in 2027.

The Technologies: The Banking Rails in Brief

With so much money changing hands every minute, it's worth exploring a few core technologies that power banks and allow this vast stream of international payments to settle.

COBOL

Launched back in 1959, Common Business-Oriented Language served as the infrastructure for many financial institutions. For decades, it's been long in the tooth. Sadly, you're still likely to find it running key systems and applications. In 2017, *Reuters* reported the following astonishing statistics. At the time, COBOL powered:

- 95 percent of swipes at automated teller machines.
- 80 percent of in-person transactions.
- More than 43 percent of all international banking systems.[32]

Given the rate at which large, successful organizations tend to adopt new technology, it's doubtful that these stats have changed much since then. A significant percentage of transactions each day continue to rely on the wildly antiquated programming language.

The dangers of running critical financial infrastructure on sixty-year-old technology are manifold. Forget for a moment COBOL's lack of native interoperability to other systems. Ignore its deficient performance compared to Python, Java, and other contemporary, general-use programming languages. Beyond these, there's a far more pragmatic concern: Financial institutions are simply running out of people who know how to write and debug it. For nearly a decade, banks have been "scrambling to fix old systems as IT cowboys ride into the sunset."[33]

Swift

Founded in 1973 in Belgium by a consortium of banks and other member organizations, the Society for Worldwide Interbank Financial Telecommunication (Swift) remains the primary rail system for contemporary cross-border payments. In her 2023 book *Reimagining Payments*, Michelle Gitlitz writes:

> Cross-border payments typically settle through correspondent banking networks. These are arrangements where one bank (correspondent) holds deposits owned by other banks (respondents) and provides payment and other services to those respondent banks. This often requires a network or intermediary institution to ensure everything goes smoothly. An example is the Society for Worldwide Interbank Financial Telecommunication. SWIFT is a global financial messaging network that enables financial institutions worldwide to securely exchange information and electronic messages about financial transactions.

Much like COBOL, Swift has been showing its age for years. Among its major deficiencies are high costs, low speed, limited access, and insufficient transparency.[34] (We'll return to Swift in Chapter 3.)

We live in an era of instantaneous payments. Within seconds, you can remit funds to people in different countries via Venmo, Zelle, AndroidPay, ApplePay, Alipay, Paytm, and scores of other apps. Yet, bank wire transfers are expensive and slow. Waiting three to five business days to access your new funds might have made sense in 1980. In 2024, it's downright absurd.

More contemporary mechanisms for international payments would fuel economic growth, international trade, global development, and financial inclusion. The financial establishment has largely resisted them so far. The rationale is straightforward: money.

In 2019, the consulting firm McKinsey found that "international payments revenues total up to $200 billion globally, split roughly evenly between transaction fees and foreign exchange revenues."[35] In other words, their inaction is perversely logical: Why fix what costs us money and only makes them more?

Now that we understand a little better the way money moves and the world financial system, it's time to focus on how the US has turned its national currency into a global cudgel.

Key Points

- The financial crisis of 2008 illustrated the complexity and interconnected nature of our global financial system.
- Money that doesn't move or spend is virtually useless; the global financial system is supposed to ensure that individuals and organizations face as little friction as possible in this regard.
- An array of international and domestic organizations and regulators attempt to ensure that the global financial system minimizes crises.
- Most financial institutions rely upon antiquated technology. They ignore more contemporary systems and protocols—and have for a long time.

CHAPTER 3
US FINANCIAL HEGEMONY

IT'S NO ACCIDENT THAT THE DOLLAR IS THE WORLD'S RESERVE CURRENCY.

> "The dollar is our currency, but it's your problem."
>
> —*John Connally, former US Treasury Secretary*

It's fair to say that the US and Iranian governments don't see eye-to-eye. They haven't for decades.

Let's start with the Iranian Revolution in 1979. Revolutionaries overthrew Mohammad Rez Shah Pahlavi's administration, in the process taking American hostages. The American reaction was swift and severe: President Jimmy Carter ended US economic and diplomatic ties with Iran, banned Iranian oil imports, and froze billions in Iranian assets.[1]

Cut to 1983. Carter's successor Ronald Reagan imposed an arms embargo on the country.[2] Ideally, these types of sanctions "coerce states and non-governmental actors to improve their behavior in the interests of international peace and security."[3]

The relationship between the two countries has ebbed and flowed. A relative high point occurred in 2015 with the Comprehensive Plan of Action. That year, parties signed an accord that significantly curtailed Iran's nuclear program in exchange for sanctions relief.[4] The Obama administration praised it as a "historic deal that will prevent Iran from acquiring a nuclear weapon."[5] Unfortunately, the accord didn't last long.

In May 2018, Donald Trump abruptly announced that the US was pulling out of the agreement. Never one to embrace subtlety, it represented, in his words, "one of the worst and most one-sided transactions the United States has ever entered into."[6]

In April 2024, Joe Biden upped the ante against America's longtime nemesis:

> Less than a week ago, Iran launched one of the largest missile and drone attacks the world has ever seen against Israel. Together with our allies and partners, the United States defended Israel. We helped defeat this attack. And today, we are holding Iran accountable—imposing new sanctions and export controls* on Iran.[7]

In this regard, Biden is no iconoclast. As Figure 3.1 shows, economic sanctions represent one of the most frequently used arrows in America's geopolitical quiver.

---

*   Indiana University of Pennsylvania defines them as "federal laws that prohibit the unlicensed export of certain commodities or information for reasons of national security or protections of trade." See https://tinyurl.com/the-cat-iup for more information.

Figure 3.1: Number of Active Economic Sanctions as of April 2024

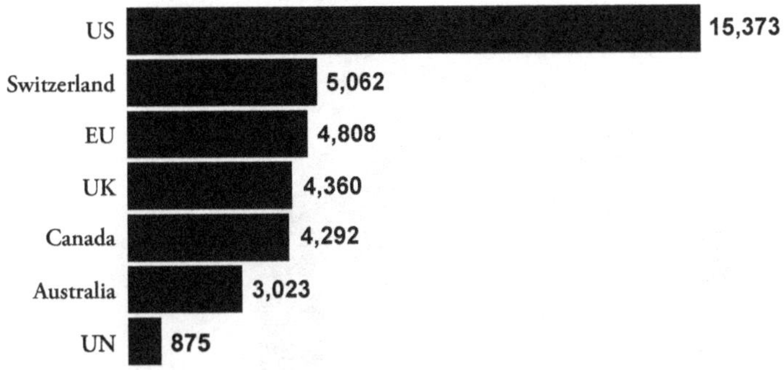

US	15,373
Switzerland	5,062
EU	4,808
UK	4,360
Canada	4,292
Australia	3,023
UN	875

Source: Castellum.ai, *The Washington Post*

Put differently, as of this writing, the US has placed at least three times as many sanctions on foreign countries as the runner-up. Their effects can be devasting, but don't take my word for it. From mid-December 2012 to mid-January 2013, the multinational analytics and advisory firm Gallup conducted a survey on the efficacy of US economic sanctions. Gallup asked 1,000 Iranian adults aged fifteen and older two simple questions:

- Do you think these sanctions have hurt the livelihood of Iranians a great deal, somewhat, or not at all?
- Have these sanctions personally hurt your livelihood a great deal, hurt it somewhat, or have they not hurt your livelihood at all?[8]

More than half—56 percent—responded "a great deal" to the first question, while 48 percent said the same about the second. That same survey asked: Which of the following groups do you hold most responsible for the sanctions against Iran? Figure 3.2 displays the results.

Interestingly, only one in ten Iranian citizens blamed its own government for the current affairs.

Figure 3.2: Groups That Iranians Hold Most Responsible for Sanctions

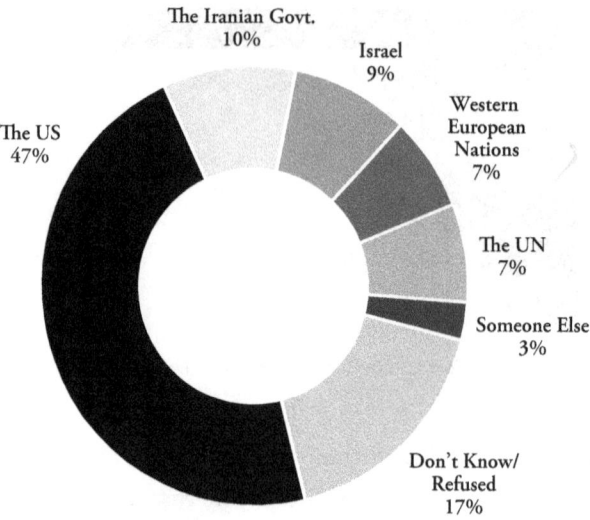

Source: Gallup | December 2012 to January 2013

US-Iranian relations aside, one thing is certain: US economic sanctions—and, by extension, those from the United Nations—have historically worked. For the duration of the current world financial order, US-imposed, dollar-based embargoes have served as powerful political cudgels. America has long used them to persuade its friends and enemies to do certain things—and refrain from doing others. Even the *threat* of sanctions can motivate the most intransigent of nations.

The obvious question is *why*. While we're at it, what mechanisms allow sanctions to work? Why are they so effective? What do sanctions have to do with the US dollar? And why has America been so willing to use them for its own means?

This chapter answers these questions in spades. It also explains the genesis of perhaps the single defining trait of the current world financial order: US financial hegemony. Let's begin our journey at the end of World War II.

Building the Weapon

By the summer of 1944, the world had been at war—again—for more than five years. Although battles continued to rage throughout Europe and the Pacific, the leaders of the world's democracies remained sanguine. They hoped that the second great conflict was closer to the end than the beginning. (Ultimately, the war formally ended on September 2, 1945, after Emperor Hirohito of Japan signed formal papers. The recent events in Hiroshima and Nagasaki left him with little choice.)

Bretton Woods: The Birth of the Current World Financial Order

On July 1 of that year, 730 delegates from all forty-four allied nations descended on the remote Mount Washington Hotel in Bretton Woods, New Hampshire. Attendees included US President Franklin Delano Roosevelt (FDR), influential economist John Maynard Keynes, and Harry Dexter White, a senior US Treasury Department official.

Formally called the *United Nations Monetary and Financial Conference* at the time, the event took place over three pivotal weeks. During this time, the UN delegates created "a series of new rules for the post-WWII international monetary system."[9] Now known widely as the *Bretton Woods Conference*, the parties birthed both the International Monetary Fund (the same one mentioned in the previous chapter) and the International Bank for Reconstruction and Development (the World Bank's lending arm). These organizations would promote free trade throughout the globe. Long-term international prosperity and peace would ensue.

Ironing Out the New World Financial Order

Given those overarching goals and the desire to avoid repeating previous post-war mistakes, it's reasonable to assume that the parties quickly and amicably agreed on how the new international financial system would function. In fact, nothing could be further from the truth. As Benn Steil writes in his riveting 2013 book, *The Battle of Bretton Woods*, two types of conflict cast a pall over the conference.

First, there was considerable conflict between and among the representatives from different nations. Most significantly, Great Britain's Keynes advocated a system prioritizing stable exchange rates and international cooperation. White disagreed. Instead, he advocated for a US-centric system with the dollar at its core.

Second, internal conflict plagued the US. American bankers and politicians weren't exactly on the same page. The former were willing to continue financing the war, but they sensed:

> an opportunity to supplant their London counterparts as the dominant players in the international market, and looked at Washington as a hindrance rather than an ally. Benjamin Strong's* New York Fed, barely two years old, had its sights set on supplanting the Bank of England as the leading force in international monetary affairs. In Washington, however, many in Congress viewed the bankers with outright hostility for having, in their view, dragged the country into the war. Treasury Secretary William Gibbs McAdoo, Wilson's son-in-law, for his part viewed Britain, New York, and Congress all as rival political powers, and was determined to keep them in check.[10]

Steil adeptly reveals the behind-the-scenes machinations of key Bretton Woods players. In so doing, he dispels the myth that the US acted exclusively as a benevolent force for world peace and prosperity. Rather, its actions reflected its leaders' ambitious geopolitical agenda. America saw a chance to stack the deck in its favor *and* eliminate Great Britain as its chief economic and political rival.

---

* Strong served as governor of the Federal Reserve Bank of New York for fourteen years until his death in 1928.

Reserve Currency

Under the Bretton Woods system, the US pegged its dollar to gold. Although not mandatory, other countries could peg their own currencies to the US dollar.[11] A few of the forty-three allied nations held out. (The USSR and France expressed concerns about handing the US so much power and declined.) A few stragglers aside, the US dollar, at that point, became the world's *reserve currency*.

Definitions of *reserve currency* are plentiful. The Council on Foreign Relations defines it as:

> a foreign currency that a central bank or treasury holds as part of its country's formal foreign exchange reserves. Countries hold reserves for a number of reasons, including to weather economic shocks, pay for imports, service debts, and moderate the value of their own currencies. Many countries cannot borrow money or pay for foreign goods in their own currencies—since much of international trade is still done in dollars—and therefore need to hold reserves to ensure a steady supply of imports during a crisis and assure creditors that debt payments denominated in foreign currency can be made.[12]

When making decisions about which currency they'll use for reserves, foreign central banks and major financial institutions typically look at the following variables:

- The size of the nation's domestic economy.
- The importance of its economy in international trade.
- The size, depth, and openness of its financial markets.

When it comes to these dimensions, the US has historically fared well against other nations. As a result, over the past eight decades, the dollar has been the most widely used currency for international trade. What's more, "high global demand for dollars allows the United States to borrow money at a lower cost and use currency as a tool of diplomacy."[13]

"That the US realized advantages over other nations hasn't exactly gone unnoticed. Most famously, consider the words of French Finance Minister Valéry Giscard d'Estaing. At some point in the 1960s, he succinctly described the benefits the US realizes because of the dollar's status as the world's reserve currency with two immortal words: *privilège exorbitant*, or exorbitant privilege.

He wasn't wrong.

We'll see next how even a massive, unexpected restructuring of the financial order hasn't displaced the dollar's standing.

Modernizing the World Financial System

The US didn't just see Bretton Woods as a unique opportunity to establish the dollar as the world's reserve currency. America could also expedite extricating itself from a nineteenth-century financial relic that had become a thorn in its side.

The End of the Gold Standard

In its simplest form, the gold standard was "a long-standing monetary system whose name became synonymous with the precious metal's benchmark."[14] At least in theory, precious metals such as gold are relatively stable. They maintain their value over time and serve as stores of value. (See the related discussion on the functions of money in Chapter 2.) A nation's unpegged currency, however, is inherently volatile.

As late as 1929, the US dollar had, to varying legal extents, tied the value of its national currency to gold for roughly a century. America was no outlier; the majority of nations abided by the same practice at the time. Nevertheless, the clock was ticking on the gold standard. An unprecedented economic cataclysm that year started a chain of events that accelerated gold's eventual demise.

The 1929 Reckoning

As the Roaring Twenties came to an end, the US entered the Great Depression. It wouldn't fully escape from the historic economic downturn for a decade. (Historians argue about whether FDR's New Deal or the arrival of WWII ultimately righted the ship and ushered in an era of prosperity.)

At its height in 1933, a full quarter of the nation's workforce was unemployed—nearly 13 million people.[15] During the financial crisis that March, the Federal Reserve Bank of New York announced that it could no longer honor its commitment to convert currency to gold."[16]

It's impossible to overstate the precarity of the situation at the time:

> Large quantities of gold flowed out from the Federal Reserve. Some of this outflow went to individuals and firms in the United States. This domestic drain occurred because individuals and firms preferred holding metallic gold to bank deposits or paper currency. Some of the gold flowed to foreign nations. This external drain occurred because foreign investors feared a devaluation of the dollar. Together, the internal and external drains consumed the Federal Reserve's free gold.[17]

The US was at a crossroads; it faced the real possibility of bank runs and a full-blown financial panic. Widespread social unrest wouldn't be far behind. One wrong monetary policy move could sound the death knell of the already-struggling country at the most inopportune time: Adolf Hitler's Nazi Party had recently come to power in Germany.

Critical Moves

FDR knew he had to tread lightly. He declared a national banking holiday and suspended the gold standard. The president "prohibited exports of gold and prohibited the Treasury and financial institutions from converting currency and deposits into gold coins and ingots. The actions halted gold outflows."[18]

THE CATALYSTS

On April 5, 1933, FDR signed Executive Order 6102 "forbidding the hoarding of gold coin, gold bullion, and gold certificates within the continental United States."[19] US citizens had until May 1, 1933, to hand over all quantities of the precious metal. For more on the terms:

> In exchange, they would be compensated $20.67 per ounce. The penalties for refusing to turn in gold were set by an amendment of the Trading with the Enemy Act of 1917 and were set as a fine of up to $10,000 and/or a prison sentence of up to ten years.[20]

On January 30, 1934, FDR signed into law the United States Gold Reserve Act. The legislation "transferred ownership of all monetary gold in the United States to the US Treasury and prohibited the Treasury and financial institutions from redeeming dollars for gold."[21]

The US recognized the increasing impracticality and inevitable end of the gold standard. Along these lines, the US used Bretton Woods to reorient its monetary policy. Instead of looking at the past (gold), it embraced a vastly different future. Consider the words of Ben Bernanke, the fourteenth chairman of the Federal Reserve from 2006 to 2014. Since that time, he has worked as a distinguished fellow at the Brookings Institution. In 2016, he wrote:

> The goal was to replace the gold standard, which had collapsed during the Depression, with something more flexible. In practice, however, the system afforded the greatest flexibility to the United States, which enjoyed substantial freedom to pursue its domestic policy objectives as well as the ability to run sustained balance-of-payments deficits.* [22]

Bretton Woods allowed the US to start untethering itself from gold's shackles once and for all. Within three decades, it completed the decoupling process.

---

* In its simplest terms, this deficit occurs when a nation imports more commodities, capital, and services than it exports.

The Nixon Shock

Republican Richard Milhous Nixon is famous for many things. The thirty-seventh US president took office on January 20, 1969, and governed for an eventful five-year period.* Thanks to the Watergate scandal, he remains the only American commander-in-chief to resign from office.

Most relevant for our purposes is August 15, 1971. Up until that day, the values of *all* national currencies were indirectly tied to the US dollar (USD). Other governments pegged their national currencies to the USD, "while the dollar was (loosely) pegged to gold."[23] Governments, individuals, and organizations could easily convert their dollars to gold at a fixed rate. That was about to change.

As Nixon told the American public that day:

> I have directed Secretary Connally to suspend temporarily the convertibility of the dollar into gold or other reserve assets, except in amounts and conditions determined to be in the interest of monetary stability and in the best interests of the United States. Now, what is this action—which is very technical—what does it mean for you? Let me lay to rest the bugaboo of what is called devaluation. If you want to buy a foreign car or take a trip abroad, market conditions may cause your dollar to buy slightly less. But if you are among the overwhelming majority of Americans who buy American-made products in America, your dollar will be worth just as much tomorrow as it is today. The effect of this action, in other words, will be to stabilize the dollar.†

In one fell swoop, Nixon singlehandedly redefined the global world financial order. Historians today refer to the speech as the *Nixon shock*. More than half a century later, its effects continue to reverberate around the world. Not only did Nixon's actions represent the de facto end of the Bretton

---

* After his initial four-year term, Nixon won his reelection bid in 1972 against Democratic candidate George McGovern.
† Watch it yourself at https://tinyurl.com/mgnixon.

Woods era, it signaled something far more ominous—something that we're only beginning to understand.

In his excellent 2021 book *Three Days at Camp David*, Jeffrey Garten makes the compelling case that the roots of America's recent retrenchment in world affairs began at that precise moment. By actions if not words, America was admitting that it was unable—or, perhaps, unwilling—to uphold the centralized global monetary system. (We'll return to this theme in Part II.)

Fiat Currency and a Whole New World

Nixon's 1971 gambit ushered in a decentralized, floating system of currency exchange rates. Under the status quo, the price of a Japanese yen stems from the relative supply and demand of other currencies. Ditto for the Australian dollar, the Canadian dollar, the British pound, and every other national currency.

The Bretton Woods system ultimately collapsed in 1973. As Ben Bernanke explains:

> The Bretton Woods system ultimately broke down in part because the US, as the "anchor" country, didn't live up to its obligation to maintain price stability. Since the early 1970's the international monetary system has been effectively decentralized, with each country setting its own exchange-rate framework and with the values of the major currencies being determined by markets ("floating" rather than fixed exchanged rates).[24]

This lack of centralization represents a tectonic shift between the monetary system of the Bretton Woods era and today's, but it's not the only one. The current global world financial order is predicated on *fiat currencies*. This type of currency derives its value because its issuing government declares the currency to be legal tender. Nothing else. In the case of the United States, Uncle Sam decrees the worth of each dollar; no gold is required. (As a means of backing a national currency, gold is downright passé. Switzerland finally severed ties between the Swiss franc and gold in 1999.)

It's worth briefly restating this stunning transformation. As it stands, the US dollar is untethered to gold—or any other commodity for that matter. Rather, its backing stems from the full faith and credit of the American government, pledging to fulfill its payment obligations in a timely manner. Loaning money to the US represents "a safe bet."[25] Put differently, the US dollar remains the world's reserve currency "because of the safety, security, and depth of the US markets. The dominance of the dollar is based on the belief the US will pay its obligations."[26] (We'll see in Chapter 5 how America's political and economic dysfunction and staggering national debt stand to knock the dollar off its perch—for good.)

While Nixon's actions suddenly and fundamentally changed the world's monetary rules, one thing has remained constant: The US dollar has endured as the most important global currency.

Let's examine why.

Dollarization and US Dominance

The most public display of US trade embargoes and sanctions arguably took place in October 1962. The Cuban Missile Crisis represented the height of Cold War tensions between the US and the USSR. President John F. Kennedy ordered a quarantined Cuba to prevent a nuclear war. (The moniker *naval blockade* connoted war.) By comparison, though, these actions were child's play compared to what would come.

Before explaining the ramifications of that short statement, a little background is in order.

The decision of most Bretton Woods participants to accept the US dollar as the world's reserve national currency effectively *dollarized* the world. As but one example of the dollar's continued ubiquity, consider Figure 3.3. It reflects the share of USD global foreign exchange reserves, export invoicing, and foreign exchange transactions.

THE CATALYSTS

Figure 3.3: US Dollar Dominance as of March 8, 2025

Source: Atlantic Council's Dollar Dominance Monitor

With respect to the former, a little context is in order. Specifically, how dominant is the USD relative to the second most popular currency used for foreign exchange reserves? Figure 3.4 answers that question.

Figure 3.4: Currency Composition of Official Foreign Exchange Reserves

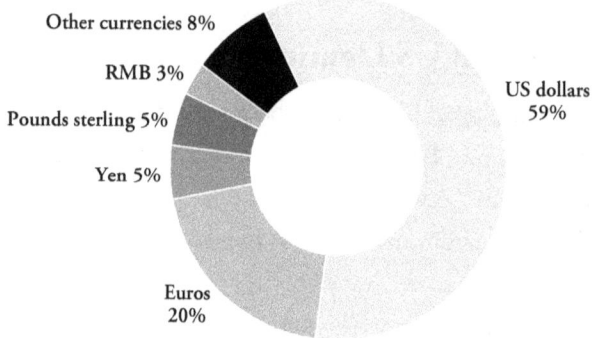

Source: International Monetary Fund. Notes: 149 reporting countries.

Many events and trends explain the status quo, but I'd like to call out one in particular. The fall of the Soviet Union on December 26, 1991, only made the world more dependent on the US dollar. Put differently, America hasn't realized one-time or diminishing benefits from the USD's status as the world's reserve currency. In fact, quite the contrary. In June 2019, the

European Central Bank published research suggesting that "the exorbitant privilege has gradually increased over time."[27]

The Rails: How the US Weaponizes Its National Currency

Banks and other financial institutions hold nearly three times as much currency in USD as they do in euros. Figures 3.2 and 3.3 illustrate the sheer power of the dollar—something that America hasn't exactly been shy about using over the past eighty years. The obvious question: How?

Swift

Chapter 2 referenced the Society for Worldwide Interbank Financial Telecommunication. By way of brief review, Swift is the world's global and centralized financial communications network. Through it, financial institutions securely exchange key messages with each other about transactions.

American senior officials pressure Swift to exclude target countries from its network, and Swift almost always complies with American requests. Governments and terrorist organizations quickly find themselves effectively isolated from the global financial system. At a minimum, the US hampers bad actors' efforts to move their money. Usually, though, these individuals, governments, and organizations find their funds frozen and effectively useless. (Remember from the previous chapter that money needs to be able to move. Freezing accounts and other assets effectively renders them moot.)

As Dante Disparte of the Bretton Woods Committee astutely observes:

> When people speak of weaponizing a currency, it is mistaken to assume a currency can be used as a weapon beyond merely being a pecuniary "dumb bomb." Rather, the currency, in military and economic parlance, is merely the payload. The real weapon, however, is the underlying rails on which currencies and corresponding payment and economic activity are transmitted. The countries, companies and consortia that control those rails ultimately wield real power and thus you weaponize payment rails, more so than you weaponize currencies. Herein, the soft power of dollar hegemony, or the accrued natural

advantages to US foreign policy from 80 years of the dollar being the world's reserve currency, come to light.[28]

The dollar has been the ultimate financial weapon. America's ability to track and intercept financial transactions, especially those related to terrorist financing, gives it even more leverage over global banking networks. Armed with this capability, the US exerts control and pressure on global banking institutions. The latter faced little choice but to comply and cooperate with its financial intelligence operations to avoid sanctions or other punitive measures.

Economic Sanctions and Financial Warfare

After the terrorist attacks on September 11, 2001, America accelerated its use of economic sanctions to effectuate its foreign policy. The US Treasury Department began undermining rogue nations, terrorists, criminal syndicates, and other bad actors.

Juan Zarate is a former senior official at the US Treasury and the White House. His 2013 book, *Treasury's War: The Unleashing of a New Era of Financial Warfare*, is nothing if not illuminating. In it, he explains how America is using its financial weapons more than its military ones.

Zarate pulls back the curtain on how the US has used sanctions, blacklisting, and international cooperation in all sorts of ways. Sometimes, the objectives are unassailable, such as disrupting terrorist plots. Other times, the morality of pressuring adversaries is a little nebulous. North Korea, Syria, and Iran serve as some of the highest-profile recent examples.

OFAC

A little-known office within the US Treasury Department plays an outsize role in modern geopolitical battles. The Office of Foreign Assets Control (OFAC):

> administers and enforces economic and trade sanctions based on US foreign policy and national security goals against targeted foreign

US FINANCIAL HEGEMONY

countries and regimes, terrorists, international narcotics traffickers, those engaged in activities related to the proliferation of weapons of mass destruction, and other threats to the national security, foreign policy or economy of the United States.[29]

Few criminal organizations or rogue nations have historically wanted to duel with OFAC—and for good reason. The agency maintains *the list*: an actual collection of *specially designated nationals* (SDNs) with whom no individual, corporation, or nation can legally trade or do business.[*]

The SDN list isn't short. Figure 3.5 shows the additions to it from 2001 to 2023.

Figure 3.5: New Additions to OFAC Sanctions Lists by Year

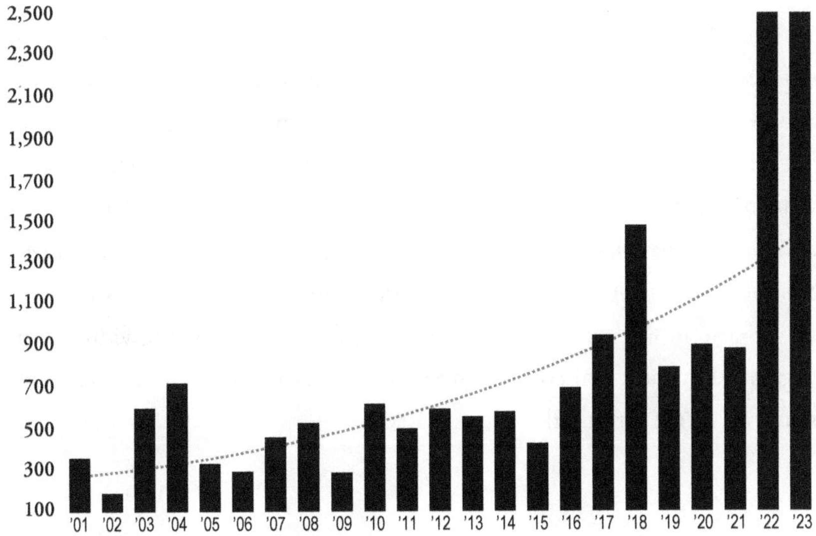

Source: Gibson, Dunn & Crutcher LLP | Data: https://tinyurl.com/the-cat-ofac24

---

[*] Go to https://sanctionssearch.ofac.treas.gov to search current US sanctions.

THE CATALYSTS

Sanctions' Unintended Effects and Collateral Damage

Beginning in 2005, the US has imposed targeted economic sanctions on "Venezuelan individuals and entities that have engaged in criminal, antidemocratic, or corrupt actions."[30] The Center for Economic and Policy Research, an American think tank, has found that these sanctions have harmed more than 300,000 Venezuelans' access to healthcare:

> This startling number includes 80,000 HIV-infected patients, 16,000 individuals in need of dialysis, and 16,000 cancer patients. Food imports have also dramatically decreased over the last decade—from $11.2 billion of purchases in 2013 to $2.46 billion in 2018—unequivocally due to a collapse of government revenue directly tied to restrictive sanctions.[31]

Finally, there's the issue of secondary sanctions. The US penalizes foreign entities that do business with sanctioned countries. Even the threat of this action often compels organizations to comply with questionable US policies.

What's more, OFAC adheres to a strict liability standard, which means that "a US person may be held civilly liable for sanctions violations even *without having knowledge or reason to know it was engaging in such a violation.*"[32] (Emphasis mine.) Translation: Ignorance of illicit behavior is no defense in the eyes of US law. As a result, companies, individuals, and organizations face real consequences for not getting in line. Astonishingly, many aren't even aware the queue exists.

The final chapter in this part explains how America's past willingness and ability to constrain private enterprise have played a pivotal role in creating the current financial world order.

Key Points

- Over the past century, the US has weaned its currency from the gold standard while retaining its status as the world's reserve currency.
- America has reaped significant rewards from the dollar's standing.
- Via powerful economic sanctions, the US has long rattled its saber for its own political and economic ends.
- Venezuela and Iran are just two of the countries that have struggled in the wake of US sanctions.

CHAPTER 4

CONSTRAINED CAPITALISM

MEANINGFUL REGULATIONS, INSTITUTIONS, AND US COURTS MINIMIZED THE EVILS OF FREE MARKETS.

> "We may have democracy, or we may have wealth concentrated in the hands of a few, but we can't have both."
> —Louis Brandeis

The name Vannevar Bush probably doesn't ring a bell, but his work—and the philosophy behind it—still underpins much of our lives a half-century after his death in 1974.

The renowned engineer and inventor cut his teeth at the storied Massachusetts Institute of Technology (MIT). In 1922, he, Laurence Marshall, and Charles Smith founded the company that became Raytheon and is now known as RTX Corporation. (The defense contractor remains a leviathan a century later. As of 2023, it employed roughly 183,000 people.[1])

THE CATALYSTS

With his country at war in the early 1940s, Bush answered the call and began a distinguished career in public service. He served as the head of the US Office of Scientific Research and Development (OSRD) from 1941 to 1947 under two presidents: FDR and Harry S. Truman. Both men correctly surmised that superior science and technology wouldn't just determine who would win the war. It would decide the peacetime winners as well.

To this end, Bush laid out a bold hybrid vision for the future: a "government-science partnership that resulted in the National Science Foundation. The core idea: governments need to fund basic research."[2] As a corollary, the private sector couldn't undertake massive projects on its own. Both the public sector and academia would need to drive key innovations for today's world and tomorrow's.

On the evening of October 4, 1957, the USSR launched the first artificial Earth satellite. Sputnik 1 sent shockwaves across the highest levels of the US government. America's dollar may have been the world's reserve currency, but the Russians weren't going to play second fiddle. President Dwight D. Eisenhower quickly marshaled his country's resources. Four months later, he established a formal agency under the US Department of Defense responsible for researching and developing advanced military technologies.

The Advanced Research Projects Agency (ARPA) addressed critical needs based on perceived and real enemy threats. For example, what if a nuclear attack knocked out America's centralized communications networks? The nightmare scenario was all too real back then. In 1949, the USSR conducted its first successful tests on atomic weapons.[3]

Soon rebranded as the *Defense Advanced Research Projects Agency*, DARPA developed the Advanced Research Projects Agency Network. ARPANET represented the world's first modern distributed or decentralized computer network. Without getting into all the technical minutiae, ARPANET could reliably deliver data packets between devices. Think of it as a talking postman, a necessary precursor to today's internet.

Let's look at the present day. The US government and scores of Silicon Valley *unicorns*—privately held companies valued at more than $1 billion—have reaped massive rewards from the profound public-private partnerships forged during WWII. Examples are everywhere, but consider the iPhone as one. As economist Mariana Mazzucato writes in her excellent 2015 book, *The Entrepreneurial State*:

> Every technology that makes the iPhone smart and not stupid owes its funding to both basic and applied research funded by the State. This of course does not mean that Steve Jobs and his team were not crucial to Apple's success, but that ignoring the 'public' side of that story will prevent future Apples from being born.

And it's not just high-tech phones. Amazon founder Jeff Bezos acknowledged how much his company benefited from America's vast infrastructure. As he said in 2018, "I didn't have to build a transportation network to deliver the packages. It existed: It was called the post office."[4]

In this way, Bezos wasn't unique. Both private corporation CEOs and elected officials recognized the invaluable and mutually beneficial nature of their longstanding collaboration. Margaret O'Mara's masterful book *The Code: Silicon Valley and the Remaking of America* delves deeply into this topic.

That's not to say that these two sides didn't occasionally clash. They most certainly did, but business didn't overrun regulators. At its core, the world financial order has reflected one simple fact: The US government routinely kept its private industry in check. For-profit enterprises with outsize power that became monopolies faced opposition and real consequences. US legislators, institutions, regulatory bodies, and the courts routinely stepped in.

As we'll see in this final chapter of Part I, for the majority of the twentieth century, these entities have collectively ensured that corporate influence didn't approach that of the polity that governed them.

Antitrust Law 101

One need not be a Karl Marx disciple to acknowledge the inherent limitations of—and problems with—laissez-faire capitalism. Most relevant for our purposes is the need for effectual antitrust law.

An Insanely Brief History of Checking Corporate Power

Antitrust law is old hat. In fact, the notion dates back at least two millennia. As the prominent South African political scientist D. V. Cowen has written:

> The oldest criminal enactment against monopolies which has been preserved to the present day, the *lex Julia de annona*, relates to the corn trade and probably dates from the time of Julius Caesar. This law, which is phrased in wide terms, imposed a heavy fine on any person who alone, or in association with others, did any act which artificially increased the price of corn.
>
> But the effect of the *lex Julia* was not encouraging. The Roman lawgiver was soon to find that monopoly grows easily and dies hard. Liability to prosecution and a fine under the Imperial decree did not prevent the practice from gradually extending to the whole of the trade in foodstuffs and, indeed, to most other articles in daily use. Records show that numerous imperial decrees were promulgated from time to time to deal with the situation. Criminal sanctions, which in the first instance had been directed against corn monopolies, were later extended to monopolies of provisions generally, and then to monopolies of all kinds of goods—*ne dardanari ullius mercies sint*. Moreover, the penalties for the offence were increased. Thus, besides the fine provided for by the lex *Juli de annona*, which remained in force, subsequent decrees introduced the penalties of withdrawal of the right to trade and even deportation.[5]

Laws designed to outlaw unfair competition continued to evolve in the thirteenth and fourteenth centuries. The latter saw the first court cases involving restraint of trade. This key legal tenet represents "any activity that tends to limit a party's ability to enter into transactions."[6] In the seventeenth and eighteenth centuries, Kings of England Charles I and Charles II both found monopolies useful for raising revenue.

Count Adam Smith among those who argued for responsible antitrust laws around that time. As the free-market champion wrote in his seminal 1776 text:

> People of the same trade seldom meet together, even for merriment and diversion, but the conversation ends in a conspiracy against the public, or in some contrivance to raise prices.

Throughout the twentieth century, the US and Europe* emerged as the world's antitrust exemplars. Their leaders created the most expansive and influential regimes that—at least in theory—ensured fair competition for all parties concerned.

It's enlightening to note, though, that not *that* long ago, national antitrust legislation was hardly ubiquitous. From 1900 until the end of World War II, "only 13 countries adopted competition laws."[7] During the Cold War, another twenty-eight nations passed similar statutes.

Why Meaningful Antitrust Legislation and Enforcement Have (Largely) Prevailed

Politicians, economists, policy wonks, and informed citizens can and do debate the specifics of individual antitrust bills. Still, the fundamental argument for reining in the excesses of unfettered capitalism is as unimpeachable now as it was in Caesar's day. Through legislation, enforcement, and penalties, governments *should* curtail big business. How else can society prevent excessive market concentration, massive income inequality, and the financial crises mentioned in Chapter 2? And what about negative externalities, such as pollution, congestion, and secondhand smoke?

---

* And later the European Union.

By and large, democratic leaders throughout the twentieth century realized what history has repeatedly taught us: Without adequate guardrails, a few individuals and corporations inevitably hold an unhealthy concentration of economic wealth. All else being equal, consumers pay higher prices for goods and services, and with less choice to boot.

Countless studies and analyses have confirmed other adverse effects of monopolies and oligopolies. For instance, workers in concentrated markets regularly face fewer employment options and lower pay. A recent working paper from the US Bureau of Labor Statistics found that "employer concentration at the county-industry level has been growing in the manufacturing sector, with a negative impact on wages."[8] (Chapter 6 explores how for-profit companies are usurping government functions at an alarming rate.)

Describing the overarching need for antitrust legislation provides the requisite context for this chapter. At this point, though, it's natural to ask a few specific questions:

- Which laws and rulings have shaped the United States's business environment and, by extension, allowed the country to become the fulcrum of the current world financial order?
- How has America's antitrust environment changed throughout the twentieth century?

This chapter addresses these two queries.

Examining America's Relationship With Antitrust Law

It's fair to split US antitrust legislation into several eras. Let's begin at the turn of the nineteenth century.

American historians refer to the twenty-year period beginning in the late 1870s as the *Gilded Age*. For two decades, monopolies and trusts dominated industries. They acted in decidedly anticompetitive ways and, even worse, with impunity. Yes, this was the heyday of robber barons:

These men used union busting, fraud, intimidation, violence and their extensive political connections to gain an advantage over any competitors. Robber barons were relentless in their efforts to amass wealth while exploiting workers and ignoring standard business rules—and in many cases, the law itself.

They soon accumulated vast amounts of money and dominated every major industry including the railroad, oil, banking, timber, sugar, liquor, meatpacking, steel, mining, tobacco and textile industries.[9]

A groundswell for change was building, and something had to give.

The Progressive Era

Republican Theodore Roosevelt took office as the twenty-sixth US president in 1901 after the assassination of his predecessor, William McKinley. He won reelection and served until 1909. Perhaps no single quote expresses the Trust Buster's thoughts on big business better than this one from Roosevelt's speech in Providence, Rhode Island, in 1902:

> The great corporations which we have grown to speak of rather loosely as trusts are the creatures of the State, and the State not only has the right to control them, but it is duty bound to control them wherever the need of such control is shown.[10]

Roosevelt, a progressive Republican, set an unambiguous tone for what would become the first era of American antitrust legislation. American politicians finally and forcefully responded to the excesses of the Gilded Age by passing remarkable, pro-consumer laws. It's impossible to overstate the magnitude of the statutes passed during this period. Even today, the effects of these laws resonate throughout the country and, in fact, the world.

The Sherman Antitrust Act

This revolutionary piece of legislation aimed to prohibit monopolistic practices and promote fair competition. In retrospect, Sherman launched the country's incipient antitrust enforcement movement. It represented Congress's first attempt to prohibit trusts. Interestingly, its name comes from "Senator John Sherman of Ohio, who was a chairman of the Senate finance committee and the Secretary of the Treasury under President Hayes."[11]

Clayton Antitrust Act

Passed in 1914 by President Woodrow Wilson, Clayton strengthened the Sherman Act. Specifically, this act proscribed many contemporary practices businesses used that reduced competition. Examples included price discrimination, exclusive dealings, and merger-and-acquisition (M&A) activity.

The Federal Trade Commission Act

That same year, the US also passed this piece of landmark legislation: the Federal Trade Commission Act. This law established the eponymous Federal Trade Commission (FTC) with a broader charter: to enforce antitrust laws and prevent unfair business practices. It's fair to say that the law and agency ushered in the era of consumer protection, competition, and innovation.

Before continuing, a short disclaimer is in order: The US may have been among the first to pass certain antitrust laws and create specific agencies. In most cases, though, America isn't alone. On the contrary, most nations have passed comparable legislation and, in the process, empowered their own enforcement agencies.

The New Deal Era

Beginning in 1929, the Great Depression led to a surge in the public sector. The 1930s and 1940s saw unprecedented government intervention designed to stabilize the economy and protect consumers, workers, and investors. Specifically, FDR passed two laws within a year of each other with far-reaching effects on the business community.

The Glass-Steagall Act

With the wounds of 1929 still fresh in Americans' minds, this 1933 act sought to prevent another national financial cataclysm. Ideally, Glass-Steagall would "provide for the safer and more effective use of the assets of banks, to regulate interbank control, to prevent the undue diversion of funds into speculative operations, and for other purposes."[12] That is, it would reduce consumer financial risk by drawing a firm line of demarcation between commercial and investment banks. (See the discussion in Chapter 2 for more about the differences between these types of financial institutions.)

Glass-Steagall also created the Federal Deposit Insurance Corporation. Since its inception, the FDIC has guaranteed its depositors' funds. Not surprisingly, other nations have emulated this agency as well. The nonprofit International Association of Deposit Insurers reports that most industrialized countries offer their citizens similar financial protections to America's FDIC.[13]

The Securities Exchange Act

Less than a year later, FDR signed this pivotal piece of financial legislation into law. The Securities and Exchange Commission (SEC) also protects individual and institutional investors by regulating the stock market and other markets selling securities. Importantly, the agency would ultimately serve as the sole arbiter of:

- The assets that constituted securities.
- Which parties would have to register as securities brokers.

(Chapter 9 will explore the considerable logistical problems of the status quo.)

The Communications Act of 1934

This statute conceived the Federal Communications Commission. The FCC regulates "interstate and international communications by radio, television, wire, satellite, and cable."[14] Its importance would rise at the end of the twentieth century as the main vehicle to regulate Big Tech. (Chapter 6 will discuss the ramifications of insufficient regulation.)

Maintaining the Status Quo

From the 1940s to the late 1970s, US lawmakers largely focused on areas other than consumer protection and antitrust. They had bigger fish to fry. Notable legislation of the era included the Civil Rights Act of 1964, the Voting Rights Act of 1965, and the Civil Rights Act of 1968. With matters of free enterprise, "antitrust came to represent the Magna Carta of free enterprise. It was seen as the key to preserving economic and political freedom."[15]

In this period, US courts didn't mince words during trials and in verdicts. With rare exceptions, they placed the burden of proof on private companies to prove that their proposed actions didn't cause harm. Put differently, corporations had to conclusively demonstrate that their M&A activity didn't now—and, arguably just as important, *wouldn't*—adversely affect competition in the future.

Dr. Laura Phillips-Sawyer is a law professor and noted antitrust expert. In a working paper for Harvard Business School, she writes about two fascinating cases that typified the Supreme Court's ethos of the time:

> One of the best-known mergers and acquisitions cases of this era denied a merger between two of the three largest banks in Philadelphia at the time, even though their overall market share was low and competing banks and economists alike welcomed the merger because it would allow the newly formed bank to compete with other, larger banks, particularly those in New York. In essence, *Philadelphia National Bank* (1963) created a parallel to the per se rule in the form of a rebuttable presumption that a merger between large companies was deemed unlawful unless there was clear evidence that it would not have anticompetitive effects. In *United States v. Von's Grocery Co.* (1966), the Court invalidated a merger between grocery firms that would have led to a meager 7.5 percent market share—a decision that

CONSTRAINED CAPITALISM

underscored just how high the justices had set the bar for companies to prove that a merger would not lead to anticompetitive effects.[16]

Think about it. The highest court in the land refused to let two food stores merge because the new entity would capture a mere $1 out of every $14 Americans spent in an admittedly essential area. By way of contrast, consider Amazon today. Its leadership has long disputed any monopolistic claims—and is gearing up for a prolonged legal battle as I write these words.[*] In 2024, the Everything Store is on track to snag a staggering 40 percent of US e-commerce sales.[17]

To be sure, antitrust laws don't exactly qualify as page-turners. Maybe they're even boring. What's more, some undoubtedly imposed undue hardships on businesses looking to make a legitimate buck. Don't be fooled, though: These bills—and many others for that matter—were downright necessary to prevent the evils of laissez-faire capitalism Americans experienced at the end of the nineteenth century. As New York University professor and author of *Adrift: America in 100 Charts* Scott Galloway astutely notes:

> The NHTSA[†] is one of the many boring state and federal agencies critical to a healthy society. Before the Food and Drug Administration, the sale and distribution of food and pharmaceuticals was a free-for-all. The Federal Aviation Administration is the reason your chances of dying in a plane crash are 1 in 3.37 billion. Next time someone tells you they don't trust government, ask them if they trust cars, food, pain killers, buildings, or airplanes.[18]

Sadly, the tide against responsible antitrust legislation in America has begun to turn. (The next two chapters revisit this topic in different contexts, but it's worth briefly mentioning it here.)

---

[*] We'll return to this topic in Chapter 6.
[†] Short for the National Highway Traffic Safety Administration.

THE CATALYSTS

Retrenchment: The Rise of Deregulation and Neoliberalism

The past forty years have seen a stark change in both US antitrust policy and judicial interpretation of antitrust law. Its precise genesis is impossible to pinpoint, but one need not possess an MBA from Harvard to know that businesses generally scoff at the thought of *any* regulation. As Dr. Phillips-Sawyer observes:

> By the 1960s, criticism of active antitrust enforcement had begun to mount. This critique, which argued for minimal government intervention into economic activities, found a home at the University of Chicago. What would become known as the Chicago school of antitrust policy held that markets were more robust and self-correcting than existing antitrust policy allowed—and moreover, that government interventions often exacerbated market inefficiencies rather than making them more competitive. Thus antitrust policy should prohibit naked price fixing or market division, but otherwise it should allow markets to function independently.[19]

The movement was afoot in the 1970s. Exhibit A: Democratic President Jimmy Carter signed the Airline Deregulation Act in 1978. To be sure, it accelerated during the next decade and beyond. Starting with the election of Ronald Reagan in 1980, America moved swiftly and steadily toward deregulation, buoyed by the University of Chicago's free-market acolytes.

Bill Clinton signed off on the Telecommunications Act of 1996. Three years later, he did the same with the Financial Services Modernization Act—aka, the Gramm-Leach-Bliley Act. This legislation repealed key parts of Glass-Steagall. In November 1999, Clinton had publicly declared, "The Glass–Steagall law is no longer appropriate."[20] (The ensuing Great Recession of 2008 made that naive pronouncement look patently ridiculous.)

I'd be remiss if I ended this section without mentioning the Communications Decency Act (CDA) of 1996. Congress sent it to Clinton's desk under the aegis of primarily limiting minors' access to pornography over the burgeoning World Wide Web.* That bill contained an obscure yet key provision that has become more and more topical.

Section 230 "provides immunity to online platforms from civil liability based on third-party content and for the removal of content in certain circumstances."[21] For example, say that you sell illegal drugs on eBay or slam your neighbor on Facebook, Nextdoor, or Twitter/X. As of this writing, legally speaking, each company is immune from any type of prosecution. In their view, they're merely neutral platforms, absolved of any legal—much less ethical—responsibility to police their users. As we saw in this book's introduction, this dangerous belief includes horrific events such as January 6. (Chapter 6 will briefly return to this subject.)

The Courts

It's instructive to view any nation's antitrust legislation from a historical perspective—and US law is no exception to this rule. It's equally valuable—if not more so—to examine how courts have interpreted these statutes. More specifically, legally speaking, have US lawmakers overstepped their bounds? And what have judges had to say about the legality of the cases that have appeared before them?

Note that US case law stems from two sources:

- The government bringing cases against companies it believes to be violating existing legislation.
- Businesses bringing actions against each other for illegal or unfair trade practices.

When the executive branch has generally opted not to rigorously enforce laws, private actors can fill the gap and stop anticompetitive processes through the courts. Such was the case during the Reagan years.

---

* Although many people mistakenly conflate the two, the web and the internet aren't identical. In a nutshell, the former is the software built upon the internet's hardware.

THE CATALYSTS

Key US Tech Antitrust Cases

Passing legislation is one thing; enforcing it is another. During the twentieth century, at key points, the US Department of Justice stepped up to the plate. The result: The government curbed the excesses of individual companies. On a macro level, though, the effects were more profound. Each legal action ensured that a single corporation couldn't become more powerful than the officials and agencies that governed it.

Let's look at four examples of US antitrust regulation of tech goliaths.

AT&T

Founded in 1885 as a subsidiary of Alexander Graham Bell's American Bell Telephone Company, AT&T was a beast. Beginning in the 1960s, "AT&T completely dominated the telecommunications industry in the United States."[22] Within a decade, AT&T employed nearly one million people, becoming the largest firm in the world. AT&T's total assets exceeded those of General Motors, Exxon, and Mobil *combined*.[23] Among its most profitable divisions was Long Lines, the provider of long-distance phone service.

It had clearly become a monopoly and, in 1974, the DOJ filed an antitrust lawsuit alleging that the Bell System companies were illegally suppressing competition in the telecommunications industry. In its suit, the government cited a violation of Section 2 of the Sherman Act.[24]

Ultimately, the telecom giant settled the case. Seven regional Bell Operating Companies (RBOCs) took control of the nation's local phone networks. The AT&T breakup "probably helped upstart fiber-optic long-distance firms Sprint and MCI, who did not own local lines and had to compete with the integrated AT&T network."[25]

IBM

International Business Machines was the very type of company poised to benefit from the computing era. Much like AT&T, at the time IBM was breathing rarefied air. In 1969, it was the sixth-largest company in the world.[26]

That same year, the DOJ sued the firm under the Sherman Antitrust Act:

> The 1969 action alleged that IBM had undertaken exclusionary and predatory conduct with the aim and effect of eliminating competition so that IBM could maintain its monopoly position in general purpose digital computers.[27]

More than a decade of courtroom back-and-forth ensued before the conservative Reagan administration* predictably scuttled the case:

> William F. Baxter, the Assistant Attorney General in charge of the antitrust division, said today that the Government's decision to drop its 13-year-old antitrust suit against the International Business Machines Corporation was "the only sensible thing to do" and that the case against the computer giant was based on "flimsy" evidence.[28]

The suit may not have resulted in the outcome that prosecutors originally wanted. At a minimum, though, the increased scrutiny slowed down Big Blue. Although it's a counterfactual, it's not hard to imagine an unencumbered IBM obliterating its rivals, the forthcoming personal computer (PC) industry.

Microsoft

By 1995, the web for which our friend Vannevar Bush and his colleagues laid the groundwork had finally taken off. Although not the first commercial browser, Mosaic Netscape had launched the previous October with great fanfare.

---

* Although both technically Republicans, Ronald Reagan and Teddy Roosevelt diverged on many policy matters. The reason is simple: The former was conservative, whereas the latter was not.

THE CATALYSTS

As modern computing morphed in front of our eyes, Microsoft was asleep at the wheel. It quickly cobbled together its alternative, Internet Explorer. Bill Gates and company weren't exactly shy about euphemistically *encouraging* Windows customers to use it in lieu of Mosaic. As *The New York Times* reported at the time:

> A close look at Microsoft's no-holds-barred push into the Internet software business offers a window into the ways the company uses its market muscle to influence the behavior of virtually every player in the industry.[29]

Microsoft's leadership and legal department knew the company could easily crush its rivals. Optics mattered more than ever. To this end, in August 1997 the company "promised to invest approximately $150 million or shares of Apple non-voting preferred stock."[30]

It's rare that a corporation throws its major competitor a giant lifeboat to ensure its survival. (Questions about Apple's long-term viability pervaded the company at the time. Iconic cofounder Steve Jobs had just returned to the helm. Remember that the iPod hadn't launched yet, never mind the über-successful iPhone.)

Was Microsoft's investment a shrewd business move, or did it represent an attempt to keep US regulators at bay? More than one thing can be true, but the latter gambit didn't appease US regulators. In May 1998, the DOJ, along with twenty states, sued Microsoft, claiming that the software giant's business practices violated the Clayton Act.

Facing a prolonged legal battle, the two sides ultimately settled. On September 6, 2001, the DOJ announced that it no longer sought the breakup of Microsoft. The two agreed on concessions.*

Had it not been for US antitrust statutes or the DOJ's willingness to enforce them in the late twentieth century, it's likely that two multitrillion-dollar tech companies today wouldn't exist. Consider the arguments that

---

* See https://tinyurl.com/the-cat-ms-timeline for a timeline of events.

CONSTRAINED CAPITALISM

"Apple co-founder Steve Jobs had raised in 1998 against Microsoft's 'dirty tactics' while urging regulators to take steps to force the PC software maker 'to play fair.'"[31] But for antitrust, we may have never heard of Google, now part of the parent company Alphabet.

Google

Those of us of a certain age remember the early days of web search. The early engines of the mid-1990s included Alta Vista, AskJeeves, Yahoo!, and Lycos. None of these tools could reliably return user results.

And then came Google.

While at Stanford working toward PhDs in computer science, Larry Page and Sergey Brin founded Google in 1998. It immediately exploded, quickly becoming the world's largest search engine. As of this writing, its market share exceeds 90 percent—nine times higher than its next five highest competitors combined.[32] In April 2024, the market capitalization of Alphabet, its parent company, cracked $2 trillion USD.[33]

It was a Pyrrhic victory for Google's leadership. For years it had faced increased scrutiny over its business practices. Four years prior, the US Justice Department[34] and numerous state attorneys general sued the company under antitrust laws. On August 5, 2024, Judge Amit P. Mehta of the US District Court for the District of Columbia issued his 277-page ruling. In one of his most damning findings, he plainly wrote, "Google is a monopolist, and it has acted as one to maintain its monopoly."[35]

Unsurprisingly, Google has vowed to appeal. If the previous anti-trust cases in this section serve as any guide, don't expect a resolution anytime soon. Cases of this magnitude have historically gone to the Supreme Court—a process that plays out over years or decades. Management at Amazon, Apple, Meta, and Alphabet know that they can probably run out the clock. After all, history has shown them as much.

THE CATALYSTS

Throughout the twentieth century, US regulators and courts generally reined in corporate power when it became excessive. As we'll see in the next chapter, that trend is ending. Tech startups have rapidly become goliaths and de facto independent nation-states. Government actions—if and when they arrive—can't undo the damage they've wrought.

Key Points

- As far back as the Roman empire, elected leaders have relied upon antitrust statutes to protect markets and society from unfair and anticompetitive trade practices.
- The US and Europe have historically promulgated the biggest and best regimes for competition regulation.
- Despite underlying philosophical differences, for most of the twentieth century, both major US political parties showed a willingness to keep big business at bay and fulfill their obligations.
- The rapid proliferation of global tech giants has made it difficult for governments to respond quickly enough to prevent monopolistic practices.

This concludes Part I of the book. To be sure, it has quickly covered a great deal of historical ground. Table 4.1 briefly summarizes the first four chapters of this book and explains the current world financial order.

Table 4.1: Summary of Previous World Financial Order

Dimension	Description
Default mode	Relative stability
Financial services	Centralized
Ability to constrain big business	Considerable, if inconsistent
World's reserve currency	US Dollar

Dimension	Description
Citizens' trust in their government and institutions	Relatively high
Ability of organizations and countries to circumvent US sanctions	Relatively limited
Power of technology	Limited, local, and controllable

We now shift our focus to Part II.

The following eight chapters describe the accelerating forces forging a new, vastly different financial world order. I've tried to disentangle them as much as possible. As you'll soon see, though, they're inextricably linked.

Make no mistake: The near future will differ drastically from the past.

PART II

THE CATALYSTS

CHAPTER 5
US POLITICAL AND ECONOMIC DYSFUNCTION

HYPER-PARTISANSHIP HAS WEAKENED THE FULCRUM OF THE WORLD FINANCIAL ORDER.

> "A great civilization is not conquered from without until it has destroyed itself from within."
>
> —*Will Durant*

American Airlines Flight 11 left Logan International Airport in Boston without much fanfare on the morning of September 11, 2001. Soon after takeoff, five members of Al-Qaida hijacked the Boeing 767 and diverted the plane toward New York City—the World Trade Center (WTC), to be exact.[1]

THE CATALYSTS

At 8:46 a.m. that morning, the terrorists crashed the plane into its North Tower. Unfortunately, the carnage didn't stop there.

In a massively coordinated effort, three other teams of hijackers seized three other US aircraft on that fateful September day. A second plane crashed into WTC's South Tower seventeen minutes later. Chaos erupted. A third hit the Pentagon in Arlington, Virginia. Courageous passengers on a fourth flight attacked terrorists and brought their plane down in an open field in Somerset County, Pennsylvania. The heroic efforts undoubtedly saved the Capitol Building, a symbolic building roughly two miles from the White House.[2]

George W. Bush addressed a bewildered and shell-shocked nation that night. He concluded his remarks as follows:

> This is a day when all Americans from every walk of life unite in our resolve for justice and peace. America has stood down enemies before, and we will do so this time. None of us will ever forget this day. Yet, we go forward to defend freedom and all that is good and just in our world.[3]

Thus began the US war on terrorism. Ten days after 9/11, a Gallup poll found that a remarkable 90 percent of Americans approved of President George W. Bush's performance as president.[4] It marked the highest approval rating of any chief executive in the country's history.

To be sure, Bush's post-9/11 actions weren't above reproach. Count the American Civil Liberties Union among the many organizations that formally objected to his administration's legislation and actions during his two terms. Of particular interest was the Patriot Act. Passed on October 26, 2001, the law "authorized unprecedented surveillance of American citizens and individuals worldwide without traditional civil liberties safeguards."[5] Despite these objections, Americans largely supported their commander-in-chief in a time of existential crisis.

US POLITICAL AND ECONOMIC DYSFUNCTION

Throughout his administration, Bush spent much of his time dealing with an array of catastrophes. He left office in early 2009 as the subprime mortgage crisis crippled the economy. In between, Hurricane Katrina ravaged the southeastern US on August 29, 2005, killing nearly 1,400 Americans and causing more than $125 billion in damages.[6] After Katrina, Bush began contemplating how to prevent yet another unthinkable disaster.

Preventing the Next Crisis

In his bestselling 2021 book *The Premonition: A Pandemic Story*, Michael Lewis provides an insider's guide into President Bush's immediate post-Katrina mindset. At that time, Bush read a book that profoundly influenced his thinking for years: *The Great Influenza: The Story of the Deadliest Pandemic in History.* John Barry's definitive account of the 1918 Spanish flu left an indelible impression on Bush. As Lewis writes:

> Inside of eighteen months, a virus had killed somewhere between forty and sixty million people around the world, but Barry focused on the American carnage. At least half a million Americans, most of them young, had died.
>
> A similar culling of the far larger population in 2005 would kill a million and a half Americans. If anything like Barry described were to occur again, it would distort American life in the most fantastic ways, and leave it forever changed.
>
> Bush returned to the White House from his summer vacation with a new interest in pandemics.*

During the remainder of his administration, Bush devoted significant resources to developing extensive preparation plans for a worldwide pandemic. As he said at the time, "If we wait for a pandemic to appear, it will be too late to prepare. And one day many lives could be needlessly lost because we failed to act today."[7] His words became frighteningly prophetic.

---

* Michael Lewis, *The Premonition: A Pandemic Story* (W. W. Norton & Company, 2021).

THE CATALYSTS

The date January 20, 2020, doesn't evoke the same memories as 9/11. In a way, though, it's equally significant. On that winter day, a relatively young 35-year-old man entered a Washington State hospital. As for his conditions, he:

> had been experiencing a cough, fever, nausea, and vomiting, had tested positive for COVID-19. He was hospitalized, where his condition grew worse and he developed pneumonia. His symptoms abated 10 days later.[8]

George W. Bush worried a great deal about the possibility of a pandemic and developed detailed plans to contain one. By contrast, the actions of his Republican successor, Donald Trump, immediately before and during COVID-19 made the pandemic political. In so doing, Trump put countless lives at stake. Table 5.1 details just a few of Trump's pandemic-related actions and statements.[9]

Table 5.1: Partial Timeline of Donald Trump's Pandemic-Related Behavior

Month and Year	Action
May 2018	The Trump Administration disbands the White House pandemic response team.
July 2019	The Centers for Disease Control (CDC) epidemiologist embedded in China's disease control agency left the post, and the Trump Administration eliminated the role.
Jan. 22, 2020	Trump publicly says, "We have it totally under control. It's one person coming in from China. It's going to be just fine."

Trump's COVID-19 statements were routinely uninformed and irresponsible. The word *incompetent* aptly describes the way he handled the pandemic.* And the brickbats didn't just come from across the aisle. Even some principled Republicans expressed their outrage. Case in point: In

---

* For much more on this topic, read *The Big Fail: What the Pandemic Revealed About Who America Protects and Who It Leaves Behind* by Joe Nocera and Bethany McLean.

December 2020, Utah Senator Mitt Romney called the president's leadership on COVID-19 "a great human tragedy."[10] He was neither alone nor wrong.

Now for the sad, but utterly fascinating part of the story. Figure 5.1 shows that, despite Trump's truly abysmal pandemic track record, nearly half of Americans approved of his early performance.

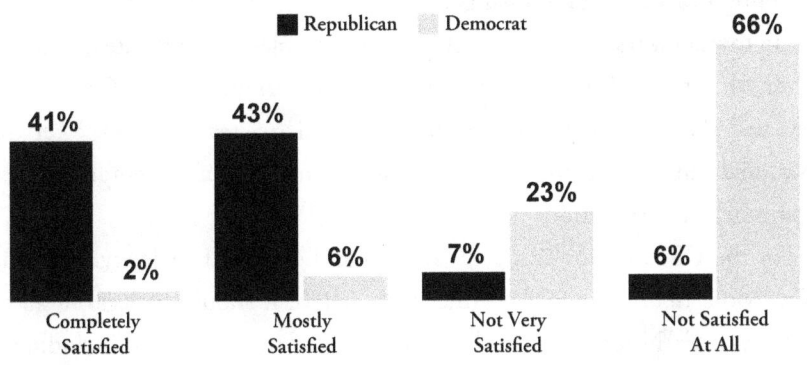

Figure 5.1: Satisfaction With Federal Response to COVID-19 From Feb. 25, 2020 to Apr. 1, 2020

Source: Civiqs

No surprise: Responses split across party lines. The post-9/11 country-above-party ethos that benefited George W. Bush was long gone—a relic of a bygone era.

Since its inception in 1776, the United States has never been completely united. (Exhibit A: the Civil War.) The fissures of the past two decades, though, have ossified. Toxic political dysfunction has crippled the once-great nation and left it on the brink of economic collapse. As we'll see in this chapter, the US is imploding as we speak. As a direct consequence of this implosion and the other catalysts discussed in Part II, it's a matter of *when*—not *if*—the US loses its place as the world's financial superpower.

Unprecedented Political Dysfunction

On November 19, 1863, Abraham Lincoln gave one of the most powerful and iconic speeches in American history: the Gettysburg Address. Delivered during the Civil War, the sixteenth president of the United States—again, a Republican—spoke of a "government of the people, by the people, for the people."

More than 160 years later, how is America doing in this regard? Is it fulfilling Lincoln's aspirational goal?

In myriad ways, the answer is no. A few examples will illustrate this point.

In the wake of another spate of mass shootings, a 2023 Gallup poll revealed that 56 percent of US adults favored stricter gun laws.[11] Yet the National Rifle Association has successfully thwarted all attempts to pass commonsense legislation.

In the US, abortion is a polarizing issue, but a clear majority leans one way. More than three in five Americans believe it should be legal in all or most cases.[12] Nearly two-thirds of women are in that camp, including a significant percentage of Republicans.[13]

Surely, Republican and Democratic lawmakers can agree on apolitical issues such as infrastructure, right? As was the case with COVID-19, the answer is no.

In 2023, the Association for Materials Protection and Performance reported that "approximately 30 percent of the bridges are structurally deficient or functionally obsolete. The annual direct cost of corrosion for highway bridges is estimated to be $13.6 billion."[14]

Early in his first administration, Trump attempted to pass legislation that addressed the nation's glaring need to upgrade its decaying infrastructure. Citing disagreements around renewable energy and combatting climate change, Democrats thwarted his entreaties.[15] In November 2021, President Biden signed the Infrastructure Investment and Jobs Act into law. Thirteen Congressional Republicans put country over party. They voted for a bill that would modernize American ports, rails, public transport, and other areas in desperate need. Soon after, Rep. Marjorie Taylor Greene, the outspoken Republican from Georgia, tweeted out their names while labeling them "traitors."[16] No good deed goes unpunished.

Much of the problems in American politics stem from its two-party system. By contrast, European governments generally benefit from multiparty arrangements. The constant need to foster coalitions tends to minimize the vitriol so prevalent in the US.

Some ideological clashes are inevitable in *any* democracy—and even healthy. The US, however, has long crossed the Rubicon. Toxicity has become the norm. Writing for *The Hill* in 2021, Harlan Ullman summarizes America's current state:

> A loyal opposition is vital to a functioning democracy. Hypocrisy is always present. Despite promising to tell the truth, presidents dissemble and many lie. Politicians promise one thing and act on others. Yet, today, hyper-hypocrisy appears to be infecting the entire political spectrum. Many blame Trump, whose record of distortions, untruths and outright lies is unmatched in American history. Yet, Trump is more a symptom than a cause of a failing political system.[17]

Brass tacks: The US empire is rapidly declining. Many lengthy tomes detail its polarization and dysfunction. For our purposes, the most galling tragedy is the deterioration of America's proudest and most impressive achievement: its formerly robust middle class.

The Erosion of the American Middle Class

Few books were as influential in the nineteenth century as Alexis de Tocqueville's seminal 1835 treatise, *Democracy in America*. The French sociologist and political scientist writes eloquently about the fundamental importance of equality in society. What's more, the United States offered the most advanced example of egalitarianism in action—at least for nonsocialist nations.

THE CATALYSTS

The GI Bill Ushers in an Era of Middle-Class Prosperity

A little over a century later, on June 22, 1944, President Franklin D. Roosevelt signed into law the Servicemen's Readjustment Act. Most Americans know it as the GI Bill of Rights.* The landmark legislation "provided returning servicemen with funds for education, government backing on loans, unemployment allowances, and job-finding assistance."[18]

The GI Bill undoubtedly achieved its goals. For starters, it prevented the US from entering a post-war depression. Arguably more important, the law ushered in an era of unprecedented prosperity for white middle-class Americans. Throughout the 1950s, the group "had more money to spend than ever—and, because the variety and availability of consumer goods expanded along with the economy, they also had more things to buy."[19]

The average white American at the time could easily afford to purchase suburban homes, cars, and modern appliances. Annual family vacations were typical. Tocqueville would have been proud. A few decades later, though, that version of the US began to unravel.

FDR understood two simple yet profound concepts. First, the fundamental purpose of an economy is to build a resilient middle class. Second, sustaining a healthy middle class isn't a natural occurrence; it takes work. Sadly, many of his successors forgot this lesson—or never learned it in the first place.

Trials and Tribulations of the Middle Class

Not that long ago, a clear majority of American adults comfortably identified as middle class. In the past five decades, however, that cohort has significantly contracted. Pew Research found that the share of adults who lived in middle-class households was 61 percent in 1971. By 2021, that number plunged to 50 percent.[20]

---

* Many Americans may not realize that it represented one of America's first major DEI programs—short for *diversity, equity, and inclusion*. For an excellent explanatory video, see https://tinyurl.com/the-cat-tik.

One needn't wonder what Tocqueville would say today if he traversed modern-day America. Income inequality is rampant and, even worse, intensifying.[21] As a result, the United States is quickly becoming economically unviable for most of its citizens. The data is indisputable.

Wage Stagnation

From 2000 to 2023, the US experienced overall inflation of 76.1 percent.[22] Figure 5.2 shows the outsize price increases in middle-class staples.

Figure 5.2: Increases in Selected US Consumer Goods and Services From 2000 to 2023

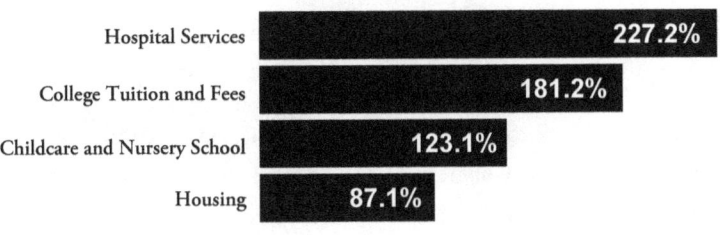

Source: Bureau of Labor Statistics

On one hand, Figure 5.2 isn't terribly revelatory. Things cost more now than they did at the turn of the century. In theory, wages should keep up with inflation and productivity. In other words, in a healthy economy, things balance out. When the absolute price of both college and healthcare rise, so should wages. In the end, the relative effect of these price increases should be minimal.

But here's where theory and practice diverge.

US wages began stagnating in the early 1970s.[23] Between 1979 and 2020, workers' earnings from labor grew by 17.5 percent. During that same period, worker productivity grew at a rate of nearly 62 percent—over three times as high.[24]

These trends aren't exactly news to US economists and policymakers. On the contrary, the data has been undeniable for a long time. Back in 2015, the

THE CATALYSTS

Economic Policy Institute analyzed the wages of the American middle class. Among its grim findings, since 1979:

> The wages of middle-wage workers were totally flat or in decline over the 1980s, 1990s and 2000s, except for the late 1990s. The wages of low-wage workers fared even worse, falling 5 percent from 1979 to 2013. In contrast, the hourly wages of high-wage workers rose 41 percent.[25]

Elected leaders in a responsive, properly functioning polity would see these statistics and react with shock. They would take immediate, decisive steps to ameliorate the situation. At the federal level, however, such action has been wanting. As the National Employment Law Project notes:

> The federal minimum wage was last raised on July 24, 2009, when it rose from $6.55 to $7.25 per hour, the last step of a three-step increase approved by Congress in 2007. Before 2007, the minimum wage had been stuck at $5.15 per hour for 10 years.[26]

To be sure, some progressive states aren't idly standing by as Congress dillydallies. For example, as of this writing, California's minimum wage is $16, and worker groups are pushing for much more.[27] Even residents of Florida—a conservative state—have earned more than the federal minimum wage since 2005.[28] It's important to note, however, that no government policies can completely isolate citizenry from major trends, such as globalization, the rise of social media, artificial intelligence, and the like.

Holding aside the economic merits of increasing the federal minimum wage, consider one of the most disturbing consequences of decades-long US middle-class wage stagnation: Most Americans are unable to handle unexpected costs, especially health-related ones.

US POLITICAL AND ECONOMIC DYSFUNCTION

Health, Debt, and Humans

Here's a particularly scary statistic—one that many non-US citizens justifiably find staggering. Roughly one in twelve Americans with medical debt claimed in 2022 to have lost their homes to eviction or foreclosure. The oft-cited culprit: healthcare-related debt.[29] Along these lines, a 2023 survey found that 63 percent of American employees can't cover a $500 emergency expense.[30] As the nonprofit Public Citizen reported in 2019, "Each year, nearly 650,000 people are pushed into bankruptcy by medical bills, accounting for more than 60 percent of all personal bankruptcies." In other industrialized countries, that number is typically zero.[31]

Many Americans are gallantly struggling to pay their bills. The average US consumer now carries $6,329 in credit card debt.[32] The buy-now-pay-later market is thriving. At the end of 2013, Affirm sported a market cap of nearly $15 billion.[33] The company reached a deal with Apple to embed its loans into ApplePay in late 2024.[34]

Is it any wonder that the US fertility rate has reached its lowest point in more than a century?[35] In many instances, twenty-somethings simply can't afford to start families. Forget stagnant wages for a moment. Netflix, Microsoft, and some other large organizations offer paid maternity leave, but US law doesn't mandate it.* In this vein, America stands in stark contrast to the rest of the world. As of 2021, only the US, the Marshall Islands, Micronesia, Nauru, Palau, Papua New Guinea, and Tonga refuse to pass relevant legislation.[36] To be fair, industrialized nations that offer paid medical leave to new parents are also seeing drops in the number of babies born each year. (Chapter 14 will return to this subject.)

---

* The Family Medical and Leave Act (FMLA) only offers limited job protection under certain circumstances.

THE CATALYSTS

The Death of the American Dream

There are many definitions of the *American dream*. Its lineage is fascinating:

> The phrase "American dream" was invented during the Great Depression. It comes from a popular 1931 book by the historian James Truslow Adams, who defined it as "that dream of a land in which life should be better and richer and fuller for everyone."[37]

Implicit in the phrase is the notion that Americans will, by and large, experience more prosperity than their parents did.

In July 2024, Pew reported that only half of US citizens currently believed in it.[38] Parse through the data, and you'll find many schisms. Wealthier Americans over the age of 50 are far more likely to buy into it. Younger, poorer citizens are far more skeptical of it as a group.

Other indicators suggest that Americans are far less sanguine about the present and future than they were even a few decades ago.

Launched somewhat ironically on April 1, 2012, the World Happiness Report attempted to compare levels of contentment across nations. America ranked in the top twenty consistently until 2024:

> Out of the more than 140 nations surveyed, the U.S. landed in 23rd place, compared to 15th place in 2023. While the U.S. is still in the top 10 happiest countries for those 60 years old and above, its overall ranking fell due to a significant decline in the reported well-being of Americans under 30.[39]

Many young American adults can't even afford to live on their own. As *Bloomberg* reported in 2023:

> Covid-19 lockdowns in 2020 drove the share of young adults living with parents or grandparents to nearly 50%, a record high. These days, about 23 million, or 45%, of all Americans ages 18 to 29 are living with family, roughly the same level as the 1940s, a time when women

US POLITICAL AND ECONOMIC DYSFUNCTION

were more likely to remain at home until marriage and men too were lingering on family farms in the aftermath of the Great Depression.[40]

Political polarization and a battered middle class are two forces driving America's decline. In this chapter's final section, we'll see how a third—economic dysfunction—has become far too big to continue ignoring.

The Clock Is Ticking on America's Economic Dominance

America is an enormous, complicated beast. In a way, though, it's not unlike any small business. The restaurateur who wants to borrow $100,000 for a kitchen makeover needs to take out a loan. The US does as well. In both cases, the states of their businesses matter—and will affect the terms of their loans.

A Massive Debt Crisis Is Looming

Governments often borrow money to finance different endeavors. As shown in Figure 5.3, the US is no exception to this rule.

Figure 5.3: US National Debt in Billions of Dollars (Rounded)

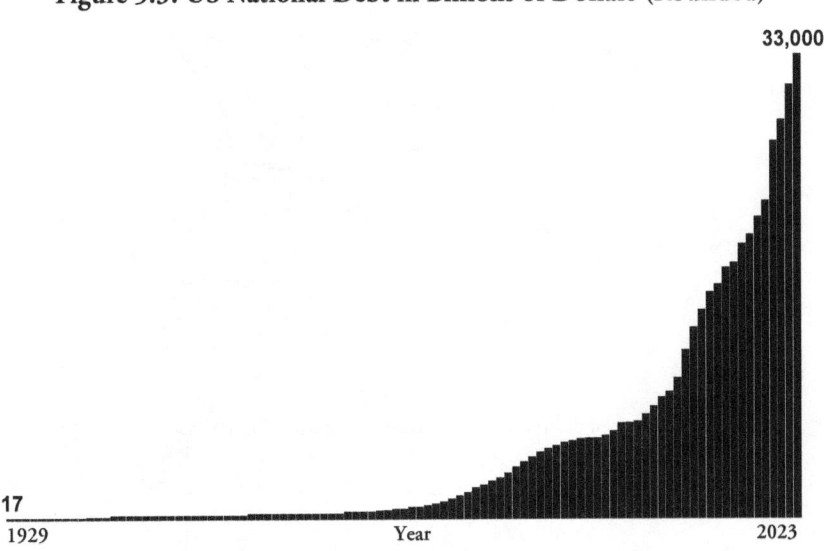

Source: Investopedia | Data: https://tinyurl.com/the-cat-debt

Debt is expected to increase over time. Thanks to inflation, a dollar ten years ago was worth more than a dollar today, and economies tend to grow over time. The US gross domestic product (GDP) was $815 billion in 1966 but $25 *trillion* in 2024.[41] To truly compare apples to apples, we need to view US debt as a function of its GDP. Figure 5.4 does just that.

The US national debt in this context is just as alarming—a fact that real and potential US creditors understand all too well.

Just like any organization seeking funds, credit markets offer terms commensurate with perceived risk. Historically, America has been able to acquire capital on the cheap. (See the discussion in Chapter 3.)

In August 2023, Fitch Ratings, one of only three private credit rating firms, downgraded America's credit rating from AAA to AA+. The relegation happened only once before in the nation's history.[42]

Figure 5.4: Total US Public Debt as Percent of Gross Domestic Product

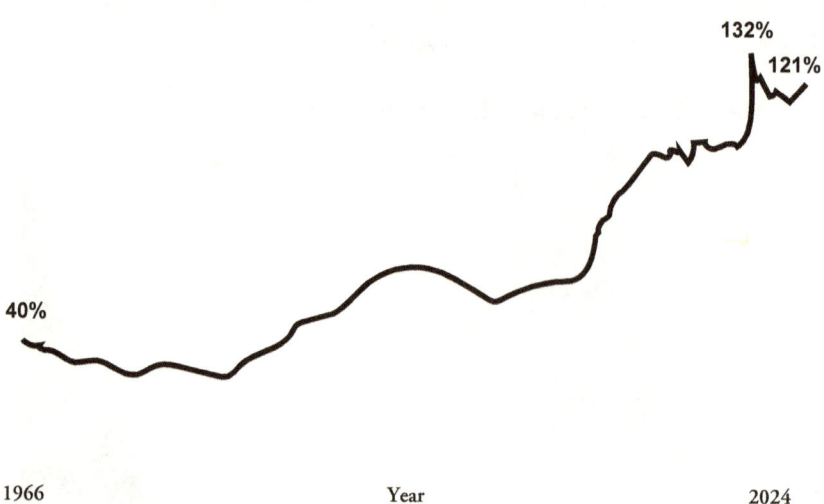

Source: Federal Reserve Bank of St. Louis | https://tinyurl.com/the-cat-deb

Three months later, the bond-ratings agency Moody's followed suit. America's large fiscal deficits and the portion of its budget devoted to paying interest on the federal debt were becoming untenable. In their words:

> Federal spending and political polarization have been a rising concern for investors, contributing to a selloff that took U.S. government bond prices to their lowest levels in 16 years.
>
> "It is hard to disagree with the rationale, with no reasonable expectation for fiscal consolidation any time soon," said Christopher Hodge, chief economist for the U.S. at Natixis. "Deficits will remain large ... and as interest costs take up a larger share of the budget, the debt burden will continue to grow."[43]

Many reasons explain the explosion of America's national debt. For our purposes, the two most relevant are its tax code and how moneyed individuals have been able to regularly avoid paying their fair share.

Disparate Tax Burdens

The flamboyant billionaire American real estate mogul Leona Helmsley once famously said, "We don't pay taxes. Only the little people pay taxes." In 1989, Helmsley went to prison for evading $1.2 million in federal income taxes.[44]

Sadly, in 2024, her words remain largely—if not entirely—accurate. A detailed discussion of the US tax code is far beyond the reach of this book. Suffice it to say, however, that America taxes labor at a higher rate than it does capital gains.* Wealthy Americans hire tax-avoidance experts to find loopholes, hide money, and minimize what they pay Uncle Sam.

ProPublica analyzed the tax records of the wealthiest twenty-five American households from 2014 to 2018. The results are flabbergasting. Despite

---

* For a much longer discussion on this topic, see Scott Galloway's post at https://tinyurl.com/the-cat-taxes.

collectively earning $401 billion, the group paid a mere $13.6 billion in taxes.[45] Do the math, and you wind up with a paltry tax rate of 3.4 percent.

Tax avoidance partially explains why rich Americans keep getting richer. The Congressional Budget Office (CBO) in 2020 found that "inequality based on income before transfers and taxes was the highest it has ever been in CBO's analyses."[46] (Chapter 11 revisits this subject in a global context.)

Salt in the Wound: Trump's 2017 Tax Law

Nearly a year after he first took office the first time, Donald Trump signed into law the 2017 Tax Cuts and Jobs Act. By all accounts, it was "a major tax code overhaul that cut taxes for both individuals and businesses."[47] Republicans argued that the measure would bolster the economy. For their part, Democrats slammed the bill as an unabashed transfer of wealth from future generations to current fat cats. Who was right?

Heres' a hint: Trump told wealthy friends after signing the legislation, "You all just got a lot richer."[48] In 2024, the Center on Budget and Policy Priorities analyzed the legislation. The bill disproportionally favored already-affluent Americans, eroded the country's revenue base, and failed to deliver promised economic benefits.[49]

An Underfunded IRS

In 2019, the Internal Revenue Service calculated that the US lost $470 billion annually to tax cheats.[50] Odds are, though, the number is much larger. A few years later, the head of the IRS testified before Congress that the figure probably runs as high as $1 trillion annually.[51]

The IRS has had to make do with insufficient financial and human resources since the first Reagan administration.[52] The results of the deficiencies have been predictable. In 2020, the Center on Budget and Policy Priorities reported that audits of millionaires had dropped 61 percent in less than a decade.[53] For those making over $5 million, the audit rate had dropped by 87 percent.[54]

In a perverse way, über-wealthy tax cheats are acting rationally, if unethically and illegally. They know full well that their odds of getting caught are minuscule.

Defaulting on Debt

At this point, it's necessary to ask a downright terrifying question. What happens if the US defaults on its burgeoning national debt? In this nightmare scenario, we can expect:

- Financial market volatility.
- An additional credit downgrade of outstanding US debt.
- A devastating economic recession or even depression.
- Ripple effects on interest rates.
- A massive disruption of government operations.[55]

In a way, the likelihood of whether the US ultimately defaults on its debt is immaterial. Capital markets are *already* bracing for the possibility. In March 2024, the prices of both Bitcoin and gold began precipitously rising. Some market analysts think that these upticks have already factored in a crisis scenario. The same holds true with the recent rises in interest rates.[56]

Lest you think that a debt default would only affect the US, think again. As we saw in Chapter 2 with the subprime crisis, the contagion would quickly spread across the globe. It's entirely possible—if not likely—that the resulting market chaos could ape that of Brexit. The British pound crashed to record lows against the US dollar. Former UK Prime Minister Liz Truss now holds the distinction of presiding over the shortest government in British history.

Penn Wharton Budget Model (PWBM) is a nonpartisan, research-based think tank that analyzes the economic impact of different public policies. Here's a damning snippet from its October 2023 research:

> PWBM estimates that—even under myopic expectations—financial markets cannot sustain more than the next 20 years of accumulated

deficits projected under current U.S. fiscal policy. Forward-looking financial markets are, therefore, effectively betting that future fiscal policy will provide substantial corrective measures ahead of time. If financial markets started to believe otherwise, debt dynamics would "unravel" and become unsustainable much sooner.[57]

Financial projections such as these should serve as a clarion call to US politicians to finally get their acts together—and fast. Unfortunately, partisan gamesmanship and downright ignorance are exacerbating America's economic problems.

Politicians Behaving Badly

Elected leaders have always shaded reality. Here are a few examples of politicians telling lies or expressing particularly egregious sentiments.

Throughout 2013, President Obama advocated for one of his greatest legislative triumphs: the Affordable Care Act. At the time, he repeatedly said, "If you like your health care plan, you can keep it."

As it turns out, that wasn't necessarily the case. The fact checkers at the *Tampa Bay Times*' nonpartisan PolitiFact project named it the 2013 lie of the year.[58]

More recently, consider a January 2023 tweet from Republican Speaker of the House Kevin McCarthy.* Figure 5.2 displays the ostensibly shocking number of IRS agents he claimed Democrats sought to add to the woefully underfunded tax-collection agency.

McCarthy didn't just mildly embellish the truth to play to his audience. He lied by orders—*plural*—of magnitude. The actual number was fewer than 200.[59]

---

* Mind you, US law stipulates that the person who holds this position would assume the role of commander-in-chief if something disastrous happened to both the president and the vice president.

US POLITICAL AND ECONOMIC DYSFUNCTION

Figure 5.5: Tweet From House Speaker Kevin McCarthy

Source: Twitter/X

When it comes to America's admittedly complicated financial system, American politicians routinely fail to grasp many of its basics, never mind its intricacies. Case in point: In 2016, while campaigning for the highest office in the land, Donald Trump stated the US will never default "because you print the money."[60] And then there's the almost comical story of Representative Liz Cheney and her staffers in the following sidebar.

Cheney's Crypto Confusion

In 2018, Matt Mead was serving his second term as the governor of Wyoming. At the time, he oversaw the creation of the Wyoming Blockchain Task Force (WBTF), one of the first of its kind in the country. Mead appointed blockchain expert Caitlin Long as a key task force member. She'd previously cofounded the Wyoming Blockchain Coalition and later founded Custodia Bank.

Mead wanted to ensure that the WBTF didn't catch the Feds by surprise. To that end, Long and prominent crypto lobbyist Jason Brett went to Washington, DC, to make the rounds and assuage any legislator's concerns. Meeting with influential Representative Liz Cheney's staff was particularly crucial. Brett called her staffers and booked an appointment with her team. They didn't expect Cheney herself to attend.

To make a long story short, Cheney's staff suddenly changed the meeting time, location, and attendees. Long and Brett furiously sprinted across the Capitol grounds. When they finally arrived, they saw Cheney and five staffers—the same ones they were scheduled to meet on the other side of the Capitol until just minutes before—sitting across the table with unwelcoming looks on their faces. It was an ambush.

Cheney's opening salvo set the tone early. She made it abundantly clear where she was coming from and whose interests she was there to represent. "My friends at the National Security Council (NSA) are appalled by what Wyoming is doing," she began.

Ouch.

Long and Brett immediately recognized the problem. Either the NSA, Cheney's staff, or the Representative herself were under a fundamental misapprehension. The attendees mistakenly believed that the WBTF wanted to change the federal requirement that all US money-services businesses register with the Financial Crimes Enforcement Network (FinCEN). However, doing so would create a national security risk.

Long understood why Cheney and her group were confused: The Wyoming statute affected a different but similarly named *state* requirement without touching the federal one. Long politely tried to explain to Cheney as much, but the representative and her staff weren't in a listening mood. They peppered Long with a barrage of questions, never letting her give complete answers. The team seemed intent on intimidating Long into halting the WBTF's work, but Long remained steadfast and calm.

Finally, Cheney had had it and barked the following order: "Well, we're going to need you to share who the CEO of Bitcoin is." She

> repeatedly demanded to know whom she could call at Bitcoin to get the answers she wanted.
>
> Long tried to explain that Bitcoin isn't a company headed by a CEO. It was—and still is, for that matter—a decentralized open-source protocol. (We'll return to this subject in Chapter 7.) The correct answer to Cheney's query was, "No one."
>
> Anyone in the country can spend five minutes doing rudimentary research on Bitcoin and cryptocurrency. You'd think that Cheney's Congressional staffers would at least appear to be vaguely informed before meeting with members of a task force investigating such an important subject. But they weren't.
>
> Sadly, this story illustrates the astonishing level of technological ignorance surrounding digital finance in most US political circles. Unfortunately, ignorance is the rule, not the exception.

America Is Built for Bureaucracy, Not Innovation

Who regulates banks? It's a simple yet essential question, especially given the damage rogue institutions can do to the financial system.

A Confusing Patchwork of Regulatory Bodies

The regulation answer, of course, depends on each country. Japan and many European countries have streamlined their regulatory bodies. Clear lines of responsibility separate each regulatory authority. Overlap is rare. Private companies generally know which agencies do what and when.

The US, however, is an entirely different kettle of fish. Three government agencies can claim responsibility for bank regulation:

- The Office of the Comptroller of the Currency (OCC).
- The Federal Reserve System.
- The Federal Deposit Insurance Corporation (FDIC).[61]

But what about nonbank financial institutions and markets in the US?

THE CATALYSTS

The Commodity Futures Trading Commission (CFTC) maintains supervisory authority over derivatives markets, including futures, options, and swaps. Technically speaking, the Securities and Exchange Commission (SEC) oversees the stock market and investments that qualify as *securities*. Additional regulatory bodies include:

- The Financial Crimes Enforcement Network (FinCEN).
- The Financial Industry Regulatory Authority (FINRA).
- The Securities Investor Protection Corporation (SIPC).

And we haven't even broached pension plans, real estate, and cryptocurrencies. Oh, and don't forget the Consumer Financial Protection Bureau (CFPB), an agency that recently survived a conservative-led legal challenge.[62]

If keeping all these agencies and their charters straight seems challenging, it is. This veritable alphabet soup irritates many a bank CEO. It also means that the US government faces an uphill battle as it tries to concurrently regulate financial products, foster responsible innovation, and combat society's ills.

Jennifer Pahlka is President Obama's former deputy chief technology officer and the founder of Code for America. Her 2023 book, *Recoding America: Why Government Is Failing in the Digital Age and How We Can Do Better*, is nothing if not eye-opening.

Pahlka persuasively argues that a rigid, industrial-era culture has effectively hamstrung the US polity. The American government's systems are both bureaucratic and outdated. The policymakers who pass laws rarely interact with the people who implement them, much less the citizens who benefit from them. Consequently, despite its best efforts, the US struggles to turn policy into actual societal improvement. Simply adding more money or technology won't fix the problem. Instead, the US needs to fundamentally reexamine how government operates. It would do well to emphasize a more contemporary, efficient, data-centric approach.

US POLITICAL AND ECONOMIC DYSFUNCTION

The Consequences of Paralysis

Due to its political and economic dysfunction, the US is unlikely to create clear regulatory frameworks for key financial innovations in the short term. Examples include cryptocurrencies, stablecoins, and central bank digital currencies (CBDCs).[63] Other nations, however, are proceeding full steam ahead. Chapter 9 covers this subject in far more detail.

If the US only faced the issues described in this chapter, it would be hard-pressed to maintain its position at the top of the world's financial totem pole.

Key Points

- As COVID-19 proved, the US no longer unifies around a crisis. Americans would rather scorch the other's earth rather than improve it.
- The underfunding of the IRS is evidence of a broken system. The US is inhibiting a key agency from doing its job.
- America has become a far riskier financial investment to credit markets. Its economic hegemony is on thin ice.
- A patchwork of regulatory institutions and a bureaucratic mindset have stifled US innovation, especially around new financial products and services.
- Early signals strongly indicate that the second Trump administration will ossify the dysfunction.

CHAPTER 6

THE RISE OF THE TECH NATION-STATE

UNREGULATED INNOVATION IS DESTABILIZING THE WORLD.

> "Technology is neither good nor bad; nor is it neutral."
> —*Melvin Kranzberg*

On December 2, 2015, a man named Syed Farook and his wife, Tashfeen Malik, suddenly opened fire in San Bernardino, California. The two ultimately murdered fourteen innocent people, including thirteen government employees. As CNN soon reported, "The couple, radical Islamists who supported ISIS, later died in a shootout with police."[1] The coming months would speak volumes about the unprecedented power of Big Tech—and its willingness to exert it.

THE CATALYSTS

At the time of the attack, people around the world had been using iPhones and Android devices as *de facto* computers and communications devices for nearly a decade.* US government officials worried about the possibility of further attacks on its citizenry. The fear was justified. Perhaps the terrorists' iPhones contained information that would avert further carnage?

There was just one problem: Law enforcement authorities couldn't access the information on Farook's and Malik's devices. No person or corporation could—not even Apple itself.

On February 16, 2016, a federal judge in California ordered the company to help the Federal Bureau of Investigation (FBI) break into Farook's phone. Apple emphatically opposed the order. CEO Tim Cook penned a letter stating the firm's position. In his words:

> The United States government has demanded that Apple take an unprecedented step which threatens the security of our customers. We oppose this order, which has implications far beyond the legal case at hand.[2]

In its refusal, one of the world's most valuable companies cited security and user privacy as its main reasons—drums it has banged for years. To be fair, Apple's relative history in these critical areas eclipses those of Google and Facebook (rebranded as Meta in October 2021).

It would be disingenuous, however, to label Apple a pure beacon of user privacy and security. For years, it has reaped massive profits from its partnership with Google, a corporation with an admittedly spotty record of protecting its users' data.[3] In 2023 alone, Google reportedly paid Apple an astonishing $18 billion to serve as the default search engine on Macs, iPads, and iPhones.[4] At the time, Apple was printing money, and its market capitalization hovered around $520 billion.[5] It's not as if Tim Cook couldn't have ordered his underlings to create a bespoke, privacy-first search engine.†

---

* Apple launched the iPhone in 2007. Android smartphones quickly followed.
† Rumors that Apple would do this very thing have persisted for years.

Faced with a potential protracted legal stalemate, the FBI turned to Azimuth, an intentionally opaque Australian firm that had produced "hacking tools for the US, Canadian, and UK governments."[6] Azimuth successfully unlocked the iPhone in question. Not long after, Apple sued the company.[7]

Apple may be the most powerful tech company to defy or resist government demands, but it's neither the only one nor the most recent. This chapter explores one of the most powerful catalysts: the rise of the tech nation-state. As you'll see in the following pages, for-profit tech corporations are usurping essential government functions, operating in dangerous manners, and attempting to set public policy. In so doing, they're redefining the world financial order.

Public No More: The Privatization of Government Responsibilities

Say that you were given a time machine in 1990. If you decided to travel thirty-five years into the future, you'd be downright amazed at the number and variety of key societal roles that private companies now fulfill or attempt to fulfill.

Determining What Constitutes Free Speech

Ratified on December 15, 1791, the Bill of Rights represents the first ten amendments to the US Constitution. Amendment I states:

> Congress shall make no law respecting an establishment of religion, or prohibiting the free exercise thereof; or abridging the freedom of speech, or of the press; or the right of the people peaceably to assemble, and to petition the Government for a redress of grievances.[8]

The right to free speech, however, isn't absolute. Those who argue otherwise tend to be anarchists or sociopaths. Examples of reasonable limitations in a civilized society include:

- No one can yell, "Fire" in a crowded theater—unless there's an actual fire.[9]
- If you defame a person or organization, they can sue you for libel or slander, depending on your medium of choice.
- It's generally illegal to leak classified information.

Unfortunately, the nuances and legalities of free speech elude many people, most famously Elon Musk.

Twitter/X

On October 27, 2022, the controversial billionaire closed his contentious acquisition of the popular social network Twitter.[10] To be fair, Twitter had long struggled and failed to contain bad actors who were intent on spreading lies. In 2018, three scholars at the Massachusetts Institute of Technology (MIT) "found that false news spreads more rapidly on the social network Twitter than real news does—and by a substantial margin."[11]

In July 2023, Musk inexplicably rebranded Twitter as X,[12] but that ill-advised semantic change* paled in comparison to the more substantive ones Musk would make.

In his first weeks as Chief Twit,† he quickly committed to radical free speech and, in the process, created a veritable "hellscape."[13] One month after assuming control, Musk summarily fired "outsourced content moderators who track abuse on Twitter."[14] Scores of other layoffs followed. Predictably, misinformation, disinformation, and hate speech—again, already prevalent on the platform—immediately exploded. Researchers found that each rose to "unprecedented levels."[15] Advertisers understandably wanted no part of the tire fire and terminated their relationships with Twitter.[16] In August 2024, Musk sued them. Many media outlets called him out for such abject hypocrisy.

Despite widespread criticism and a user exodus including Elton John, Trent Reznor, and Whoopi Goldberg,[17] Musk refused to back down. His

---

* Many noted branding experts called the move insipid.
† The title that Musk gave himself.

appalling actions manifest his arrogant belief that he—and he alone—should determine what constitutes free speech, consequences be damned. (Chapter 13 briefly returns to this subject.)

Case in point: Musk had long ignored the demands of Brazilian Supreme Court Justice Alexandre de Moraes to block accounts that spread hate speech and misinformation. On August 30, 2024, "X began to go dark across Brazil."[18] In response, Musk called the judge "an evil dictator."[19] Ultimately, Musk relented, fearing dire financial consequences for his satellite business, Starlink—itself a subsidiary of his space corporation, SpaceX.[20]

Telegram

Tweets are public by default. People looking to secure their messages can choose from a bevy of options, including the popular app Telegram. Much like Signal and WhatsApp, Telegram encrypts all user chats, though its specific encryption model varies by chat type. Uniquely, Telegram intentionally designed its app to make it difficult for authorities to retrieve its data. Retrieval requires law enforcement to obtain court orders from multiple jurisdictions. Not surprisingly, the app facilitates all sorts of illegal activities. Its thirty-nine-year-old Russian-born founder and CEO, Pavel Durov, is another free-speech zealot who has routinely dismissed government pressure and ultimatums.[21]

On August 25, 2024, French officials arrested Durov after his private jet landed north of Paris.[22] In placing him under formal investigation, authorities cited his "suspected complicity in allowing illicit transactions, drug trafficking, fraud and the spread of child sex abuse images to flourish on his site."[23]

Musk, Durov, and other CEOs of influential private companies believe that they—not a nation's democratically elected officials and judges—should determine matters of public policy. The rest of this section briefly describes other examples of this disturbing and far-reaching trend.

Determining Fair Use

Next up is fair use, "a legal doctrine that promotes freedom of expression by permitting the unlicensed use of copyright-protected works in certain circumstances."[24] Fair use is everywhere, including in this very book. As you've undoubtedly noticed, I liberally cite articles, books, blog posts, and interviews with attribution. If I excessively borrow from others' work and fail to cite my sources, I run afoul of this longstanding legal principle.

OpenAI burst onto the scene on November 30, 2022. On that day, the previously obscure company launched a powerful upgrade to ChatGPT. Version 3.5 of its artificial intelligence could do previously unimaginable things. The world noticed. Within five days, more than one million people were using it.[25]

But how did ChatGPT acquire such human-like skills?

As it turned out, OpenAI scraped as much data as it could from the web. In so doing, it may well have violated fair use. Once details leaked about how OpenAI made its sausage, outrage in certain circles ensued.

On December 27, 2023, *The New York Times* filed suit, claiming that OpenAI used millions of its proprietary articles sans attribution, permission, and payment.[26] A few days later, OpenAI refuted those claims on its blog. In its view, its use of content to train ChatGPT and other tools constitutes fair use.[27] Other publishers and news outlets piled on, citing copyright infringement.[28]

As Rachel Reed writes for *Harvard Law Today*:

> In its suit, the Times alleges that, when prompted by users, ChatGPT sometimes spits out portions of its articles verbatim, or shares key parts of its content, such as findings uncovered through investigations by Times reporters, or product endorsements carefully researched and vetted by Wirecutter, an affiliate site. ChatGPT has also "hallucinated"—or made up—articles attributed to the Times, according to the filing. All this violates copyright law and undercuts

the Times's business model, which relies on licensing, subscriptions, and ad revenue, say its attorneys.[29]

Who will ultimately prevail? The outcomes of each case are uncertain, but legal experts expect them to take decades to resolve. Less uncertain, however, is whether OpenAI has benefited from moving fast and breaking things, to borrow from the early Facebook credo. The answer here is an obvious yes.

Sam Altman's company wouldn't be worth a staggering $100 billion[30] as of this writing if it negotiated content-licensing deals with partners instead of gobbling as much data as it could as quickly as possible. For PR reasons, Meta may be formally eschewing its former internal religion. Make no mistake, though: The ethos is very much alive and well in American tech companies. Those who contend otherwise are sorely mistaken.[31] The only difference today is these firms' targets, and if not curtailed, their eventual victims.

Subverting Employment Laws

The United States passed many pieces of landmark legislation during the twentieth century. Apart from the laws mentioned in Chapter 4, America began regulating the workplace—specifically, child labor, overtime, safety, minimum wage, unemployment insurance, and job protection during pregnancy. Although individual states imposed their own requirements, no company could effectively exempt itself from the floor set by federal law. Few possessed the audacity to even try.

You needn't be a labor economist to see what would invariably happen: US manufacturing increasingly moved abroad to countries with cheaper labor and questionable employment practices. "Offshoring, particularly of manufacturing and low-skilled jobs, like factory-based assembly jobs, began on a large scale in the 1970s and 1980s."[32] Note that reshoring has gained steam considering the nationalism-driven trade tensions discussed in Chapter 9.[33]

But large tech corporations no longer take as a given that they must play by the same rules as everybody else, even those imposed by the US federal government. As we'll see next, some particularly audacious ones want to adhere to a different set than their contemporaries do: their own.

The explosion of smartphones and apps ushered in what many economists have dubbed the *gig economy*. It has birthed many Silicon Valley unicorns: privately held startups whose valuations exceeded $1 billion. Dozens have since gone public, making their founders and early investors insanely rich as a direct consequence.

Call them *unicorns* if you like. In a way, though, they aren't special at all. Presumably, they must abide by all legislation in the countries in which they do business, including labor statutes. Yet at some point over the past decade, their leaders began asking themselves a simple yet disturbing question: What if we *didn't* have to follow these laws?

This brings us to California. In 2020, Uber, Lyft, and DoorDash led a coalition to get a radical referendum on the November ballot. If passed, Proposition 22 would:

> exclude ride-hail and food-delivery app-based workers from nearly all employee rights under state law, including the right to a minimum wage, time-and-a-half for overtime, expenses reimbursement, and benefits such as unemployment compensation and state workers' compensation.[34]

These companies wanted voters to put personal profit over protecting workers' rights. They also wanted workers to vote against their economic interests. Doing so would take plenty of convincing and, by extension, money. In total, the coalition spent a whopping $224 million to pass the measure.[35]

Despite its questionable legality at the time,[36] Prop 22 passed. An astonishing 59 percent of California voters endorsed it. Given that number, the math is unmistakable: Many supporters effectively voted to forgo legal protections guaranteed to virtually all Americans, including themselves.*

Subverting Safety Protections

Among all fifty US states, arguably none took COVID-19 as seriously as California. Its representatives continually erred on the side of caution, especially in relation to Florida, Texas, and Alabama. During the early days of the pandemic, many CEOs of California-based companies scoffed at what they believed were superfluous safety restrictions. And then there's Elon Musk.

The Workplace

On March 16, 2020, public safety officials in Alameda County issued a shelter-in-place order (SIPO). In short, it required:

> residents to remain in their homes for all but essential activities such as purchasing food or medicine, caring for others, exercise, or traveling for employment deemed essential. The authority to issue SIPOs rests with state and local officials.[37]

In this case, Musk, the perennial rule-breaker, was acting in his capacity as CEO of the electric car maker Tesla. He publicly defied county orders so Tesla's Freemont plant could resume production. Days later, hundreds of Tesla workers tested positive for the coronavirus.[38]

Lodging

Musk isn't alone in attempting to skirt laws. Let's turn to hotels for a moment. Say what you will about accommodations; at least guests can quickly report problems. Hotels that fail to meet local health and safety requirements face stiff fines and penalties. The same hasn't held true, though, for another pioneer of the sharing economy: Airbnb.

---

* Sadly, it's one of many instances in which governments, lobbyists, industry groups, and political parties have tricked citizens into voting for collectively harmful policies.

Brad Stone describes many of the horror stories Airbnb guests have faced in his bestselling book, *The Upstarts: How Uber, Airbnb, and the Killer Companies of the New Silicon Valley Are Changing the World*. In some cases, Airbnb has quietly settled potential lawsuits for fear of negative publicity, especially when it was nearing its December 2020 initial public offering. A chilling 2015 *New York Times* piece detailed how the company "wants sexual assault victims to be able to decide for themselves when, how or if to report a crime."[39] More recently, a family sued the company after its nineteen-month-old died of fentanyl toxicity during a stay in a Florida rental property.[40]

Privatizing Space Exploration

The US won the space race in the late 1960s thanks in large part to an independent agency within its federal government: the National Aeronautics and Space Administration (NASA). Back then, the agency accounted for more than 4 percent of America's annual federal budget.

In 2024, the US government allocated $24.9 billion to NASA. That number may seem enormous, but the opposite is true. It represents a mere 0.36 percent of the federal budget.[41] Put another way, America has cut funding to its national space program by more than 90 percent.

Today, NASA's mission is to "pioneer the future in space exploration, scientific discovery, and aeronautics research."[42] Sadly, the agency is hamstrung. Its paltry budget prevents it from achieving its lofty and praiseworthy goals.

This raises the question: Who's making up the slack?

Two private companies—Elon Musk's SpaceX and Jeff Bezos's Blue Origin—are mostly fulfilling former NASA functions. Each has secured valuable government contracts, with plans to ramp up soon. And then there's Project Kuiper, Amazon's endeavor to beam internet service from orbit. In October 2023, the Starlink competitor completed the first launch of its satellite internet network.[43] Nearly one year later, United Airlines shook up the satellite broadband market by announcing it would replace its Wi-Fi providers with Starlink in SpaceX's largest aviation Wi-Fi deal.

And why *wouldn't* these private firms double down? One research firm recently estimated the value of the current global space technology market at $443 billion, a number that may rise to nearly $1 trillion by 2033.[44]

Providing Essential Technologies, Utilities, and Infrastructure

Private companies—especially tech ones—play an outsize role in US government affairs. A few examples will illustrate this point.

In 2018, the US government was on pace to become Amazon's largest customer,[45] at least until Donald Trump involved himself.* The Department of Defense had for years relied heavily on the company's cloud-computing business, Amazon Web Services (AWS).

On October 1, 2013, the US government launched healthcare.gov, an essential ingredient of the Affordable Care Act (ACA). Almost immediately, issues plagued the site, making many Republican opponents smile. Later that month, the Obama administration tapped software engineers from Google, Oracle, and Red Hat "to assist in untangling the problems with its online health insurance marketplace."[46]

One could write an entire book—and many have—about how private American corporations have usurped what were once public functions. It's time to move on, though, and unpack why this has happened.

Corporate Taxes

As he has proved over his career, Jeff Bezos is nothing if not shrewd. In 2017, his company publicly announced that:

> it was seeking a second North American headquarters which, once built out, would employ up to 50,000 high-tech workers. This set off a race among big cities eager to house the world's most valuable company and its well-paid employees.[47]

---

* See https://tinyurl.com/aws-the-cat.

Bezos expected local governments to line up for the chance to break ground. He wasn't disappointed. Hundreds of proposals rolled in. Ultimately, Amazon settled on two locations: Arlington, Virginia, and New York City. (The latter ultimately fell through in February 2019 after a high-profile backlash erupted over unionization and tax incentives.[48])

In April 2023, Amazon asked Virginia "for nearly $153 million in state incentive payments, which would be the first tranche of funds to be paid out since the tech giant agreed in 2018 to build a headquarters complex in the state."[49]

Amazon is hardly the only company to extract massive tax abatements from local governments. Sometimes, even the *threat* of moving corporate headquarters and jobs is sufficient to get state politicians to cut deals that ultimately harm taxpayers.

Causes, Considerations, and Accelerants

No single factor caused Amazon, Apple, Meta, and Google to occupy outsize power worldwide. Multiple factors were at play, but we'll explore the most significant ones.

Toothless, Dated American Legislation and Regulation

Given the political polarization detailed in Chapter 5, US Senators from opposing parties shouldn't agree on much. Yet, despite their differences, Iowa Republican Chuck Grassley and Minnesota Democrat Amy Klobuchar found common ground. On June 15, 2023, the two US Senators introduced the American Innovation and Choice Online Act. If passed, the bipartisan legislation "would put in place common sense rules of the road for major digital platforms to ensure they cannot unfairly preference their own products and services."[50]

For example, consider Amazon, a company that has long operated an online marketplace in which third-party resellers can hawk their gear. The company has contended that it doesn't use data in a way that would give it an unfair advantage. Yet, when testifying before Congress in July 2022, company founder and then-CEO Jeff Bezos admitted that the practice may have nonetheless taken place on his watch, but without his knowledge.[51]

In her superb 2024 book, *The Everything War: Amazon's Ruthless Quest to Own the World and Remake Corporate Power*, *The Wall Street Journal* reporter Dana Mattioli depicts the actions Amazon took to scuttle the Grassley-Klobuchar bill. The company spared no expense in ensuring its demise, but here's the flabbergasting part: Amazon concurrently claimed that it wasn't engaging in the very actions the legislation would forbid.

Amazon's peers have also recognized the growing import of setting the national legislative agenda. A 2019 Public Citizen report analyzed the 2018 election cycle. It detailed how "Big Tech corporations have blanketed Capitol Hill with lobbyists and lavished members of Congress with campaign contributions."[52]

Big Tech regularly quashes bills that are designed to constrain it. One area of proposed legislation scares tech behemoths more than all the rest.

Section 230

Chapter 4 referenced Section 230 of the Communications Decency Act of 1996. (See its section titled "Retrenchment: The Rise of Deregulation and Neoliberalism.") By way of background, Section 230 "provides immunity to online platforms from civil liability based on third-party content and for the removal of content in certain circumstances."[53]

The fact that Section 230 remains US law reflects Big Tech's profound power. Repealing it wouldn't immediately solve all the world's problems, but Mark Zuckerberg, Elon Musk, and other tech CEOs would need to take significant steps to make their products far safer. The costs of inaction would be too great to ignore.

When called before Congress in March 2019, Zuckerberg asked for regulation.[54] It was a smart move. He appeared genuinely concerned for America's well-being on the brightest of stages. At the same time, he knew full well that meaningful government intervention would never arrive, at least in the US.

Why Big Tech Took Root in the US and Not Europe

The simple reason that Big Tech took off in the US but not Europe is regulation—or, more specifically, the lack of it in the US. As the following examples demonstrate, European countries take the responsibility of regulating private business seriously; America doesn't, and its politicians are paid quite well not to.

GDPR

Taking effect in May 2018, the EU's General Data Protection Regulation scared the CEOs of many US tech companies. The measure:

> sets out detailed requirements for companies and organisations on collecting, storing and managing personal data. It applies both to European organisations that process personal data of individuals in the EU, and to organisations outside the EU that target people living in the EU.[55]

At least sixteen other countries have passed data privacy legislation similar to GDPR, if different in scope.[56] The closest equivalent to GDPR in the US is the California Consumer Privacy Act, passed in 2018 over staunch business opposition.

Digital Markets Act

On May 2, 2023, the EU's Digital Markets Act (DMA) went into force. The act:

> establishes a set of clearly defined objective criteria to qualify a large online platform as a "gatekeeper" and ensures that they behave in a fair way online and leave room for contestability. The Digital Markets Act is one of the centrepieces of the European digital strategy.[57]

THE RISE OF THE TECH NATION-STATE

Progressive leaders in the US would love to pass comparable legislation, but the dysfunction described in Chapter 5 has repeatedly proved too difficult to overcome. Lest you think that only one American political party is responsible, think again. Both Democrats and Republicans have blood on their hands. Brody and Luke Mullins describe the sad affairs in their illuminating 2024 book, *The Wolves of K Street: The Secret History of How Big Money Took Over Big Government*. The book traces the rise of lobbying dynasties from both major American parties. Both are complicit in turning Washington into a powerful pro-business force. Wages, healthcare, and safety have suffered as a result.

Meaningless Fines

Compared to their US analogs, EU laws regulating Big Tech are more potent. (Admittedly, the bar is low.) Still, EU penalties have often served as minor annoyances or speeding tickets for affluent tech corporations intent on building monopolies. Consider the circumstances surrounding a massive Facebook acquisition:

> The European Union's powerful antitrust chief fined the social network 110 million euros, or about $122 million, for giving misleading statements during the company's $19 billion acquisition of the internet messaging service WhatsApp in 2014.[58]

Do the math. To placate European regulators and ensure the completion of the company's most ambitious play to date, Facebook effectively paid a 0.6 percent tax. Would Zuck have ponied up if the fine were thirty times higher?

Ireland

Europe is becoming less attractive to American tech companies for another reason. Ireland has long served as a tax haven for large US tech corporations, including Google, Facebook, and Apple. But in 2021, the country ratified an EU deal that "aims to reduce tax avoidance."[59]

THE CATALYSTS

The Nature of Digital Technologies

On many levels, we live in a very different world than we did in the twentieth century.

Bits vs. Atoms: The Rise of Assetless Business Models

As of September 9, 2024, Uber's market capitalization was $147 billion, but the company owns not a single automobile. That same day, Airbnb was worth $73 billion—nearly seven times as much as Hilton.[60] The world's most valuable hotel chain by brand owns its 8,000 locations; Airbnb owns no land or properties. Nvidia has become one of the world's most valuable companies while outsourcing all its manufacturing.[61] Forgoing physical stores and warehouses hasn't stopped women's apparel darling Shein from taking off.[62]

Wall Street clearly adores asset-light companies. They don't have to worry about deteriorating buildings and cars. Plus, they often turn full-time, benefits-eligible employees into far cheaper contractors.

Radical Portability and the Jobs Threat

The American robber barons of the twentieth century couldn't just pick up their railroads, tobacco farms, and steel mills and move them to other countries. Factories, land, and other physical assets kept them decidedly immobile.

Today, CEOs and founders are more willing to use the threat of moving their operations to extract lucrative tax credits and abatements.

In 2024, California Governor Gavin Newsom signed several laws expanding protections for LGBTQ+ students. That July, X and SpaceX CEO Musk announced that he was moving both companies to Texas.[63] Odds are, though, that Musk was just looking for a reason. His new home won't impose a state income tax, unlike California.

Legal Complexities and Unresolved Issues

With physical assets located in a country, it's easier for governments to function, collect taxes, enforce rules, and the like. Big Tech makes this difficult, however. Simple questions like the following require complex answers:

- Where does data live?
- In the event of a criminal case and guilty verdict, what do you seize?
- In which country do you prosecute?
- How does a government hold its leaders accountable?

The presence of cryptocurrencies only complicates matters, as we'll see in Chapter 11. After all, enforcement requires governments and borders.

Consequences

It's hard to overstate the effects of Big Tech's ascension. The following section illustrates some of their most important ones.

Distorted Geopolitics

Global policymakers must pine for the relatively simple days of the early aughts. Yes, the internet and email existed, but smartphones and social media had yet to arrive. Big Tech hadn't yet run amok. With rare exceptions, world leaders and politicians had to worry about their contemporaries, not CEOs of largely unregulated behemoths.

Fast-forward to February 2023 and the World Economic Forum. Diplomats from twenty-five countries met in the San Francisco Bay Area and launched the Tech Diplomacy Network. The Silicon Valley–based global group offers resources for governments and the tech industry to collaborate and address the geopolitical implications of innovation.[64]

If the previous world financial order resembled checkers, the one currently evolving is tantamount to four-dimensional chess. Writing for *Foreign Affairs*, the American political scientist Amy Zegart astutely notes:

> Foreign policy has always been a two-level game; US officials have to wrangle both domestic actors and foreign adversaries. But more and more, the decisions of private companies are shaping geopolitical outcomes, and the interests of the US private sector are not always aligned with national objectives. Meta, the parent company of Facebook, Instagram, and WhatsApp, is determining what constitutes truth for the three billion people worldwide that use its platforms.[65]

In the past year, American CEOs with vested Chinese business interests have met face-to-face with Chinese leader Xi Jinping with roughly the same frequency as US Secretary of State Antony Blinken. And when war erupted in Ukraine, the tycoon billionaire Elon Musk singlehandedly decided whether, where, and when the Ukrainian military could communicate using the Starlink satellite network he owns.

Zegart is hardly the only one to note this tectonic shift. On an August 2024 *New York Times* podcast, Casey Newton and Kevin Roose delved into unchartered waters. The two journalists asked the simple but disturbing question: Can Musk get Trump elected?[66]

Before Musk's disastrous Twitter acquisition, the query was absurd. In the fall of 2024, however, it was a reasonable one to ask. And now we know: A private citizen *can* impact the results of a US presidential race.

The Continual Spread of Misinformation, Disinformation, and Illicit Content

Consider the following anecdote from a 2019 *New York Times* exposé on YouTube:

> Christiane C. didn't think anything of it when her 10-year-old daughter and a friend uploaded a video of themselves playing in a backyard pool.
>
> "The video is innocent, it's not a big deal," said Christiane, who lives in a Rio de Janeiro suburb.

A few days later, her daughter shared exciting news: The video had thousands of views. Before long, it had ticked up to 400,000—a staggering number for a video of a child in a two-piece bathing suit with her friend.

"I saw the video again and I got scared by the number of views," Christiane said.

She had reason to be.

YouTube's automated recommendation system—which drives most of the platform's billions of views by suggesting what users should watch next—had begun showing the video to users who watched other videos of prepubescent, partially clothed children, a team of researchers has found.[67]

The obvious question is: Who programmed YouTube to suggest videos of scantily clad young girls to potential child molesters? No one. The answer is a bit counterintuitive: No one programmed YouTube *not* to do so.

And that story, in a nutshell, explains perhaps the most dangerous effect of tech gone mad. Powerful and opaque algorithms determine what we see and think. The mathematician and data scientist Cathy O'Neil conducts this autopsy in her excellent 2016 book, *Weapons of Math Destruction: How Big Data Increases Inequality and Threatens Democracy*.

And it's not just what we see and think; these tools ultimately affect what we *do*—and often in horrifying ways.

That social media causes real-world violence and even fatalities at this point should shock no one. We saw in the preface how Facebook's recommendation engines facilitated the January 6 riots. That same year, the *Columbia Journalism Review* directly linked the social network to "violence in the Philippines, Libya, Germany, Myanmar, and India."[68]

What's the fix? There may not be one in a largely regulated environment, much less the current, unregulated one.

THE CATALYSTS

David Auerbach is a prolific writer and former Microsoft and Google software engineer. He chronicles a terrifying reality in his 2023 book, *Meganets: How Digital Forces Beyond Our Control Commandeer Our Daily Lives and Inner Realities*. Even the leaders of these companies don't fully understand how their own products work.

If that last sentence doesn't frighten you, then the following ones will. Generative AI only exacerbates this problem. It's not as if programmers can pinpoint the specific lines of code in Open AI's ChatGPT, Google Gemini, Anthropic's Claude, and similar tools that propagate hate and deepfakes. Large language models are unique; they don't work like traditional software programs that the employers' coders can debug.

What's more, nationalism is on the rise, and democracy and institutional trust are eroding. Chapters 7, 8, and 12 will return to these topics at length.

The Erosion of Privacy and the Weaponization of Data

Let's return for a moment to the 2016 US presidential election. In the spring of 2018, Mark Zuckerberg faced the largest scandal in his company's history:

> A data analytics company has harvested information from more than 50 million Facebook users. That data was used to "change audience behavior" and advance political projects like Brexit and Donald Trump's White House bid.[69]

That firm, Cambridge Analytica, ultimately harvested the data of 87 million users—a number that Zuckerberg revised upward from his earlier estimate.

The status quo is blurring any notion of truth. Thanks to a less informed populace, bad actors can easily manipulate citizens to promote their own agendas.

Maybe Mark Zuckerberg was right when he said in 2010 that "privacy is no longer a social norm."[70] If that's the case, maybe there's a silver lining.

With so much data and sophisticated analysis, we can predict the next January 6 attack.

More Frequent Financial Chaos

GameStop bills itself on its website as "the world's largest retail gaming, trade-in and trading card destination."[71] Thanks to smartphones and high-speed internet connections, the publicly traded company struggled for years. Plenty of market analysts thought GameStop's demise was inevitable. Many large institutional investors bet on its price falling further and shorted the stock.[*] On January 8, 2021, $GME traded at a meager $4.42 (USD).

On January 29, 2021, GameStop's stock price skyrocketed to $81.25. The rise didn't stem from a change in the company's fundamentals or profits or a rumored acquisition. No, a *short squeeze* caused all hell to break loose. One can:

> quickly move a stock price higher, often much higher. It can be an exciting event, as traders rush in to buy, pushing up a stock's price. The stock spikes, potentially leading to even more buying as short sellers are forced to "cover" their shorts. Metaphorically, think of a short squeeze as investors rushing to get out of a crowded theater after someone yells "fire."[72]

In hindsight, the perfect storm consisted of:

- Reddit users rallying behind influential trader Keith Gill, aka "Roaring Kitty."
- Historically low interest rates.
- Young people stuck at home during the pandemic's lockdown period, many of whom received stimulus checks.
- Aggressive promotion by a relatively new, youth-oriented trading app, Robinhood.[†]

---

[*] Effectively, this is a bet that its price will drop. If it increases, the ones holding the short positions will have to buy back stock at its current (read: higher) price.

[†] See https://tinyurl.com/the-cat-gs for a more detailed breakdown of its causes and effects.

THE CATALYSTS

GameStop was just one meme stock to inexplicably pop in recent years. On May 22, 2024, shares of bookseller Barnes & Noble Education rose 73 percent. Users of the r/WallStreetBets subreddit may have coordinated their efforts to artificially move the market again.[73]

Many Davids want to stick it to the Goliath that is traditional finance. Expect more of these massive, unpredictable, and coordinated financial swings from emboldened, tech-savvy users.

Corporate Profits and Power Balloon

Finally, it's safe to say that US corporations are making more money than ever. Figure 6.1 shows the increase in post-tax profits since 1929.

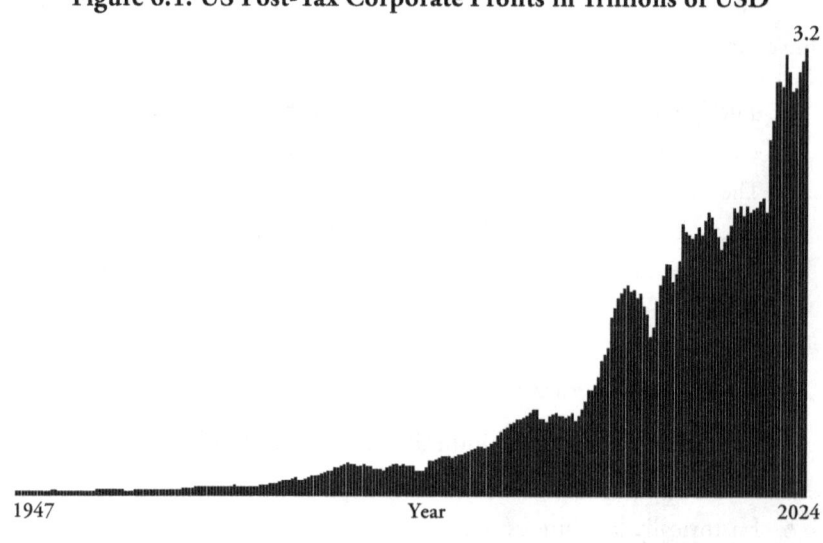

Figure 6.1: US Post-Tax Corporate Profits in Trillions of USD

Source: Federal Reserve Bank of St. Louis | Data: https://tinyurl.com/the-cat-stl
Note: Excluding IVA ad CCAdj | IVA= Inventory valuation adjustment, CCAdj = Capital consumption adjustment

If Uber and Lyft don't need to pay their drivers expensive but legally required overtime and benefits, their CEOs won't donate those considerable savings to charities. That's especially true now that each company is publicly held. Microsoft and Amazon profits don't shrink after they ink massive cloud computing contracts with the federal government. OpenAI paid content providers exactly nothing in building its groundbreaking chatbot, although the company has since begun negotiating deals after the fact as a legal prophylactic.[74]

A detailed econometric analysis of the sources of corporate profits lies far beyond the scope of this book. Still, we know that US middle-class wages have remained largely stagnant since the 1970s. (See the discussion in Chapter 5.) What's more, for-profit firms haven't increased earnings so rapidly *solely* because they've been able to privatize functions the government once performed.

Suffice it to say that the topics covered in this chapter are, at some level, contributing to greater corporate profits.

The next chapter looks at one of the major effects of tech gone wild: the rise of nationalism.

Key Points

- American tech companies are effectively setting global public policy and usurping the role of elected officials.
- US regulation has been largely ineffectual at curbing the power of Big Tech.
- Under current US law, leaders of tech companies aren't legally obligated to police the content on their platforms. Opaque algorithms are doing immeasurable harm.
- The erosion of privacy and data weaponization are just a few of the effects of the status quo.

CHAPTER 7

FINANCIAL DISINTERMEDIATION

NEW TECHNOLOGIES ARE LAYING THE GROUNDWORK FOR A MORE DECENTRALIZED WORLD FINANCIAL ORDER.

> "A government monopoly on money is the last chain binding man to the state. Break it, and true freedom begins."
> —Robert Nozick

At the end of the twentieth century, the record industry was high on the hog. In total, EMI, Sony, Vivendi Universal, EMI, BMG, and their ilk were collectively shipping nearly one billion compact discs each year.[1] Times weren't just good; they were great. "Accounts from US record retailers and mass merchandisers indicated a banner 1997."[2] Little did they know that a freshman at Northeastern University in Boston would plant the seeds that would quickly lead to their demise.

THE CATALYSTS

On June 1, 1999, Shawn Fanning released Napster, a simple, insanely powerful, and disruptive file-sharing application. Anyone could download and use it for free, and it required zero technical knowledge. The app allowed anyone to install the software to discover digitized songs on other users' personal computers (PCs). The only caveat: Other users needed to install the program as well. Napster was no mere discovery tool, though. Users could easily download songs from each other's computers for free.

Eight million people eagerly hopped on the Napster bandwagon, especially tech-savvy college students eager to check out their favorite artists' new songs. The statistics were downright remarkable. At Indiana University, the "computer department reported that Napster use was consuming 61% of its bandwidth before they blocked access to the site."[3]

Everyday consumers loved Napster, but that adoration was hardly universal. Musicians and record executives were appalled that anyone could steal their songs and albums—sometimes even before their official release. Six months after Napster launched, the Recording Industry Association of America (RIAA) sued the company for copyright infringement.[4] Napster lawyers argued that its service did no such thing, citing the fair use doctrine. It was a Hail Mary.

In 2001, US courts ultimately agreed with the RIAA and deemed Napster illegal.[5] In a more profound way, though, the verdict was moot. Napster's meteoric rise demonstrated that consumers were unwilling to revert to the previous method of buying music: paying $15 for a compact disc with two good songs and a bunch of chaff.

Legality aside, no entity could ultimately put the genie back in the bottle. Napster didn't last long, shutting its doors in 2002.[6] But even before its demise, scores of other quirkily named file-sharing apps had quickly sprouted up, including LimeWire, Kazaa, Gnutella, and Wrapster. The days of artists and record companies profiting from album sales were numbered.

As David Bowie presciently said in 2002, "You'd better be prepared for doing a lot of touring because that's really the only unique situation that's going to be left."[7] In February 2004, Tower Records filed for bankruptcy.[8]

FINANCIAL DISINTERMEDIATION

Spotify, Apple Music, and other streaming services have replaced CD sales. There's a reason many sixty-something rockers are still on tour: They earn very little money from other sources.

The rise of Napster strongly parallels a far more disruptive innovation: cryptocurrency. As we'll see in this chapter, the similarities between the two inventions are striking. Both posed existential threats to mammoth industries that, as you might expect, actively have fought the introduction of new technologies. What's more, in each case, tech bros in hoodies have pushed a new mousetrap that threatens legacy "suits."

Before getting to the guts of this chapter, a brief disclaimer is in order.

Assumptions and a Disclaimer

I believe in truth in advertising. This chapter does *not* serve as a primer on every conceivable emerging financial technology. Instead, I briefly summarize how cryptocurrencies, stablecoins, and decentralized finance are disintermediating traditional finance and, in the process, forging the new world financial order. You can read entire tomes about each of the topics covered in the following pages. To help with that, I've included valuable supplemental resources where appropriate.

To be fair, I'm operating under the assumption that you've heard a thing or two about cryptocurrencies. You may not, however, fully grasp the problems they address, much less their underlying tech. Much like the other chapters in Part II, I'll cover material in a manner that's far more broad than deep.

Along these lines, please don't expect an in-depth tutorial on the technical differences between the thousands of cryptocurrencies that now exist. We won't be exploring the ins and outs of decentralized finance (DeFi). Rather, we'll focus on the high-level impact of these technologies, the ramifications of their evolution, and their effects on the new world financial order.

Let's start with a few technological building blocks before moving on to cryptocurrencies and asset tokenization.

THE CATALYSTS

Blockchain and Distributed Ledger Technologies

The American statistician and prominent management theorist W. Edwards Deming famously said, "In God we trust. All others must bring data."

Like David Bowie, Deming wasn't wrong.

To properly function, *every* financial system needs to meet certain basic requirements. At a bare minimum, individuals, governments, corporations, and other institutions must be able to quickly and easily record, store, retrieve, and share their data. Accurate financial information allows banks to make loans, publicly held companies to report quarterly results, payroll departments to process checks, merchants to take payments via credit cards, and a myriad of other things that allow the world economy to function efficiently. Take away accurate data, and none of this happens.

The Centralized Status Quo

The world financial system is centralized, and it has been for a long time. (Flip back to Figure 2.2 in Chapter 2.) That is, essential data exists in colossal databases—sometimes even antiquated mainframes with roots dating back decades.[9] These centralized systems generally work, but no one can call them *perfect*. As we saw in Chapter 2, they suffer from significant limitations, many of which stem from archaic technology. These systems are costly, inefficient, and not terribly secure.

The centralized nature of financial systems encourages hackers and other bad actors to target them. When—not if—they can breach these systems, they collect valuable personally identifiable information (PII). The Identity Theft Resource Center reported that the number of data compromises in 2023 was 3,205—a 78 percent increase from the previous year.[10] Odds are these numbers are grossly understated.

To be sure, centralized financial systems haven't remained entirely stagnant over the past decade. Most notably, corporations are embracing cloud computing. In a fundamental way, though, nothing has changed. Firms have merely charged Amazon, Google, Oracle, and IBM with the task of hosting their internal systems and databases.* For the most part, large corporations have relieved their internal IT departments of the responsibility.†

But what if there were a different, more efficient, more secure, and fundamentally better way to store PII and financial transactions? The roots of such a system lay in cryptography and digital signatures, but early efforts weren't ready for prime time. The year 2008 served as the requisite tipping point.

Satoshi Nakamoto: Mysterious Genius

By way of background, eCash and other early digital currencies suffered from the *double spend problem*: It was impossible to prevent people from using a digital dollar or coin multiple times. This issue made their widespread adoption a nonstarter.

On October 31, 2008, the pseudonymous Satoshi Nakamoto‡ released *Bitcoin: A Peer-to-Peer Electronic Cash System*.[11] The seminal white paper proposed a peer-to-peer electronic cash system built on an entirely new foundation. Much like Napster, Bitcoin's distributed nature allowed it to circumvent centralized third parties, including financial institutions. (We'll return to Bitcoin later in this chapter.)

Nakamoto proposed creating a computer network that stitched together different blocks of transactions into chains. They posited that doing so would enable more secure financial transactions. (Ironically, you won't find the word *blockchain* once in the white paper.) Nakamoto brilliantly solved the vexing double-spend problem. Absent that solution, digital currencies wouldn't have flourished.

As it turned out, Nakamoto had underestimated the power of his ideas. Blockchain has evolved into a "distributed data structure that contains blocks chained together in chronological order."[12] A network of computers

---

* To learn more, check out Nicholas Carr's 2008 book titled *The Big Switch: Rewiring the World, from Edison to Google*.
† For the sake of simplicity, I'm deliberately glossing over the topic of private clouds.
‡ As of this writing, Satoshi's identity remains a mystery.

verifies and connects the blocks to ensure safe transactions for all parties involved. The resultant chain automatically joins the entire, unaltered ledger of transactions in an agreed-upon sequence. That's not to say, though, that all blockchains *are* created equal.

Types of Blockchains

When people talk about blockchains, they may not be comparing apples to apples.* Many times, they refer to permissionless blockchain networks or public blockchains. Popular examples here include Nakamoto's Bitcoin and Ethereum, launched in 2015. These networks are truly open; anyone can join sans a proper invitation.

By contrast, permissioned or private blockchains are members-only networks. A central authority, often a private company, makes its key decisions. It decides

- Who can join the network.
- What they can access.
- Which actions they can take.

As but one example, consider JPMorgan's Kinexys (formerly known as Onyx), a private and permissioned blockchain. It incorporates the technological benefits of blockchain technology into traditional banking offerings that are, by the bank's own admission, slower and more inefficient.[13]

More Than Just Blockchain: DLTs

Others have expanded upon Nakamoto's core idea of blocks. Today, as we saw with Kinexys, others have joined the party. It's best to think of the original idea of the blockchain as a specific type of what industry leaders now broadly call *distributed ledger technologies* (DLTs).

DLTs are an entirely different type of animal than their older, centralized antecedents. These powerful, modern systems still record, store, and share

---

* In the same way, *cloud computing* is a catchall term. Types of clouds include public, private, and hybrid. Yes, they overlap, but there are substantial differences among them.

financial data, but in a decidedly decentralized manner. Data doesn't exist in a single database; rather, it exists in disparate, secured blocks across an entire network.

In terms of security, data storage via DLT represents a vast improvement over centralized systems for one simple reason: There's no single point to attack, no lone vulnerability. Hacking data from a DLT network isn't a small chore; criminals and cyberterrorists must breach all or most of the nodes on the network. In layperson's terms, a bank robber can't break into a single Chase branch and abscond with bags of cash anymore. He would have to rob thousands of mini-branches to leave with the same payoff.

One of the most critical elements of DLTs is their immutability. Let's contrast them with internal bank ledgers—some of which, remarkably, remain simple Excel spreadsheets. Once a DLT appends blocks to a chain, no one can modify or delete them. Ever. This is a big deal. I once prosecuted a defendant for bank embezzlement. Astonishingly, he had committed the crime by simply hiding cells in an Excel spreadsheet. Antics such as these are impossible; DLT recordkeeping is tamper-proof and, consequently, invaluable.

Consensus Mechanisms

Banks rely largely on consumer trust. We wouldn't entrust our funds with people or institutions that couldn't secure and protect them. Few of us would pay by credit card if the company's fraud department refused to let us dispute errant charges. Trust is paramount.

Remember that blockchain supplants human beings with technology. People don't verify that two parties want to conduct a financial transaction. This brings us to the notion of a *consensus mechanism*.* This type of tool verifies individual transactions and maintains the security of the underlying blockchain.[14]

---

* Also known in some circles as *consensus protocols* or *consensus algorithms*.

Proof of Work

Bitcoin relies upon a validation process called *proof of work* (PoW). After a party initiates a transaction, computers on the network compete to solve a series of math problems to validate it on the blockchain and confirm that it took place. A winner's block is added to the ledger. For their efforts, these *miners* receive a small amount of bitcoin for winning. After this process culminates, the system automatically closes the block and opens a new one.

The computing power needed to validate all these transactions is downright staggering. In 2022, Bitcoin surpassed Sweden for overall energy consumption over the previous year.[15] Governments are justifiably worried about their countries' energy grids.* To this end, Kazakhstan president Kassym-Jomart Tokayev signed legislation to limit energy usage of crypto mining in February 2023.[16]

One needn't be a scientist to realize that the status quo wasn't tenable. As cryptocurrency and related technologies started to gain traction, the DeFi industry soon realized that it needed to address its negative environmental impact.

Proof of Stake

Much like PoW, proof of stake (PoS) is, as McKinsey puts it, "a way to decide which user or users validate new blocks of transactions and earn a reward for doing so correctly."[17] The biggest difference between PoS and PoW is efficiency. Research suggests that PoW can reduce overall mining energy consumption by nearly half.[18]

---

* For a fascinating report from the *Journal of Environmental Management*, see https://tinyurl.com/the-cat-environ.

Ethereum

As of February 2, 2025, Ethereum is the second-largest cryptocurrency by market capitalization.[19] It resembles Bitcoin in many ways, but one key feature differentiates the two: programmability. Nakamoto invented Bitcoin as a currency substitute. By contrast, Ethereum is a network that applies what coders call *conditional logic*: if this, then that. In the process, Ethereum opens a world of exciting possibilities. Most important for our purposes is the smart contract:

> Smart contracts are self-executing contracts with the terms of the agreement directly written into code. These contracts automatically execute when predefined conditions are met, eliminating the need for intermediaries. Stored on a blockchain, they are immutable and transparent, meaning that once the contract is deployed, it cannot be altered, and all parties can view its terms.[20]

For this reason, Ethereum's applications aren't confined to finance; they run the gamut.* Put differently, Bitcoin has been an important trailblazer but a relatively limited one: It only allows the transfer of value. Smart contracts executed on Ethereum, however, can automate payments, lending, borrowing, and other finance functions that currently require humans.

Decentralized Finance

It's time to discuss decentralized finance (DeFi). Think of it as an "umbrella term for peer-to-peer financial services on public blockchains, primarily Ethereum."[21]

The history of DeFi is nothing if not mixed. Like many new technologies, it exploded on the scene only to take a step back—a point that Google Trends confirms.† Although DeFi has recently started to come back,[22] it remains a thorn in the side of overworked financial regulators. Their already-full plates

---

* For far more information on this topic, see the 2023 book *Ethereum for Business: A Plain-English Guide to the Use Cases that Generate Returns from Asset Management to Payments to Supply Chains.*

† See https://tinyurl.com/the-cat-defi for an interesting chart.

contain cryptocurrencies, stablecoins, and other digital assets. (Once again, we'll return to that subject later in the chapter.)

DeFi has evolved a great deal since its inception. No one can accurately claim, though, that it's nearly as mature as its counterpart, centralized finance (CeFi). The following sidebar illustrates my point.

> ### A Conference Call Yields a Valuable Insight
>
> For a year, I served as the chief of legal affairs at Chainalysis, a Manhattan-based blockchain analytics firm. At one point early in my tenure, I hopped on a call with a major DeFi company. (Call it Acme here, although it's obviously a pseudonym).
>
> Acme's general counsel (GC) specifically asked me to attend so I could chime in on whether DeFi companies even needed blockchain analytics tools to track illicit activity and bad actors. I agreed, with the caveat that I wouldn't be providing Acme with legal advice on the call.
>
> At the time, Acme wasn't doing anything to patrol against money laundering and terrorist financing. I argued that it should probably step up its efforts lest it be responsible for the next 9/11.
>
> The GC's response shocked me then and does even today. He was surprised that I still felt that way. After all, I had left the government and now worked in the industry. Why did I even care about terrorist financing?
>
> I had naively thought that everyone in the business of moving money recognized the harms of terrorist financing and the need to prevent it. It turns out that some people ignore matters of public policy and national security if they're not legally required to care. They're happy to turn a blind eye, especially when it's in their financial interest to do so.

DeFi Culture

That story illustrates how DeFi culture has evolved since its inception; much of it is no longer the Wild West. Although exceptions remain, the DeFi community now largely acknowledges its moral and legal obligations. Companies have started to innovate in a more responsible manner than in years past. For instance, they're building tools into their products that address both:

- Anti-money laundering (AML).
- Countering the financing of terrorism (CFT).

These developments aren't coincidences, and they don't stem from benevolence. We'll discuss in Part III how getting in front of these issues is in the industry's best interest. By patrolling themselves, they're betting that they'll ultimately discourage regulators and policymakers from overreaching when they pass new laws.

Fintech, Tensions, and the Banking Status Quo

Throughout the history of capitalism, established powers have fought new technologies tooth and nail. Harvard professor Clayton Christensen detailed this fundamental tension in his classic 1997 text, *The Innovator's Dilemma*. No industry is immune, and traditional banking is no exception to this rule. Its leaders have actively resisted new financial technologies—aka, *fintech*—over the past decade.

Better tools have arrived that can vastly improve the efficiency of what have traditionally been core banking functions. Money transfers and cross-border payments are just two of many examples.* And these new tools are maturing as we speak. It's not hard to imagine fintech even eliminating many of these legacy activities altogether—a fact that largely explains why historic resistance to them has been so palpable.

---

* For more on this subject, see *Web3 in Financial Services: How Blockchain, Digital Assets and Crypto Are Disrupting Traditional Finance* by Rita Martins.

That's not to say that resistance has been universal, though. Part III examines examples of early fintech adopters in the private and public sectors. We'll see how Standard Chartered Bank and the Monetary Authority of Singapore (MAS) have already reaped sizeable rewards from embracing new financial technologies.

Cryptocurrencies Enter the Mainstream

The financial world today is a far different, even quainter one than its 2007 counterpart. The subprime crisis resulted in additional regulations aimed at curbing the excesses of unfettered capitalism. In the US, President Obama signed the Dodd-Frank Wall Street Reform and Consumer Protection Act on July 21, 2010. (Bankers and their well-funded lobbyists were none too pleased. We'll see how they extracted their revenge in Chapter 11.)

Apart from new—and much needed—legislation, exciting and promising technologies have arrived in earnest. Blockchain, DeFi, and DLTs are inherently disruptive in nature, but they don't represent the sole tension in traditional financial circles today. CEOs of large financial institutions are losing sleep over the very nature of money.

Bitcoin: The First Tectonic Shift

It's no overstatement to call Nakamoto's innovations *revolutionary*. The first part of this chapter focused on blockchain. Now it's high time to discuss its cousin: Bitcoin.

By birthing the first true cryptocurrency, Nakamoto enabled any person, group, or institution to independently move what we loosely call *money*. For years now, buying a pizza or paying for a digital product no longer requires traditional intermediaries or even the exchange of fiat currency between parties. What Napster did for—or really, *to*—music, Bitcoin has done to money.

FINANCIAL DISINTERMEDIATION

A Simple Example

Say that I want to purchase a good or service from a local merchant. Under the current world financial order, my options include using a physical check, cash, or a credit or debit card. In any event, to process the payment, I need an intermediary to complete the transaction. I'm talking about payment processors, banks, or other money-transmitting entities. Think Venmo or Western Union. But Bitcoin represents a stark departure from the status quo. It allows for the direct, peer-to-peer transfer of value, with no limits, between any two people or entities anywhere in the world.

A Different Way to Bank

Bitcoin is a fully decentralized store of value that users can send in a peer-to-peer (P2P) fashion. Against this backdrop, it provides the missing puzzle piece to complete the disintermediation of traditional finance, as Figure 7.1 displays.

Figure 7.1: Bitcoin P2P Decentralized Digital Ledger

BITCOIN: P2P DECENTRALIZED DIGITAL LEDGER

Network participants agree on a set of rules; those rules dictate bitcoin issuance

The master ledger is secured by cryptography and stored across a completely decentralized network of participants

CRYPTOGRAPHIC PROOF INSTEAD OF TRUST

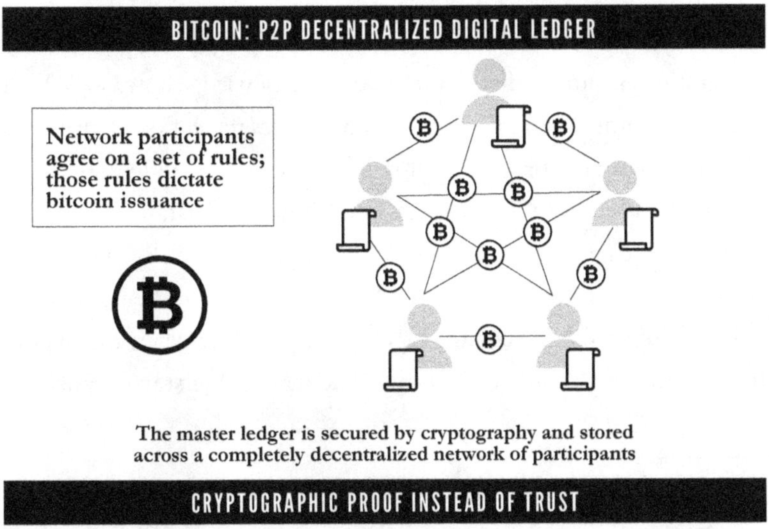

Banks rely on trust and people. In contrast, Bitcoin eschews personal interaction. It's predicated on an immutable, transparent ledger of transactions. In other words, technology replaces trust.

At some point in your life, you may have signed up for a bank account or credit card. If so, you know that financial institutions tie user transactions to their true identities. Outsiders can't view them without due process. By design, Bitcoin and other open crypto ledgers eschew collecting PII. Still, they're not entirely anonymous. They post all transactions on a public ledger.

Bitcoin and several subsequent cryptocurrencies operate on *decentralized* networks[*] of thousands of computers. Take away centralized systems, and modern banks as we know them cease to exist.

For all these reasons, cryptocurrencies make traditional finance types uncomfortable. Put simply, they change the game and threaten their livelihoods.

Dimon Waffles on Crypto and Blockchain

Flagrant self-interest has plagued crypto since its inception. Perhaps there's no better example of this reality than JPMorgan CEO Jamie Dimon.

The über-influential banker and billionaire spent years publicly denigrating crypto. He flat-out refused to acknowledge how blockchain tech could improve financial services, much less revolutionize them. As Upton Sinclair once remarked, "It is difficult to get a man to understand something when his salary depends on his not understanding it."

During that period, however, JPMorgan internally spent millions of dollars hiring some of the brightest minds in the industry to build its internal blockchain program, Onyx. Only when the hypocrisy became untenable did Dimon backtrack. He started publicly

---

[*] While Bitcoin is widely considered to be the most decentralized cryptocurrency, decentralization exists on a spectrum. Cryptocurrencies have differing degrees of decentralization, and some are quite centralized.

> distinguishing Bitcoin from blockchain. Dimon has only recently admitted that JPMorganChase is now one of the "biggest users" of blockchain technology.[23]

Beyond Banking

Let's rewind to 2005 for a moment. Say that I told you that you could pseudonymously, digitally, and instantly transfer millions of dollars nearly for free. Oh, and you needn't worry about regulatory checks or controls. You'd have called me *crazy*—for good reason.

The invention of Bitcoin and subsequent P2P cryptocurrencies isn't just changing finance. Let's talk about governments. Since the advent of central banking, only sovereign nations have been able to mint anonymous currencies, like cash. The entire process is bulky, difficult to move in large amounts, and impossible to move digitally without an intermediary. But governments today no longer possess a monopoly to issue what we now call *money*. As we'll see in later chapters and Part III, crypto's tentacles have stretched into geopolitics as well.

Asset Tokenization

This chapter began by discussing massive technological advancements in finance. Thanks to them, we can now authenticate and securely move photos, videos, audio files, graphics, and just about every digital asset.[*] Remarkably, we can now do the same with most physical ones as well.

That is, we can easily digitize baseball cards, barrels of whiskey, or whatever we like. The process is called *asset tokenization*, and it "involves representing the ownership rights of real-world assets (RWAs) as digital tokens on a blockchain."[24] While we're at it, we can tokenize liabilities and

---

[*] For an excellent summary on how to approach the classification and taxation of digital assets, see the recommendations that the Digital Asset Markets Subcommittee made to the CFTC Global Markets Advisory Committee (GMAC) on March 6, 2024. See https://tinyurl.com/the-cat-reco.

trade them for good measure. The ramifications of tokenization on global finance are impossible to overstate.

Benefits

Count increased liquidity, fractional ownership, immutability, transparency, and around-the-clock access and trading among the manifold benefits of asset tokenization. To state the obvious, however, an unclear or absent regulatory framework will ultimately hinder the adoption of tokenization.

Maturation

Still, it stalled in its early days because of the relative immaturity. In the past few years, though, the scaffolding supporting tokenization has narrowed the gap between theory and practice.

Eric Chen is the CEO of Injective Labs, a company that builds the infrastructure for RWAs. In his words:

> Simply tokenizing something without utility or considering adoption by applications and ecosystems was ineffective back in 2018. However, now there is a flourishing ecosystem of DeFi applications with infrastructure to support tokenization.[25]

As the sufficient infrastructure around RWAs develops, people are beginning to think bigger. Why not tokenize buildings, bonds, and carbon credits? The value proposition seems clear. However, hurdles remain in many jurisdictions and nations, but not all of them. Others are paving the way with regulatory clarity that enables innovation to flourish. (Part III will return to this topic.)

Access and Challenges

Tokenization democratizes access to investments, but significant obstacles are thwarting its progress. Most importantly, governments need to ensure that they enact sensible laws around who can participate in certain asset classes.

In many industrialized nations, one must be an accredited investor to access riskier asset classes that tend to offer higher returns. (The list of requirements to attain this legal status in the US isn't short. Net worth and income top the list.[26]) Countries that fail to expand this legal status can expect predictable results: The investor pool that can use tokenization to access a broader range of assets will remain limited.

Types of Tokens

Broadly speaking, tokenized assets come in two categories: fungible and non-fungible tokens. As for their difference, the former:

> are types of cryptographic tokens that are basically identical or uniform and can be interchanged with other fungible tokens of the same type without any issues. Such tokens relate to the things we use every day, and it applies to real-world as well as digital assets. Non-fungible tokens are special tokens that represent unique, collectible items.[27]

Let's explore each in more detail.

Non-Fungible Tokens

The first non-fungible token (NFT) arrived in 2014 without much fanfare.* NFTs began gaining mainstream momentum in 2017,[28] but March 2021 caused quite the stir when:

> A JPG file made by a digital artist known as Beeple sold Thursday for almost $70 million by Christie's auction house. That price set a new record for the increasingly popular market for digital-only art—and makes Beeple's piece the third most-expensive work sold by a living artist at auction, according to a statement by Christie's.[29]

---

* See a timeline at https://tinyurl.com/the-cat-nft.

THE CATALYSTS

The NFT cat was out of the bag. In 2022, American media personality Paris Hilton infamously appeared on NBC's *The Tonight Show* with host Jimmy Fallon talking about cartoon apes. Pretty soon, the noise around the image and collectible NFTs became deafening—especially given COVID-related travel restrictions.* The near-incessant buzz muted their true import and value: the ability to electronically track unique, non-fungible assets.[30]

Authenticity and Scarcity

During my talks, someone invariably asks me about art and NFTs. The audience member tends to be, in a word, skeptical. The question stems from a fundamental misunderstanding of the topic. The NFT is *not* the image itself; it's the digital certificate of authenticity for that image.

To make things more concrete, I respond by comparing an NFT to a Rolex watch, Prada handbag, or another luxury good. Prada could have manufactured its handbag in China for a fraction of its cost. I then query the audience: Where does the bag's value come from? Typical responses include:

- The bag.
- The demand.
- The cachet of the brand.

All these answers are understandable but false and incomplete. The bag's value stems not from its materials or even its design. The correct answer is the small paper card consumers receive when they purchase it. This document confirms two things. First, it proves that the bag is authentic, but that's not the only source of its value.

Second, it contains a unique number, such as number 26 out of 2,000. That declaration connotes scarcity. It symbolizes that the manufacturer—Prada in this case—intentionally reduced supply in the face of high consumer demand. Whoever owns this product can show the world that they can

---

* Let's just say that people had a little too much free time to pump meme stocks and engage in crypto speculation.

afford to buy an expensive, authentic luxury item. (Recall our discussion in Chapter 1 on the distinction between use and exchange value.)

At this point, lightbulbs typically start going off over attendees' heads. They begin to realize the true value of an NFT: It represents the digitized version of that old-school physical authenticity card. Rather than seeing NFTs as a gimmick, they start to view them as a useful technology for tracking unique, non-fungible assets.

Real Estate and the Future

Yes, one can use an NFT to tokenize a painting or digital image, but it can do much more. As but one example, in the US, many county land ownership offices operate in a tech vacuum. They keep centuries-old property records in dusty, flammable paper books or filing cabinets. Sometimes messy title disputes erupt over the legitimate owner of land and homes. For this very reason, NFTs may represent the future of real estate.[31]

Expect NFT momentum to rise and spread. Local and national government agencies will eventually digitize their constituents' property records. After that happens, the entire title insurance industry may be on the same path as the recording industry.

Fungible Tokens

Now that we've covered unique tokens, let's turn to interchangeable ones. As with the Prada example, it's easiest to understand fungible tokens through a simple real-world analog. Say that you visit your local farmers market one Saturday morning. If you want to pay for some organic vegetables in cash, it doesn't matter which $20 bill you hand the vendor. In this sense, there's no difference between the physical store of value.

The same principle applies to fungible tokens. Put differently, "Each token is identical and can be exchanged for another of the same type without any loss of value."[32]

THE CATALYSTS

Stablecoins

Fungible tokens come in many types. The most popular one is a *stablecoin* backed by fiat currency. This backing provides stability—or at least the aegis of it. Generally speaking, stablecoins are far less volatile than Bitcoin, Ethereum, and other cryptocurrencies. Stablecoin issuers have created them for the dollar, euro, and yuan, respectively.

Circle and Tether are two of the most prominent stablecoin issuers, though competitors are coming.[33] These companies create tokens undergirded by government-issued fiat currencies. (The ratio is one-to-one.) For example, Circle's dollar-backed stablecoin (USDC) is worth $1 USD. In theory, that should never change.

Stablecoins solve several financial problems:

- They're revolutionizing dated, clunky payment rails. They enable faster cross-border transactions.
- They can goose demand worldwide for currencies in countries that want to buy foreign currencies (usually US dollars) but, for whatever reason, struggle to do so.
- They can curb hyperinflation.
- They let citizens easily withdraw their money when they're unable to visit banks, as we saw with Ukrainians after Russia invaded their country.[34]

The future of stablecoins is nothing if not bright.

Central Bank Digital Currencies

Central bank digital currencies (CBDCs) are another type of fungible token—one closely related to what we commonly refer to as *money.*

> A central bank digital currency (CBDC) is a form of digital currency issued by a country's central bank. It is similar to cryptocurrencies, except that its value is fixed by the central bank and is equivalent to the country's fiat currency.[35]

FINANCIAL DISINTERMEDIATION

Digital money may seem like a new concept, but nothing could be further from the truth. Most industrialized countries have long recognized a digitized form of their national currencies. Think about it. Bank accounts, credit cards, and payment apps don't require hard currencies to work.

CBDCs are technically liabilities, not assets. They revert to government-issued fiat currencies. China, the Bahamas, Jamaica, and Nigeria have each launched their own CBDCs. Expect more to arrive soon. In May 2020, 35 countries were actively exploring creating their own CBDCs. As of this writing, that number exceeds 130.[36] That cohort collectively represents 98 percent of the world's annual GDP.

CBDCs make sense because they reduce friction and enable global interoperability, especially when it comes to digital assets. Important consortia and institutions are starting to realize the inevitability of CBDCs. Case in point: the Society for Worldwide Interbank Financial Telecommunications. Since the beginning of 2023, Swift has been piloting interoperability initiatives for CBDCs.[37]

The technologies discussed in this chapter are rapidly disintermediating traditional finance. No one knows how they'll ultimately play out. I'm no soothsayer, but if history in general—and Napster, specifically—is any guide, we can confidently conclude the following:

- Criminals will flock to new tech and adopt it. Condemnation will come from legacy industries that fear change.
- Banning the tech is impossible. The better approach is to intelligently regulate it and facilitate its responsible growth and evolution.
- Disruptive technologies eventually affect every aspect of society. We don't share data, listen to music, or communicate the way we did in 1995. Finance and payments are about to undergo a similar metamorphosis.

THE CATALYSTS

The next chapter looks at what happens when disintermediated finance and other catalysts combine with a global decline in institutional trust.

Key Points

- Satoshi Nakamoto's white paper ushered in the era of blockchain and crypto.
- Bitcoin is a disruptive but fairly limited technology. Ethereum is far more diverse and provides programmability.
- DeFi poses a threat to traditional, centralized finance but comes with opportunities for systemic improvement.
- Some governments are actively seeking to embrace these new financial tools.
- The lessons we learned from Napster apply directly to cryptocurrencies, blockchain, and other emerging financial technologies.

CHAPTER 8

THE EROSION OF INSTITUTIONAL TRUST AND DEMOCRACY

AUTOCRATS ARE CAPITALIZING ON PROFOUND SKEPTICISM TO SEIZE POWER.

> "Democracy is the worst form of government, except for all the others."
>
> —*Winston Churchill*

Let's start this chapter with the following thought experiment. On November 15, 2014, say you went to dinner with your significant other. A mugger hit you on the head with a blunt instrument and absconded with your wallet and brand-new iPhone 6. You survive but end up in a coma.

Ten years later, on November 15, 2024, your medical condition suddenly and inexplicably abates. You wake up to find your partner has stood by your side the whole time. You whisper, "What did I miss?"

Fearful of overwhelming your recovering brain with a deluge of information, your partner tells you that a country's democratic government has recently fallen into authoritarian hands. Its corrupt leaders have politicized its judiciary, tightened control over media outlets and universities, and cracked down on peaceful dissenters. Opposition leaders face persecution, imprisonment, or exile. Institutional trust has plummeted.

Based on the description of how far democracy has devolved, you feel compelled to guess. "Was the country Hungary? Myanmar? Venezuela?" Your partner nods to all of them.

Before you can speak again, they continue naming the rest: Tunisia, Turkey, Poland, France, India. …

You interject, "At least the US isn't on that list!" Your partner becomes upset but brings you up to speed on what has happened in the past ten years. You sit, speechless, wrapping your head around the unthinkable: The US elected a reality television star and unrepentant convicted felon to its highest office. You think it's a joke, but your partner shows you the news to confirm it's real.

This chapter is about the most depressing catalyst of them all: the twin erosions of democracy and institutional trust. Before explaining their causes and how they're driving the new world financial order, though, a section covering their critical nexus is in order.

Trust and Democracy

Remember life before smartphones, social media, and the internet? A quarter-century ago, people would have considered you crazy if you stayed at a complete stranger's house overnight. Only hippie hitchhikers in the 1970s hopped in random cars after their drivers pulled over. Sure, we bought items from people we didn't know, but only at garage sales or flea markets.

My, how times have changed.

These days, we think nothing of using Airbnb or VRBO to rent rooms or even entire homes in distant lands—sight unseen.* Uber, Lyft, and other ride-sharing companies have upended the taxi industry. And eBay, Craigslist, Amazon, and other online marketplaces make it easy to purchase goods from people we'll never meet.

The Fluid Nature of Trust

The point is that trust is—and always has been—a dynamic concept. Centuries ago, we only trusted our family members, friends, and others in our immediate circles or tribes. Today, we trust that the five-star Uber driver will safely take us to our destination and not harm us. Otherwise, we'd never get in, and at scale, Uber's market capitalization wouldn't hover around $150 billion as of this writing.

In 2017, Rachel Botsman published a landmark book, *Who Can You Trust?: How Technology Brought Us Together and Why It Might Drive Us Apart*. She defines trust as "a confident relationship with the unknown."[1] Without it, "and without an understanding of how it is built, managed, lost and repaired, a society cannot survive, and it certainly cannot thrive."[2]

Truer words about societies have never been written—especially when it comes to democratic ones.

Monarchies and Democracies: An Insanely Brief Overview

Students of history and informed citizens don't take democracy for granted. The right of a people to rule itself via elected representatives isn't enshrined anywhere, nor is it a fait accompli. Historically speaking, not that long ago, unelected monarchs ruled just about everyone on the planet, whether those folks liked it or not.

For centuries, few questioned the divine right of kings to rule as they saw fit. Consider Plato's words. In his seminal work *The Republic*, written around

---

* To be fair, though, we can view photos of these destinations. Whether they match the real homes, though, remains to be seen.

375 BC, he argued *against* letting a citizenry elect its own leaders to make societal decisions.

The tide started to turn roughly two millennia later. In the mid-seventeenth century, the philosopher and political theorist John Locke challenged kings' and queens' absolute power. In his 1689 influential book *Two Treatises of Government*, he made the case that *all persons* are endowed with natural rights to life, liberty, and property—not just those wearing crowns and their corrupt sycophants. What's more, a nation's ruling class wasn't exempt from the same standards that applied to plebians. Leaders who failed to protect their people's rights faced consequences. The latter could justifiably resist and replace them with new ones. If doing so required force, so be it.[3]

Technically speaking, Locke was a *constitutional monarchist*—a form of government in which an unelected monarch shares power with a constitutionally organized one. (Understanding political terminology, such as the difference between *democratic socialists* and actual *socialism*, is essential. The next chapter discusses the rise of nationalism.)

Regardless of his democratically impure beliefs, Locke's ideas profoundly influenced the founding fathers, the 1776 American Revolution, and the advancement of democratic forms of government. Case in point: The French First Republic convicted King Louis XVI of treason in 1792. Less than a year later, on January 21, 1793, High Executioner Charles-Henri Sanson[4] beheaded the former monarch by guillotine in the *Place de la Révolution* in Paris.[5] It's safe to say that other emperors noticed. Maybe their stations and rights to rule their people weren't so absolute or divine after all.

Of course, the democratic pendulum didn't immediately or universally swing across the globe. India and Pakistan weren't independent nations until 1947; before then, they were English colonies.[6] Even today, colonies and other non-self-governing territories persevere despite the UN's efforts to eradicate them.

The sad but unfortunate reality is that all democracies are fragile; some may even be fleeting. Barack Obama once called self-government "one of the world's boldest experiments."[7] All democracies face challenges at some point, and some will ultimately fail their inevitable tests. A 2022 study from the University of Gothenburg in Sweden found that "70 percent of the world's population now live in dictatorships."[8] Even more troubling, that number is "advancing globally."[9]

In large part, the resilience and health of any single democracy hinge upon the trust of its citizenry. The same holds true for the current world financial order. Trust is downright essential for the system to function. This begs the natural question: What's the current state of our trust in governments and institutions?

The State of Trust in Different Institutions

The question about trust is meaty and even book-worthy. There's no better place to find an answer than the Edelman Trust Institute's 2024 Trust Barometer. The annual global report provides insights into global trust levels across diverse institutions and highlights key trends influencing public sentiment.

The eighty-eight-page analysis examines trust in government, media, business, and non-governmental organizations (NGOs) across twenty-eight countries. In total, Edelman surveyed more than 32,000 respondents for its 2024 report.[10]

To be sure, variations exist among countries. Overall, however, the state of trust across the globe is, in a word, dismal. Consider just a few of the report's damning statistics:

- Only 30 percent of respondents believe democracy effectively serves them.
- More than three in five people feel they'll be worse off in five years.

On many levels, it's a sorry situation. Figure 8.1 shows the extent to which respondents view the private sector as more competent but less ethical than its public counterpart.

Figure 8.1: Perceptions of Competency and Ethics for Government vs. Business

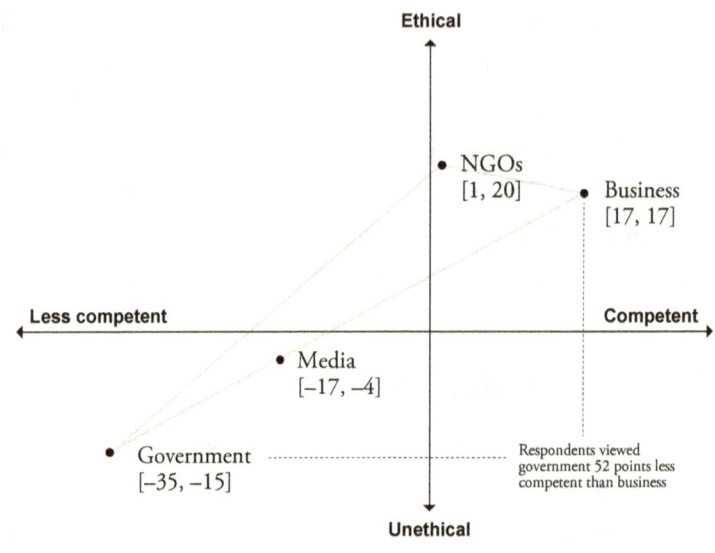

Source: Edelman

Around the same time that Edelman released its annual report, the company dropped a supplemental report called *The Empowered Patient*. Again, more bad news. Barely one-third of respondents trust journalists to tell the truth about health issues and how best to protect the public's health—a steep drop of ten percentage points from the previous year.[11]

Trust is rapidly declining, making the rise of autocrats more understandable (although still dispiriting). The next question: Why?

How We Got to Now

It's time to explain the factors causing institutional trust to plummet and, in a related vein, so many democracies to falter. Note that I could spend the remaining pages of this book—never mind this chapter—unpacking the status quo and still leave a great deal on the table. As with all the chapters in Part II, I'm intentionally sacrificing depth for breadth.

Basic Human Nature

Let's start with a simple, even prosaic reason for our current state of affairs: our humanity.

As the American biologist and neurologist Robert Sapolsky writes in his book *Determined: A Science of Life Without Free Will*, "We are nothing more or less than the cumulative biological and environmental luck, over which we had no control, that has brought us to any moment."[12]

As a species, we suffer from myriad cognitive biases that deeply color how we view the world.* We've always naturally responded to what interests us. When confronted with information that conflicts with our worldviews, we experience cognitive dissonance. As a rule, human beings don't change their minds easily. Instead, we rationalize and engage in what psychologists call *motivated reasoning*.[13] We simply reframe our arguments to justify our positions. In the process, we throw logic and common sense to the wind. (We'll return to this subject in Chapter 12.)

This superpower allows people to reconcile two contradictory beliefs. For example, an unrepentant convicted felon can stand for law and order. An anti-vaccination protester can hold a sign that reads *My Body, My Choice* while supporting laws that prevent women from making choices regarding their bodies. A Trump supporter can affix a *Blue Lives Matter* bumper sticker to her car and say January 6 was a legitimate peaceful protest, even though she knows Capitol police officers died as a result.[14]

In the latter case, what if the Trump supporter doesn't even know about those tragic deaths or, worse, doesn't believe anything she reads about them? What if she lives in a self-imposed echo chamber?

The Information Explosion and Filter Bubbles

For several reasons, countless people do live in echo chambers. First, as a species, we naturally gravitate toward data that confirms our already-held

---

* Thousands of books and experiments have proved as much, but the work of Daniel Kahneman and Amos Tversky is particularly important here.

beliefs. That fact hasn't changed. However, the amount of content available for us to consume has.* Today, it's unfathomable. Thanks to smartphones, blogs, social media, podcasts, and video-streaming sites, we can effectively create our own realities.

Eli Pariser explores this topic in his excellent but chilling 2012 book, *The Filter Bubble: How the New Personalized Web Is Changing What We Read and How We Think*. We can now choose only to receive news that confirms our beliefs. The consequences of filter bubbles are impossible to overstate. Brass tacks: If you want to develop a balanced and more accurate worldview, you must actively *work* to do it.

Omnipresent and Ubiquitous Algorithms

In 2018, YouTube chief product officer Neal Mohan revealed that 70 percent of what people watch on it stems from its recommendation algorithms.[15] A 2021 *Wall Street Journal* exposé revealed that TikTok uses only one "important piece of information to figure out what you want: the amount of time you linger over a piece of content."[16]

Tech companies personalize user and customer content feeds. In so doing, they perpetuate and exacerbate the very filter bubbles Pariser describes in his book. These algorithms don't just make people uninformed or misinformed; they can radicalize users. In 2023, researchers at the University of California, Davis found that YouTube video recommendations lead to more extremist content for right-leaning users.[17]

The Profit Motive

Compelling research shows that Facebook, YouTube, Twitter/X, and other social media platforms create partisan divisions, foster confirmation bias, polarize users, and weaken democratic processes—sometimes *intentionally*.[18] In sum, the leaders of these massive corporations are both unwilling and unable to address the problems they've created.

---

* See https://tinyurl.com/the-cata-data for some fascinating stats on how much data we create every day.

In 2021, Frances Haugen worked as a data scientist at Facebook. Her work revealed that her employer's three core products—WhatsApp, Facebook, and Instagram—were harming teenagers. Haugen presented her findings internally, but her superiors chose to ignore or minimize her research. The company routinely prioritized growth over the safety of its users.

Haugen considered the matter a public safety issue and blew the whistle on her employer. She disclosed tens of thousands of pages of internal Facebook documents to Congress and the Securities and Exchange Commission.[19] *The Wall Street Journal* ran a series of provocative pieces on the matter.[20] Behind the scenes, Mark Zuckerberg's recently rebranded Meta worked furiously to obscure the story and undermine Haugen's credibility.[21]

Mark Zuckerberg isn't inherently evil; he was protecting his business's interests. Facebook makes most of its money by running ads. Spending more time on the platform results in more ads seen, more revenue, and more profits. Capitalism rarely rewards companies for voluntarily behaving ethically, especially in the US.

So why don't lawmakers compel Facebook and other tech behemoths to behave in ways that don't wreak havoc on society?

Big Tech Staves Off Meaningful Government Regulation

Several reasons spring to mind. While I'm focusing on Facebook/Meta, I could make comparable cases for Amazon, Apple, Alphabet, and Microsoft. All of them fall under the same umbrella.

Unlimited Coffers

Meta's virtually bottomless piggy bank allows it to, put bluntly, buy off the politicians who pose the biggest threats. Like its fellow tech titans, it makes legal contributions to political action committees (PACs) and individual politicians. From 2020 to 2022, the company averaged $20 million in lobbying expenses.[22] That number represented a hundredfold increase from 2009.

THE CATALYSTS

Cowardly Politicians

Regulators and politicians are often reluctant to police the very corporations that fall under their jurisdictions. Jesse Eisinger tells this sordid but true tale in his 2017 book, *The Chickenshit Club: Why the Justice Department Fails to Prosecute Executives*. Elected officials and political appointees don't want to burn bridges. In less than four years, they could be interviewing for private-sector jobs.

The problem isn't confined to the absence of meaningful legislation in the tech sector. It's far broader. Even scandals and full-fledged crises rarely result in perp walks. In 2010, Goldman Sachs paid $550 million for its role in the subprime crisis.[23] That amount might seem significant, but it's a pittance compared to its 2010 net revenues of $39.2 billion.[24] You'd think that the threat of incarceration would keep white-collar criminals in line, but nothing could be further from the truth. A two-tiered system of justice is now blatantly evident—and not just in the US.[25] This profound lack of accountability throughout the world has reinforced perceptions that institutions are self-serving and unaccountable. (We'll return to this subject later in this chapter.)

Regulators' Ignorance and Lack of Education

Many government officials don't remotely understand the industries and companies they're supposed to regulate. Perhaps the most famous example occurred on April 10, 2018. In the wake of the Cambridge Analytica scandal, the US Senate held hearings on data privacy and invited the embattled Facebook CEO to attend.

Zuck's senior team no doubt prepared him for the inevitable maelstrom of queries for his televised testimony, but one clearly surprised him.* Utah Republican Senator and elder statesman Orrin Hatch asked how the company made money.[26] The astonishingly ignorant question caused the Facebook founder to visibly smirk before responding, "Senator, we run ads."

---

* Read his entire testimony at https://tinyurl.com/the-cat-zuck.

THE EROSION OF INSTITUTIONAL TRUST AND DEMOCRACY

The four words became a meme. Soon, people were wearing t-shirts with the response. Most important for our purposes, the naivety underscored that politicians—especially older ones—are often insulated and don't understand the technology and emerging innovations they're responsible for regulating.

Edelman's data supports this assertion, as Figure 8.2 shows.

Figure 8.2: Government Incompetence in Regulating Emerging Innovations

Thailand	66
UK	66
India	65
Australia	64
China	64
Canada	63
Ireland	63
Malaysia	63
Mexico	63
S. Africa	63
US	62
Japan	61
Argentina	60
Germany	60
Netherlands	59
Nigeria	56
Brazil	56
Colombia	56
France	55
Kenya	53
S. Korea	53
Spain	51
UAE	50
Singapore	45
Saudi Arabia	45

Source: Edelman

Fifty-nine percent of global respondents to the 2024 Trust Barometer said that government regulators lack an adequate understanding of emerging technologies to effectively regulate them.

They're right. As discussed in Chapters 4 and 6, legislation to constrain tech companies is sorely deficient. (See the discussions regarding Section 230 of the Communications Decency Act.)

Big Tech Exploits a Broken Polity and Co-Opts the Internet

Meta, Google, Amazon, and other tech titans haven't just reaped outsize profits and become de facto monopolies. (Chapter 6 explored this subject in detail.) These companies' founders have co-opted the internet's raison d'être. Their motivations are as political as they are economic—if not more so.

The prominent American cultural critic Jonathan Taplin makes this point in his 2017 book *Move Fast and Break Things: How Facebook, Google, and Amazon Cornered Culture and Undermined Democracy*. Taplin doesn't mince words, writing:

> The original mission of the Internet was hijacked by a small group of right-wing radicals to whom the ideas of democracy and decentralization were anathema. By the late 1980s, starting with eventual PayPal founder Peter Thiel's class at Stanford University, the dominant philosophy of Silicon Valley would be based far more heavily on the radical libertarian ideology of Ayn Rand than the commune-based principles of Ken Kesey and Stewart Brand.* Thiel, who was also an early investor in Facebook and is the godfather of what he proudly calls the PayPal Mafia, which currently rules Silicon Valley, has been clear about his credo, stating, "I no longer believe that freedom and democracy are compatible." More important, Thiel says that if you want to create and capture lasting value, you should look to build a monopoly.[27]

The trend has continued—if not intensified—in the years since Taplin published his book. As mentioned in Chapter 5, Elon Musk announced plans to move the headquarters of both X (formerly Twitter) and SpaceX from California to Texas in August 2024.[28] Political and economic reasons (read: state taxes) fueled his decision.

It's folly to think of this issue exclusively in economic terms, though. More perniciously, as we'll see in this chapter, oligarchs, nation-states, terrorists, and political action committees (PACs) are using tech companies' wares to actively undermine democracies across the globe.

Cracks in Capitalism: How the System Failed Us All

Chapter 5 discussed the economic struggles of US blue-collar workers. (See the section titled "Trials and Tribulations of the Middle Class.") Big business has largely neutralized global regulators. Regulation is wanting, if not toothless. CEOs are growing wealthier and generally unaccountable for

---

* We'll revisit him in Chapter 10.

their actions, and bankers are tone-deaf. In 2009, "Thousands of top traders and bankers on Wall Street were awarded huge bonuses and pay packages last year, even as their employers were battered by the financial crisis."[29] Talk about putting salt in the wound. Much of the public justifiably perceived their government as protecting corporate interests over those of ordinary citizens.

The result was a highly flammable situation. It was only a matter of time before something happened.

Occupy Wall Street

Against this backdrop, on September 17, 2011, a group of protestors descended upon Zuccotti Park in Manhattan, New York. Their grievances included economic inequality, corporate greed, political corruption, and recently bailed-out bankers. The group—ultimately dubbed *Occupy Wall Street* (OWS)—set up shop in the park, where they remained for fifty-nine days. Word spread. Organizers claimed that "there would be demonstrations in 951 cities in 82 countries."[30]

Fortunately, civil disobedience won out over violence, with the group opting for marches and rallies.[31] That OWS lacked a cohesive plan or a specific set of objectives didn't seem to matter; the movement spread to other cities around the globe. Their movement tapped into a fundamental and growing belief that the current form of capitalism lacked anything resembling social and economic justice.

Residual Effects

Many pundits callously dismissed OWS as a flash in the pan. On the contrary, its effects linger to this day. As James A. Anderson astutely wrote in *Time* in 2021, a full decade after the global protests:

> The lasting effects of Occupy are not isolated to the Left. A surge in populism is visible across the American political spectrum and much of the Right's messaging can be traced back to the discontent

Occupy crystallized. Donald Trump was able to leapfrog a crowd of Republican contenders in 2016 in part by hinting early on about raising taxation rates for the rich—only to U-turn later. His close adviser, Steve Bannon has identified a growing distrust of elites by a predominately white working class as key to Trump's popularity.[32]

Other populist leaders and demagogues recognized the opportunity. They capitalized on their citizens' vitriol and attacked other pillars of democracy, including the press.

The Decimation of Local Journalism

Newspapers used to perform many critical community functions. Journalists held power accountable, informed the community, and fostered some sense of civic engagement.

Those booming days have passed, and Big Tech bears much of the burden. As prolific technology author Phil Simon writes in his 2023 book *The Nine*:

> There's no sense in sugarcoating it: the explosion of the web in the mid-1990s caught newspapers flatfooted. Craig Newmark launched Craigslist, a remarkably plain and simple site that would siphon off want ads and job postings from local papers. In 2006, total revenue from US newspapers hit $49.3 billion, recovering nicely from the dot-com implosion. The reprieve, however, turned out to be short-lived. Pew Research estimated that, by 2020, the figure had plunged to $10 billion—an 80 percent drop.[33]
>
> When hidebound newspaper editors finally recognized the need to adapt, the die had been cast. Local presses struggled to keep the lights on.
>
> Hundreds of papers ultimately shuttered. In 2019, more than 1,400 American cities and towns had lost newspapers in the past fifteen years alone.[34] Then came COVID-19. The pandemic caused hundreds more to close their doors for good.[35]

THE EROSION OF INSTITUTIONAL TRUST AND DEMOCRACY

Newspapers can't blame Facebook and Google for all their woes, though. They bear some of the burden for the demise of their businesses. For example, *The New York Times* let Google freely serve up its articles for years until it decided to stop the ill-advised practice.[36] People became used to getting news for free. You can't unring that bell.*

Today a veritable news vacuum exists in most American cities and towns. Faced with a dearth of credible local information, unverified, biased, and politically motivated sham "news" sources proliferate. In many cases, there's not even the aegis of proper journalism, fact-checking, or objectivity.

The Unfettered Power of User Data

Meta and Google have amassed unprecedented troves of personal data on their users.[37] (The data stockpile of Twitter/X isn't nearly as impressive.) Sadly, as we saw in Chapter 6, these companies have failed to protect this invaluable asset.† (See the section titled "The Erosion of Privacy and the Weaponization of Data.")

You don't need to head to sites on the dark web, though, to access remarkably personal demographic and psychographic data on hundreds of millions of users. These platforms allow highly targeted advertising—indeed, this is how they earn the majority of their income. Meta, Alphabet, Twitter/X, and others have created tools that allow their true customers (read: advertisers) to effectively manipulate specific groups with tailored messages, all without transparency or public scrutiny.

---

*   American journalist Jeff Jarvis has written extensively on the media landscape.
†   See https://tinyurl.com/the-cat-fb-data for a list of Facebook data breaches up to 2023. It's not a short read.

> **Using Facebook Ads to Circumvent the Law**
>
> In the US and many other industrialized countries, it's illegal to discriminate against people based on age, sex, gender, and marital status. For example, a local manufacturer can't legally post a job in a newspaper that restricts applicants to single white men under thirty years old.
>
> However, on Facebook, that same manufacturer can create a targeted ad that only single white men under thirty will ever see. Doing so takes zero technical skill.
>
> Over the years, Facebook has faced several related lawsuits, but the practice continues virtually unabated. In 2019, ProPublica reported that "Facebook ads can still discriminate against women and older workers, despite a civil rights settlement."[38]

Better Exploitation and Manipulation Through Data

What happens when you combine repeated data breaches, a lack of oversight, and business models that encourage addiction and manipulation? Lots of bad things.

Domestic Economic and Political Messaging

Corporations realize that these microtargeted ads can really move the needle, influence user behavior, and directly affect their businesses and profits. Chapter 6 described how tech companies were fighting Proposition 22 in California. (See "Subverting Employment Laws.") For the most part, Uber and Lyft didn't use relics of a bygone era: taking out ads in local newspapers or radio stations. No, social media represented a far better bang for the buck. The firms "poured millions of dollars into Facebook ads to protect their business in California."[39]

American politicians and PACs have also shifted their strategies accordingly. US political digital advertising spending in the first seven months of 2022 from Google and Facebook totaled $388 million. The numbers for connected TV advertising* during that period clocked in at only $309 million.⁴⁰

This data gives these companies—and anyone who can purchase or otherwise access it—immense power. With it, they can shape opinions, voting behavior, and public discourse in ways that may not align with the democratic ideal of free and fair choice. Alternatively, they can use it to defraud Americans out of more than $250 million donated to an "Official Election Defense Fund" that never existed.⁴¹

US companies and politicians who are using new communications mediums to influence elections, referenda, and public policy is nothing new. Foreign powers intent on subverting American democracy and ideals are an entirely different ball of wax.

Deliberate Manipulation by Malign Foreign Governments

If Uber or your local mayor can run ads on Facebook, Instagram, and YouTube, why couldn't a foreign adversary with far more malicious intentions?

It's not a rhetorical question. In 2017, Facebook admitted selling $100,000 in ads to fake Russian accounts during the 2016 presidential election.⁴² Experts say that the "Russian propaganda effort helped spread 'fake news' during [the] election."⁴³

That the practice has continued unabated since should surprise precisely no one.

Facebook, Twitter/X, and YouTube are catnip for Russian forces attempting to spew propaganda and stoke divisions inside the US. Consider the words of former KGB agent Yuri Alexandrovich Bezmenov, who in 1984 claimed that:

---

* *Connected TV advertising* refers to "video ads that are delivered via a streaming service during a viewer's movie, TV show, or other video content—and viewed on an actual TV set." See https://tinyurl.com/the-cat-tv for more information.

THE CATALYSTS

Russia has a long-term goal of ideologically subverting the U.S.* He described the process as "a great brainwashing" that has four basic stages. The first stage, he said, is called "demoralization," which would take about 20 years to achieve.[44]

As Paul Ratner of *Big Think* writes:

> "As I mentioned before, exposure to true information does not matter anymore," said Bezmenov. "A person who was demoralized is unable to assess true information. The facts tell nothing to him. Even if I shower him with information, with authentic proof, with documents, with pictures; even if I take him by force to the Soviet Union and show him [a] concentration camp, he will refuse to believe it, until he [receives] a kick in his fan-bottom. When a military boot crashes his balls then he will understand. But not before that. That's the [tragedy] of the situation of demoralization."

Russia has long wanted to skew Americans' opinion on a range of issues. In 2016, it ran intentionally divisive ads on Facebook and YouTube in the US. The Kremlin effectively achieved its goals: dividing the American public and interfering with its elections. Given its success, why stop? The bottom line is that Russia's overall game plan has remained constant; only its delivery mechanisms have changed.

While we're at it, what's to prevent any country from doing the same anywhere else? Yes, some nations have banned American social networks and related apps—not coincidentally, many of which are the same that have fallen into authoritarian hands mentioned at the start of this chapter.[45] (Chapter 14 will present specific policy recommendations for countering this challenge.)

---

* Watch the terrifyingly prescient video at https://tinyurl.com/the-cat-kgb.

Sophisticated Networks

Finally, today's despots aren't rising to power and holding on to it on their own. On the contrary, they've got plenty of help. Anne Applebaum delves into this trend in her bestselling 2024 book, *Autocracy, Inc.: The Dictators Who Want to Run the World*. She describes how autocrats use sophisticated networks that rely on:

> kleptocratic financial structures, a complex of security services—military, paramilitary, police—and technological experts who provide surveillance, propaganda, and disinformation. The members of these networks are connected not only to one another within a given autocracy but also to networks in other autocratic countries, and sometimes in democracies too. Corrupt, state-controlled companies in one dictatorship do business with corrupt, state-controlled companies in another. The police in one country may arm, equip, and train the police in many others. The propagandists share resources—the troll farms and media networks that promote one dictator's propaganda can also be used to promote another's—as well as themes: the degeneracy of democracy, the stability of autocracy, the evil of America.

Popular opposition movements in Venezuela, Hong Kong, and Moscow are ultimately minor nuisances, not real threats.

Now that we've unpacked the major causes of the status quo, it's time to focus on its effects. Warning: They're not pleasant.

Ramifications

Perhaps Plato was right: Democracy will result in arrogant, power-hungry demagogues. It's just a matter of when. Writing for *Quartz* in June 2018, Olivia Goldhill observes:

THE CATALYSTS

> In the *Republic* ... Plato describes such the democratic man—by which he means a democratic leader—as one of "false and braggart words and opinions."[46]

Many of today's autocrats certainly fit the bill, including (arguably) the US president at the time Goldhill wrote those words. Still, historically low levels of institutional trust worldwide haven't just resulted in the lamentable rise of decidedly undemocratic firebrands who rule with an iron hand. The wound is far deeper.

Note that I separate the ramifications in this section by necessity when, in fact, they're anything but. Each one catalyzes and accelerates the others. That last statement should terrify you.

Amplification of Misinformation

Social media platforms have become powerful tools for spreading misinformation, creating echo chambers, and contributing to polarization. We covered this topic in Chapter 7. As but one domestic example, Twitter allowed the far-right American political conspiracy theory and political movement QAnon to blossom, ushering a minor blip on the extreme fringe in 2017 into the mainstream.[47]

Globally, China has used TikTok to further its covert influence worldwide. In February 2024, the US Office of the Director of National Intelligence released its 2024 Annual Threat Assessment. The agency found that the Communist Party of China (CCP) used the platform to "sow doubts about US leadership, undermine democracy, and extend Beijing's influence."[48]

A Widespread Inability to Distinguish Fact From Fiction

Distrust from social media and legacy media has created a perilous situation: People don't know what's real. As the following sidebar illustrates, the worst is yet to come.

> ### AI, Deepfakes, and Ukraine: A Prelude of Things to Come
>
> In 2022, a video appeared on YouTube and other social media networks. While this happens countless times every day, this clip was particularly odd. It showed Ukrainian President Volodymyr Zelenskyy standing at a podium. He told his people to lay down their arms and surrender to Russia.
>
> Many Ukrainians didn't fall for the ruse. Their fearless leader's head "appear[ed] too large for and more pixelated than his body—and his voice sound[ed] deeper."[49] Put differently, they recognized the video for what it was: a deepfake.
>
> Generative AI tools are rapidly becoming more sophisticated. At what point will manufactured photos, videos, and audio recordings become indistinguishable from real ones? That day is coming. We aren't remotely prepared for such a future.*

Weakened Social Cohesion

The name *the United States* has always been a misnomer. Very little unites it. A child growing up in New York may hear a different story about the Civil War than one raised in Alabama. The Alabama child might hear about the "War of Northern Aggression."[50] In the UK, sentiment surrounding the Brexit vote revealed tears in the country's societal fabric around economic inequality, feelings on immigration, and stark generational differences.[51]

A full discussion of this topic is far beyond the scope of this book. There's little doubt, though, that the collective erosion in trust has increased societal polarization in many countries. In the US, it has become a full-blown crisis that has exacerbated the political and economic dysfunction detailed in Chapter 5.[52]

---

* For a terrifying glimpse of what that future may entail, watch both seasons of the *BBC* show *The Capture*.

THE CATALYSTS

DeFi and Cryptocurrencies Enter the Mainstream

Chapter 7 covered the rise of decentralized finance (DeFi), cryptocurrencies, and blockchain technology. In mid-November 2023, a single bitcoin was worth $37,000. On January 20, 2025, the price reached $108,786 before pulling back.[53] Many factors explain its staggering resurgence, including the results of the 2024 US presidential election. However, the lack of trust in traditional institutions is one of the biggest.[54]

In a different, more trustworthy world, the bright future for nascent financial technologies and blockchain projects would be less politicized. "Anti-crypto armies" wouldn't exist. National priorities would include CBDCs, interoperability, and regulatory harmonization. Instead, the Bitcoin tribe is alive and well, clamoring for the replacement of the US dollar. And several countries are pulling ahead of the US in terms of innovative regulation and facilitating emerging technologies in the digital economy.

Speaking of tribes, the next chapter discusses a related by-product of an angrier, more cynical world: the rise of neo-nationalism.

Key Points

- Authoritarian capitalism is on the rise, while trust in public institutions is plummeting.
- Newspapers are no longer prominent in the media landscape. People continue to seek information from sources that confirm their biases.
- Big Tech has effectively staved off meaningful legislation, especially in the US, to the grave detriment of society globally.
- Today, misinformation and disinformation are rampant; autocratic leaders are using it to manipulate their citizens.
- Outside their borders, countries face an even more formidable threat: major powers using malign influence to spread propaganda and nationalist policies.

CHAPTER 9

THE CONTAGION OF NEO-NATIONALISM

INDUSTRIALIZED COUNTRIES ARE ESCHEWING GLOBALIZATION TO FORGE THEIR OWN ECONOMIC SOVEREIGNTY.

"Nationalism is power hunger tempered by self-deception."
—*George Orwell*

On April 18, 1968, Enoch Powell spoke at a meeting of the Conservative Political Centre in Birmingham, England. The demographic makeup of his country was changing, and the right-wing British politician was none too pleased. Almost overnight, his "Rivers of Blood" speech immediately sparked "a national debate about immigration, integration, and race relations."[1] If it happened today, we'd say it went viral.

THE CATALYSTS

Powell's divisive words rightfully offended plenty of folks—but not everyone disagreed. His message deeply resonated with one group: Britons pining for their homeland's glory days. Powell successfully tapped into a deep-seated resentment of non-Anglo-Saxons and his nation's direction. Conservative, older, white men in particular wanted "old" England to start reasserting itself.

That disaffected group of Britons, however, remained a minority—albeit a vocal one. England at the time was largely embracing economic policies promoting globalization: free trade, immigration, and foreign investment. On January 22, 1972, the UK formally joined the European Economic Community—the predecessor to the EU that the Maastricht Treaty of 1992 created.[2] The benefits of fully participating in the world economy clearly exceeded their drawbacks.

That faction's sense of disillusionment didn't entirely dissipate, however. On the contrary, it bubbled under the surface of English politics for decades. On June 23, 2016, tensions finally came to a head in the form of the historic Brexit referendum. Citizens narrowly voted to leave the European Union—a decision with far-reaching, perhaps permanent economic consequences.

The demographic data behind the Brexit vote is both fascinating and revealing. White English voters largely delivered victory for the leave side. Younger Brits were far more likely to vote to remain in the EU than their more senior compatriots.[3] The cancer lurking in British society had finally metastasized.[*]

As proof, look no further than Powell. He remains a historically relevant figure, especially among some Brits. In 2018, the left-leaning UK think tank British Future commissioned a poll on his controversial *cri de cœur*.[4] The group asked respondents to pick the name of the person associated with the phrase *rivers of blood* from a list. Only 18 percent of respondents under thirty-four years old could do so. For people 65 and over, the story was much different. Of that cohort, more than 80 percent correctly identified him.[†]

---

[*] See https://tinyurl.com/the-cat-brexit for a far deeper discussion on this topic.
[†] Read the whole speech at https://tinyurl.com/the-cat-enoch.

England is today once again a truly sovereign nation—and, by almost all accounts, economically far worse for it. Two-thirds of the British public claim that Brexit has damaged the economy. Even leave voters are experiencing buyer's remorse: Only one in five thinks the impact has been positive.[5] A 2024 Cambridge Econometrics report estimated that Brexit caused the UK economy to shrink by £140 billion.[6] One wonders how the vote would go if held today, but it's a moot point. There's no reset button.

Lamentably, England isn't the only storied nation currently grappling with a dangerous cocktail of *isms*: populism, racism, sexism, ethnocentrism, protectionism, and isolationism. As we'll see in this chapter, more and more nations are opting for nationalism over globalism. The consequences of this potent catalyst on the new world financial order are impossible to overstate.

Not Just England: Hypernationalism in Action

Britons disenchanted with Brexit and its economic fallout can at least take some solace in a simple fact: They're not alone. Across the pond, American politicians are behaving just as badly—if not more so.

US

One could fill several tomes on the counterproductive policies of the first Trump administration. I'll focus on just two, though.

Trade Wars

First, let's discuss tariffs. The first Trump administration implemented them "on products including lumber, steel and semiconductors to shield American companies from a glut of cheap imported products from China and other countries."[7] US manufacturers blamed the tariffs for inflation's rise. There's truth in that.

Rather than change course in the future, though, Trump doubled down on his plans and started slapping steep levies on imports after being reelected:

As a candidate, Trump pledged to slap 60% tariffs on all goods coming in from China and 10% tariffs on goods imported from all other countries. While aides say those pledges weren't campaign bluster, there are still questions about how to pursue them, through what legal authorities and when.[8]

Experts predict that Trump's economic plans will worsen US inflation—just as it's dropping from its decades-long highs.[9]

Trump's understanding of economics is as dangerous and deficient as his understanding of the environment. To be fair, though, Americans may be expecting too much business acumen from a man who's filed for bankruptcy six times.[10]

Climate Change

Global warming is real. It's no longer some theoretical possibility that may arrive decades down the road. As another reminder of its impending consequences, in September 2024 Hurricane Helene ravaged the southeastern US.[11] What's more, climate change will change life as we know it. The protestations of deniers don't alter this simple, immutable fact.

The health of the planet affects everyone. Against this backdrop, 196 parties at the UN Climate Change Conference signed the Paris Agreement in 2016, a legally binding international treaty to tackle the issue and preserve life on this planet as we know it.

The US and China didn't exactly see eye-to-eye at the time, but neither country let geopolitical differences cloud the big picture. Just about every elected and unelected leader on the planet recognized the need to hold "the increase in the global average temperature to well below 2°C above pre-industrial levels" and pursue efforts "to limit the temperature increase to 1.5°C above pre-industrial levels."[12]

One would think that reducing the world's carbon emissions and ensuring the health of future generations would be a fundamentally apolitical, truly international issue. In this vein, you'd expect the world's then-leading superpower to continue to lead by example. The grossly irresponsible actions of Obama's successor in November 2019 proved otherwise:

> President Trump has announced his intention to withdraw the U.S. from the Paris Agreement—the global accord which implements the objectives of the United Nations Framework Convention on Climate Change. Under the agreement, the U.S. had previously submitted a Nationally Determined Contribution (NDC) in which we committed to reducing the country's greenhouse gas emissions by 26–28% below 2005 levels by 2025. In his announcement, Trump stated that "as of today, the United States will cease all implementation of the Paris Agreement" including the NDC and contributions to the Green Climate Fund.[13]

Six weeks after taking office in 2021, President Joe Biden course corrected. The US officially rejoined the Paris Agreement.[14] Unfortunately, the move was temporary. Hours after formally beginning his second term, Trump signed an executive order withdrawing the US from the climate treaty again.[15]

The message the US is sending is clear: "We may have cared about pressing global issues in the past. We no longer do. You're on your own." We'll see later in this chapter how other countries are stepping up to the plate.

France

England's neighbor and ally hasn't embraced neo-nationalism just yet, but it's perilously close to doing so. Seeds planted years ago are starting to bloom.

Marine Le Pen is a French attorney by trade who has run for the French presidency thrice. In 2012, the mainstream press in her country dismissed her as a crackpot with Nazi sympathies. Among her well-chronicled run-ins:

- One with pop star Madonna over swastikas.[16]
- Another with Parisian non-Muslims who may have unwittingly been eating halal meat.[17]

THE CATALYSTS

Much like Trump, Le Pen unabashedly advocated for protectionist policies while running for office in 2017.[18] Despite this position (or maybe because of it), her stock kept rising. As Eleanor Beardsley wrote for NPR in April of that year:

> There's no doubt she's become a major figure in the French political landscape. In just six years at the helm of the nationalist National Front party, she has changed it from a fringe party into a national political force to be reckoned with.[19]

The trend continued in 2022. As *Politico* editor at large Nicholas Vinocur noted in 2024, she had turned "respectable":

> Marine Le Pen has made a concerted effort to rebrand her party, the National Rally, as a France-first populist movement, distancing herself from her father's controversial legacy. She has avoided major scandals and focused on abstract concepts like fundamentalist Islam. While she has achieved some success in rebranding, critics argue that her comments about Muslims and immigrants verge on Islamophobia. Le Pen's party is gaining support and is poised to make significant gains in the upcoming European Parliament election. However, concerns remain about her party's far-right associations and the potential disruption she could bring to the European Union if elected president.[20]

As of this writing, the centrist and pro-European Emmanuel Macron presides over France, but Le Pen remains a powerful political force. For two reasons, it would be foolish to dismiss her movement.

First, Figure 9.1 displays the past two election results for the French presidency. Le Pen's voter base is growing based on her revised message. Second, if she were to suddenly vanish, another dangerous right-wing politician would no doubt supplant her. Plenty of French men and women are buying what she's selling.

Figure 9.1: Voting Percentage for Past Two French Presidential Elections

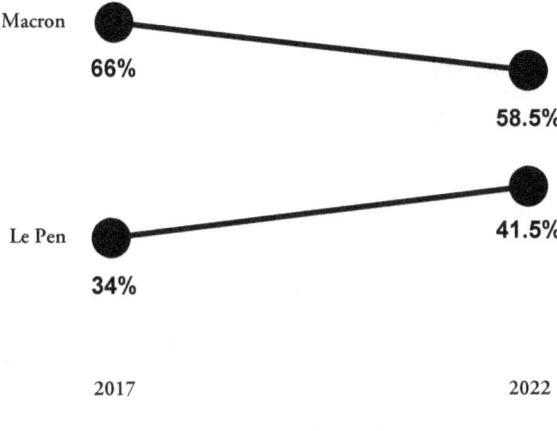

Source: *The Guardian*

Bottom line: Neo-nationalism is on the rise across the globe. Count Italy, Germany, and Hungary among the many countries seriously rethinking their economic policies and willingness to engage on the international stage. But what exactly are its acolytes rebelling against? Why have the tried-and-true bands of free trade and globalism taken such hits over the past ten to fifteen years?

Before answering those questions, let's take a brief step back.

Economics 101 and the Benefits of Globalism

All modern societies need to produce a variety of goods and services to survive. Fine, but which ones should a nation focus on?

At a high level, this question has two answers. First, a government could attempt to mandate which products to manufacture, how much of them, and what to charge for each. In a word, it could *centralize*. The USSR effected this type of command economy for decades before ultimately collapsing on December 25, 1991. The Iron Curtain fell for many reasons, but internal economic strife ranks high on the list.[21]

THE CATALYSTS

The second, far more popular way embraces *decentralization*: Let individual actors and free markets make these decisions themselves.

The Fruits of Economic Interdependence

Consider Poland. For years, the country has excelled at producing plastics.[22] It's not particularly adept at growing wheat. Australians efficiently grow the commodity—and have for a long time.[23] Economically, it makes a great deal of sense for these two countries to trade plastics for wheat. Yes, Poles could start their own wheat farms, but the opportunity cost of doing so exceeds its benefits. Ditto for Australians getting into the plastics business. When countries focus on their areas of expertise, they find themselves better off.

None of this is news. This commonly held economic orthodoxy harkens back to 1817. In that year, the British political economist and member of Parliament (MP) David Ricardo wrote an enormously influential text. In *On the Principles of Political Economy and Taxation*, Ricardo proved how all nations stand to benefit from free trade. He coined the term *the law of comparative advantage*, which remains a bedrock of economic thought. In layperson's terms, a comparative advantage occurs "when a country can produce a good or service at a lower opportunity cost than another country."[24] More than two centuries later, mainstream economists regard Ricardo's work around economic interdependence as "genius."[25]

Free trade hasn't just earned the praise of highfalutin economics and theoretical policy wonks pontificating at conferences and in their corner offices. The hard data bears out the validity of Ricardo's work.

In the twentieth century, nations around the world embraced globalization and free trade. As a direct consequence, global gross domestic product (GDP) exploded. Figure 9.2 shows its meteoric rise.

Figure 9.2: World Gross Domestic Product From 1960 to 2022

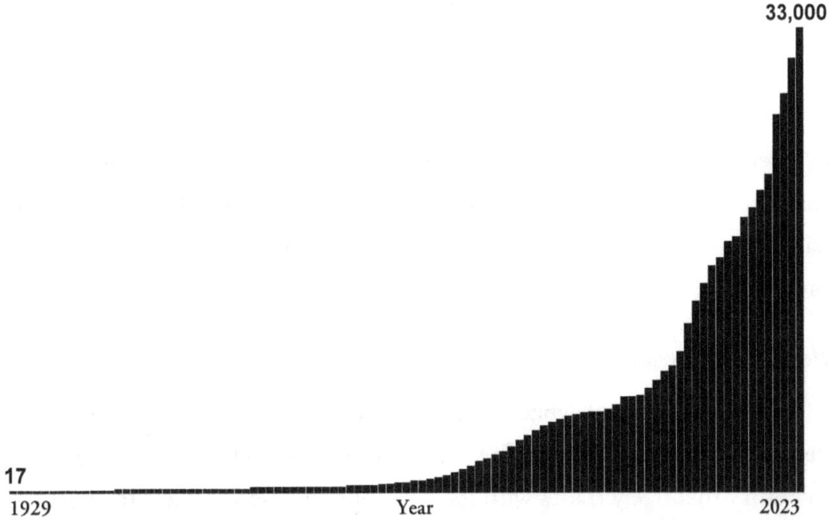

```
33,000




17
1929                            Year                            2023
```

Source: Macrotrends | Data: https://tinyurl.com/the-cat-gdp

Note: Data in trillions of USD. Dollar figures for GDP converted from domestic currencies using single-year official exchange rates.

To be sure, free trade alone doesn't fully explain Figure 9.2. Myriad technological innovations, advancements in transportation, urbanization, population growth, better healthcare, and other factors contributed to this precipitous increase. Still, it's doubtful that the world economy would have grown so much so quickly over the past six decades if a protectionist mindset and trade barriers had ruled the day.

Globalism can even weather the occasional pandemic, a point that Chairman of Chatham House and former Chairman of Goldman Sachs Assets Management Jim O'Neill makes:

> Without COVID-19, GDP growth in the past decade would have been about 3.6 percent—just below the 3.7 percent experienced in 2000–09. Not bad given all the challenges, and contrary to the mood of pre-pandemic times. Indeed, each decade has witnessed stronger economic growth than the 1980s and 1990s, each about 3.3 percent.

> Hundreds of millions of people have been taken out of absolute poverty, in part because of the growth miracle led by the so-called emerging markets.[26]

An environment that encourages free trade correlates with economic prosperity. The Mercatus Center at George Mason University found in 2018 that "free trade increases prosperity for Americans—and the citizens of all participating nations—by allowing consumers to buy more, better-quality products at lower costs."[27]

Beyond Dollars and Cents

But the benefits of what some have termed *commercial liberalism* don't just apply to money matters. Free trade reduces conflict. All else being equal, a country that freely trades with its contemporaries is less likely to engage in wars—both as instigators and as victims.[28]

Rabble-rousers in the US, England, and France either never received the memo or have actively chosen to ignore it. Globalism isn't perfect though and, as we'll see next, the flaws in its current incarnation are allowing demagogues to rise to power.

Understanding the Sudden Reemergence of Nationalism

There's something paradoxical about how, to varying extents, elected officials and politicians in the US, France, and England are rejecting globalism. Each country has reaped massive economic benefits from free markets, international trade, immigration,[29] and multiculturalism. Within a relatively short period, however, the default modus operandi has been inverted.

In 2022, Robert Schertzer and Eric Taylor Woods published *The New Nationalism in America and Beyond*. In their words:

> Nationalism's dominance in world politics today is all the more remarkable when we consider that it is a relatively recent phenomenon.

Most scholars agree that nationalism is a modern ideology, originating in Europe in earnest in the nineteenth century (although the precise timing and the degree to which nationalism builds on premodern ideas and culture are key topics of debate, as we discuss). The idea that a type of political community called a "nation" should command our allegiance above all else is a fundamentally modern idea. This exaltation of nations was unknown in premodern Europe, when allegiances were defined by one's affiliations to their rulers and to their religion. Moreover, the very idea of a nation as a community whose bonds transcend the social status of its members would have been anathema to premodern Europeans, who generally believed that the rulers and the ruled were fundamentally different categories of human (Greenfeld 2019, 7–9).[30]

An open mindset is giving way to a closed, far less economically advantageous one. The obvious question: Why?

A Failure of Elected Officials, Not of Globalism

Dave Fishwick is an immensely interesting guy.

He founded the eponymous David Fishwick Minibus Sales and soon became Britain's largest minibus supplier. During the subprime crisis, he noticed a drop-off in his business. As it turned out, large banks refused to lend his customers money. He could have just accepted reality, cashed out, and called it a day. Instead, he founded Burnley Savings and Loans with the goal of turning a profit in 180 days. The company used the advertising slogan "Bank on Dave."

Well-to-do owners of successful transportation vehicle companies tend not to take on side hustles of this magnitude. The British-owned Channel Four Television Corporation thought Fishwick's tale deserved a wider audience. The network commissioned the series *Bank of Dave* in 2012.

Fishwick then discovered that customers began arriving at his bank for a different reason: They had accumulated debt after taking out loans from payday firms with notoriously exorbitant interest rates. Curious as usual, he investigated the industry for the 2014 Channel 4 series *Dave: Loan Ranger*. Both series earned British Academy Scotland Awards. Netflix then, in 2023, chronicled his fascinating career turn in the semi-fictionalized film *Bank of Dave*.* It debuted on December 18 of that year and, as Fishwick told *American Banker*, "Within three days it was there in the top 10 alongside Tom Cruise's *Mission Impossible*."[31]

Misplaced Blame and Anger

Fishwick adroitly revealed what oligarchs in all countries on both sides of the political spectrum don't want the public to see. In many Western cultures, governments have erected significant obstacles and barriers to economic entry that let wealthy individuals and corporations preserve their power. Pure greed is alive and well.

For example, the UK's banking system is notoriously exclusionary. In 2024, the Financial Conduct Authority reported that a stunning "23% of UK adults (12.1 million people) had issues accessing a financial product or service in the two years to May 2022."[32] Indeed, prior to Metro Bank's opening in 2010, a new high street bank† hadn't opened in the country for 150 years.[33]

The United States largely follows the same playbook. A bevy of American laws has for decades limited certain categories of assets to "accredited investors." The goals are twofold:

- To restrict certain investments to wealthy folks who can gobble up an even bigger slice of the pie and absorb more financial risk.
- To protect consumers they consider too poor or ignorant to be trusted with determining their own investment risk tolerance.

These regulations work. Leaders could open currently closed avenues to financial independence and increased wealth. Instead, demagogues are

---

* Watch the trailer at https://tinyurl.com/the-cat-dave.
† These commercial institutions provide retail banking services to individuals and small to midsize businesses.

blaming globalism, other nations, and immigrants—basically, anyone but the people responsible for their stations in life. Sadly, a significant percentage of citizens believe these lies. In large part, nationalism and the election of autocrats are direct results of their deliberate deception to preserve current levels of wealth inequality.

Irrational, Fear-Based Voting

Why do so many people around the world routinely vote against their own self-interests?

John P. Watkins, a professor of economics at Westminster College, squares the circle in a 2021 piece for *The Salt Lake Tribune*:

> How do Republicans promote globalization and free trade, tax cuts for the wealthy, de-regulation and shrinking the federal social safety net while opposing raising the minimum wage, mitigating climate change, opposing policies that benefit lower-income workers? How do Republicans convince these voters that Republicans best represent their interests?[34]

The honest answer: They skillfully and routinely exploit people's cognitive biases to win elections. (See the discussion in Chapter 8 titled "Basic Human Nature.") To paraphrase from Rob Reiner's 1995 film *The American President*, starring Michael Douglas and Annette Bening, nationalists aren't interested in solving any given issue. They want to do two things and two things only: to make people afraid of it and to tell them who's to blame for it.

Residual Racism

Returning to Schertzer's and Taylor Woods's book for a moment, "Neo-nationalists are tapping into long-established ethnic myths and symbols to garner support from white majorities." Fox News, *The Daily Mail*, and other right-wing media outlets decry the challenges that white people routinely face. On the former, an ex-host unapologetically—even proudly—promoted racist, white-supremacy theories hundreds of times.[35]

Go back more than 150 years, though. From a military perspective, the Union defeated the Confederacy in the American Civil War. Yet the latter's Southern oligarchic values prioritizing the interests of wealthy white men over democracy and equality remained—and, in fact, spread west. That viewpoint continues to influence American politics today. Heather Cox Richardson deconstructs this especially toxic aspect of US society in her 2020 bestseller *How the South Won the Civil War: Oligarchy, Democracy, and the Continuing Fight for the Soul of America*. The same historical racism that drove Brexit and resurrected the ghost of Enoch Powell is firmly on display in the United States.

Social Media: The Perfect Weapon to Advance Neo-Nationalism

As discussed in Chapters 6 and 8, tech nation-states bear some of the burden for the current situation. They've routinely allowed bad actors to use their tools with, at most, minimal restriction. When news breaks to this effect, leadership at these companies typically resists admitting what happened until regulators compel them to do so.[36] The US in 2022 even witnessed a tech mogul purchase one of the largest social media platforms in the world. Elon Musk soon weaponized Twitter into his own targeted, growing "misinformation machine."[37] With zero guardrails in place, the mind boggles at what will happen in the 2026 midterm elections.

Putting It All Together

No, globalism isn't perfect. Many of the societal and economic problems facing countries today don't inherently emanate from globalism and free trade per se. Far too often, people blame globalization, immigrants, and other countries for their stations in life. But they ought to be pointing fingers squarely at their elected leaders for failing them. Existing policies are directly exacerbating a whole host of problems.

The Ramifications of Neo-Nationalism

Before wrapping up this chapter, a few brief words on the effects of increasing levels of nationalism are in order. Again, one could write entire books about these topics.

The Increasingly Viable BRICS+ Alternative

For decades, countries across the globe knew where their bread was buttered. Accordingly, they hitched their wagons to the US and the USD. Their pros exceeded their cons. For at least three reasons, however, that statement probably no longer holds water.

- America's acute political and economic dysfunction discussed in Chapter 5 should deter other wagons from following it over a cliff.
- The maturation of new financial instruments discussed in Chapter 7 is creating alternatives to fiat currencies.
- America is shifting America toward authoritarian capitalism and away from democracy.

An isolationist, protectionist US incentivizes governments to forge an independent, non-USD-linked financial future. Donald Trump will invariably galvanize many countries already aspiring to de-dollarize to cut as many monetary ties with America as possible. (Chapter 13 will return to this subject.)

Hello, crisis. Meet opportunity. As the Indian journalist Hindol Sengupta wrote in *The Sunday Guardian*:

> In a world divided between the West and the Rest, Western inability to comprehend a changing world order gives a common platform for grievances of "the Rest," no matter the friction between individual countries.[38]

Let's see what the rest looks like in 2025.

THE CATALYSTS

Brief History and Overview

In 2001, the aforementioned Jim O'Neill coined the term *BRIC*.[39] At the time, he referred to Brazil, Russia, India, and China. He posited that those growing nations would dominate the world economy and challenge the dominant G7 wealthy economies.

In 2006, representatives of the BRIC countries met informally during the United Nations General Assembly. Three years later, the group held its first summit in Yekaterinburg, Russia.[40] BRIC leaders bandied about key economic issues. The docket included:

- Improving the global economy in the wake of the subprime banking crisis.
- Reforming existing international financial institutions, such as the World Bank and the IMF.
- Finding ways to de-dollarize and conduct international commerce while circumventing the current, US-based system.
- Developing a viable alternative to Swift.

In 2011, the acronym changed to BRICS with the inclusion of South Africa. The new moniker also reflected the group's more inclusive focus on emerging nations.

Struggles and Sources of Friction

Some have argued that BRICS is an ineffectual entity representing no significant threat to US economic hegemony.[41] However, it's more accurate to say that the first incarnation of BRICS didn't achieve its ambitious initial goals. Beyond that, the group has stagnated because of the world's general comfort with the existing financial oligarchy.

Early tensions have existed among different members. Here, I'll highlight three key examples. First, the larger, wealthier countries (read: Brazil, Russia, India, and China) have at times strengthened their voting blocs at the expense of their smaller BRICS counterparts.

Second, the leaders of BRICS nations certainly resent American imperialism, dollar dominance, and the willingness of the US to rattle its economic saber. As a group, though, the group suffers from its own internal pecking order. Patrick Bond, the coauthor of *BRICS and Resistance in Africa*, has referred to this phenomenon as *BRICS subimperialism*.[42] The following sidebar explains just one of the conflicts of interest hampering the reforms that BRICS members may like to make.

> ### India Resists BRICS Reforms
>
> The BRICS nations have collectively expressed a strong interest in "creating a new currency to compete with the US dollar, and recently announced plans for a blockchain-based payment system."[43] Although these projects faltered for several reasons, the main culprit is internal.
>
> India put the kibosh on these plans. In 2023, the number of billionaires in India grew from 16 to 131.[44] The country now sports the fourth highest number of über-affluent individuals, behind only the US, China, and Germany. These folks understandably don't want to rock their own economic boats.
>
> Beyond the self-interests of its richest citizens, there are other financial and geopolitical concerns. Two-thirds of the country's trade is still in USD and Euros. That same number for the Chinese yuan is a mere 3 percent. Indian officials have been reluctant to use the yuan because of high currency-conversion costs and border disputes.[45]

Other manifestations of intra-BRICS tensions include:

- The 2010 vote to restructure the International Monetary Fund.[46]
- Russia's 2022 invasion of Ukraine.

Although conflict around key issues continues to exist, the group has expanded.

THE CATALYSTS

Additional Expansion, Name Change, and Bright Future

Today, BRICS has emerged as a major political and burgeoning force, albeit an imperfect one. Its recent ascension presents the clear desire of nations to "create a counterweight to Western influence in global institutions."[47] In 2024, Egypt, Ethiopia, Iran, Saudi Arabia, and the United Arab Emirates (UAE) formally joined BRICS.[48] Now christened *BRICS+* in certain circles, "the ten BRICS countries now comprise more than a quarter of the global economy and almost half of the world's population."[49] What's more, it is poised to add additional members in the years ahead.

Will an empowered and resolute BRICS+ minimize the global importance of the US dollar? It's more than just a theoretical question. The maturation of new financial technologies in Chapter 7 offers hope to countries looking to wean themselves off US financial hegemony as quickly as possible. I'll revisit that very scenario in Chapter 13.

China Builds Figurative and Real Bridges in Africa

Protectionist and America First policies under the Trump administration have led to the US withdrawing from critical foreign matters. This regression has opened an opportunity that Chinese leadership has intelligently capitalized on.

Chinese head Xi Jinping has promised Africa billions in fresh financial support, including specific funds earmarked for agriculture, infrastructure, trade, and investment projects. The alliance makes sense for both sides. Africa receives much-needed support and financial assistance. China builds figurative bridges through more substantial relationships with the continents' countries, leaders, and citizens. It augments its soft power and fills the vacuum that the US has created.

"China and Africa account for one-third of the world population. Without our modernization, there will be no global modernization," Xi said.[50] If only Western leaders remembered as much.

Economic Consequences of Withdrawing From the Global Economy

Marine Le Pen, Boris Johnson, and Donald Trump have all repeatedly banged their drums to put their countries first. Will neo-nationalism help their economies and the citizens who voted for them?

The short answer is no.

Trade: Lessons From Brexit

What lessons should Brexit teach leaders and politicians flirting with neo-nationalism?

For starters, to state the obvious, isolating and alienating your main trading partners is bound to boomerang and cause economic difficulties. Nobel prize-winning economists warned the UK of the long-term damage that would result if it proceeded with Brexit.[51] England couldn't easily replace its single biggest trading market (the EU) with separate US, Australia, and New Zealand free-trade agreements.

Inflation

Countries that slap tariffs on foreign goods can expect the prices that their citizens pay for goods and services to rise. No less an authority than the World Bank found in 2021 that "higher tariffs lead to an increase in inflation after two years."[52]

Lower Unemployment and Misguided Policies

A 2021 study on US-China trade concluded that "Trump's trade policies cost the US economy nearly a quarter million jobs. But his obsolete understanding of international trade flows ends up pointing trade policymakers in the wrong direction."[53]

Other Effects

One need not be an expert on contemporary geopolitics to see where the spread of neo-nationalism is leading us. The prior world wars serve as an

THE CATALYSTS

instructive guide on what to expect. A less global economy means each of the following:

- Imperialism is on the rise. Russia invaded Ukraine. Will China soon do the same to Taiwan?
- Alliances are disintegrating.
- As autocracy expert Anne Applebaum has noted, tyrants today are talking alarmingly like 1930s dictators.[54]
- Even worse, they're acting with relative impunity.
- US financial hegemony is starting to crack.

That puts a bow on this chapter. Next, we discuss a natural outgrowth of neo-nationalism. Some countries are choosing to zig rather than zag. They're opening their borders and encouraging immigration and foreign investment. Innovation hubs are now blooming in unexpected places.

Key Points

- Hyper-nationalism is replacing globalism as the dominant economic mindset/model. The consequences for the new world financial order are profound.
- Disaffected (often white) groups from Anglo-Saxon world powers want to reassert their dominance. They want to revert to a prior and, in their mind, better time.
- Britian, France, the US, and other countries are withdrawing from the global economy.
- BRICS+ countries are poised to fill the economic, financial, and geopolitical vacuum that US isolationism has created.
- The powers-that-be need to continue to convince the have-nots to vote against their economic self-interest to keep the current power structure.

CHAPTER 10

NEW INNOVATION HUBS BLOOM

AS AMERICA STUMBLES, UNEXPECTED DESTINATIONS ARE STEADILY DRIVING ENTREPRENEURSHIP.

> "Our ancestors crossed oceans and deserts; movement is our oldest story."
>
> —*Rebecca Solnit*

Anthony Tan came from means. His is not a rags-to-riches story. Born into one of Malaysia's wealthiest families in 1982, he could have coasted through life.

Tan wasn't wired that way, though. The self-described "rebel without a cause"[1] met classmate Tan Hooi Ling at Harvard University and remained in touch after graduation. In 2012, the two entrepreneurs founded MyTeks, a startup intent on making taxi rides safer for Malaysian citizens and tourists.

In 2013, the company moved its headquarters to Singapore and rebranded as Grab. The opportunity was larger than the company's two cofounders had realized, so they increased their ambitions. Tan, Ling, and their colleagues doubled down, building and developing new products for couriers. The company began its regionwide expansion, launching in Thailand, the Philippines, and other nations.

Grab methodically forged new partnerships throughout Southeast Asia. Its popularity spread, and it soon became the region's leading super-app. Deliveries, mobility, and financial services are now among the services its customers can access from a single app on their smartphones.

On December 2, 2021, at 9:30 a.m. Eastern Time (10:30 p.m. in Singapore), the two cofounders rang the NASDAQ bell to celebrate Grab's first day as a publicly traded company. The ceremony didn't just mark the company's coming-of-age, though. It served as a milestone for the entire region.[2] Never before had a new listing from Southeast Asia started the day's trading. Grab's success has continued in subsequent years, with revenues exceeding $2 billion in 2023. What began as the crazy idea of two Harvard students has grown into a company offering rides in 465 cities. As of November 2024, 42 million people (yours truly included) are using the app per month.[3]

The significance of Grab far exceeds Singapore or even Southeast Asia. As we'll see in this chapter, the popular app represents an unmistakable, intensifying, and profound trend. It's time to explore the fifth catalyst: the blossoming of new innovation hubs across the globe.

The Changing Nature of Global Innovation

As we saw in Chapter 4, Silicon Valley has unquestionably driven a great deal of worldwide innovation in the past half-century—maybe even most of it. Indeed, for any startup intent on changing the world over the past two decades, San Francisco's Bay Area has been *the* place to be. Facebook was just one of the successful startups whose founders and financial backers quickly realized the importance of moving there.

These days, though, successful entrepreneurs need not follow the old California- or US-centric playbooks to make it. Formerly ignored regions are closing the innovation gap and, in the process, birthing impressive startup ecosystems of their own. Figure 10.1 displays the related changes that have taken place in the past quarter-century.

Figure 10.1: Changes in the Venture Capital Landscape

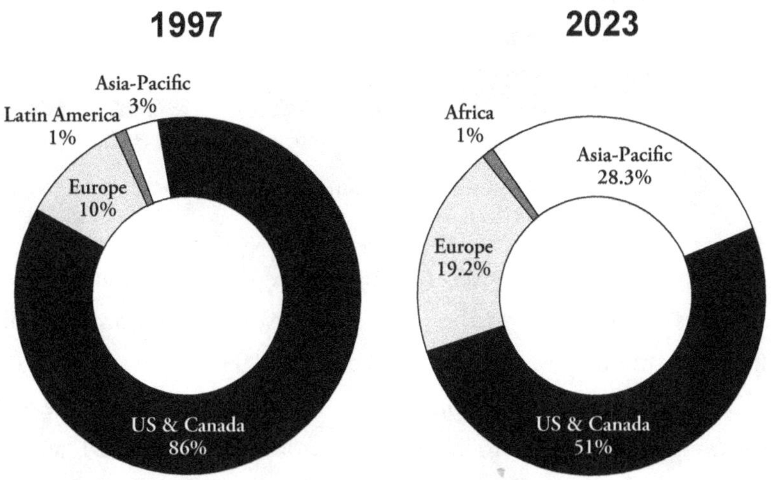

1997

- Latin America 1%
- Asia-Pacific 3%
- Europe 10%
- US & Canada 86%

2023

- Africa 1%
- Asia-Pacific 28.3%
- Europe 19.2%
- US & Canada 51%

Source: 2024 Global Innovation Index, WIPO | Data from Refinitiv Eikon

In a word, the evolution has been drastic. Compared to 1997, far more VC funding today goes to startups based outside of North America. Any serious, well-researched ranking of entrepreneurial cities will reflect this seismic shift. Let's look at one of them.

Digging Into the Data

Launched in 2012, Startup Genome works with economic and innovation ministries and public/private agencies across the globe. In June 2023, the organization published its annual Global Startup Ecosystem Report (GSER). Among the report's goals: to rank cities by their levels of innovation and entrepreneurialism. Figure 10.2 aggregates the top thirty cities in the most recent list.

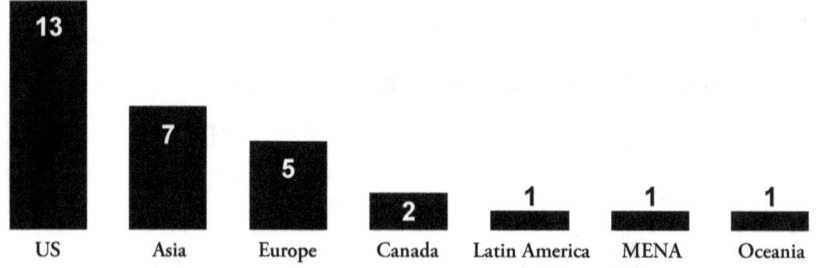

Figure 10.2: Global Startup Ecosystem Ranking—Summary of Top Thirty by Region

Source: Startup Genome | Data: https://tinyurl.com/the-cat-genome

American cities currently sport an impressive thirteen of the three top-thirty spots (43 percent) on the GSER. Ever wonder what a comparable ranking and summary would have looked like in 1997?

Unfortunately, Startup Genome's formation date prohibits a true 1997 apples-to-apples comparison. Based on the data in Figure 10.1 and the trends discussed in this chapter, however, it's reasonable to conclude that US metropolises on such a list would exceed 43 percent—probably by a considerable amount.

Figures 10.1 and 10.2 illustrate that non-US cities have become more viable places to start what may turn out to be billion-dollar enterprises. But why? That simple question underpins the rest of this chapter.

Explaining Singapore

There's no simple solution to my earlier question, and we don't have the space to adequately explain the seventeen non-American cities on the GSER. We can, however, delve deeper into one.

Let's look at Grab's current base of operations. As the journalist Gina Marrs wrote in 2024, "In recent years, Singapore has become a leading financial hub, with plenty of banks, venture capital firms and financial institutions offering opportunities for budding startups."[4]

The data certainly supports her claim. Figure 10.3 displays the meteoric rise of foreign investment in Singapore since 1970.

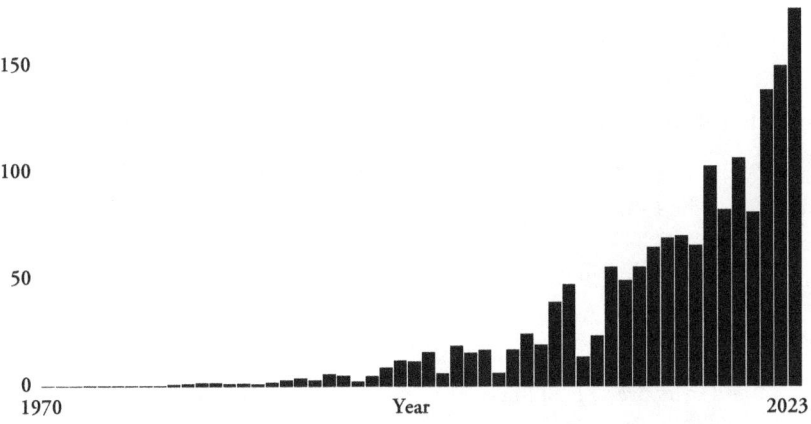

Figure 10.3: Singapore Foreign Direct Investment From 1970 to 2023 (Billions, USD)

Source: Macrotrends | Data: https://tinyurl.com/the-cat-sing-fdi

With exponentially more money flowing into the country, one would expect more of these bets to hit. As Figure 10.4 shows, that's exactly what's happening. As of 2024, each of the following Singaporean companies is a *unicorn*—a privately held entity worth at least $1 billion.

THE CATALYSTS

Figure 10.4: Top Unicorns in Singapore as of 2024 (Billions, USD)

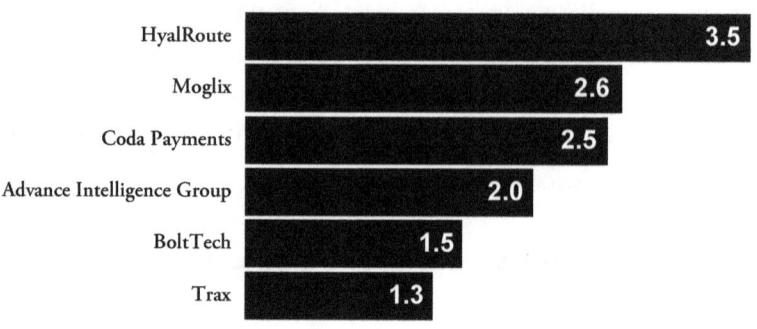

Source: Techround | Data: https//tinyurl.com/the-cat-sing

What's more, Figure 10.4 is unicorn-centric and, as a result, not remotely comprehensive. In fact, it *understates* Singapore's success in launching new ventures. The GSER confirmed as much:

> Singapore has jumped 10 places in the ranking to #8, the second-highest ranked Asian ecosystem after Beijing. A 100% increase in exits over $50 million since the GSER 2022 helped boost its placement, and exits over $1 billion have risen from 0 to 4. Delivery app Grab is the highest valued at $40 billion.* Singapore now boasts 18 unicorns, including cryptocurrency exchange KuCoin,† which is valued at $10 billion.⁵

Note that Figure 10.4 ignores Grab. As a publicly traded company, it no longer qualifies as a unicorn.

Even COVID didn't cause Singapore or, more broadly, Southeast Asia, to lose investment momentum. Beginning in April 2020, investors started rethinking funding for early-stage ventures. Interestingly, though, Asia was "the least impacted region" in this regard. Related funding dropped a mere 1 percent from 2021 to 2022.

---

* As of November 30, 2024, its market capitalization was roughly half of this amount.
† The company formed in China in 2017 but later moved to Singapore in response to the Chinese government's restrictions around cryptocurrencies.

> **Some Crude Unicorn Math**
>
> Solely judging a nation's level of innovation based on its number of unicorns might seem a bit primitive. Still, it's a useful—if crude—gauge.
>
> As of February 2024, India sported 117 unicorns.[6] It's an impressive number, but 1.43 billion people live in the world's most populous country.[7] Think of it this way: In India, every 12.2 million citizens has a unicorn.
>
> Now consider the Republic of Singapore. Only about six million people live in the country, but it has birthed eighteen unicorns. That's one for every 333,333 inhabitants.
>
> India's population is 238 times the size of Singapore's, yet the former can "only" claim 6.5 times as many unicorns. By this admittedly simple measure, Singapore is clearly ahead of the curve.

Understanding Innovation Hubs

The data is unequivocal: Singapore has emerged as a true innovation hub, but what does that really mean?

McKinsey defines the umbrella term as a:

> geographic are[a] that bring[s] together R&D* institutions (such as tech-enabled corporations, universities, and medical facilities), as well as venture capital, incubators, and start-ups.[8]

Of course, not all innovation hubs are created equal. They vary by size, scale, duration, emphasis, long-term impact, and, especially today, location. As we'll see throughout this chapter, North America no longer dominates the playing field. (As but one recent example of how innovation continues to diffuse, Microsoft invested $1.5 billion in Abu Dhabi-based G42 to develop artificial intelligence in April 2024.[9]) Despite their considerable differences,

---

* Short for *research and development*.

though, one aspect remains constant: They correlate with increased productivity, economic growth, and job creation.[10]

In the aggregate, perhaps no country sports the same track record on innovation as American corporations. In the same report, McKinsey found that "annual productivity growth for US innovation industries has averaged 2.7 percent since 1980—nearly double the rate of all other sectors." But competitors are snapping at the gate.

Why Innovation Hubs Are Emerging in New Locales

Policymakers want in on the action. Let's explore a few of the key underlying reasons for Figure 10.1.

Immigration

It's trivia time again.

What do Australia, Canada, Ecuador, France, Germany, Malta, Mexico, Montenegro, New Zealand, Panama, Portugal, Spain, and Thailand have in common?

As of February 2024, these countries weren't just welcoming certain types of immigrants; these nations were actively seeking them.[11] As for why, the keys to America's economic success aren't exactly secrets. Other countries' policymakers have long studied the strengths and weaknesses of the US system and adapted it as needed.

The Manifold Benefits of Open Immigration Policies

Many factors explain why America has led the world in innovation for so long. Vast natural resources, a culture that tolerates failure, political stability, and relatively cheap access to capital top the list. Most relevant here, though, has been its consistent willingness to open its doors and let people from other countries in.

In 2023, the American Immigration Council released its latest annual research. Fortune 500 companies with "immigrant roots generated more money than the GDP of most western nations."[12] Whether immigrants or the children of immigrants, they either directly or indirectly founded nearly half of today's Fortune 500 companies. This list includes four of the top twelve:

- **Apple:** Steve Jobs arrived in America after his parents emigrated from Syria.
- **Google (now Alphabet)**[*]**:** In 1979, the Brin family immigrated to the United States from what was then the USSR. Their son Sergey cofounded the search engine in 1998 along with Larry Page.
- **Amazon:** Mike Bezos, speaking no English, came to the US alone at the age of 16 from Cuba. Ultimately, his son Jeff cofounded the e-commerce giant.
- **Costco:** Cofounder Jeffrey Brotman arrived from Canada after his parents had emigrated from Romania.

In fiscal year 2023, these four companies alone employed nearly 2.2 million people. They posted a combined revenue of $1.4 *trillion*—yes, with a *t*. That number exceeds the GDP of most Western nations.

Immigrants haven't just started a handful of companies that ultimately morphed into massive corporations. They've started—and, in fact, continue to start—dental offices, clothing stores, restaurants, and myriad other businesses. A 2024 survey from payroll services provider Gusto once again confirmed longstanding economic dogma that immigrants start an outsize proportion of small businesses:

- **Immigrants routinely punch above their weight.** In 2023, they comprised 14 percent of the US population but founded a disproportionate 19 percent of new companies.
- **The entrepreneurship gene is contagious.** The children of immigrants started 17 percent of new businesses in 2023.[13]

---

[*] Alphabet is Google's parent company.

- **Immigrant-owned businesses create more jobs.** In 2023, 91 percent of new, immigrant-owned businesses employed more than one individual. That number exceeds the norm of all respondents: 84 percent.[14]

The data is undeniable. Immigrants "on balance are net contributors to the US economy when considering their contributions to the labor market, to overall economic growth, and to government coffers."[15] Across the board, immigration is a net gain.

Staff Augmentation

Remember from Chapter 6 that most of today's tech nation-states sprouted in the US. In the absence of a welcoming immigration policy, it's entirely possible—if not probable—that these titans wouldn't have ascended to their current heights. Over the last quarter-century, Facebook/Meta, Cisco Systems, Google/Alphabet, Oracle, and scores of other American tech companies have relied upon immigrants to perform key functions and overcome national labor shortages. In fact, some have called H1-B visas "the lifeblood of US tech innovation."[16]

Counterproductive Policies

Overall, American companies and Americans have accrued manifold benefits from immigration. With this in mind, intelligent US policymakers have been scratching their heads over the past decade.

Policy-wise, the first Trump administration's fervent anti-immigration stance and rejection of Lady Liberty didn't make a scintilla of economic sense.* It damaged the US economy and harmed US workers.[17] It also belied his own party's platform. Republicans generally promulgate pro-business policies and, as we just saw, immigration creates countless companies, jobs, and economic growth.

---

* The hypocrisy rankled as well. Trump's father emigrated to the US from Kallstadt, Germany. Trump's first wife was born in Czechoslovakia, and his current wife was born in Slovenia.

To be fair, not every nation is willing to open its borders to highly skilled immigrants, never mind unskilled ones and political refugees. America's own history on the matter is decidedly mixed. Since 1965, Gallup has asked Americans: "In your view, should immigration be kept at its present level, increased, or decreased?"[18] Only during the pandemic did more than one-third of respondents claim that Americans need *more* immigrants. The number currently lies at one in six.

I don't mean to trivialize the issue's hefty political ramifications, especially today. Trump, Le Pen, and their ilk publicly demonize the group and score cheap points with their misinformed constituencies regularly.

Trump's frequent ramblings aside, immigration "has an overall positive impact on the long-run economic growth in the US."[19] No person can credibly claim otherwise, which is why other nations want in on the action. America's loss can be their gain.

While important, the Trump administration's war on immigration is but one factor in explaining the rise of innovation hubs outside of the US. Let's explore the rest.

Governments Want to Neutralize Tech Nation-States

Stewart Brand is an American writer and the author of the counterculture magazine called *Whole Earth Catalog*. Brand's still alive as of this writing, but his epitaph may very well read:

> Information wants to be free.

Brand first uttered those words as part of a longer, typically forgotten quote at the first Hackers Conference in 1984.* In one context, the abbreviated maxim portended the existential financial struggles journalists and musicians would face when the web matured. (See the discussion in Chapter 7 on Napster.) On a different level, though, it meant that contemporary technology makes it more difficult—maybe even impossible—to keep

---

* See https://tinyurl.com/the-cat-brand for the complete story behind the quote.

information private. (Google "Ashley Madison data breach" or "Wikileaks" if you doubt me.)

Starting in 2006, Google began a multiyear effort to introduce an altered (read: censored) version of its best-in-class search engine in China. I'll cut to the chase: The company struggled to appease a government that wanted to restrict access to information.[20] Internally, executives were deeply conflicted about the project. After all, Google's longstanding mission was "to organize the world's information and make it universally accessible and useful."[21]

Ultimately, Google lost the battle of wills and decided to cut its losses in 2010. I don't know if Chinese officials knew about the second interpretation of Brand's words, but they undoubtedly didn't *want* information to be free.

For our purposes, the China-Google episode is instructive on a few levels:

- The goals of a private, for-profit corporation may fundamentally conflict with those of a nation.
- Goals aside, a company's core technology or product may do the same.
- All things considered, it may be best for a country to build its own technology, even if it's inferior to existing ones. (Indeed, as of this writing, Baidu owns 70 percent of the Chinese search market.[22])

Few countries practice outright censorship at present. (As we saw in Chapter 9, though, more are heading down that dangerous path.) Still, governments have finally realized they can't sit idly on the sidelines. They can't let foreign-based tech nation-states wreak havoc and cause civil strife on their watches. To some extent, everyone needs to be in the innovation business. Those who ignore it do so at their peril.

The COVID-19 Effect: WFH Gives Way to WFA

The pandemic expedited what management gurus call *digital transformation*. Companies and employees quickly adopted Slack, Zoom, Microsoft Teams, and other communication and collaboration tools designed to promote asynchronous work. Even relatively hidebound professions such as accounting were able to "leapfrog decades ahead."[23]

The lessons from COVID are too many to list here. For our purposes, the pandemic demonstrated these things:

- People can effectively work from home.
- Home need not be any particular country or even a quasi-permanent one.
- As a result, people can really work from anywhere.

In many cases, working from home (WFH) became working from anywhere (WFA). I should know. For the past year, I've lived as a digital nomad.

Life as a Digital Nomad

The legal professor Ayelet Shachar once said, "The right to move is as fundamental as the right to stay."

In 2024, I found myself spending more time abroad than in my apartment, so I decided to stop wasting money on rent. I put nearly all my belongings in storage and packed a carry-on roller bag and backpack. I rented an Airbnb in Italy, house-sat for a friend in France, and stayed in a friend's apartment in Madrid. I was just getting started.

Between 2023 and 2024, I visited fifteen countries, stayed in numerous hostels, and surfed on many a couch. Being "unhoused" turned out to be a life-changing experience. People asked me where I lived. I looked down at the carry-on roller bag that contained everything I needed and answered, "Right here."

In those countries where I didn't speak the language, it was more challenging, but I was a quick study. My Spanish improved instantly when I was robbed in Madrid, and I learned how to say thank you in more than ten languages.

> The occasional unfortunate incident aside, I found the people in every country welcoming and, more often than not, amazing. After COVID, most of the people I met told me that they had met other digital nomads. For three years, they encountered people just like me.
>
> I've found living abroad and experiencing so many other cultures rewarding for a few reasons:
>
> - Learning that I could do it.
> - Seeing alternative ways of living than the US one. Some were better than others.
> - Making global friends who taught me so many different perspectives from which to view the world.
>
> Because of my work, I was able to pull this off. Some time zones were more amenable to working from anywhere (WFA) than others. Still, if I had a reliable Wi-Fi connection, headphones, and a laptop, I could run my company from anywhere on the planet. I could *live* anywhere in the world. I could choose to live somewhere in line with my personal values.
>
> I'm an infinitely richer person for the experience.

Virulent Opposition to Policies, Politicians, and Politics

People leave their native lands for all sorts of reasons. For starters, there's war. As of November 2024, the non-profit United States Association for the United Nations High Commissioner for Refugees (USA for UNHCR) reported that 6.8 million Ukrainian refugees have crossed into Poland, Hungary, Moldova, and other neighboring countries.[24] Next, beyond military conflict, disaffected citizens of certain countries have historically sought political asylum in the US and other countries. Finally, highly skilled white-collar workers sometimes land international assignments as foreign nationals or ex-patriots.

For several reasons, though, we may see vastly more movement in the next decade than we've seen in the past century.

Russia

Apart from the mass Ukrainian exodus, "huge numbers" of Russians have voluntarily fled their homeland since Putin invaded Ukraine.[25] Estimates vary, but some put the number as high as 650,000.[26] "This wave of emigration is highly political, as many that left the country opposed President Putin's regime and the war against Ukraine."[27]

And it's not just Russia. Over the past decade, more Americans have been looking to leave the Land of the Free.

Oh, Canada

When it became evident that Donald Trump would win his 2016 presidential bid, Americans started googling a very specific phrase. Canada's immigration website crashed during the vote.[28]

When it became evident that he would win the November 2024 election, Americans once again began googling "moving to Canada." Searches "were highest in Vermont, Oregon and Washington, states that voted overwhelmingly for [Kamala] Harris."[29]

Companies Facilitate Employee Abortion-Related Movement

On May 2, 2022, a draft of a US Supreme Court ruling leaked. The official-looking document indicated that abortion's continued constitutional protections were ending abruptly.[30] The fact that the über-conservative justices overturned *Roe v. Wade* six weeks later shocked few informed US citizens. More surprising and encouraging, though, was the reaction from some leaders at organizations such as the customer relationship management behemoth Salesforce.

A few weeks after the draft leaked, the company announced that it would help employees pay abortion-related travel costs and possible indefinite relocation.[31] Dozens of companies soon followed suit.[32]

By itself, a few organizations relocating employees won't cause innovation hubs to bloom. When combined with the other causes listed in this section, though, the trend is clear: More than ever, people can find places to work and live that agree with their morals. We aren't living in the mid-nineteenth or even mid-twentieth century.

America's Secret Innovation Sauce Isn't So Secret Anymore

In the 1980s, cottage industries and management consulting gurus appeared on the scene. Michael Hammer's and James Champy's book *Reengineering the Corporation* launched lucrative consulting practices. Jim Collins struck gold with his bestselling—but fundamentally flawed—*Good to Great*. There's big money in helping companies become more innovative.

No one would label increasing a country's level of innovation as *easy*. Still, plenty of blue-chip consulting firms and boutique agencies are willing to help nations emulate America's success. Startups Genome, Deloitte, Boston Consulting Group, McKinsey, and Bain[33] are just some of the talent policymakers and government officials can hire to help:

- Foment an entrepreneurial culture.
- Build a supportive network of mentors and investors and a vibrant community of entrepreneurs.
- Foster collaboration among different stakeholders, including universities, government agencies, and large corporations.
- Enact policies that foster innovation.

Chapter 14 will return to this subject.

Economic Incentives: The Gold Rush Is On for Digital Nomads

While the US discourages or even bans immigrants, other countries are recognizing the unique opportunity to attract knowledge workers.

Europe

This is especially true in Europe. A 2024 report found that "nine out of the top 10 digital nomad programs are located in Europe."[34] It's so competitive that countries are actively evaluating their policies to ensure that they sufficiently attract these coveted workers. Case in point: Portugal "implemented a favorable tax incentive for digital nomads,"[35] although in 2024 the country modified the program.

Canada

Based in the university town of Waterloo-Kitchener, Communitech has served Canadian tech founders for more than a quarter-century. During that time, it has smartly forged broad partnerships. Communitech has worked with hundreds of higher education institutions, corporations, innovative startups, and government agencies.

Tulsa (Yes, Tulsa)

American hipsters and techies have long flocked to Portland, Austin, Brooklyn, Seattle, and other cool locales—basically, anywhere but Oklahoma. Leaders in Tulsa, however, saw an opportunity to lure folks from costly cities. The year 2018 saw the birth of Tulsa Remote. The "one-year program … offers a $10,000 grant and additional benefits to eligible remote workers who move to and work from Tulsa."[36]

The program has been wildly successful. In its first seven years, it has attracted 3,000 talented remote workers to the area. As the following sidebar illustrates, though, not all efforts to build a startup ecosystem succeed or even survive.

> **Vegas Struggles to Build an Innovation Hub**
>
> Las Vegas had long been known for its casinos, organized crime, and adult entertainment. Sin City had earned its nickname.
>
> Zappos cofounder Tony Hsieh wanted to change that, and he was willing to put his money where his mouth was. In January 2012, the eccentric Zappos cofounder invested $350 million of his own money in the area. He dubbed his new creation *The Downtown Project*. The following year, he relocated Zappos's headquarters to Las Vegas.
>
> Hsieh believed that he could "accelerat[e] the revitalization of the Fremont East Entertainment District and its surrounding area in Downtown Las Vegas."[37] His varied ambitions included real estate, small business, tech, education, arts, and culture. Dozens of startups quickly flocked to the Nevada desert, buoyed with funding and promises from Hsieh himself.[38]
>
> Aimee Groth details in her book *The Kingdom of Happiness: Inside Tony Hsieh's Zapponian Utopia* how Hsieh's dreams of grandeur didn't materialize. All but a few startups failed or left the area altogether. Sadly, Hsieh died after sustaining severe injuries in a fire at his Connecticut house on November 27, 2020.

Millennial Malaise

In the US and other countries, young people have become disenchanted with their current economic and political systems.* Pessimism about the future is rampant, particularly among younger individuals in wealthy nations. In a 2021 survey, more than half of respondents claimed that "children today will be less economically successful than their parents."[39] The reasons run the gamut, but I'd like to point out a fundamental one: affordable housing.

---

* See https://tinyurl.com/the-cat-dis for an excellent PBS documentary on the subject.

As is the case with many countries over the past few years, the US housing market has been wildly out of whack. The demand for homes far exceeds their available supply. More than two-thirds of American construction firms say their job applicants lack the skills they need.[40] Canada is also struggling to build enough homes for its citizens. Interest rate cuts will help, but they alone won't solve the problem.[41]

Be honest with yourself. Imagine that you're a twenty-six-year-old upwardly mobile professional who's unable to put down firm roots in your home country. Factor in policies that restrict your fundamental rights. (More on that later in this chapter.) Wouldn't you at least consider giving another country a try for a few years?

The Rise of Mobile Payments

Finally, as anyone who traveled in the 1980s knows, one aspect of living in a foreign country today is easier by orders of magnitude: paying for basic items. Thanks to smartphones and mobile payment methods, we no longer have to exchange dollars for pesos. Using my phone to "tap-to-pay" all over Europe visibly showed me how behind the US is in payments technology.

How New Innovation Hubs Are Changing the Game

The rise of innovation hubs in new areas means different things to different nations, industries, companies, groups, and people. To state the obvious, there will be winners and losers. Let's start with the country that stands to lose the most.

An Ever-More Vulnerable America

For decades following World War II, the American steel service industry flourished—one of the fulcrums of the US economy. In 1969, American steel production hit a record 141 million tons.[42] From there, it was all downhill.

Chapter 7 described the threats of new financial instruments and technologies to US hegemony. Of this I'm certain: The rise of alternative innovation hubs will only advance its expiration date. A quick history lesson will illustrate the point.

Mini-Mills

The mid-twentieth century represented the halcyon days for American steel companies. Senior executives at established integrated mill companies thought they and their firms were impregnable. Before long, though, an obscure technology arrived that would soon eat the industry's lunch in the form of mini-mills. The move turned out to be a critical mistake.*

Compared to integrated mills, the smaller models required fewer raw materials and less energy.[43] Even better, new market entrants typically avoided the United Steelworkers and other unions. By doing so, mini-mill operators faced significantly lower labor costs.

The writing was on the wall. As is often the case, though, the incumbents didn't know it yet. As Lydia Chavez wrote in *The New York Times* in 1981:

> The truncated steel mill is to the integrated steel mill what the Volkswagen was to the American auto industry in the 1960's: smaller, cheaper, less complex and more efficient.[44]

Over the past fifty years, annual variations aside, US domestic steel production has declined.[45] In response, America has had to supplement its supply of this essential metal alloy through imports. Canada, Brazil, and Mexico are among the countries that help the US keep the lights on.[46] (Remember that, in and of themselves, imports aren't inherently disadvantageous. See the discussion in Chapter 9 on the law of comparative advantage.)

Mini-mills are enlightening on two fronts. First, as Christensen describes in his book, *all* industries and companies face disruption from unexpected sources—even and especially critical, ostensibly healthy ones.

---

* This discussion resembles the one in Chapter 7 on *The Innovator's Dilemma*. See the sidebar "Dimon Waffles on Crypto and Blockchain."

Long-term success isn't guaranteed; permanent prosperity is a myth. Second, complacency is rampant. Executives frequently ignore new technologies and trends because they generally want to preserve the status quo. If it isn't broke, they don't fix it.

The Semiconductor Conundrum

Today, steel continues to power the modern way of life. Indeed, the alloy is "essential to the world's water and food supply, energy generation, and national security."[47]

When tech-obsessed American teenagers and millennials think of today's must-haves, they're more likely to name semiconductors and chips than steel. Forget your laptop, smartphone, or other favorite gadget. Today, "if it's got a plug or a battery, it's probably got a chip."[48] The list includes cars, dishwashers, microwave ovens, televisions, washing machines, refrigerators, and other appliances.[49]

Intel used to dominate the US chip industry. Now the company is "struggling to stay relevant."[50] In terms of market capitalization, the AI darling Nvidia is worth 16 Intels.[51] On December 2, 2024, the former's CEO Patrick Gelsinger resigned after a "disastrous tenure."[52]

The idea of a national chip shortage justifiably terrifies Americans—and it's not just a theoretical risk. Taiwan Semiconductor Manufacturing Company (TSMC) makes an estimated 90 percent of the world's cutting-edge logic chips.[53] If China invades Taiwan, it's hard to envision TSMC chip production not plummeting.*

Against this backdrop, Joe Biden signed the bipartisan CHIPS and Science Act on August 9, 2022.[54] The statute earmarked a considerable $52.7 billion in federal funds to address this critical national vulnerability and lessen its dependence on foreign chipmakers. (America is no anomaly here. Many countries have passed laws that have designated funds to buttress key industries.[55])

---

* As of December 2024, the company was nearing completion of a US facility in the Arizona desert north of Phoenix. See https://tinyurl.com/the-cat-tsmc for more details.

THE CATALYSTS

The victory may be ephemeral, though, because the Biden administration disbursed the funds too slowly. During his campaign, Trump threatened to repeal CHIPS. But after winning the election, Trump conferred with economic advisors, and it appears likely that he'll leave the act intact.[56] Also uncertain is whether the legislation will save American chip manufacturers and resurrect this critical industry.

So where does this leave the US?

America faces formidable economic obstacles around innovation, even with the backing of its federal government. An unsupportive or even hostile administration will only hasten its demise.

Population and Economic Decline: Why We Should Embrace Legal Immigration

Countries that restrict population growth undermine their own efforts to sustain their populations and levels of economic growth. The University of Pennsylvania at Wharton reports that American:

> population growth is projected to decline, and the population will become much older over time. Preventing these outcomes will require faster immigration by several multiples of its current rate.[57]

It's just bad policy—and the US economy and its citizens will ultimately suffer for their leaders' shortsighted, grossly misinformed decisions.

Brace yourself: The next chapter is a grim one. It examines how criminals are exploiting technology and regulatory gaps to operate with near free rein.

Key Points

- US innovation used to be unparalleled, but other countries have been catching up.

- COVID-19 forced many individuals, companies, and countries to conduct radical remote work experiments. The surprising results have profoundly impacted immigration policies.
- In the Olympics for global talent, the US won't be winning medals anytime soon. By rescinding fundamental rights and creating an autocracy, the US is encouraging emigration.
- America's dented brand means that other countries will more easily attract talented workers.

CHAPTER 11

THE WAR OVER TRANSPARENCY

POWERFUL ENTITIES AND INDIVIDUALS ARE OPERATING WITH ANONYMITY AND IMPUNITY.

> "Secrecy is the enemy of efficiency, but also of justice."
> —*Jeremy Bentham*

At some point in 1618, tensions between European states and religions reached a tipping point. Actions replaced words, and the Thirty Years' War began. The deadly conflict engulfed France, the Holy Roman Empire, and essentially all major European powers. Some historians have dubbed it "the first modern war."[1]

The results were nothing short of devastating. "Three decades of violence, famine and disease … swept across the continent and decimated its population."[2] Anywhere from four to twelve million people lost their lives. Around 450,000 people died in combat alone. The 1648 Treaty of Westphalia formally brought the bloodshed to an end. It also marked Switzerland's independence from the Holy Roman Empire and its neutrality.[3]

As a newly sovereign nation, Switzerland was free to create its own laws. At the time, France's King Louis XV and his minions wanted to obscure its dealings with banks in a "heretical" protestant country.* Against this backdrop, in 1713, Switzerland's Council of Geneva "banned bankers from divulging their clients' details to safeguard the interests of the French monarch."[4]

The move worked. As Kalyeena Makortoff wrote in 2022 for *The Guardian*:

> French kings found the ideal refuge for their wealth: a city-state nestled between the snow-capped Alps and the pristine waters of Lake Geneva. Catholic royalty flocked to Geneva in the 18th century in an effort to conceal their dealings with Protestant bankers.[5]

French aristocrats weren't the only ones to benefit from Switzerland's laws designed to ensure financial secrecy. The country's decision has reverberated through the world financial order for centuries—and, in fact, continues to do so today.

And Swiss officials didn't stop there. They proposed and passed deliberate legislation to bolster their country's rep for protecting financial privacy:

> By 1934, politicians agreed to put banking secrecy—the "duty of absolute silence"—into law, making it a crime for anyone to share clients' banking information, particularly with foreign authorities.
>
> Controversially, the law, combined with Switzerland's political neutrality, made the country a haven for Nazi officials. Swiss bankers collaborated heavily with Adolf Hitler and his regime, offering financial credit and helping fleeing Nazis hide their loot after the second world war.[6]

---

* At the time, two major Christian denominations dominated Switzerland: Protestantism and Catholicism.

It's important to note that Swiss law at the time did *not* explicitly prohibit German citizens from reporting financial crimes. Rather, the country's statutes primarily served to protect banking clients' privacy and financial information.[7] Switzerland's prioritization resulted in an unintended consequence: Whistleblowers faced legal risks for reporting financial improprieties.

Not surprisingly, gobs of illicit funds flowed into Swiss banks. Executives earned untold fortunes for looking the other way. A massive 2022 leak revealed that criminals, fraudsters, and corrupt politicians held an eye-popping £80 billion in the Swiss bank Credit Suisse alone.[8] Adding fuel to the fire, Switzerland's elected officials passed friendly tax laws giving affluent individuals even more incentive to immigrate to the country—and, of course, to bring their prodigious funds with them.

Sebastian Guex, a professor of history at the University of Lausanne in Switzerland, has extensively studied the country's storied banking industry. In his words, "To add something that other countries didn't have, they also adopted tax measures to stimulate rich people coming from outside to stay long in Switzerland."[9]

Switzerland's tale of financial secrecy underscores the long, ongoing war between financial transparency and privacy. As we'll see in this chapter, bad actors have always wanted to conceal their dealings, and diligent regulators have always wanted to bring their activity to light. Given the catalysts already discussed in Part II, this conflict is intensifying and taking on new fronts.

Transparency and Traditional Finance: A Quick Overview

Before continuing, we need to briefly review the remarkable opacity of the world financial system that dominated for so long.

THE CATALYSTS

Opaque by Default

Switzerland took its clients' financial privacy to an unhealthy extreme, but global financial transactions have historically been siloed and opaque. Efforts to pass anti-money laundering laws and reporting regulations routinely faced significant opposition.* (I'll focus on the US in this section, but most industrialized, capitalist nations encounter similar obstacles to financial reform.)

For this reason, up until 1970, American law didn't require domestic financial institutions to keep records or report suspicious transactions. As a direct result, money laundering, tax evasion, and other financial crimes ran amok. For example, beginning in the 1960s, "the value of the illegal drug trade grew" and "money laundering became more lucrative and increasingly sophisticated."[10]

The Tide Finally Begins to Turn

Faced with burgeoning problems, the US Congress responded in full force by passing the Currency and Foreign Transactions Reporting Act (CFTRA). On October 26, 1970, President Richard Nixon signed it into law. At a high level, the CFTRA mandated transparency. More specifically, it required:

> many financial institutions to create "paper trails" by keeping records and filing reports on certain transactions. These reports are submitted to the U.S. Department of the Treasury's Financial Crimes Enforcement Network (FinCEN). FinCEN collects and analyzes the information to support law enforcement investigative efforts and to provide U.S. policy makers with strategic analyses of domestic worldwide money laundering developments, trends and patterns.[11]

---

* For an exhaustive review of the history of anti-money-laundering efforts in the US, see https://tinyurl.com/the-cat-aml.

Nonbank enterprises also faced new regulatory requirements. Businesses had "to keep records and file reports that are determined to have a high degree of usefulness in criminal, tax, and regulatory matters."[12]

The CFTRA represented landmark legislation. In theory, it would curb money laundering and other financial crimes.[13] Note that today, the law is better known as the *Bank Secrecy Act* (BSA).* Nineteen years later, the G7 countries, the European Commission, and eight other countries have followed suit. The group in 1989 created the Financial Action Task Force (FATF) with a strict mandate "to prevent the utilization of the banking system and financial institutions for the purpose of money laundering, … including the adaptation of the legal and regulatory systems so as to enhance multilateral judicial assistance."[14] More specifically, FATF:

- Examines money-laundering techniques and trends.
- Reviews what's happening at the national and international levels.
- Makes recommendations to combat money laundering and, effective 2001, to counter the financing of terrorism (CFT).

The FATF evaluates countries around the world. It issues public warnings after deeming countries' anti-money laundering (AML) and CFT programs deficient. If those nations want to maintain their positions within the global economy, then they'll have to address those deficiencies.

Before we get to whether the global AML/CFT system has worked, we need to answer an even more profound question: Why was the traditional financial system so opaque to begin with?

Original Emphasis, Considerations, and Limitations of Bank Secrecy Laws

It's imperative to understand a few basic concepts about bank secrecy laws. Ironically, the moniker is a bit of a misnomer. Related legislation aims to:

---

* Technically speaking, the BSA doesn't exist. See https://tinyurl.com/the-cat-bsa for more information on the genesis of the term.

- Prevent bank secrecy by mandating transparency.
- Require banks to keep records and report suspicious activity to authorities.

Initially, regulators wanted to stop money laundering. On two levels, regulatory frameworks required banks to treat their customers in a decidedly non-Swiss manner. First, they introduced *Know Your Customer* (KYC) rules.[15] Collectively, the mandates represented "a set of standards used in the investment services industry to verify customers and their risk and financial profiles."[16]

Next, banks needed to perform customer due diligence (CDD) or enhanced due diligence (EDD). As for the distinction between the two, garden-variety CDD applies "to all customers, while EDD is reserved for high-risk customers requiring further scrutiny."[17] In either case, original AML rules mandated that banks focus on their customers. How much in assets does Company X or Individual Y hold in the financial institution, and what do we know about them? The framework functioned moderately well, given the banks' siloed information systems.

A better approach would involve capturing all bank transactions. Regimes that analyze *all* transaction-level activity would help regulators and authorities immensely. For starters, they could easily view, analyze, and share valuable data. Authorities could ask critical questions, such as:

- How specifically did Company X or Individual Y manage to acquire such wealth?
- With which other parties did each conduct business?
- When and where did those transactions take place?

Vast troves of data and metadata make answering these queries far easier, if not always easy. Take it from an AML expert and former prosecutor: A transparent, transaction-based system would yield far more apprehensions, arrests, and convictions. (We'll come back to how well transaction tracing works with cryptocurrencies later in this chapter.)

THE WAR OVER TRANSPARENCY

9/11: The Day That Changed Everything

Chapter 3 touched upon the impact of 9/11 on the US financial system. Now it's time to dig a little deeper. We need to understand how the terrorist attacks and their subsequent fallout fundamentally changed the game.

On October 26, 2001, President George W. Bush signed into law the USA Patriot Act. In his words:

> We will direct every resource at our command to win the war against terrorists: every means of diplomacy, every tool of intelligence, every instrument of law enforcement, every financial influence. We will starve the terrorists of funding, turn them against each other, rout them out of their safe hiding places and bring them to justice.[18]

Almost immediately, the financial services industry began playing a pivotal role in detecting and reporting financial crimes—specifically, money laundering and terrorist financing.

By way of background, Congress had considered—but not passed—several anti-money laundering statutes before 9/11. Many of these reforms ultimately found their way into the Patriot Act. As internationally recognized regulatory expert and attorney John Byrne wrote in September 2021:

> Prior to 9/11, the Bank Secrecy Act was facing criticism and potential limitations. However, the attacks led to swift legislative action, primarily through the USA PATRIOT Act, which significantly expanded AML obligations. While the Act was presented as a direct response to 9/11, many of its financial provisions were actually drawn from previous unsuccessful legislative attempts addressing traditional money laundering.[19]

Recall our discussion in Chapter 4 of how the US has effectively employed sanctions. By weaponizing its currency, the US has attempted to meet key policy objectives:

- To choke off terrorists and money launderers by cutting off their access to the global financial system.
- To penalize third parties that assist these bad actors.
- To prevent these individuals, groups, and governments from playing jurisdictional arbitrage and finding countries with weaker laws.

With the requisite background out of the way, let's return to the key question: Has the global AML/CFT framework achieved its ambitious aims?

The Verdict: Mixed Results

A different book would fully review the original BSA, subsequent revisions, enforcement efforts, and similar laws and regulations passed throughout the world. We lack the space. It's fair to say, though, the results are mixed. We saw in Chapter 3 the power of US sanctions. In some cases, they work *too* well. What's more, as the following sidebar illustrates, US law didn't merely hinder foreign terrorists from carrying out unspeakable actions. At least in some small part, the BSA led to one of the most iconic events in American history.

> **Following the Money**
>
> June 17, 1972, lives in infamy.
>
> On that summer day, operatives acting on behalf of President Richard Nixon's reelection campaign broke into the Democratic National Committee headquarters at the Watergate office complex in Washington, DC. It's impossible to overstate the import of the subsequent scandal—Watergate—on many levels.[*]
>
> What role did the BSA play in the investigation?
>
> I don't want to exaggerate things. At a bare minimum, though, it helped two heralded *Washington Post* journalists who investigated the

---

[*] Read Bob Woodward's superb 1974 book *All the President's Men* or watch the 1976 film starring Robert Redford and Dustin Hoffman.

> "so-called third-rate burglary that ... ended the presidency of Richard Nixon."[20] Bob Woodward and Carl Bernstein largely succeeded by following the money—and the sums involved left the very type of paper trail that the CFTRA intended. As but one example, Bernstein "was able to confirm the burglar's calls to Hunt through telephone records, and also traced a check in one burglar's bank account to the CRP."[21] (CRP was the acronym for the Committee to Reelect the President.) If banks didn't need to keep detailed records, perhaps things would have turned out differently for the disgraced former president.

Merely an Inconvenience?

The Cato Institute, the prominent libertarian thinktank, is among the BSA's most ardent contemporary skeptics. In its view, current legislation and its resultant framework have collectively "proven a minor inconvenience for criminals but a major burden on law-abiding citizens."[22] Coin Center has also joined the fray. It has slammed the BSA as "a sweeping delegation of law making power."[23]

Future Challenges

Bush resolutely vowed to "rout out" bad actors using any means necessary. In this case, though, theory and practice collided. First, the US couldn't accomplish this goal in 2001 by itself. Cooperation with allies would be essential, but many sovereign nations resisted—and not just Switzerland.

In October 2014, ministers from fifty countries adopted landmark common reporting standards (CRS) that allowed officials from these nations to easily exchange taxpayer information with each other.[24] Still, many problems remained. Put another way, nearly thrice as many countries *didn't* sign on.

THE CATALYSTS

DeFi, Crypto, and Courts Can Enable the Untraceable Transfer of Funds

Second, no one in 2001 could have possibly anticipated the technological innovations that made Bush's pledge downright risible two decades later. Chapter 7 discussed the rise of digital currencies—a technological innovation that could render the BSA and other twentieth-century legislation largely impotent.

Cryptocurrency mixers or tumblers "obfuscate the provenance, possession, and movement of cryptocurrencies through a process of 'mixing.'"[25] Tornado Cash is a particularly dangerous one because it runs on immutable smart contracts. The only way to stop it requires "shutting down the entire Ethereum blockchain, which would be nearly impossible."[26] Before its 2019 launch, the open-source software would theoretically let authoritarians and terrorists effectively launder their money and commit sanctions evasion out in the open.

In practice, that's exactly what happened. Myriad bad actors have used it "to launder more than $7 billion worth of virtual currency," causing the US Department of the Treasury to label Tornado Cash "notorious."[27] Today, American law enforcement officials aren't just battling cybercriminals. Remarkably, their own country's judicial system is actively thwarting their efforts.

In late November 2024, the US Fifth Circuit Court of Appeals ruled in the Van Loon case that "immutable smart contracts cannot be classified as 'property' under existing law."[28] A portion of Tornado Cash's code—the one that relies upon immutable smart contracts—is "exempt from US Treasury sanctions."[29] The solution would have likely required Congress to amend the relevant sanctions statute. The point, however, is now moot. On March 21, 2025, the Trump Administration "remove[d] the economic sanctions against Tornado Cash."[30] This will undoubtedly make it easier to mix clean funds with illicit finance from Iran, North Korea, and other malign foreign actors.

Bottom line: Governments are rapidly losing the ability to stop or even slow criminal activity.

Conflicting Goals

In an ideal world, everyone would be on the same page. That is, all law-abiding regulators, business leaders, privacy experts, advocacy groups, politicians, judges, and law-enforcement authorities on the planet would agree on the need to impede financial criminals, hackers, and terrorists. As such, they would immediately begin working on balanced solutions to the formidable problems that cybercrime presents. While we're at it, let's magically give everyone extensive knowledge of cryptography, coding, and all things tech. Sufficient tools, resources, and education for all.

To be sure, stopping money laundering and related financial crimes would still pose alarming challenges. DeFi and cryptocurrency would still be tough nuts to crack.

Even in this mythical reality, cybercrime wouldn't instantly cease. Still, getting everyone up to speed would at least represent a significant step in the right direction.

As we'll see next, though, we're nowhere close to universal agreement on the problem, let alone the solution. Sadly, it's not just hackers, terrorists, and other bad actors who want to operate with complete anonymity. Plenty of "respectable" folks want to effectively kill AML/CFT and return to the anonymous free flow of money.

The Powerful Forces Opposing Financial Transparency

Even before the advent of the internet, the web, DeFi, and cryptocurrency, no piece of legislation—up to and including the CFTRA—could eliminate financial crimes. No law ever will. If current legislation is to remain effective, however, it must evolve in response to new tools and techniques.* Minor tweaks to decades-old legislation won't come close to cutting it.

As we'll see next, a powerful cohort of forces wants to preserve the status quo—and even remove the few, largely antiquated enforcement weapons available to regulators.

Bankers Resist Attempts at Regulation

In Chapter 7, I broached the Dodd-Frank Act. (See the section titled "Cryptocurrencies Enter the Mainstream.") In the aftermath of the subprime crisis, bankers paid themselves handsome bonuses. But here's perhaps an even more stunning lack of self-awareness: Bankers then paid their lobbyists to fight US regulations that aimed to prevent another banking crisis. Clearly, they were capable of doing that themselves.

Their absurd argument didn't pass the smell test. Thankfully, the executive and legislative branches weren't buying it.

With a different party in power, though, the banking industry found a receptive audience. In June 2018, the same folks who caused the world economy to ground to a halt were able to dilute the bill:

> Bank regulations adopted in the wake of the 2008 financial crisis are rolling back under a bipartisan bill approved by Congress and signed by President Trump last month. The effects of freeing thousands of banks from the stricter federal oversight imposed by the Dodd-Frank Wall Street Reform and Consumer Protection Act are a matter of debate, with some predicting wide-ranging impacts on the banking industry and consumers.[31]

It's only a matter of time before the next financial crisis arrives. The elites want capitalism on the way up but socialism on the way down in the form of bailouts. Privatize the gains. Socialize the losses.

---

* See https://tinyurl.com/the-cat-money for a comprehensive history of American anti–money-laundering laws.

DeFi Is Enabling a Libertarian Resurrection

Through her books, essays, and talks, the Russian author Ayn Rand built a loyal following. *The Fountainhead* in 1943 and *Atlas Shrugged* in 1957 codified her philosophy: objectivism. (Let's just say she wasn't a fan of social safety nets.) In conservative circles, she became an icon and intellectual heavyweight.

Although she died in 1982, Rand's philosophy has found new life in the digital age. Nowhere is this truer than in DeFi. Extremists believe that even the goals of hindering money launderers, criminals, and terrorists pale in comparison to absolute privacy. One wonders what Rand herself would say if she were alive today. Will techno-anarchists and libertarians change their tune when the next 9/11 happens? Or will they continue adhering to their misguided, absolutist philosophies? Faced with mass destruction or even bioterrorism, will they still contend that the right to financial privacy supersedes public safety interests?

Former Coinbase chief technology officer Balaji Srinivasan takes these ideas to their illogical extreme in his web-based manifesto *The Network State: How to Start a New Country*. He advocates starting a country—you read that correctly—from your computer. This state would recruit citizens like a startup hires employees. As for physical land, don't ask.

The Growth of Private Equity

The American banking industry isn't the only one suffering from a visibility problem today. Many nonfinancial institutions no longer must deal with the Securities and Exchange Commission (SEC) for one simple reason: They either have gone private or are now in the hands of private equity. Figure 11.1 shows a visual of this pronounced recent trend.

Privately held companies don't face anywhere near the same regulatory and compliance requirements as their publicly held counterparts.

Here are just a few of the corporations that have, for one reason or another, decided to go that route:

- X Corp (formerly Twitter).
- Heinz.
- Burger King.
- Dell.
- Hilton.
- Panera Bread.
- Reader's Digest.[32]

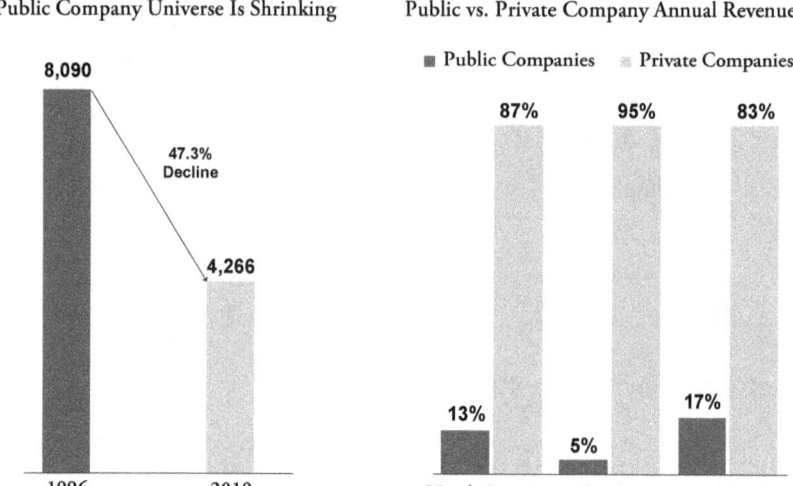

Figure 11.1: Growth of Private Equity

Source: 2024 Global Innovation Index, WIPO | Data from Refinitiv Eikon

Additional sources: US Bureau of Labor Statistics, World Bank, KKR, as of October 28, 2022, and Capital IQ, last 12 months, as of February 2023. Note: The number of private firms includes those firms with more than fifty employees.

It's inaccurate to claim that privately held companies face zero reporting requirements. Generally speaking, though, they're far less cumbersome.

A Flurry of Coming Legal Challenges

As of this writing, plenty of well-funded pro-business groups have used the US legal system to challenge different aspects of the BSA. Three cases made it to the Supreme Court:

- *California Bankers Assn. v. Shultz* (1974)
- *United States v. Miller* (1976)
- *Bittner v. United States* (2023)

Expect that number to skyrocket in the coming years. For instance, consider the bipartisan Corporate Transparency Act (CTA), enacted in 2021. The legislation attempts to "combat illicit activity including tax fraud, money laundering, and financing for terrorism by capturing more ownership information for specific U.S. businesses operating in or accessing the country's market."[33]

As part of the law, all businesses must provide "identifying information about the individuals who directly or indirectly own or control a company."[34] This is the crucial Beneficial Ownership Registration (BOR). The CTA may not be perfect legislation, but its goals are indisputably essential: to capture criminals and prevent future catastrophes. BOR's actual burden on even small enterprises is minimal, and it's not as if cybercrimes such as ransomware attacks are theoretical risks. In 2023, there were "only" 317.5 million of the latter, as Figure 11.2 displays.

If anything, regulatory bodies and enforcement officials need more arrows in their quiver, not fewer. This is especially true in an era of cybercrime-as-a-service:

> Budding cybercriminals now only need a rudimentary understanding of cybersecurity, access to the internet, and a few dollars in their pocket to initiate an attack. As such, cybercrime has become indiscriminate, with cybercriminals attacking any organization, regardless of its size.[35]

Figure 11.2: Annual Number of Ransomware Attempts Worldwide From 2017 to 2023

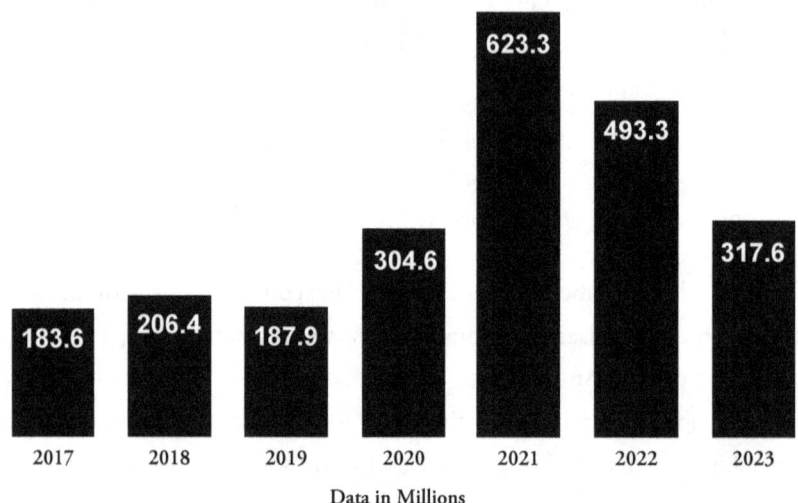

Source: SonicWall via Statista | https://tinyurl.com/the-cat-ran

Note: Data based on SonicWall Capture Labs characteristics. Wider industry metrics may vary.

These daunting realities and statistics, however, haven't stopped a variety of trade associations from deriding the BOR.

These folks aren't just tweeting their dismay and trolling people justifiably concerned about little things like their personal safety and the good of society. Rather, they've launched nationwide lobbying campaigns to sway popular opinion. As but one example, the National Federation of Independent Business has called BOR "burdensome."[36] Nothing could be further from the truth. For small businesses, filing takes minutes to complete and costs nothing. For obvious reasons, larger enterprises with complex ownership structures may need to devote more resources to comply.

Beyond spreading falsehoods, trade associations have attempted to repeal the CTA or have courts declare it unconstitutional. Even worse, they're finding friendly judges.[37]

THE WAR OVER TRANSPARENCY

One can only imagine a deliberately opaque world that effectively bans authorities from tracking sophisticated criminals and malign foreign actors.* Today, America's enemies know better than to execute another 9/11. That event temporarily united the country. The attackers, planners, and financiers quickly faced the wrath of the US government.

America's enemies are taking a decidedly different tack: employing ransomware attacks, hacking its infrastructure, and spreading propaganda. Those that want to do the US harm have realized that a far more effective strategy involves death by a thousand cuts. Vicious partisanship and political infighting prevent America from properly defending itself.

Entrepreneurs Abdicate Responsibility for Their Wares

Chapter 6 covered the rise of the tech nation-state. Facebook (now Meta), Google (now Alphabet), and their ilk have developed well-earned reputations for irresponsible innovation.

Consider Beacon, Facebook's 2007 default e-commerce feature that worked as follows:

> When users bought things on Beacon-affiliated sites (such as Fandango or Overstock.com), their friends were automatically notified of the purchase. This notification happened before the purchaser had a chance to approve it.

It was hardly his company's first—or last, for that matter—privacy gaffe, but let's move beyond the beleaguered social network. The Silicon Valley ethos of innovating first and asking critical questions later remains alive and well. It's clear that OpenAI is employing the same playbook as its predecessors. In October 2024, the company announced that it was:

---

* I'm reminded here of the George Carlin joke from his 1988 special *What Am I Doing in New Jersey?* The acerbic comedian opined, "Now they're thinking about banning toy guns ... and they're going to keep the fucking real ones."

disbanding its "AGI* Readiness" team, which advised the company on OpenAI's capacity to handle artificial intelligence that could potentially equal or surpass human intellect and the world's readiness to manage such technology.[38]

In response, the company's safety czar, Miles Brundage, resigned. In a later interview, he sounded the alarm. Neither his ex-employer nor the world is ready for what the company is building.[39] In a way, nothing has changed: Those who move fast and break things see no need to slow down. They don't care what they're breaking, much less what it will cost to fix.

Where We Are Now

A transparency problem is plaguing the current world financial order. I'll focus on identifying its major consequences next. In Chapter 14, I'll offer policy recommendations.

Current Regulatory Frameworks Are Broken

On October 26, 2023, the Economic Crime and Corporate Transparency Act received royal assent in the UK. The bill aims to do the following:

- Reduce economic crime through corporate transparency.
- Require companies, limited partnerships, and other kinds of corporate entities to verify the identities of those who form them and their beneficial owners.
- Enhance verification requirements of directors and beneficial owners of overseas entities with a UK branch.[40]

The EU also mandates many of the same logical disclosure requirements that have yet to take hold in the US. Under EU rules, "issuers of securities on regulated markets must disclose certain key information to ensure transparency for investors."[41]

---

* Short for *artificial general intelligence*.

Despite such encouraging signs in some jurisdictions, the problems exceed their solutions. Right now, regulators and law enforcement agencies are bringing knives to a gunfight. Banks find the current system burdensome.[42] More importantly, it simply doesn't work.

Money Launderers Are Winning

Bad actors have gamed the system since time immemorial. So what's changed? The system has never lagged so far behind the technology. For the past two decades, most transnational criminal organizations have successfully evaded enforcement authorities. I remember a popular maxim from my days as a prosecutor: "We only catch the dumb, lazy ones."

The stats are scary. The US Treasury Department estimated in 2016 that money launderers and terrorists concealed the movement of more than $300 billion around the country. That number represented an increase of more than 40 percent from 2003.[43]

That same year, the US Federal Bureau of Investigation (FBI) released the report "Combating the Growing Money Laundering Threat." From it:

> Transnational criminal organizations, foreign intelligence services, and terrorist groups—as well as Internet fraudsters and other criminals—move billions of dollars each year through the international banking system and across borders to conceal the origin of the funds.[44]

At that point, DeFi and cryptocurrencies hadn't matured to the same extent they have now. Can anyone credibly argue that, in the current environment, it's harder for bad actors to move funds wherever and whenever they want?

Organized crime is meeting a disorganized response. The criminals are winning, and it's not even close.

Compliance Conundrums

When it comes to catching the bad guys, the status quo doesn't just fail us. It's woefully inadequate at compliance. For the most part, financial institutions have lacked the incentive to comply with existing laws. Just as in any other industry, the financial industry has its fair share of questionable behavior.[45]

It's simple math. As we saw with the subprime crisis, industry types doing untoward things earn fortunes. At the same time, they know that their odds of being caught are low. Even if they are, will they serve prison time for their crimes? Or, more likely, will they pay the equivalent of speeding tickets? Two high-profile examples illustrate my point.

Proof That Crime Pays

In 1992, Steve A. Cohen founded SAC Capital. The aggressive hedge fund, at its peak, managed more than $16 billion in assets.[46] As Sheelah Kolhatkar describes in her 2017 book *Black Edge*, Cohen's high-risk outfit, SAC Capital, was a "magnet for market cheaters."

Several SAC Capital employees went to prison for insider trading, but Cohen himself avoided incarceration. Yes, the disgraced ringleader ultimately paid a fine of $1.8 billion in 2013. Yet the largest insider-trading penalty ever at the time didn't exactly leave Cohen destitute.[47]

Seven years later, Cohen purchased his favorite baseball team, the New York Mets, for a cool $2.4 billion.[48] Oh, and his new hedge fund, Point72—effectively the continuation of SAC Capital—held more than $35 billion in assets under management (AUM) as of December 2024.[49]

Cohen's wildly successful second act isn't exactly serving as a deterrent to would-be financial criminals. Quite the contrary.

Binance

Changpeng Zhao, known commonly as CZ, knew plenty about finance and tech. At one point, the Chinese-born Canadian built high-frequency trading software. In 2017, he founded the cryptocurrency exchange Binance, nearly two years before Sam Bankman-Fried started FTX.

Like many of his fintech contemporaries, CZ wasn't too keen on compliance. Growth and money were far higher on his list of priorities.

For three years, CZ effectively operated a transnational money-laundering business. Finally, in November 2023, the US Justice Department charged him with willful violations of AML and sanctions laws.[50]

As acting Assistant Attorney General Nicole M. Argentieri of the Department of Justice's (DOJ) Criminal Division said, CZ "threatened the U.S. financial system and our national security."[51] For his heinous crimes, CZ served—wait for it—a mere four months in prison.[52] As part of its plea with the US DOJ, Binance agreed to pay a $4 billion fine* and submit to two separate monitorships.†

Lesson learned, right?

The jury is still out.

In September 2024, I attended the Digital Asset Compliance & Market Integrity Summit (DACOM) in Manhattan. Among the speakers was Noah Perlman, Binance's chief compliance officer (CCO). Before working for CZ, Perlman served in the same capacity at Gemini, the far smaller, US-based crypto exchange founded in 2014 by Cameron and Tyler Winklevoss of Facebook fame.

Perlman cheekily remarked about the two companies' drastically different market shares in relation to their inapposite attitude toward compliance. In other words, he boldly said the quiet part out loud:

- If companies have to pay penalties that represent a pittance of the profit, then why obey the law?
- If you can become the market leader, plead guilty to horrific and illegal conduct, and remain on top, then what is the real reputational risk?

---

* It's worth noting that $4 billion represented one-fifth of Binance's daily trading volume. Yes, daily.
† As FTI Consulting describes the term, "When an investigation reveals employees have engaged in misconduct such as corruption, anti-competitive behavior, export controls and sanctions violations, or consumer protection laws, it may be necessary for a court or regulatory agency to appoint a monitor, examiner, receiver or assessor." For more on this subject, see https://tinyurl.com/the-cat-monitor.

As the late Charlie Munger of Berkshire Hathaway once succinctly put it, "Show me the incentive and I'll show you the outcome."

Fintech Is Exposing Significant Regulatory Gaps

In April 2024, the American banking-as-a-service outfit Synapse Financial Technologies declared bankruptcy. In the end, $85 million in funds were unaccounted for, spread out over more than 200,000 accounts. The debacle "raised serious questions about accountability and oversight in fintech-bank partnerships."[53]

It's clear that legislators and regulators understand little about fintech. For this reason, parts of the industry are operating in an unfettered, often galling manner. Fintech startups are identifying legal loopholes and regulation gaps. (Some use attorneys for this purpose; others don't even bother.) They're releasing risky, poorly managed tools that, as we saw in the case with Synapse, can wreak havoc on the lives of hundreds of thousands of customers.

Tax Havens Persevere—and Let the Rich Fleece the Poor

In his 2022 book *Butler to the World*, Oliver Bullough peels back a curtain that many oligarchs would prefer to keep closed. Thanks to its overly permissive legal and financial systems, Britain has become *the* global enabler for wealthy and corrupt individuals to hide and stash their illicit funds. By one estimate, London and the three UK crown dependencies[*] launder 40 percent of all dirty money today.[54] The UK network of tax havens drives a full third of corporate tax abuse risks. Yet, the Organisation for Economic Co-operation and Development (OECD) rates the UK as "not harmful."[55]

Not to be outdone, the US has also become "the world's refuge for dirty money."[56] The reasons vary, but much of the blame stems from one financial instrument. As Michael Casey wrote for the nonprofit American progressive magazine *Mother Jones*:

---

[*] The Bailiwicks of Jersey, Guernsey, and the Isle of Man.

THE WAR OVER TRANSPARENCY

The rise of the American shell company stretches back to the late 19th century, when New Jersey enabled the formation of holding companies—helping create America's first monopolies—without requiring them to transact business in the state. So many firms re-registered in the Garden State that people in other states, which were suddenly losing out on taxes and fees, began calling it the "Traitor State."[57]

But how much are we talking about?

Far more than you probably realize.

The Panama Papers revealed the shocking global value of hidden assets. As one estimate put it:

> The global stock of unrecorded private financial net assets—including currency, bank deposits, stocks and bonds, and other tradable securities—invested in or through offshore havens already totaled $21 trillion to $32 trillion by the end of 2010, about 10–15 percent of global financial wealth.[58]

The current financial system allows the wealthy to easily hide their income and assets and, critically, avoid paying taxes. In 2023, the Tax Justice Network estimated that, in total, countries are projected to lose $4.8 trillion to tax havens over the next decade.

Those tax havens are closer to home than most Americans realize. Wyoming, South Dakota, North Dakota, and Nevada want to entice the world's wealthiest individuals. To this end, these states have passed laws that make them highly attractive for establishing trusts. Their statutes include language that provides strong asset protection, privacy, and favorable tax treatment, among other features. Specific examples include:

- **South Dakota:** Laws around perpetual trusts and robust privacy protections let the affluent easily hide massive amounts of wealth.[59]
- **Nevada:** Dynasty trusts and domestic asset protection trusts (DAPTs)[60] metastasize opacity.

- **Wyoming:** The state offers thousand-year trusts and other enhanced privacy features.[61] Not coincidentally, it consistently ranks as a top jurisdiction for trusts and tax avoidance.[62]

For obvious reasons, these states claim that their trust industries are well regulated and comply with federal anti-money laundering laws. As a former federal prosecutor, however, I'm less confident; I've seen firsthand the level of secrecy and the sheer volume of assets held in these trusts. This lack of transparency is problematic on a couple of levels.[63] First, it creates a significant challenge in assessing the true scale and nature of the wealth held in these trust structures. Second, it poses potential risks to financial system integrity and US national security.[64]

The Wealth Gap Is More Evident Now

Only a privileged few know where money is moving. It's becoming more and more evident, however, where it's *not* going: to the majority of the world's citizens. The 2021 World Inequality Report found that "[c]ontemporary global inequalities are close to their early 20th century level, at the peak of Western imperialism."[65]

This brings us to a fascinating paradox: In 2024, the world's top 1 percent owned more wealth than 95 percent of humanity.[66] Given that, how and why do so many people continue supporting a system that heavily disenfranchises them?

The next chapter—and our final catalyst—resolves that paradox.

Key Points

- Transaction-based regulatory requirements for transparent systems allow authorities to improve their odds of apprehending individuals and groups committing financial crimes.

- Cryptocurrency and other digital assets are shining a light on how badly we were doing AML/CFT and how much dirty money is in the system.
- Digital asset technologies are a double-edged sword; they enable money laundering and criminal activity while making them more transparent.
- The penalties for financial criminals are laughably light and often nonexistent.
- Oligarchs and criminals can easily hide their wealth. The impact on global inequality has been pronounced.

CHAPTER 12

SOCIAL ENGINEERING

WE ARE LIVING IN AN ERA OF UNPRECEDENTED MASS MANIPULATION.

> "In a time of deceit, telling the truth is a revolutionary act."
> —*George Orwell*

June 4, 1919, represented a historic triumph for American women. On that day, the US Congress passed the Nineteenth Amendment to the Constitution. The legislation, ratified a little over a year later, "prohibit[ed] any citizen of the United States from being denied the right to vote on the basis of sex."[1]

The battle over women's suffrage took more than four decades to play out. (Members of Congress proposed the Amendment *annually* starting in 1878.) Progressive types saw its enactment as a long-awaited victory for equality—further proof that the burgeoning women's rights movement had arrived in full force.

The tobacco industry immediately saw dollar signs. Philip Morris, Chesterfield, Lucky Strike, and other cigarette manufacturers quickly started plotting. How could they capitalize on this shift in American sentiment? Was it, in fact, a massive business opportunity? Could they market their products to this newly empowered class of customers by pushing the buttons of women's suffrage, freedom, and equality?

To each of these questions, the answer was a resolute yes. "The number of women aged 18 through 25 years who began smoking increased significantly in the mid-1920s."[2]

Over the ensuing decades, tobacco companies' slogans changed in response to social mores and the regulatory environment. Let's start with the former. In 1968,[3] against the backdrop of the women's lib movement, Philip Morris released an infamous *Virginia Slims* female-targeted ad declaring, "You've Come a Long Way, Baby."* Today, manufacturers of e-cigarettes attempt to lure female customers via "themes of independence, glamour, fun, and health-consciousness."[4] (In case you're curious, Big Tobacco didn't forget about men, but they required different triggers, such as appeals to their "rugged masculinity."[5])

Now, on the regulatory front. Despite their incessant protestations, cigarette manufacturers knew full well that their products killed their customers and posed massive public health dangers and costs. For decades, Big Tobacco executives, lobbyists, and PR firms acted as *merchants of doubt*—to paraphrase the excellent book of the same name. The industry excelled at obscuring the truth, fighting new legislation, and lying to the American public[6] until it no longer could.

Once again, the tactics worked. In 1965, the Centers for Disease Control (CDC) first assessed cigarette smoking via the National Health Interview Survey (NHIS). A full 42 percent of American adults regularly smoked.[7]

---

* View one ad at https://tinyurl.com/the-cat-tobacco.

On April 1, 1970, President Nixon signed legislation banning cigarette companies from running TV and radio ads.[8] Twenty years later, the numbers dropped. Roughly one-quarter of the American population ignored the health risks and continued to smoke regularly.

The cat has long been out of the bag. In the US, by law all packs of Marlboros, Newports, and Camels must contain "textual warning statements accompanied by color graphics, in the form of concordant photorealistic images, depicting the negative health consequences of cigarette smoking."[9]

And yet, despite everything we know about the subject, consider this remarkable fact: Nearly one in five Americans still smoked in 2022.[10] Put differently, American tobacco companies continue to convince millions of existing and future patrons to buy an expensive product[11] that unquestionably harms them, although at a decreasing rate.[12] In 2021, the US remained "the fifth largest tobacco-producing country in the world, following China, India, Brazil, and Indonesia."[13]

Unfortunately, as we'll see in this chapter, there's nothing special or unique about how Big Tobacco manipulates tens of millions of Americans. In fact, its means of persuasion are relatively tame by comparison. These days, powerful forces are successfully convincing masses of people all over the world to think, vote, and even act in ways that empirically belie their self-interest.

It's time to talk about our final catalyst: the ubiquity and effectiveness of social engineering.

Modern Social Engineering Explained

Before we arrive at how we got to now, a little background information is in order.

Origins and Trailblazers

Movements and phenomena don't just inexplicably happen. Whether they're working independently or on behalf of their governments, organizations, or groups, individuals make discoveries and advancements that ultimately reverberate years or even centuries later. As is often the case, those reverberations often cause unexpected waves. Jacob Cornelis van Marken is no exception to this rule.

Jacob Cornelis van Marken

Born in 1845, Van Marken studied manufacturing techniques in Austria.[14] He ultimately founded the Royal Dutch Yeast and Spirit Factory in 1869. His entity laid "the foundation for industrial biotechnology."[15]

In many ways, the Dutch industrialist's socially progressive management philosophy was far ahead of its time. "His factories boasted profit sharing, a cooperative printing press, schools, libraries, athletic and social clubs, and insurance funds for accidents, sickness, and old age."[16] If you described a company that offered similar employee perks today, people would probably think you were talking about Google.

Like his contemporaries, Van Marken employed proper engineers who fixed broken machines on the factory floor. Nothing earth-shattering there. Throughout his career, though, Van Marken had an epiphany: Fully functioning appliances and gadgets were necessary but insufficient to optimize productivity. Achieving that lofty goal required another type of technician.

In 1894, Van Marken penned a series of essays crystallizing his views on management. Running a successful enterprise required a different type of specialist, whom he called *sociale ingenieurs*.[17] These social engineers would provide the requisite technical expertise to solve human-centric problems. By doing so, they could improve society in much the same way as engineers designed and developed machinery. At least, that was the theory.

Van Marken died in 1906. He couldn't have envisioned what would become of his managerial benevolence.

SOCIAL ENGINEERING

Sigmund Freud

Sigmund Freud arrived on this planet in 1856. Born in Příbor, Czechia, he emigrated to Austria in March 1938 to escape Nazi persecution.[18] Freud's work as a neurologist led him to study the human unconscious and to birth a critical field of clinical research called *psychoanalysis*. A proper book was only a matter of time.

Freud released *The Interpretation of Dreams* in 1900. The text is one of the most important books of the twentieth century because it:

> provides a groundbreaking theory of dreams and an innovative method for interpreting them that captivates readers to this day.
>
> The book represents Freud's first major attempt to set out his theory of a dynamic unconscious, created in childhood, which operates continuously in every human mind.
>
> For Freud, dreaming is a mental activity that follows its own logic. By identifying its mechanisms, Freud also shed new light on the workings of the unconscious and its powerful role in human life.[19]

Psychoanalysis today isn't nearly as popular as it was a century ago. Over the years, science hasn't been too kind to Freud.[20] Nevertheless, his influence lives on.

Edward Bernays

Freud's nephew, Edward Bernays, was born in 1891 in Vienna, Austria. He studied his famous uncle's work and understood all too well the frailties of the human condition. Those who understood the group mind could alter people's behavior and influence their opinions. People generally believed what they read in print, but radio, cinema, and other nascent technologies offered even greater promise for mass manipulation. (We'll see in the next section how laughably primitive those tools were in comparison to today's counterparts.)

Bernays effectively invented modern public relations (PR). Consequently, *LIFE* magazine named him as one of the 100 most important Americans of the twentieth century. In the parlance of our times, he's "the original influencer."[21]

In 1929, Bernays published the aptly titled book *Propaganda*. From it:

> We are governed, our minds are molded, our tastes formed, our ideas suggested, largely by men we have never heard of. This is a logical result of the way in which our democratic society is organized. Vast numbers of human beings must cooperate in this manner if they are to live together as a smoothly functioning society. In almost every act of our daily lives, whether in the sphere of politics or business, in our social conduct or our ethical thinking, we are dominated by the relatively small number of persons … who understand the mental processes and social patterns of the masses. It is they who pull the wires which control the public mind.

American corporations eagerly hired Bernays to employ his by-any-means-necessary approach, including Big Tobacco. He unabashedly also used fear to sell products. "For Dixie cups, Bernays launched a campaign to scare people into thinking that only disposable cups were sanitary."[22]

Social Engineering

Today, we think of social engineering in two contexts. First, it's an effective means for cybercriminals "to communicate with the intended victim by saying they are from a trusted organization. In some cases, they will even impersonate a person the victim knows."[23] Once bad actors gain access to prized accounts and systems, all hell typically breaks loose.

The second is more relevant for our purposes. In his book *Social Engineering: The Science of Human Hacking*, Christopher Hadnagy defines it as "any act that influences a person to take an action that may or may not be in their best interests."

Note that social manipulation isn't inherently bad.* For instance, late 2021 saw the widespread release of the COVID-19 vaccine in the US. Alabama, Arkansas, California, and Colorado were just a few of the states that offered residents nominal financial rewards for getting the shot and slowing the pandemic's spread.[24]

Why Social Engineering Works So Well Today

In season three of the FX show *Fargo*, David Thewlis's sinister character V. M. Varga utters the line, "We see what we believe, not the other way around."† It's a dismal assessment of the human condition, but an accurate one. Our ability to ascertain what's best for us remains imperfect at best.

Human Beings' Flaws Have Metastasized

Chapter 8 covered some of the cognitive biases that all people suffer from. (See the section "Basic Human Nature.") To some extent, we're all subject to manipulation. The fleas come with the dog. Understanding a few of our shortcomings will explain the increasing effectiveness of social engineering. As we'll see in this section, these facets of humanity exacerbate problems, and the consequences couldn't be more dire.

We Lack Perfect Information in Making Decisions

Herbert Simon of Carnegie Mellon conducted extensive research on how people make decisions. We human beings have never possessed complete information, and we never will. As a result, we *satisfice*. Put differently, we follow a heuristic when making decisions that helps us arrive at "acceptable outcomes."[25] Our rationality is fundamentally *bounded*. The perfectly rational person, *Homo economicus*, doesn't exist. For his seminal work, Simon won the 1978 Nobel Memorial Prize in Economic Sciences.

---

* See *Mindmasters: The Data-Driven Science of Predicting and Changing Human Behavior* by Sandra Matz for more information on this topic.
† From the 2017 episode, "Somebody to Love."

More recently, Richard Thaler, Dan Ariely, and others have popularized the related field of behavioral economics. In short, "People do not always make what neoclassical economists consider the 'rational' or 'optimal' decision, even if they have the information and the tools available to do so."[26] Perhaps that is the single biggest irony of the era of Big Data, but I digress.

Our Collective Intelligence May Have Peaked

In 1948, Dr. Read Tuddenham at the University of California published an article in *The American Psychologist*.[27] The professor had conducted extensive research examining human intelligence and its measurement. He wondered quite simply: Are we getting smarter?

In large part due to educational advances, the answer seemed to be yes. The New Zealand moral philosopher and researcher James Robert Flynn subsequently built on Dr. Tuddenham's work. A review of scientific literature today reveals that:

> Average Intelligence Quotient (IQ) scores have been found to increase across time in developed countries at a startlingly consistent rate of approximately 0.33 points per year, or 3.3 points per decade.[28]

Advancements in education, nutrition, medical care, and technology mean that humanity has *generally* grown smarter each decade. Put differently, *The Flynn Effect* today is "widely accepted."[29] (Interestingly, the term only entered the zeitgeist in 1994 after the publication of Richard Herrnstein's and Charles Murray's controversial book, *The Bell Curve*.)

Of course, these gains aren't evenly distributed. For example, Brazil, Russia, India, and China "are currently seeing the greatest increases" in IQ scores.[30] What's more, some evidence suggests that our collective intelligence is peaking.[31]

Maybe it's dropping, even in wealthy, industrialized nations. Evidence supporting this assertion is hardly lacking. IQ scores in Denver and Norway have declined in recent years.[32] In the US, 10 percent of citizens believe that

SOCIAL ENGINEERING

the world is flat.[33] In 2022, YouPoll asked Americans to assess the proportion of citizens who identified as gay, bisexual, or transgender, among other topics.[34] Table 12.1 displays a partial listing of the poll's results.

Table 12.1: Partial Results of 2022 YouPoll Survey

Group(s)	Estimated Percentage	Actual Percentage
Gays and lesbians	30%	3%
Bisexuals	29%	4%
Transgender	21%	0.6%

Similarly laughable and horrifying discrepancies exist across the board regarding Muslims, millionaires, Texas residents, and more.*

But what if we somehow wave a magic wand and eliminate those chasms in knowledge? Everyone could access all the relevant information about global warming, national elections, immigration, economic growth, and other worldly issues. If we did, would we make optimal decisions?

Probably not, and certainly not all the time.

In 2018, bestselling author and prominent historian Yuval Noah Harari appeared on CNBC to discuss several topics, including the rise of authoritarians and populists. Among his astute observations, the latter are selling "nostalgic fantasies about the past instead of real visions for the future." Harari continued by warning, "We should never underestimate human stupidity."[35] In this way, he echoed the words of the American showman P. T. Barnum. As he observed in the nineteenth century, "No one ever went broke underestimating the intelligence of the American people."

---

* Technology may in fact be making us stupid. See Nicholas Carr's excellent 2010 book, *The Shallows: What the Internet Is Doing to Our Brains*.

THE CATALYSTS

We Are Less Patient Than Ever

Political soundbites have been shrinking for more than a century. During the 1968 US presidential election, the average TV sound bite was forty-three seconds. In the 1988 election, it had plunged to nine.[36] The finding caused one of the US major TV networks to significantly alter its policy:

> CBS announced a new policy for its nightly news. Starting immediately, the network would not use any sound bite—that is, any footage of a candidate speaking uninterrupted—that lasted less than 30 seconds.

As Democrat nominee Michael Dukakis carped at the time, "If you couldn't say it in less than 10 seconds, it wasn't heard because it wasn't aired."[37]

CBS's policy change reflected the grim reality of the time that remains true today: Our attention spans are waning. Cell phones have only intensified the problem. In the 1990s, they were rare. Plenty of people lacked proper computers, even in industrialized nations. As a result, we looked at screens an average of 1.5 hours per day. That number in 2024 has ballooned to 7.5 hours every day.[38] Device addiction is so pronounced that *digital detox* has entered the zeitgeist.

As NYU professor Scott Galloway put it, "We live in a society where everyone fast-forwards to the end, believing we know what happened and why."[39] We've lost the ability to understand nuance—or even try. Even the noble concept of truth is dying on the vine. In fairness, it has never been more difficult to ascertain what's true.

We're Less Willing and Able to Determine Fact From Fiction

Bullshit, of course, is hardly a new advent. In the second half of the fifth century BCE, the Sophists, a group of for-hire vagabond rhetorical educators in Greece, taught their clients persuasion techniques to win arguments. Truth to them was an afterthought.[40] Their position angered Plato.

The philosopher took them to task in *Euthydemus*, one of his most famous Socratic dialogues, in 380 BCE.

Fast-forward a few millennia, give or take. At some point, software programmer Alberto Brandolini read Daniel Kahneman's epic book *Thinking Fast and Slow*. Inspired, he tweeted what has ultimately become known as the *bullshit asymmetry principle*. Brandolini's Law states that "the amount of energy needed to refute bullshit is an order of magnitude bigger than that needed to produce it."[41]

Brandolini's shrewd observation predated the arrival of today's crop of generative AI tools. Deepfakes, synthetic voices, and the like will only intensify and democratize misinformation and disinformation.

Stories Continue to Motivate Us—for Better and Worse

In 2016, Wiley Ink posted a one-page cartoon online titled "Science vs. Everything Else."* If you were concerned about the world, the sketch made you both laugh and cry. It showed two lines of people seeking two antithetical groups of answers:

- Simple but wrong.
- Complex but right.

You can guess which line was longer.

The cartoon illustrates what cognitive psychologists call the *narrative fallacy*. Since our inception as a species, we've relied upon stories to keep us alive. Remember that codified knowledge via books is a relatively recent advent. (Johannes Gutenberg only invented the printing press in 1436.)

In and of themselves, stories don't cause objective harm, but they simplify cause and effect. Many of the autocrats discussed in Chapter 9 aren't just telling stories that gloss over important details, though. They're fabricating the entire thing.

---

* See it yourself at https://tinyurl.com/the-cat-science.

Politicians Are Lying More Than Ever

In 2007, Bill Adair launched PolitiFact, a "fact-checking website that rates the accuracy of claims by elected officials and others on its Truth-O-Meter."[42] Writing for *The Atlantic* in October 2024, he laments today's sad state:

> When I launched PolitiFact in 2007, I thought we were going to raise the cost of lying. I didn't expect to change people's votes just by calling out candidates, but I was hopeful that our journalism would at least nudge them to be more truthful.
>
> I was wrong. More than 15 years of fact-checking has done little or nothing to stem the flow of lies. I underestimated the strength of the partisan media on both sides, particularly conservative outlets, which relentlessly smeared our work.[43]

Adair—perhaps naively—thought the threat of being caught demonstrably lying would prevent politicians from doing it in the first place. (See Figure 5.5 for a particularly blatant example.) It hasn't, and research has proved as much. The Oxford Internet Institute found in 2020 that social media manipulation by political actors is an "industrial scale problem."[44] What's more, "private firms are increasingly involved in manipulation campaigns."[45]

The Most Dangerous Man You've Never Heard of

Between November 2020 and the January 6 attack on the US Capitol, Donald Trump's campaign raised more than $250 million. Three of its four best fundraising days came after Trump *lost*. Their most lucrative pitch? Donate to the "Official Election Defense Fund" to overturn the stolen election.

There was just one problem: It was all a scam. No such fund existed. Trump's team knew he had legally lost, and they knew funds raised would flow to a leadership PAC Jared Kushner and others had created.* The campaign's own lawyer had investigated claims of election fraud and found no evidence. They all knew it was a lie, but it was generating *enormous* amounts of money.

The "Official Election Defense Fund" was one of many effective marketing tactics crafted by Gary Coby, founder of the digital agency Direct Persuasion and the peer-to-peer texting company Opn Sesame. Few people have even heard of these shadowy firms—by design. But don't let their lack of name recognition fool you. They helped secure Trump's 2016 victory and helped him amass his unprecedented war chest after his 2020 defeat.

Since 2016, Coby has emerged as a master of social manipulation. He pioneered aggressive fundraising tactics by blending traditional marketing strategies, peer-to-peer texting, legal loopholes, and an "act first, apologize later" approach. His methods evaded content moderators on social media platforms, allowing his team to spread misinformation to millions. Their fundraising appeals were sometimes so duplicitous that donors unwittingly contributed and then had to demand refunds.

While Coby blazed this trail, others have followed suit. Teams of writers now work in bullpens. They use sophisticated tactics in misinformation, marketing, and technology to throw red meat to their political base and manipulate them into donating.†

Fine, politicians are lying more, but why do their lies resonate so strongly with us?

---

* Save America, Trump's leadership political action committee, was founded on November 9, 2020, two days after the election results were announced. The money they raised has paid for expenses like travel, Melania's fashion stylist, presidential portraits, and more than $20 million in Trump's legal bills.

† *Red meat* was the actual term that Kevin Zambrano, former chief digital officer of the Republican National Committee, used during his interview with the January 6 committee.

THE CATALYSTS

People Are Angry

On March 6, 2020, Yale law professor Daniel Markovits appeared on *Amanpour & Company* to talk about his new book, *The Meritocracy Trap: How America's Foundational Myth Feeds Inequality, Dismantles the Middle Class, and Devours the Elite*.

In the interview, Markovits claims that American meritocracy is a sham that disenfranchises the middle class and allows the wealthy to preserve their privilege across generations. In his words:

> If you're told your own struggles are your fault and your inadequacy, then a demagogue who comes in and says, "No, no, no, the system is against you," is going to be extremely appealing. … What's happening in our politics now is that the anger of people who are excluded structurally, and then the economic injury is coupled with a moral insult—they're told it's their fault—are understandably frustrated and lashing out.*

I'll save the human race's most galling deficiency for last.

We're Followers—Even When Our Leaders Behave Immorally

Beginning in February 1963, the German-American historian and philosopher Hannah Arendt penned a series of articles in *The New Yorker*.[46] The reporting focused on the trial of German Nazi leader Adolf Eichmann. The key member of Hitler's Final Solution ordered untold numbers of innocent Jews to death in Nazi concentration camps.[47] Eichmann didn't singlehandedly send myriad people to gas chambers, though. He had plenty of help. Arendt wanted to know how so many ordinary people could carry out these atrocities.

Arendt's subsequent book, *Eichmann in Jerusalem: A Report on the Banality of Evil*, shed light on the unthinkable. Eichmann's minions weren't

---

* Watch the entire interview at https://tinyurl.com/the-cat-merit.

necessarily malignant; they were just following their superior's orders. As her book's subtitle suggests, evil was banal.

For obvious reasons, Jews across the world erupted in outrage—and they weren't the only skeptics of Arendt's journalism. Ordinary, civilized folks justifiably thought that, under similar circumstances, they would have responded differently if put in the same situation. Few of them knew, however, that one psychologist had already proved Arendt's central thesis. His study's results were still undergoing peer review. The journal article was published in 1963.[48]

In August 1961, Yale University psychologist Stanley Milgram conducted a series of experiments that now live in infamy.* Milgram effectively tricked participants into believing that they were administering electric shocks to a patient who needed to learn. The increasingly powerful shocks, of course, weren't real—and neither were the "learner's" ostensible cries for help.

When the true subjects resisted continuing the experiment, an authority figure told them to proceed. In the end:

> Milgram found that, after hearing the learner's first cries of pain at 150 volts, 82.5 percent of participants continued administering shocks; of those, 79 percent continued to the shock generator's end, at 450 volts.[49]

Dismiss the experiment as a controversial and unethical one-off if you like, but the finding is valid. In 1984, Dr. Jerry Burger at Santa Clara University got as close as ethically possible to Milgram's original parameters.

> People learning about Milgram's work often wonder whether results would be any different today. ... Many point to the lessons of the Holocaust and argue that there is greater societal awareness of the dangers of blind obedience. But what I found is the same situational factors that affected obedience in Milgram's experiments still operate today.[50]

---

* Check out the 2015 film *Experimenter*.

THE CATALYSTS

The verdict is unambiguous: It's in our nature to follow our leaders, even if they ask us to do the unspeakable. When you come to terms with that reality, you begin to understand the precarious state of many democracies.

Superior Weapons

Let's return for a moment to the start of this chapter. Big Tobacco's continued survival in 2025 in the US is nothing short of astonishing, especially when you consider the following:

- Including deaths from secondhand smoke, more than 480,000 people perish from smoking annually.[51]
- The economic costs of smoking in the US clock in at more than $300 billion a year.[52]
- Smokers typically pay a considerable tobacco surcharge on their health insurance premiums.[53]

The inimical health effects and addictive nature of cigarettes have been obvious for decades. Moreover, the US government severely restricted the industry's ability to advertise its products, even requiring them to affix highly visible—if diluted—warnings on them. And yet, tens of millions of Americans routinely continue to smoke themselves to death.

Now imagine today's largely *unregulated* companies, political action committees (PACs), rogue states, wealthy individuals,* and other organizations. They wield each of the following:

- **The weapons:** Extraordinary tools to influence others' opinions and behavior.
- **The ammunition:** Troves of highly personal user data that enable precise microtargeting.

And if that weren't enough, these entities can easily customize their messages in real time to maximize impact—and, by that, I mean *damage*.

---

* Leading up to the 2024 election, an Elon Musk–funded PAC microtargeted Muslims and Jews with diametrically opposing messages. See https://tinyurl.com/the-cat-elon.

SOCIAL ENGINEERING

As we saw in Chapter 8, that's precisely what Russia's KGB has attempted to accomplish for more than sixty years. Instead, Americans are *willingly* doing it for them.

Here's an apropos analogy: Bernays's clients in the 1920s and '30s used slingshots. By comparison, the tools available to organizations today to shape public opinion resemble the cheap, precise drones that militaries are using.[54] Big Tobacco, Big Oil, and Big Pharma remain alive and well, but Big Tech and Big Data dominate our era.

Unlimited, Remarkably Accurate Ammunition

Chapter 6 covered the power of Big Tech, but we've yet to delve too much into the shady world of data breaches. The stream has become incessant, and we've become immune to them.

Former Cisco Systems CEO John Chambers once quipped, "There are two types of companies: those that have been hacked, and those who don't know they have been hacked." I'll point out two of the largest hacks in recent memory.

Yahoo!

Between 2013 and 2016, Russian hackers attacked Yahoo! and obtained the names, email addresses, phone numbers, birthdates, passwords, calendars, and security questions of more than three billion users.[55] Making matters worse, the company's management initially lied about the scale of the breach. Further, it failed to disclose the incident to users. In the end, the US Securities and Exchange Commission fined the corporation $35 million.[56]

Equifax

At some point in 2017, the Chinese military allegedly hacked the systems of the consumer credit reporting agency.[57] The cybercriminals absconded with the highly sensitive personal data of more than 148 million Americans. Data included names, home addresses, phone numbers, birthdates, social security numbers, and driver's license numbers.

At first glance, the Equifax hack may seem inconsequential compared to the Yahoo! one. After all, the number of users affected in the latter is pittance compared to the former. The difference is the gravity of the information stolen in the Equifax incident. Changing your Yahoo! password or security questions is a nuisance. You can't say the same about the data that the Equifax hackers obtained: birthdates, driver's license numbers, and social security numbers. The US government makes this information difficult or impossible for people to change. Not surprisingly, criminals often use this critical data to commit identity theft.

The Status Quo: Our Nightmare Is a Bad Actor's Dream

Confining our discussion to illegal data breaches minimizes the problem. Corporations—especially private data brokers—hoover up gobs of data and then *lawfully* release or sell it.

We lack the space to explore all the dimensions of the problem, but mobile advertising is worth calling out here. As former *Washington Post* reporter Brian Krebs put it:

> Collectively, these stories expose how the broad availability of mobile advertising data has created a market in which virtually anyone can build a sophisticated spying apparatus capable of tracking the daily movements of hundreds of millions of people globally.[58]

Until countries pass meaningful data privacy laws and require greater investment in data security, the threat will only intensify.

Ramifications

Because of the reasons described in the previous section, social engineering is rampant. Chapter 14 will discuss containment strategies, but first we must understand its effects.

We Actively Harm Ourselves—and Others

In 2022, only four states in the US produced more coal than Kentucky.[59] The sedimentary rock is deeply embedded in its culture. For example, the local library in Greenville, Kentucky, in 2021 displayed a book called *Coal Mining Equipment at Work* by the American author Michael D. Davis. From his 2011 text:

> So many times we forget that Coal is what made this country what it is. Without it, we have no electricity, no cars, no trains, no buildings—nothing. It's the fundamental building block of everything we see and use in society.[60]

We can argue over the veracity of Davis's claims all day long. Less debatable, though, is whether fossil fuels have caused significant global warming and climate change that affects everyone, irrespective of location and political party.[61] The evidence is incontrovertible.

Try relaying that inconvenient truth to Kentuckians, though. Dr. Keith Mountain previously served as the chair of the Geography and Geosciences Department at the University of Louisville. Giving an interview in 2021, he explained:

> There is no ambiguity. Humans are a major cause of climate change. ... It isn't guesswork anymore. People in Kentucky aren't interested in the issue, so they don't care. They don't think of coal as a finite resource, he says, and the political structure reflects that ignorance. The challenge isn't in providing evidence anymore.[62]

This is the same type of motivated reasoning we discussed in Chapter 8. Making matters worse, politicians on the right have clouded the issue. They've made it acceptable for someone to identify as a *climate change denier*. Many have. Tens of millions of people vote against their self-interests—and those of their children.

The contagion is far bigger than climate change, and it spreads far beyond the US.

Worldwide, right-wing parties and populists have excelled at getting their constituents to shoot themselves in the foot—and then promptly reload. (See the discussion in Chapter 9 on Brexit.) As Great Britain nears the seventh anniversary of its historic vote to leave the EU, many Brits are suffering from "Bregret."[63] Similarly, on taxes, healthcare, minimum wage, and social security, the US Grand Old Party (GOP) has consistently tricked its own members into immolating themselves.[64]

The Death of Truth

Chapter 8 discussed several related ramifications of the status quo as it pertains to the erosion of institutional trust. (See the sections "A Widespread Inability to Distinguish Fact From Fiction" and "Amplification of Misinformation.")

Perhaps political strategist Stephen Bannon said it best: "Flood the zone with shit."[65] People won't know what to believe.

Ubiquitous Scams and Schemes

Thanks to sophisticated tools and troves of data, scammers are fishing with dynamite. It's easier than ever for them to manipulate their prey in all sorts of devious ways.[66] Recent advances in generative AI drastically increase their targets and payoffs.

Deepfakes

Just ask the finance worker at the engineering firm Arup who, in 2024, remitted $25 million upon request to the company's chief financial officer (CFO).[67] The only problem: Arup's CFO made no such request. The employee fell for a sophisticated deepfake.

Pig Butchering

It's common for farmers to intentionally overfeed their livestock. Doing so fattens up their animals before they go to slaughterhouses—and increases the animals' value.

Along these lines, Chinese criminals have invented *Sha Zu Pan*. The term—roughly translated to "killing pig game"—is:

> a scam named after the practice of farmers fattening hogs before slaughter—often starts with what appears to be a wrong-number text message. People who respond are lured into crypto investments. But the investments are fake, and once victims send enough funds, the scammers disappear. As far-fetched as it sounds, victims routinely lose hundreds of thousands or even millions of dollars. One Kansas banker was charged this month with embezzling $47.1 million from his bank as part of a pig-butchering scam.[68]

Researchers at the University of Texas at Austin have used blockchain tracing tools to determine the amount of money stolen from victims of pig butchering. The total from January 2020 to February 2024 exceeded $75 *billion*—far more than even experts had estimated.[69]

Run-of-the-Mill Scams

Finally, as I know all too well, old-school swindling hasn't gone anywhere.

A Stockholm Apartment: Debunking a Scamming Myth

In November 2024, I had the honor of speaking at the Singapore Fintech Festival. Along with four others, I spoke on a panel titled "Anatomy of a Scam." At one point, the five of us discussed the common misperception that only old, uneducated, unintelligent people get scammed. I understood the myth, but I knew from personal experience

> plenty of tech-savvy folks fell prey as well. To prove my point, I relayed the following story.
>
> In 2007 I was temporarily living in Stockholm, Sweden. I needed to find an apartment and began searching online ads. Once I found one that appealed to me, I sent my deposit via Western Union. I then waited to meet the landlord to pick up the keys. It turned out to be a scam.
>
> Two of the other panelists—both tech-savvy financial services types—admitted that they'd fallen victim to cons as well. That is, three of the five panelists had been duped.
>
> Is that 60 percent figure comparable to the global number? Unfortunately, we may never know. Blame victim shaming and underreporting. The lesson here is that we all need to be vigilant against today's egalitarian fraudsters.

Every Organization Is Embracing Tech and Data

Churches used to raise funds by passing around a basket during services. Some still do, but that quaint practice is changing. Many religious organizations are adopting a high-tech, analytics-oriented approach to filling their coffers. In some cases, they're even targeting the disabled.

On a since-retired 2023 press release on its website,[70] the Christian app company Gloo branded itself as:

> the leading technology platform dedicated to connecting the faith ecosystem and releasing its collective might, announced a new effort, the AI & the Church Initiative to empower the Church to responsibly navigate and engage the evolving landscape of artificial intelligence (AI).[71]

Yes, even churches recognize the power of technology, analytics, and AI—and not for benevolent purposes. Pastors and preachers aren't learning how to code on their own time. Rather, churches are receiving plenty of financial support from the powerful right-wing Koch brothers.*

Charles Kriel is a specialist advisor to UK Parliament on disinformation. In his words:

> Koch brothers–funded charity commissioned Cambridge Analytica, along with a software company called Gloo, to build a software platform that could be used by churches in order to target vulnerable people.[72]

This is appalling on two levels. First, targeting the weak and vulnerable is unconscionable—and anathema to the spirit of Jesus Christ. Second, Kriel is referring to the same Cambridge Analytica that illegally harvested a trove of Facebook user data to sway the 2016 US presidential election.†

Increased Market Volatility and Manipulation

Haley Welch, known more commonly as *Hawk Tua Girl*, is facing a backlash. On December 4, 2024, the American influencer launched her eponymous cryptocurrency. The HAWK digital coin "hit a $490m market cap shortly after it launched on Wednesday, before suddenly losing more than 95% of its value within hours."[73] Analysis of the coin's transaction history upon launch raised claims of fraud. The case is headed to the courts.[74]

None of this should surprise you. Thanks to smartphones and trading apps like Robinhood, people carry always-on casinos in their pockets. Add to that the fact that many are financially illiterate, and you've created a perfect storm for manipulation. (See Figure 1.4 in Chapter 1.)

---

* *Kochland: The Secret History of Koch Industries and Corporate Power in America* offers a unique look into the brothers' empire.
† Watch the documentary *People You May Know* at https://tinyurl.com/the-cat-camb.

Virtual Societal Warfare

The nonprofit organization RAND improves policy and decision-making through research and analysis. In October 2019, several of its employees collaborated on a book, *The Emerging Risk of Virtual Societal Warfare*.

They correctly identify the serious risks to peace that social engineering poses. From the text:

> Conflict will increasingly be waged between and among networks. State actors are likely to develop such networks to avoid attribution and strengthen their virtual societal warfare capabilities against retaliation. It will be much more difficult to understand, maintain an accurate portrait of, and hit back against a shadowy global network.[75]

The challenges facing governments, leaders, non-governmental organizations (NGOs), regulators, and policymakers have never been slight. But RAND's research indicates that they're about to become even harder to address.

Key Points

- The roots of social engineering date back more than a century.
- Big Tobacco was able to preserve its business using primitive tools in a highly regulated environment. That fact doesn't bode well for those who want to minimize the degree of negative social engineering and its pernicious effects today.
- Our failings and foibles as human beings are precisely what make social engineering so effective.
- Thanks to robust tools and an endless stream of available user data, scammers and hackers shoot fish in a barrel. The arrival of generative AI only makes their lives easier.

This concludes Part II. We now shift our focus to Part III and the book's final two chapters. Where are we headed, and how do we change directions?

PART III

THE NEW WORLD FINANCIAL ORDER

CHAPTER 13

THE CATALYSTS COLLIDE

A VOLATILE FINANCIAL WORLD ORDER IS RAPIDLY APPROACHING.

> "Chaos was the law of nature. Order was the dream of man."
>
> —*Henry Adams*

Part II examined each of the eight catalysts in relative isolation. I'll be the first to admit that my analyses barely scratched the surface. Plenty of scholars have written lengthy, incisive tomes about tech-nation states, the erosion of societal trust, and the like.

But to understand the future, we need to broaden our aperture. Specifically, what happens when we synthesize the catalysts? What does the new world financial order look like if we take a 360-degree view?

THE CATALYSTS

This chapter offers five educated predictions. Even if some of the following prognostications don't completely come to fruition, our world will look drastically different in the next five years.

Authoritarian Capitalism Overtakes Liberal Democracy

One need not be a history professor to recognize the precarious nature of democracy. In the twentieth century, the twin systems of democratic rule (politics) and market-based self-determination (economics) ruled the day. After WWII, undemocratic dictatorships represented the exception to the rule. As we saw in Part II, however, autocrats have been silently whittling away these ideologies—if not overtly attacking them altogether.

Sadly, right-wing despots are winning, and the new world financial order will reflect this staunch new reality.

What Comes After Democratic Rule

In his 2018 book, *Digital Demagogue: Authoritarian Capitalism in the Age of Trump and Twitter*, Christian Fuchs discusses *right-wing authoritarianism* (RWA). In a separate piece, he articulates its four main elements:

- Belief in the need for top-down leadership.
- Nationalism.
- The friend/enemy scheme.
- Militant patriarchy.[1]

If this sounds awfully close to 1930s fascism, you know your history.

A more commonly used term these days is *state* or *authoritarian capitalism*. As Kevin Rudd wrote in 2018 for *The New York Times*:

> As Western democracies look increasingly sick, other systems of governance are now on offer. Russian nationalism represents a departure from Western political, economic and diplomatic norms.

China has become increasingly confident in its own model, described as authoritarian or state capitalism. And its "Beijing consensus" is held up to the non-Western world as an example of a more effective form of national, and even international, governance.[2]

Are there technical differences between and among fascism, RWA, and authoritarian capitalism? Probably, but for us they're differences without distinctions; long, theoretical, and semantic discussion here isn't necessary for our purposes. It's essential, though, to underscore several points about today's brand of authoritarian capitalism.

First, the far right is exclusively driving the movement, and the left has been ineffective against it. Second, in Fuchs's words, authoritarian capitalism "serves the ideological purpose of distracting attention from the role of class structures and capitalism as foundations and causes of social problems."[3]

Put differently, the über-rich are actively deceiving the middle and lower classes to preserve profits. It's the ultimate red herring. If that means the end of true democratic rule, that's a price they're willing to let others pay.

Examining Brazil

It's instructive here to examine the rise of Jair Messias Bolsonaro. From 2019 to 2023, he served as the country's thirty-eighth president. How the retired military officer rose to power isn't a distinctly Brazilian story:

> As the appetite of the economic and political elites grows, the space for democracy around the world shrinks. Bolsonaro's Brazil is a case in point. The elites got fed up with all the redistribution, so they looked for a strongman to stop the profit rate from falling, discipline the poor and shift the focus of political debate from economic redistribution to the culture war. Same as in Hungary. The only difference is that the Brazilian left has found itself, and the voters have shunned the right-wing populist Bolsonaro. The same dynamic was behind the political success of Duterte, elected in the Philippines, on the other side of the world.[4]

THE CATALYSTS

Bolsonaro, Duterte, Trump, and Le Pen are hardly unique.

Commonalities

If you look at Bolsonaro in Brazil, Le Pen in France, Duterte in the Philippines, Orbán in Hungary, and Putin in Russia, you'll find remarkable consistencies. These autocrats rely upon the same seven basic tactics to obtain and preserve their power:

- Politicize independent institutions.
- Spread disinformation.
- Aggrandize executive power.
- Quash dissent.
- Scapegoat vulnerable communities.
- Corrupt elections.
- Stoke violence.[5]

Brazilian voters struck an essential victory for democracy by electing Luiz Inácio Lula da Silva in January 2023. In July 2023, a panel of judges barred Bolsonaro from running for office until 2030.[6]

Opportunism

Think of today's authoritarians as modern-day analogues to Mussolini and Hitler. Each demagogue reflects the same fundamental disease.

Globalization has exacerbated inequality. The gap between the haves and have-nots has angered the latter and forced the former to identify scapegoats. Thanks to social engineering, disillusioned voters will blame immigrants and trade agreements rather than their elected officials and capitalism itself. Polarization and bad leadership are weakening democracies from within.

The Post-Democracy World

To be sure, the events in Brazil served as encouraging news during grim times. Still, how many nation's leaders, judges, institutions, citizens, and voters will be able to withstand the constant and proficient assault of right-wing

THE CATALYSTS COLLIDE

tyrants and their media machines? (Recall the discussion in Chapter 12 on social engineering.)

Even worse, what if power-hungry autocrats benefited from the considerable financial support of hostile powers? Thanks to current US campaign finance laws, proving as much is difficult. Efforts to improve those laws face herculean opposition. In September 2022, US Republicans blocked the DISCLOSE Act. The legislation "would have required dark money* groups to reveal large donors."[7]

If you believe in democracy, it's difficult to be optimistic.

Extremists will continue to exploit cultural divides over immigration, identity politics, and other issues. Trump, Le Pen, and their ilk will continue to make the difficult but necessary work of building consensus even more so. Decisive authoritarians seem like effective alternatives to these thorny battles over complicated issues. Many voters—consciously or not—consider democracy ineffective compared to the singular vision of a decisive tyrant.

Democracies across the globe—especially those with leftist leadership voids—will continue struggling to deliver on economic and social promises. This battle will open the door for populist leaders all too willing to exploit longstanding grievances against elites and institutions. As a result, democracy will continue backsliding nearly everywhere—a sad reality that Trump's 2024 successful reelection bid only underscored. Think about it. A significant percentage of the American public reelected a convicted felon who facilitated an insurrection because his economic rhetoric was better than the opposition's. If authoritarian capitalism flourishes in the "shining city on a hill," what message does that send to the rest of the world?

---

* *Dark money* refers to "political spending meant to influence the decision of a voter, where the donor is not disclosed and the source of the money is unknown." See https://tinyurl.com/the-cat-dm for more information on this topic.

THE CATALYSTS

The US Dollar Loses Dominance

Chapter 3 covered how the US established its dollar as the world's reserve currency. By weaponizing its currency over the past eighty years, America has been able to achieve key economic and geopolitical goals. Since the mid-1990s, nearly every US Treasury secretary or head of the Federal Reserve has acted and lived by this mantra: A strong dollar is in America's interest.[8]

America needs to brace for impact. The dollar's run as the big kahuna will likely end in the not-too-distant future. Saleha Mohsin of *Bloomberg News* details the tenuous status quo of the USD in her seminal 2024 book, *Paper Soldiers: How the Weaponization of the Dollar Changed the World Order*. Indeed, the dollar's role and future are very much in question—to say nothing of America's status as the world's economic superpower.

The reasons for this coming tectonic shift are manifold. For starters is the US's profound political and economic dysfunction, discussed at length in Chapter 5. Any realistic examination of its affairs leads to a single, damning conclusion: The greatest threat to America's future is America itself. US volatility and dysfunction are hardly a secret. It's a matter of when—not if—America implodes. The sole remaining question is what other nations and regions intend to do about it.

Accelerating De-Dollarization Efforts

Many nations have seen the writing on the wall. For instance, on December 20, 2023, Russia and China announced "their intent to abandon the US dollar in their bilateral transactions."[9] The BRICS+ countries—some of which are hardly America's friends—are surely the most vocal about getting off the dollar. They're not, however, the only ones taking concrete steps to forge a new, far less USD-centric world financial order. Even America's nominal allies are getting in on the action.

The EU has taken decisive steps to reduce its level of dollar dominance. As but one example, consider Germany. In 2018, its leaders called for creating a new EU-based payment system that operates independently of the

THE CATALYSTS COLLIDE

US and the Society for Worldwide Interbank Financial Telecommunication (Swift).[10]

Nations' increasing efforts to wean themselves off the USD are noteworthy on several levels. First, they should surprise no one paying attention to world affairs. Second, these efforts collectively mark "a noteworthy development within the ongoing trend of de-dollarization."[11] How noteworthy?

Stephen Jen is the ex-Morgan Stanley currency guru famously known for coining *dollar smile theory*.* From a 2023 *Bloomberg* piece:

> The dollar is losing its reserve status at a faster pace than generally accepted as many analysts have failed to account for last year's wild exchange rate moves, according to Stephen Jen.
>
> "The greenback's share in global reserves slid last year at 10 times the average speed of the past two decades as a number of countries looked for alternatives after Russia's invasion of Ukraine triggered sanctions," Jen and his Eurizon SLJ Capital Ltd. colleague Joana Freire wrote in a note. "Adjusting for exchange rate movements, the dollar has lost about 11% of its market share since 2016 and double that amount since 2008," they said.
>
> "The dollar suffered a stunning collapse in 2022 in its market share as a reserve currency, presumably due to its muscular use of sanctions," Jen and Freire wrote.[12]

In a word, yikes.

Third, because countries are buying and holding fewer US dollars, they're investing in different asset classes.

You might reflexively think that the Chinese yuan stands to benefit the most, but that's not the case. Many major global financial institutions don't use it or accept it today to settle debts. The US dollar is far more universal,

---

* Here's the theory in a nutshell: "When the US economy significantly under- or out-performs the rest of its peers, the dollar tends to be strong and increase in value compared to other currencies." See https://tinyurl.com/the-cat-smile for more information and a graphic visual that says it all.

so don't expect China's national currency to become the leading reserve asset any time soon.

Where's the money going? The answer is a mix of old and new destinations.

The Resurgence of Gold

Reserve diversification is taking several traditional forms, including alternative national currencies or commodities—especially gold. The latter's price ballooned roughly 75 percent in the two years beginning in late 2022 before slightly retreating.[13] The simple reason: a surge in demand. Specifically, central banks from advanced economies have been upping their reserves of the stuff.

A World Gold Council survey released in June 2024 found that, in the prior year, "central banks added 1,037 tonnes of gold—the second highest annual purchase in history—following a record high of 1,082 tonnes in 2022."[14]

In fact, it would be foolish for their leaders *not* to explore viable financial alternatives to the USD. But why gold? The old standby has long served as a partial hedge against inflation and other economic cataclysms. Unlike the era marked by Bretton Woods, though, many other exciting options exist. And this brings us back to the third catalyst: financial disintermediation.

The Maturation of Digital Currencies

Startups hopped on the decentralized finance (DeFi) train in the early 2010s. And why not? Airbnb and VRBO disrupted hotels. Uber and Lyft blew up the taxi industry. Why wouldn't the same class of ambitious entrepreneurs do the same with money and payments? Sure, we saw high-profile debacles such as FTX, but what if these folks were onto something revolutionary, more efficient, and even necessary?

Government officials and CEOs of large financial institutions have asked themselves that question for the past decade. Crypto may be volatile, but its underlying technology is here to stay. Case in point: The price of Bitcoin topped $100,000 (USD) on December 5, 2024.[15]

Crypto and other digital currencies are making good on their fifteen-year-old promise: to provide alternative forms of value that facilitate global trade and cross-border payments. In doing so, they're also accelerating de-dollarization. As discussed in Chapter 7, many countries are actively developing cryptocurrency projects that will ultimately yield interoperable digital currencies—and sooner than many American policymakers and leaders would like.

Stablecoins

Much of the retail world uses dollar-backed stablecoins as an alternative to the international US dollar. But these are run by private companies, some of whom have opaque governance and reserve management practices. As of this writing, El Salvador-based Tether holds roughly 70 percent of the US dollar-backed stablecoin market.[16] It's also the eighteenth largest holder of US Treasury bills.[17] Despite its dominance, it operates sans formal regulation or supervision by an authoritative body.

Regulations and global principles are emerging around these cryptocurrencies designed to minimize price volatility. Common tenets include:

- Stablecoin issuances require explicit regulatory approval.
- Reserves must be liquid and stable, ensuring they can cover all issued stablecoins on a one-to-one basis.
- Stablecoin payment services must align with existing financial regulations.[18]

A common set of standards will undoubtedly expedite the introduction and use of stablecoins worldwide, though each regulator will likely include a preference for its own non-USD currency. America's continued failure to pass federal stablecoin legislation will create a dangerous situation: Other countries will shape regulations that could impact the stability and liquidity of the US treasury bill market.

THE CATALYSTS

Central Bank Digital Currencies

Chapter 7 also introduced CBDCs, a topic that clearly crossed the chasm at some point in late 2022. During that time, Google revealed that worldwide searches for the term exploded 769 percent above average levels and reached an all-time high. The same held true in both the US and the UK.[19]

These aren't just curious folks googling to kill time at work. CBDCs are happening. Consider this statistic from the Atlantic Council, an American think tank: "By the end of 2023, over 130 central banks representing 98 percent of global GDP will have initiated programs to develop central bank digital currencies (CBDCs)."[20]

> ### The Anti-Bretton Woods
>
> You'd think that the self-anointed greatest nation in the world would be leading the charge here. As of this writing, however, the likelihood of the US creating a CBDC to compete with a privatized digital dollar is low. A pernicious combination of social engineering and right-wing fearmongering has politicized what should have been an apolitical issue.
>
> America will find itself in a unique economic and political situation: The rest of the world will be discussing the development and implementation of a critical financial instrument while the US and its leaders struggle to find a seat at the table. Think of this as the antithesis of Bretton Woods.
>
> What if the US gets its act together in the next few years?
>
> Even in that unlikely event, America will start the marathon an hour after all the other runners have heard the starting gun. Bottom line: American CBDC inaction and foot-dragging will further weaken the USD.

THE CATALYSTS COLLIDE

The US Dollar's Place in the New World Financial Order

Grizzled US policymakers have seen this movie before. Many consider the threat of de-dollarization abstract and old hat. As Robert H. Wade of the London School of Economics and Political Science correctly observes:

> People have been forecasting the end of dollar hegemony for half a century and more, for reasons to do with the inherent difficulties for the US central bank to balance supplying enough dollars for global transactions and few enough dollars to sustain confidence in the value of the dollar.[21]

American Pollyannas—mainly on the right—are quick to dismiss the events discussed in this section. In the short term, they're right. The US dollar will, likely, remain the global reserve currency. That argument, however, largely misses the point. De-dollarization is not binary; there are degrees. (See Figure 3.3.)

We've reached the beginning of the end of the US dollar's global dominance. As former Congresswoman Stephanie Murphy said at the 2023 National Security and Digital Assets Seminar hosted by Georgetown Law's Institute of International Economic Law, "If our friends are working hard to get off the US dollar, imagine how hard our foes are working."

Even if Kamala Harris had won the 2024 election, nations wouldn't have immediately curtailed their de-dollarization efforts. "Most central banks said they expected the US dollar's share in global reserves to fall in the next five years."[22]

But there's no question that Trump's victory—and the volatility he's already creating—will increase de-dollarization efforts. His proposed tariffs, tax cuts, and other inflationary and protectionist policies will do irreparable damage to the USD precisely when legitimate alternatives are flourishing.[23] Trump's win only emboldens nations to increase their efforts around alternative and digital currencies.

The Global Financial System Forks

Nations have always disagreed on core economic, political, and social issues. Countless millions have died in subsequent conflicts. Over the past eighty years, though, global mechanisms existed to *attempt* to peacefully resolve conflicts before war erupted. No, given their charters, NATO, the UN, the World Bank, and the IMF haven't been perfect—not that any institution could be. Still, much of the world has greatly benefited from their existence, even if the benefits have been distributed disproportionately.

These institutions will face even greater difficulties in resolving regional and global conflicts. Solving global issues is about to become exponentially harder for one simple reason: The current global financial system will soon splinter or fork.*

One System Becomes Many: The Rise of Regional Blocks

Increased nationalism and geopolitical tensions will keep fragmenting trade blocks and alliances. More countries will prioritize their own policies over international collaboration. New trade blocks will invariably form around nationalist agendas and common enemies—most likely, the US under an erratic, self-interested, and protectionist Trump.

More nations will engage in friendshoring: the "growing trade practice where supply chain networks are focused on countries regarded as political and economic allies."[24]

Moreover, as we saw in Chapter 8, trust in IMF, the World Bank, and other multilateral institutions is rapidly diminishing. Expect financial volatility to increase.

In place of a single, global financial system, expect a group of smaller, localized ones. Countries and regions looking to minimize their exposure to the USD will create their own financial systems.

---

* *Forking* refers to a longstanding practice in the software development world. When coders disagree on the direction of a project, they create a new version of it and a basic set of rules.

As for when, that day isn't far off. Viable alternatives to Swift already exist. Expect them to proliferate.

Unpacking BRICS+

Chapter 9 introduced the genesis of the BRICS+ nations. Technically speaking, it's not a region. Rather, it's a loose amalgamation of countries with ostensibly overlapping economic interests. BRICS+ is poised to become a crucial geopolitical block in the new world financial order. Its collective population growth, economic strength, and rising geopolitical influence all but guarantee as much.

Although they may not agree on every issue, they share one fundamental priority: ensuring their country's key role in the new multipolar world. On an individual level, each is making the most of America's decline in its own unique way. Let's briefly examine three of its charter members.

China

On many levels, the Red Dragon is filling the power vacuum that a more isolationist US is creating. China is laying down the gauntlet, both directly and subtly challenging US hegemony. Consider its massive economic and diplomatic initiative, named the *Belt and Road Initiative* (BRI):

> China is expected to spend over $1 trillion—seven times the size of the Marshall Plan in real dollars. This initiative seeks to build new markets for Chinese goods and increase China's economic connectivity in 130 countries around the world, encompassing more than 60% of the world's population and one-third of global GDP—including 40 out of 54 African countries.[25]

Here's a partial breakdown of Chinese funds dispersed as of 2021:

- **Latin America:** $150 billion since 2005.
- **Africa:** A 520 percent increase in the past fifteen years.
- **Asia:** $48 billion in diplomacy and development.[26]

THE CATALYSTS

These investments often serve multiple purposes, including infrastructure development and diplomatic leverage—and they're paying major dividends. The Regional Comprehensive Economic Partnership (RCEP) is the world's largest free trade agreement; it positions Asia as a central player in global trade while excluding the US. Of note is the Digital Silk Road initiative. This key part of the BRI promotes Chinese technology across the globe. At the same time, it sets international standards in artificial intelligence, telecommunications, and other emerging technologies.[27] It's abundantly clear that China is attempting to build bridges with other nations while a Trump-led US is burning them. Those wounds won't heal when—or if—he eventually leaves office for good.

Brazil

Rather than choose sides between the present and the future, Latin America's largest economy is straddling both sides of the fence. It's concurrently trying to placate the world's *current* economic superpower (America) while playing nice with the country perhaps best positioned to supplant it (China).[28] In short, its relationships are complicated.

China is justifiably interested in Brazil's considerable natural resources—as are many others. In 2023, Brazil led the world in exports of seven food commodities, including soybeans, corn, coffee, sugar, beef, and chicken.[29] Brazil *already* occupies a critical role in the global food supply. Soon, expect that role to expand. What's more, it's poised to become a significant oil exporter. In 2024, the "value of Brazilian crude exports rose 5% to $44.8 billion in 2024, the first time oil eclipsed all other foreign sales for Latin America's biggest economy."[30]

The US may want Brazil to be politically and ideologically monogamous, but Brazil clearly wants to see other people. Trump's volatility only intensifies Brazil's need to establish some distance.

India

As US-China trade tensions have increased, India's leaders have stepped up to the plate to strike trade deals. In the 2023 fiscal year, Apple produced $14 billion worth of iPhones in the country.[31] Apple now makes one-seventh of its iPhones in India—a fraction that doubled from the previous fiscal year.

Like Brazil, India is attempting to please multiple masters with antithetical goals: America, Russia, and China. Whether the world's most populous nation can pull off this herculean feat remains to be seen. Less uncertain, though, is India's ability to create remarkably useful financial technologies, specifically around payments.

Launched in April 2016, India's Unified Payments Interface (UPI) has grown quickly and remarkably. The revolutionary digital payment system:

- Processed more than nine billion transactions in May 2023 alone.
- Handled 80 percent of India's digital payments.
- Drastically improved India's level of financial inclusion by 300 million people.
- Saved the Indian economy approximately $67 billion as of 2023.[32]

These results have piqued the interest of other nations looking to modernize their financial rails. More broadly, India is looking to engage other countries in what some have called *technological diplomacy*:

> India's ambition to export UPI to other countries represents a strategic move to enhance its positioning as a trusted development partner, particularly in digital finance. The success of UPI domestically has sparked interest from several countries, say, Japan, UAE, France and now Maldives, as part of their pursuit for financial modernization. By promoting UPI globally, India is engaging in technological diplomacy. Successfully implementing UPI in other markets could establish India as a leader in providing scalable and secure digital payment solutions.[33]

UPI faces many challenges in other countries,* but the signal the country is sending to the rest of the world is incontrovertible: We can help you modernize how your citizens and institutions move money.

The Endgame

The BRICS+ countries are clearly capitalizing on America's decline and filling the power vacuum. In the new world financial order, other regional blocks will emerge. No one knows when or where, but it's a good bet that they'll use digital currencies. Parallel financial systems will eventually enable all countries to avoid the USD, Swift, and other financial relics of the twentieth century.

Some of these blocks will attempt to weed out dirty money; others won't. As it stands now, the largely opaque traditional financial system is a mix of clean and illicit funds. The more transparent digital financial system will move from its current glass house toward frosted glass. Digital currencies will always provide more risk monitoring visibility than siloed traditional finance, resulting in a bifurcated system. The issue will be which jurisdictions move toward privacy while balancing transparency with strong laws. These benign, law-abiding regimes will attract institutional investors. On the other hand, they'll innovate more slowly to meet regulatory and compliance requirements.

Privacy-focused, laissez-faire hubs will innovate first and ask questions later. The tradeoff, however, is fundamentally the same: A lack of regulatory scrutiny will result in reputational risk and a morass of legal issues. Individuals, corporations, groups, and even entire nations will take advantage of more favorable laws in Jurisdiction A and circumvent less favorable regulations in Jurisdiction B. (We call this practice *jurisdictional arbitrage*.)

What will the US be able to do about the future circumstances? Very little, if anything.

---

* Privacy, security, and integration with other nations' traditional payment systems lie at the top of the list.

THE CATALYSTS COLLIDE

Dangerous Criminals Operate Freely at Home and Abroad

Say that you put Chapters 5, 7, 11, and 12 in a microwave oven and cooked them for ten minutes. What would you create? Or what would happen if you mixed a cocktail with equal parts US dysfunction, DeFi, forces preventing transparency, and social engineering?

Remove the metaphors from these hypothetical questions, and you'd wind up with arguably the most disturbing aspect of the new world financial order: bad actors, terrorists, and criminals (cyber and old-school) operating with near impunity.

Ineffective Legislative Responses to Clear and Present Dangers

We saw in Chapter 11 how American judges are invalidating commonsense anti-crime legislation in the name of privacy. (The practice is eerily redolent of the National Rifle Association's attack on gun reform to protect the Second Amendment in the US.) Thanks to the result of the 2024 congressional and presidential elections, we should expect fewer national bills on this key subject. Republicans are running the table—and plenty of interested cryptocurrency companies are lining their coffers to ensure as much.

Pay to Play: How Corporations Buy a Seat at the Table

The nonprofit watchdog Public Citizen has long analyzed US federal election data. In August 2024, the group released a report of all contributions of $5,000 or more by for-profit corporations to super PACs and hybrid PACs between 2010 and June 30, 2024.

Its findings were extraordinary. Public Citizen found that, "after its 2024 spending spree, crypto industry cash is poised to account for a staggering 15 percent of all known corporate contributions made since the Supreme Court's 2010 ruling in *Citizens United*."[34] (That crucial US decision "further tilted political influence toward wealthy donors and corporations."[35])

THE CATALYSTS

Here are a few more eye-popping stats from its analysis:

- As of August 2024, crypto corporations represented "by far the dominant corporate political spenders in 2024 as nearly half (44%) of all corporate money contributed during this year's elections ($274 million so far) came from crypto backers."
- Crypto corporations spent $119 million directly influencing federal elections.
- 92 percent of the corporate crypto spending is from 2024.[36]

Ask yourself this question: After being mistreated by Democrats for four years, would crypto companies spend this much money to buy politicians intent on regulating or deregulating them? The answer is obvious. The crypto industry will be able to innovate and release products with less government interference, but at what cost? A more relaxed regulatory environment will be a field day for bad actors.

The season of influence is perpetual; it's not confined to elections.

Buying Off Politicians: The Cost of Doing Business

Chapter 8 covered the deleterious effects that social media corporations inflict upon the world. (See "The Profit Motive.") Criminals systemically carry out illicit activity on today's platforms. These companies won't address the problem unless legislators and regulators compel them to do so.

And let's not forget other societal ills, such as how Facebook routinely causes mental health issues among minors. The company's internal research has found as much. Of course, Meta's leadership subsequently disputed those results in front of the US Congress in 2021.[37] Other social issues include cyberbullying and sextortion.[38] Untold minors consider self-harm and suicide as a direct consequence. Horrifically, many succeed.

None of this should be news. The time for action has long passed. Against this backdrop, in his 2023 State of the Union Address, Biden urged Congress to pass legislation to protect kids online. The resulting proposal, the Kids Online Safety Act (KOSA), "set[s] out requirements to protect minors from online harms."³⁹ The law would create a *duty of care*: "a legal term that requires companies to take reasonable steps to prevent harm—for online platforms minors will likely use."⁴⁰

The bipartisan bill appeared to be headed for Biden's desk for signature. Finally, Facebook (and its related properties), Snap, Twitter/X, and others would be legally obligated to protect children.

Passage seemed inevitable, and then Mark Zuckerberg and his lieutenants used a tried-and-true tactic to successfully stall it. On December 4, 2024, Meta announced it would build a $10 billion data center in northeast Louisiana—not precisely a hotbed of tech expertise.⁴¹ That location was no accident. Guess where US House Speaker Mike Johnson and House Majority Leader Steve Scalise hail from? When asked about the matter, Johnson's spokeswoman, Athina Lawson, had the unmitigated gall to "dismi[ss] any connection between the project and the legislation's current status."⁴² She and her boss would have you believe that the two events are entirely disconnected.

In America today, you just can't make this stuff up.

Whether KOSA or a diluted alternative ultimately passes in the US is moot. Much like Big Tobacco, crypto and Big Tech lobbyists have figured out how to effectively kneecap legislation that objectively benefits society. The playbook is easy to copy. Expect this pattern to continue in the world's remaining democracies—especially in the US. Bad actors are the clear winners at the expense of society at large.

Widespread Evasion of US Sanctions Will Metastasize

It's time for another thought experiment.

Imagine a fictitious place today called Society X whose citizens are unified in their desire to catch bad actors. Its elected officials pass the strictest possible laws and penalties for breaking them. Regulatory and enforcement bodies possess the appropriate resources to do their jobs. The courts in Society X consistently back these efforts and only intervene in the rare event of clear privacy violations.

THE CATALYSTS

Would crime exist in this mystical place?

Absolutely, and one need only look at Singapore for the proof. Chapter 11 covered Tornado Cash. (See the section "DeFi, Crypto, and Courts Can Enable the Untraceable Transfer of Funds.") These dangerous, wholly private cryptocurrency mixers would pose challenges to any government serious about anti-money laundering (AML) and countering the financing of terrorism (CFT). Society X may do better than most, but plenty of malfeasance will still occur. Criminals will still get away with their crimes and be able to launder their money through the global financial system.

Now imagine the US in 2025—a far cry from Society X. A twice-impeached leader convicted of thirty-four felonies who incited an insurrection doesn't exactly scream *crime fighting and safety*. Republicans and courts will no doubt continue to weaken AML/CFT and other financial crime laws, making it easier to evade sanctions and facilitate illicit finance.

It's painfully evident that US policymakers are unwilling to give regulators and enforcement officials the tools they need to do their jobs. In fact, under the second Trump administration, they're firing career enforcement officials en masse.[43]

As for the legal system, US courts give negligible sentences to perpetrators of financial crime, and few mandatory minimums exist for white-collar crime. As a direct result, bad actors rarely face severe consequences for their deeds. Undeterred, they'll keep using Big Tech's tools to manipulate victims at scale and steal generational wealth that takes lives.

Bad actors will operate with near impunity. Countries like Russia, North Korea, and Iran will continue to conduct business entirely outside of the US financial system. As a result, America's soft power will dramatically decline, if not disappear altogether. Lest you dismiss this scenario as remote or hypothetical, think again.

Researching this book, I interviewed Juan Carlos Zarate, author of *Treasury's War: The Unleashing of a New Era of Financial Warfare*. In his words:

> I'm most worried about the systemic implications of digital currencies creating networks and payment platforms that circumvent the entirety of the US traditional financial system. This reduces America's ability to leverage the tools of exclusion. If those methods scale, it will give rogue actors access to cross-border payment networks, enabling them to move money across borders they would otherwise lack.[44]

What happens when sanctions lose all their deterrence? US military strength becomes its sole source of power. If America's only answer to another country's aggression or human rights violations is military force, look out. That's not a world anyone wants to live in.

The Flight to Safety, Sanity, and Quality of Life

Ray Dalio cofounded Bridgewater Associates in 1975. Today, it's one of the world's largest hedge funds. Dalio formally left the firm at the end of 2021 as part of an anticipated succession plan,[45] but he's stayed productive since. As of this writing, his net worth clocks in at roughly $16 billion USD.

Dalio's moves since departing speak volumes about his thoughts on the new world financial order. For instance, he's worked extensively on a lucrative investment venture in Abu Dhabi, a deal complicated by his Bridgewater departure.[46] Then, in May 2024, Dalio joined a burgeoning group of billionaires purchasing historic Singaporean houses.[47]

We saw in Chapter 10 that innovation hubs are blooming outside of the US—a trend that will only intensify. This is the fifth and final characteristic of the new world financial order.

Better Options

All jurisdictions need to strike a balance between:
- Regulatory oversight and technological innovation.
- Liberty with the punishment necessary to deter crime and ensure compliance with the rule of law.

As discussed in the previous section, America's equilibrium is out of whack. As such, expect a flight to safety—and not just among billionaires.

Some nations' criminal justice systems do deter crime. The United Arab Emirates (UAE) and the Republic of Singapore are just two examples. (In 2021, *The Economist* ranked Singapore as the third safest city in the world.[48]) As a result, people can routinely lay their phones down in public. By way of contrast, theft rings in Spain operate brazenly. Make no mistake: Harsh criminal penalties effectively deter crime.

Nations that mete out real sentences stand to benefit from American inaction in the face of formidable threats.

The Impending US Debt Bomb and Its Inevitable Fallout

As we saw in Chapter 5, America's debt crisis is at a breaking point. (See Figures 5.3 and 5.4, respectively.) America won't establish sufficient fiscal constraints to address its crippling debt. The dominos will continue to fall:

- Global investors will sour on US markets and the volatile, dysfunctional US government.
- The US will relinquish its role as the global leader in financial innovation to other, more sustainable, less toxic nations.
- Emerging markets with lower debt burdens will attract investment by offering more favorable regulatory environments for blockchain tech and DeFi.

If the US attempts to curb its debt by slashing social services, expect considerable civil unrest. Add to that an administration outwardly hostile to legal immigration, and don't expect talented students and entrepreneurs to set up shop here. Ditto for Dalio and other deep-pocketed investors.

THE CATALYSTS COLLIDE

Lessons From Frogs

For several reasons, frogs typically sit on lily pads and routinely hop to different ones.* A temperature change might cause one of the amphibians to suddenly, instinctively hop from one pad to another.

In the aftermath of the 2024 election, and given the immediate volatility that ensued, many Americans have become decidedly froglike. They're hoping for the best but preparing for the worst. (Chapter 11 discussed the rise of digital nomads, a trend I'm intimately familiar with.)

Finally, if you'll have to live with authoritarian capitalism anyway, why not move to the UAE, Singapore, or another country or region? Benefits include an exponentially better quality of life, less crime, and a healthcare system that doesn't involve medical bankruptcy.

In an era of remote work from home (WFH), global communication platforms, and digital currencies, expect more and more citizens to ask themselves this question in the new world financial order.

Table 13.1 briefly compares the current world financial order to the emerging one.

Table 13.1: Summary of New World Financial Order

Dimension	Current WFO	New WFO
Ability of Small Investors to Move Financial Markets	Minimal	Significant
Ability to Circumvent US Sanctions	Difficult	Much easier
AI	Limited	Extensive
Default Mode	Relatively stable	Relatively unstable
Finance	Highly centralized	Much less centralized in certain spots

---

* See https://tinyurl.com/the-cat-frogs for more than you ever wanted to know about the subject.

Dimension	Current WFO	New WFO
Innovation Hubs	Primarily US-driven	Less US-driven; EMEA, APAC
International Trust	Relatively high	Rapidly declining
Media	Centralized and expert-driven	Decentralized and influencer-driven
Networks	Limited, local, and controllable	International, powerful, and uncontrollable
Role of the US Dollar	Critical	Important

Chapter 14, our last, offers some guiding principles and policy recommendations designed to maximize the opportunities in the new world financial order and minimize its considerable perils.

Key Points

- Authoritarian capitalism is poised to overtake many liberal democracies. The former may sadly become the norm.
- Persistent US economic and political dysfunction will continue undermining confidence in the dollar as the world's reserve currency. De-dollarization is well underway, and its consequences will be profound.
- A group of smaller, localized financial systems will replace today's US-centric financial world order.
- The US is about to enter an era of pervasive, unprecedented social engineering. The arrival of powerful generative AI tools makes a terrifying situation even more pronounced.
- Singapore, the UAE, and other regions and nations will become highly desirable living and working destinations.

CHAPTER 14

PRINCIPLES AND POLICIES

DESPITE THE CHANGES, NATIONS CAN THRIVE IN THE NEW WORLD FINANCIAL ORDER.

> "The most difficult thing is the decision to act; the rest is merely tenacity."
>
> —*Amelia Earhart*

I began this book by describing the horrific events leading up to January 6, 2021. Historians will rightfully view that day as America's tipping point. After decades of profound political dysfunction, the US finally—and permanently—fractured. The results of the 2024 presidential election removed any lingering doubt: America's cancer has metastasized. No single policy or leader can save it; its two parties are too broken to try.

At this point, it's imperative to ask a few big, hairy questions:

- Should we blithely accept the fact that the catalysts will run roughshod over their governments, elected officials, and enforcement officials?
- In other words, is it possible to slow down the catalysts and even rein them in?

The short answer to the last query is a resounding yes. The accelerating forces I've described in this book are certainly formidable. Rest assured, though: Policymakers, government officials, and regulators aren't powerless—and neither are the people they represent. Containment is the greatest challenge, but where do we begin?

This final chapter offers first principles and specific policy recommendations nations should adopt *before* the new world financial order arrives in earnest. Yes, it's still evolving, but the biggest mistake is waiting for all the catalysts to play out. Per the oft-quoted axiom, "The best time to plant a tree was thirty years ago, and the second best time to plant a tree is now."

Taking a Step Back

Before continuing, we need to cover some foundational concepts in political science.

Revisiting the Social Contract

Count Thomas Hobbes, John Locke, and Jean-Jacques Rousseau among the deep thinkers who discussed the idea of a *social contract* centuries ago. In political philosophy, it is:

> an actual or hypothetical agreement between the governed and their rulers, or among the governed themselves, defining the rights and duties of each party. This concept suggests that individuals, originally living in a state of nature characterized by freedom and equality,

consent to form a society and establish a government to ensure order and protect their rights.[1]

A great deal has changed since those influential philosophers posited their lofty ideas. In the new world financial order, we need to revisit the social contract. The following principles and recommendations promote a safe and decent society—a true commonwealth.

No perfect political or economic system has ever existed. It never will. Any type of structure has winners and losers. Capitalism and democracy—the dominant systems of the twentieth century—are no exceptions to this law.

What Are We Willing to Accept?

Accepting this reality, however, doesn't necessitate resigning ourselves to staggering wealth inequality. We need not tolerate rampant crime, the erosion of trust, and unaccountable tech nation-states. We shouldn't blindly adhere to authoritarian rule. These outcomes aren't given. As human beings and societies, we possess agency: the ability to make choices.

Policymakers, regulators, elected leaders, and enforcement officials are extensions of that agency. Not only can they take steps to minimize the catalysts' adverse effects—they must. More than that, though, in every nation, the governed must demand that their leaders fulfill their social contracts.

As we saw in Part II, confronting *any* of the catalysts isn't easy, much less all of them. The force of any one of them is formidable. Put together, they may seem unstoppable—destined to decimate everything in their path and leave a trail of casualties in their wake.

Defining Our Terms

At least in democracies, legislative bodies pass laws that regulators enforce—with varying degrees of success. For instance, in the US, physically attacking another without provocation is illegal. Do it and, all else being equal, you'll wind up in jail.

By contrast, governments establish overarching guidelines or guidance designed to achieve specific objectives, or policies. Non-governmental organizations (NGOs) do the same. As of this writing, the UN's stated policies include protecting human rights and delivering humanitarian aid.[2]

Compared to laws, policies tend to be broader in scope. Statutes need to precisely define what constitutes illegal behavior. In the previous example, playfully tapping someone on the shoulder is a far cry from slapping them across the face. Returning to the UN, its member nations may disagree on specifics, including how and when to protect human rights and deliver humanitarian aid. Still, all parties are theoretically on board with those specific policy goals.

The Need for Principle-Based Policies

Rules complicate matters—and make lawyers rich. Policies that rely on a gaggle of complicated rules can be harder to enforce. For this reason, abiding by overarching principles is often a more effective course of action. Dov Seidman expertly argues as much in his book *How: Why How We Do Anything Means Everything*.

Regulators and policymakers often find the idea of a principle-based regulation attractive for its "malleability and in the vision it evokes."[3] The lack of über-specific language is a feature, not a bug:

> Principles based regulation uses high-level, general statements often containing both explanations of the intent behind the principle and qualitative rather than quantitative terms ("fair", "reasonable"). Principles are designed to be applicable across a wide range of circumstances and as used by regulators today often focus on outcomes, rather than inputs.[4]

PRINCIPLES AND POLICIES

As an aside, Canada's Charter* has served as a model for other countries' constitutions precisely because:

> The way it safeguards fundamental freedoms is flexible, in comparison to the somewhat more rigid US guarantees. For starters, it directs courts to interpret any law that might infringe on rights in a way that allows limits "justified in a free and democratic society."[5]

Some of the principles in this chapter may appear so obvious that explicitly stating them here may seem superfluous. I disagree. Doing so is essential for two reasons:

- It reminds decision-makers of overarching goals.
- It increases the odds of true alignment. If you and I can't agree on core principles, what are our odds of achieving specific policy objectives?

With the requisite background out of the way, we can now turn to this chapter's specific principles and the policy recommendations that will enable their achievement.

I've grouped them into natural categories, but these buckets are neither distinct nor comprehensive. What's more, following them won't guarantee permanent economic prosperity in perpetuity. Instead, think of them as essential tenets necessary to confront the catalysts and flourish in the new world financial order.

---

* Canada's Charter refers specifically to the Canadian Charter of Rights and Freedoms, part of the larger Constitution of Canada.

The Freedom of Speech

Let's begin by addressing a key cause of several catalysts: the freedom of speech. To be sure, it's been a thorny issue since time immemorial. The days of the newspaper and snail mail, however, have long passed.

The rampant spread of lies is eroding institutional trust, causing people to vote against their self-interests, polarizing society, and obliterating the very notion of truth. Even more galling, as we saw in Chapter 6, Big Tech and its leaders have been effectively deciding many critical free-speech issues on their own for at least a decade. (See the section "Public No More: The Privatization of Government Responsibilities.")

First Principles

The status quo in many nations is simply untenable. It requires a reset.

Even in a Democracy, the Freedom of Speech Should Not Be Absolute

Elon Musk has frequently proclaimed to be a "free speech absolutist." He's anything but. Many of his decisions since acquiring Twitter—now rebranded as X—reflect his utter hypocrisy on the subject.[6] Musk's words belie his actions. He wants anyone to be able to say and tweet anything unless those words affect one of his many businesses or attack him personally. At some level, even he recognizes that reasonable limits on speech should exist. Courts have historically agreed, balancing freedom of speech with public safety, national security, and other societal needs.

Elected Officials Should Determine Public Policy

Say for a moment that Musk's viewpoint on freedom of speech was universally correct. The eccentric multibillionaire somehow crafted the perfect policy about what all earthlings could say and how they could say it. There's a larger question: Should Musk, Mark Zuckerberg, and other unelected business leaders be able to determine important policy matters independently?

The answer is no.

PRINCIPLES AND POLICIES

Preventing the Spread of Misinformation and Disinformation Is Paramount

Using artificial intelligence on your smartphone to remove an innocent passerby from an otherwise perfect photo of your friends is one thing. Routinely promoting fake news and lies is quite another. The latter presents a clear and present danger to countries around the world.

Solutions and Recommendations

The following policy recommendations won't magically cure all abuses of free speech, but they represent a good start.

Strengthen Defamation Laws Worldwide

As I wrote in the introduction, after the 2020 US election, then-President Trump repeatedly made false claims about the legitimacy of Joe Biden's victory. He was hardly alone. One America News Network (OAN) and Fox News were two of the largest media organizations all too willing to spread his lies and conspiracy theories.

These weren't just cries of, "This isn't fair." Rather, the attacks targeted voting equipment companies, including Dominion Voting Systems (DVS) and Smartmatic. Each enterprise suffered irreparable reputational damage as a direct result.

Ultimately, both had to pay large financial settlements to resolve their lawsuits. In the case of DVS, Fox News was determined to avoid apologizing on air for its employees' actions.[7] To that end, it ponied up a whopping $787 million to settle the defamation case.[8] On an individual level, a court ordered right-wing media personality Alex Jones to pay $1.5 billion in damages to the families of Sandy Hook shooting victims in 2022, rendering him nearly bankrupt.

Except for criminal perjury cases, prison may not represent a viable option for serial fabricators. Significantly strengthen the laws and increase the financial penalties for their prevarications, though, and maybe they'll think twice about spreading falsehoods that irrevocably damage the fabric of society.

Along these lines, governments—especially those outside of the US—need to hold Big Tech companies liable for the behavior that their platforms allow and even promote via their algorithms. Recall from Chapter 4 how, in the US, Section 230 of the Communications Decency Act shields companies and their employees from any civil or criminal prosecution. That law is unlikely to change anytime soon. However, if other countries enacted laws holding tech platforms liable, the Brussels Effect* would make social networks less toxic. Evidence that it will work? In January 2025, Mark Zuckerberg whined that Trump should intervene to prevent the EU from reining in Meta.[9] Hopefully, the EU won't remain alone in passing laws that try to save humanity from Big Tech.

Prevent Bad Actors From Using the Legal System as a Cudgel

All of us make honest mistakes and occasionally shade the truth. No one is suggesting that that behavior warrants severe punishment. But promulgating lies on the scale of Trump, OAN, Fox, and Alex Jones is an entirely different beast.

Allow me to put on my lawyer hat for a moment and define a specific legal term. A *cause of action* is:

> a set of predefined factual elements that allow for a legal remedy. The factual elements needed for a specific cause of action can come from a constitution, statute, judicial precedent, or administrative regulation.[10]

Without a cause of action in a defamation case in the US, a plaintiff's case can't proceed. In the US, "To make out a claim for defamation, the

---

* This is the ability of the European Union, the world's largest single market, to pass regulations that influence global standards and policies. For more on this subject, see Anu Bradford's 2020 book, *The Brussels Effect: How the European Union Rules the World*.

statement at issue must be false."¹¹ Sadly, those realities don't stop people and organizations with means from blatantly abusing the legal system.

Consider the following story:

> Back in 2006, when Donald Trump was known as a media personality, not a politician, Trump filed a defamation lawsuit against *New York Times* reporter Timothy O'Brien over O'Brien's claim that Trump was not a billionaire. Trump ultimately lost the case.
>
> When asked about the lawsuit years later, Trump said, "I spent a couple of bucks on legal fees, and they spent a whole lot more," Trump said. "I did it to make his life miserable, which I'm happy about." That kind of legal action, intended to harass or intimidate, rather than uphold a legal principle, is so common, it has a name: "strategic lawsuit against public participation," or "SLAPP."¹²

In February 2024, the European Parliament adopted Daphne's Law, an anti-SLAPP directive. Its name emanates from Daphne Caruana Galiza, a Maltese investigative journalist who faced forty-eight lawsuits when two brothers assassinated her in 2017.¹³ The directive gives the EU member states two years to adopt their own Anti-SLAPP laws.

Journalists should spend their time breaking stories of regional and national import, not defending themselves against frivolous lawsuits. The fact that their employers must allocate funds to defend them is absurd and downright horrifying. Governments should take immediate measures to prevent this type of activity—and enact stiff penalties for those who attempt to intimidate and silence reporters for doing their jobs.

Combat Misinformation and Disinformation at an Early Age

In October 2022, the Open Society Institute in Sofia, Bulgaria, released its latest survey on resilience against misinformation.¹⁴ For the fifth consecutive time, Finland ranked first out of forty-one European nations.* As Jenny Gross wrote for *The New York Times*:

> Officials say Finland's success is not just the result of its strong education system, which is one of the best in the world, but also because of a concerted effort to teach students about fake news. Media literacy is part of the national core curriculum starting in preschool.[15]

Will teaching kids critical-thinking skills prevent all Finns from seeing and acting on fake news? Of course not, but Finland stands a better chance at avoiding those perils than other countries do. The skill will become even more important as artificial intelligence and deepfakes become commonplace.

Crime, Enforcement, and the Right to Privacy

The Electronic Frontier Foundation (EFF), American Civil Liberties Union (ACLU), libertarians, and other staunchly pro-privacy groups today advocate for extreme privacy. The lack of nuance in the current debate is killing us.

First Principles

No one would deny that privacy is an important human right; some would call it fundamental.

Also, you need not be a former federal prosecutor like I am to know that crime will always exist.

Investigators can't do their jobs without reasonable access to data. Anyone with a modicum of knowledge about national security and financial crimes will agree with that simple statement.

---

* See https://tinyurl.com/the-cat-fin for a video on the subject.

PRINCIPLES AND POLICIES

Bad Actors Will Always Attempt to Hide Their Actions—and Usually Succeed

No newsflash here but, as Chapter 11 described, you don't have to be a master hacker to access powerful tools that effectively cloak your activities. Bank robbers no longer need to pull up to your local savings and loan. They can pilfer from afar, often leaving nary a single digital footprint.

Much Like Free Speech, the Right to Privacy Shouldn't Be Absolute

Perhaps the idea of absolute privacy appeals to you. If so, ask yourself if it's worth the tradeoff: Criminals can operate with impunity. Should a medical emergency cause you to go to the hospital, imagine that a doctor can't treat you because of a recent ransomware attack. Or what if bad actors hacked your bank account or crypto wallet?

Data Collection and Use Are Legal and Essential Government Activities

Governments, regulators, and enforcement officials must legally collect and use a reasonable amount of information to protect their citizens. The idea that enforcement agencies can magically identify and catch criminal actors without essential data and metadata is absurd.

Solutions and Recommendations

I don't purport to know all the ways to reduce crime while maximizing individual privacy. I do know, however, that the following recommendations will bear fruit.

Use Technology to Optimize Data Privacy

Governments and organizations need to modernize their collection and use of data. Current efforts are downright primitive—and related regulations reflect this reality.

The past few years have seen the arrival and maturation of several technologies and strategies that allow governments to balance privacy concerns with the need for data collection and usage. Techniques like differential privacy, secure multiparty computation, and federated learning protect sensitive information while enabling governments to provide public services.

For example, consider zero-knowledge proofs (ZKPs). These cryptographic tools allow verification or validation of information without exposing sensitive information.[16] Say you go to a liquor store to buy alcohol, and you need to provide identification. The liquor store clerk only needs to see your age, but your driver's license provides your address and other private data. ZKPs only show people what they need to see.

Criminal Sentences Must Deter Illegal Behavior

Paul Manafort is many things. Donald Trump's former campaign chairman also occupies a place on the short list of the most corrupt men in America. In no order, he:

> spent a decade laundering tens of millions in criminal proceeds, defrauded the IRS of millions of dollars in tax revenue, lied to the FBI, tampered with witnesses, and acted as an unauthorized foreign agent for a corrupt, pro-Russia Ukrainian strongman. And this all somehow added up to an "otherwise blameless life" in the eyes of our justice system.[17]

In March 2019, a federal judge sentenced him to what may appear to be a laughably light forty-seven months in prison.[18] (Sadly, in the US, four years in a white white-collar facility* represents severe punishment.) Manafort didn't even serve that limited time. In December 2020, Trump pardoned him.[19]

Perhaps Manafort wouldn't have committed his crimes if he faced lifelong imprisonment or, at least, decades behind bars. Ditto for CZ and Steve A. Cohen, discussed in Chapter 11. The appalling lengths of these sentences send an unmistakable message in the US. Rich (and often white) people not

---

* That's not a typo. In these low-security facilities, you'll find far fewer non-Caucasians.

only don't play by the same rules as everyone else; they can make their own rules.*

Many jurisdictions are adopting frameworks like the EU's 6th AML Directive (6AMLD). It increases minimum prison terms and expands the definition of money-laundering offenses. More countries must strengthen enforcement through higher prison terms and fines, especially for financial crimes.

Bolster Legal Frameworks and Infrastructure

In 2024, Tigran Gambaryan spent eight months in a Nigerian prison. Authorities there charged him with tax evasion and unlawfully detained him.[20] His actual crime: He was attempting to assist Nigerian law enforcement while working for a company with lax AML policies. Authorities kidnapped the compliance officer and charged him for his employer's actions.

If nations have the time and resources to wrongfully arrest and detain people like Gambaryan, they can surely invest in better legal frameworks. They need to solidify their infrastructure to investigate and prosecute crime and prevent corruption in their backyards.

As crimes such as pig butchering become more common, we must grant law enforcement officials sufficient budgets and tools to do their jobs. More illicit finance will continue moving into cryptocurrency and other digital assets. Global law enforcement lacks adequate preparation, training, and resources.

Nations must effect laws and controls regarding financial crime and corruption. Pretending that criminals will ignore sophisticated and cost-effective money-laundering tools is irresponsible and dangerous.

---

* I'm reminded here of a fantastic scene in the show *Succession*. View it at https://tinyurl.com/the-cat-rich.

THE CATALYSTS

Government, Politics, and International Relations

The following principles and recommendations discuss protecting democracy from autocrats and building bridges with like-minded nations.

First Principles

It would be arrogant to propose the solutions to all problems currently plaguing democracies and societies across the globe in a few paragraphs. Think of the following core tenets as key pieces of societal foundations, not a universal list.

Democracy Is Difficult to Preserve, but It's Worth Fighting For

Churchill was right: Democracy is the worst form of government, except for all the others. Chapters 5 and 8 covered some of the greatest challenges to consensus-driven government. Don't expect those threats to abate anytime soon.

America Won't Be Leading the Fight for Democracy and Freedom

In July 2023, Hardy Merriman, Patrick Quirk, and Ash Jain of the Atlantic Council released "Fostering a Fourth Democratic Wave: A Playbook for Countering the Authoritarian Threat." Here is one of the authors' strategic pillars for preserving democracy:

> Broadening options to enable and support civil resistance movements through training, capacity building, educational resources, and strategic assistance while respecting local ownership.[21]

At the time, the report's suggestions seemed reasonable. First, Joe Biden and his administration had assured America's allies that its longtime friend would continue the fight for democracy. US aid to Ukraine was a case in point: America was walking the talk. Second, another Trump term seemed to be a remote—if scary—possibility.

PRINCIPLES AND POLICIES

Now that America has fully leaned into authoritarian capitalism, nations must brace themselves for a starkly different future: If you want to preserve democratic rule, don't expect the US to throw you any lifelines. You're on your own.

Elected Leadership Should Be Diverse, Not Homogeneous

In 2022, five of America's fifty governors sported net worths in the hundreds of millions or even *billions* of dollars.[22] This statistic is astonishing. You need not be a demographer to accurately guess their genders and ethnicities.

Yes, the world is an increasingly dangerous and volatile place. The world's current leadership makes it so. Too many rich, old, white, technology-illiterate men are making decisions for everyone. All else being equal, a diverse set of educated, tech-savvy elected officials will yield outcomes that truly serve their constituencies, not the needs of the upper 1 percent.

Doing Something Is Almost Always Better Than Doing Nothing

The French philosopher François-Marie Arouet, aka Voltaire, uttered one of my favorite maxims: "Perfect is the enemy of good."

Pick freedom of speech, privacy, or any issue of import. Odds are that there's far too much bickering over relatively minor hypothetical issues while major problems fester and intensify. Yes, edge cases will always exist, but does it make sense to wait to pass meaningful legislation addressing societal ills because one faction may experience negative consequences down the road?

To quote Mr. Spock of *Star Trek* fame, "The needs of the many outweigh the needs of the few." Policymakers and elected officials would do well to remember those words. There will never be a perfect time to enact new laws. Think about the opportunity cost of inaction.

Trying to Eliminate Social Engineering Is a Fool's Errand

No policy prescription exists that will eradicate mass manipulation. Once Big Data proved that humans are effectively sheep, the lure of herding them—for politics or profit—became too great. If we're to achieve better societal outcomes, we must minimize social engineering's collateral damage and use it responsibly.

The Catalysts Are Far Too Powerful to Confront Alone

Misinformation, tech nation-states, bad actors' ability to evade traditional guardrails, and social engineering are formidable foes. To effectively combat them, elected officials should employ an approach rooted in cooperation, not isolationism and nationalism.

Solutions and Recommendations

Once again, it's time to operationalize these first principles. How can policymakers, regulators, and enforcement officials move the needle?

Consolidate and Coordinate Pro-Democracy Efforts

Despite being less than two years old, the Atlantic Council report seems nostalgic. It assumed that America would continue leading to preserve democracy. Because that clearly won't be the case, what do other countries do?

As of January 2025, the Worldwide NGO Directory listed 150 different institutions whose mission involved promoting democracy.[23] That many independent organizations working to achieve the same lofty goal are inefficient at best. At worst, they're duplicative. Consolidating and coordinating efforts may seem like a herculean task, but the ends certainly justify the means.

NGOs are one thing, but individual nations are quite another.

Work With Allies and Find Common Ground

Ours is a connected world, and some degree of cooperation on political, economic, and social matters is necessary. No matter how mighty, no single nation can solve climate change alone.

We saw in Chapter 12 the havoc that Brexit is wreaking on UK businesses and citizens. Given the current dysfunctional state of the US, it's understandable that a nation wouldn't want to hitch its wagon to the American star.

Fortunately, viable alternatives are available. Many groups are currently fighting global problems collaboratively while promoting democracy. They include the European Union (EU), the Nordic Council, and the Association of Southeast Asian Nations (ASEAN). Don't forget NATO and the UN, either. Who's to say that more aren't possible?

Embrace Regulatory Sandboxes

In the software world, developers often release limited alpha and beta versions of their apps and systems. The goal is simple: to identify bugs before shipping the product to a larger audience. Why can't regulators and policy officials do the same?

Think about cryptocurrency or other newfangled technology with enormous promise and potential for harm. Now imagine trying to develop every conceivable regulation around one of them. Your goals include minimizing government regulation, encouraging innovation, and ensuring the public's safety. What are the odds that you'll stick the landing?

Correct answer: zero.

What to do? Put differently, how do you solve the regulator's dilemma?[24] Some policymakers have turned to a *regulatory sandbox*. It is:

> a legal classification that creates a space where participating businesses won't be subject to onerous regulations—usually for a limited amount of time. The point is to allow these businesses to "play" in the sandbox without regulations to see if innovative ideas and products can get traction and enter the market.[25]

Policymakers have already created these types of sandboxes for self-driving cars, networked buses, and delivery drones.[26] Organizations like the Alliance for Innovative Regulation (AIR) can also assist regulators with education and tools for regulatory modernization.

THE CATALYSTS

Ban Dark Money

This one is a no-brainer—and the definition of an *apolitical* issue. Governments that allow anonymous donations to political candidates invite corruption and risk authoritarianism. Systems that rely upon disclosure as a solution only work if both the populace cares and the authorities enforce disclosure laws. Otherwise, it's the fox guarding the henhouse.

Pass Clear Statutes Before You Need to Use Them

Trump escaped successful prosecution for his role in the January 6 insurrection for many reasons, but an arguably outdated US statute dating back to the Civil War certainly contributed to the Department of Justice's ultimate failure.[27] By contrast, as Chapter 13 covered, Brazilian law allowed its courts to uphold the decision to ban its former president from running until 2030.

It's downright impossible to predict the future, but the lessons of the US and Brazil should serve as a wake-up call: Policymakers should ensure that their laws minimize offenders' wiggle room—and not just around attempted coups.

Ideally, the catalysts won't attempt an insurrection, foment widespread social unrest, or facilitate some other terrible event in your nation. Still, in the immortal words of the novelist Franz Kafka, "Better to have, and not need, than to need, and not have." Shore up your laws now, not when a catastrophe occurs.

Social Manipulation for Good

Other than perhaps *2001* and *The Terminator*, few American sci-fi movies have left as indelible a mark on popular culture as 2002's *Minority Report* starring Tom Cruise. He plays John Anderton and

> works with the PreCrime police which stop crimes before they take place, with the help of three 'PreCogs' who can foresee crimes. Events ensue when John finds himself framed for a future murder.[28]

PRINCIPLES AND POLICIES

The movie's chilling premise poses an interesting theoretical and ethical question: What should you do to prevent future crimes from taking place?

As I discovered with my work on the January 6 committee, theory has collided with practice. The tools and data exist today for a government to be able to predict which of its citizens are most likely to commit future terrorism in the homeland.

Relatively few people know as much—and that fact is no accident. During my time on the committee, Professor Bill Scherer and I worked on a project that analyzed three datasets:

- Trump's Federal Election Commission (FEC) donation records.
- Charging documents of the defendants prosecuted for their role in the attack.
- Scherer's proprietary and established marketing database on 270 million Americans.

The results were compelling. We could use advanced machine learning models to identify defendant lookalikes in the general population. Existing data would let US officials create January 6 attacker profiles. Then we could identify the 5 percent of US adults that statistically matched the defendants' profiles. We could accurately predict the states, counties, and zip codes that would birth the next insurrectionists. Deprogramming messages and antipropaganda campaigns in those jurisdictions could reduce the likelihood of another violent attack.

Not surprisingly, you won't find any mention of this in the report of The House Select Committee to Investigate the January 6th Attack on the United States Capitol. Despite our mandate to propose solutions that would prevent the next attack, the committee's leadership knew the world wasn't ready for a real-life *Minority Report*. They were likely right.

If you remember one thing from Chapter 12 of this book, make it this: Conflict profiteers excel at manipulating people for their own benefit. Fortunately, governments aren't helpless against their onslaught of misinformation and disinformation. Leaders can—and must—actively counter them. In other words, use social engineering for good.

Select More Informed, Tech-Savvy Policymakers

Up until the nineteenth century, leeching "was frequently practiced in Europe, Asia, and America to deplete the body of quantities of blood, in a manner similar to bloodletting."[29] Thankfully, the practice has all but ended. You wouldn't attempt to run the UK's National Health Service (NHS) if you advocated using segmented worms in lieu of modern day medical procedures and pharmaceuticals.

So why do we allow technologically clueless individuals to make policy decisions that affect so many different aspects of society? Even more puzzling, why in some cases do we ban government officials from using the very tools they're regulating? For example, the US Office of Government Ethics (OGE) in 2022 prohibited employees at the Federal Reserve, the Treasury Department, and other federal agencies from owning cryptocurrency if they worked on federal crypto regulation.[30] They were, interestingly, allowed to own cash even though they worked directly on USD monetary policy.

To varying extents, all the catalysts rely on emerging technologies that constantly morph. All policymakers, politicians, regulators, and enforcement officials need to possess a certain proficiency in technology. Naysayers may object, but plenty of age, citizenship, and other restrictions exist around political office and appointments—and for good reason.

Economics and Cautious Capitalism

Our final bucket involves wealth, inequality, taxes, wages, and other fundamental economic issues. After all, this is a book about the new world financial order.

PRINCIPLES AND POLICIES

First Principles

There's no secret formula for building and maintaining a financially sound society. Capitalism may be the best of all economic systems, but calling it perfect is preposterous. Every sophomore economics major knows that free markets result in pollution and countless other undesirable externalities. There's a critical role for governments and policymakers to play. Let's start by agreeing on some reasonable principles.

Left Unchecked, Capitalism Will Result in an Unsustainably Large Wealth Gap

Chapters 5 and 11 discussed the alarming levels of wealth inequality around the world. If history teaches us anything, it's that people eventually wake up to reality. At some point, the powers that be will no longer be able to use social engineering to convince the disenfranchised that immigrants or external forces are to blame for their stations in life. The system itself is the problem.

The Middle Class Is the Bedrock of a Healthy Economy

Chapter 5 covered America's robust middle class following WWII. For decades, the presence of a relatively equitable society benefited US citizenry and politicians. In a word, America was stable. China's middle class is now the largest in the world. It exceeds America's entire population.[31] Its leadership knows full well that, without the buffer of a stabilizing middle class, social tensions between the haves and have-nots will rise steadily. Unrest or violence is the inevitable result.

Policymakers Must Ensure Responsible Innovation

Tech bros incessantly pine about innovation as if it were an unalloyed good. If they had their way, they'd "disrupt" every industry, irrespective of the consequences to society at large. Even after making *The Social Dilemma*, they refuse to ask if they *should* build something, in addition to if they could.

Technology will always move faster than existing policies and regulations, a trend that will only intensify in an age of generative AI and fintech. Nevertheless, regulations allowing startups and entrepreneurs to callously "move fast and break things" are both unsustainable and downright unsafe.

Immigration Promotes Positive Economic and Societal Outcomes

That I have to explicitly cover this longstanding axiom of economic doctrine only reinforces today's sad state of affairs. For those who need further proof of what economists have long known, consider a May 2020 working paper from the National Bureau of Economic Research. Among other things, the authors found that immigration:

- Positively impacts local innovation as measured by patent activity. The arrival of 10,000 additional immigrants increases patent flow by one patent per 100,000 people over a five-year period.
- Positively affects measures of local economic dynamism, including job creation, job destruction, and wage growth. One standard deviation increase in immigration (about 12,000 immigrants) raises job creation rates by 7% and job destruction rates by 11% relative to mean levels.[32]

Solutions and Recommendations

In any country, the ruling economic class fights to maintain the status quo. This reality makes it difficult, if not structurally impossible, to unseat the powers that be. Policymakers must possess the will to improve their constituents' lives. To this end, here are concrete suggestions designed to promote economic prosperity in the new world financial order.

Promote Socioeconomic Mobility

Chapter 5 covered the struggles of America's middle class, but how is this cohort doing across the globe? A 2025 report by Oxfam International on worldwide income inequality detailed the dire situation.[33] Specifically:

- Billionaire wealth surged by $2 trillion in 2024, three times faster than the year before.[34]
- The number of people living in poverty has barely changed since 1990.
- Sixty percent of billionaire wealth now comes from largely unmerited sources, including inheritance, monopoly power, and crony connections.

China and, to a lesser extent, India, haven't just driven much of the economic growth in the past decade. They're also responsible for reducing the global wealth inequality. In 2019, researchers at the World Data Lab noted:

> Over the next decade, middle-class spending power will shift from west to east due to the huge growth in the middle-class segments of India and China. The middle classes of these two countries will represent over 83% of their respective country's spending power, meaning that businesses should consider their tastes and preferences. Combined, the world's two most populous countries are expected to represent over 43.3% of the global middle class by 2030.[35]

Although the US has clearly lost the script here and forgotten its history, Chinese and Indian leaders have long realized the importance of preserving—nay, *growing*—their middle classes.

The statistical relationships are complicated, but a robust middle class typically can access better education[36] and healthcare.[37] The result: higher productivity.[38] Policymakers should stay the course and continue to lift people out of poverty. The societal and economic benefits of letting them retain some of their productivity gains are too great to ignore.

That's not to say that policymakers and legislatures couldn't make some much-needed changes to strengthen their middle classes even more.

THE CATALYSTS

Make the Tax System More Equitable

Monaco, New Zealand, Singapore, and Hong Kong are just a few of the countries that forgo capital gains taxes. Other nations, such as the US, Canada, and Germany, tax earnings from investments at lower rates than wages earned while working.

These differentials effectively disadvantage young and poor people who can't afford to invest in stocks, bonds, and other financial vehicles. At the same time, they unfairly benefit wealthy individuals, who often earn more from investments than actual labor.

Ensure That Economic Policies Let People Live With Dignity

England is one of the countries that has experimented with universal basic income (UBI).[39] If that type of program is too progressive for your constituents, then at least ensure that wage minimums are livable. In other words, don't mirror countries such as the US, Honduras, and Pakistan. A point from Chapter 5 bears repeating: America hasn't raised the federal minimum wage since 2009.[40] In contrast, citizens in Australia, Germany, the Netherlands, and France earn livable wages. Not coincidentally, their societies reap significant rewards.

Ensure Affordable Housing for Citizens

What happens when you mix a pandemic, existing housing shortages, economic stimulus payments, and rising interest rates? In 2023, the answer depended on whether you owned your home. Existing homeowners saw their property values skyrocket, but the same toxic cocktail "diminish[ed] the prospects of home ownership."[41] Supply and demand were wildly out of whack.

Adding salt to the wound, Airbnb and VRBO have created an effect called *hotelization*. Property owners are converting houses and long-term rental units into short-term vacation rentals. Each conversion reduces the housing supply available for frustrated renters and would-be homebuyers.

PRINCIPLES AND POLICIES

For their part, private equity firms and foreign investors have exacerbated the dearth of available homes for purchase. Each has been gobbling up residences en masse. A 2024 report from Harvard University's Joint Center for Housing Studies[42] found that, in the US, "private equity firms raise rents, impose new fees, skimp on property maintenance and pursue tenants more aggressively in court."[43] North of the border, "foreign ownership has also fueled worries about Canadians being priced out of housing markets in cities and towns across the country."[44]

You can't build new homes overnight. New policies are imperative. In response, some nations have addressed the problem head-on. For example, in 2024, Canada extended its initial ban on foreign home ownership for another two years.[45]

As the following sidebar illustrates, the current housing crisis plagues countries and cities around the world.

Homeless in the Most Beautiful Place on Earth

Tourists from around the world regularly flock to Queenstown, New Zealand. Most have seen its stunning vistas in movies like *The Lord of the Rings*. The nation's annual tourism industry grew to $6 billion in 2023.[46] Visitors learn that the Middle Earth from the series is, in fact, real—not computer-generated imagery (CGI). Booming tourism requires workers who, in turn, need affordable housing. Many Kiwis, however, can't afford a place to live.

While visiting in August 2023, I talked with bar owners and restaurant managers in Queenstown. The local housing shortage was a frequent topic of discussion. Unfortunately, local government has been slow to make necessary zoning and policy changes. As a result, plenty of residents must sleep in their cars or hostels.

With nowhere to live, workers must pack up their bags. Businesses then struggle to attract and retain staff, resulting in a labor shortage that hurts the local economy.

THE CATALYSTS

Nations Should Strive for Universal Financial Literacy

It's fair to call the state of financial literacy *wanting*. By way of reminder, only one-third of adults possess financial literacy, although significant disparities exist across regions and demographics.[47] Every citizen needs to be financially literate; it shouldn't be a luxury reserved for the affluent.

Building and sustaining a successful middle class require teaching people not just how to spend, but how to invest. No one will invest wisely—much less create generational wealth—without understanding compound interest, basic investment strategies, and other core financial tenets. As the following sidebar demonstrates, I learned this invaluable lesson at an earlier age than most.

Winning the Birth Lottery

As the child of two financial planners, I grew up learning about money at the dinner table. I thought every family talked about retirement, annuities, and social security between bites. As I matured, though, I learned there were three types of people when it came to financial literacy:

- Those who learn it early on.
- Those who learn it later in life.
- Those who *never* learn it.

When I was 25, I began my first job out of law school at a DC law firm. At the time, I earned about $125,000 annually. During orientation, human resources (HR) asked us if we wanted to contribute to the company's 401(k) plan.* The maximum annual contribution back then was $15,000, or $1,250 per month.

---

* A 401(k) is an employer-sponsored retirement savings plan in the US that offers certain tax advantages.

> While I was filling out the form, a coworker asked me about the firm's 401(k) matching plan.* (I'll call him Tim here, but it's a pseudonym.) Our job titles and salaries were identical, but he was a few years older than I.
>
> Tim told me that he planned to invest only $50 per month. By doing so, he was throwing away thousands of dollars in employer-matched funds. He explained that he was the first in his family to earn that much money. Tim never learned about investing.
>
> I realized then that people making significant amounts of money often lack the knowledge to maximize their wealth. Thankfully, my coworker listened to me over lunch one day as I explained how interest compounds over time. The next day, he increased his contribution.

Counter Anti-Immigration Rhetoric on Social Media

Policymakers can effect change by implementing economic plans that foster immigration. Given the anti-immigration sentiment that generally comes from right-wing nationalistic movements, effective social media campaigns may be necessary to counter misinformation. It's time to fight fire with fire. Immigration fear-mongering is often just race-baiting. It ignores the economic benefits of immigration we've already covered.

Emulate Other Countries' Innovations Around Immigration Policy

Over the past decade, many countries creatively attacked the problem of attracting skilled workers. Here are a few examples.

- Denmark,[48] Canada,[49] and Australia[50] are just a few of the countries that admit skilled workers via point-based systems. Doing so aligns immigrant skills with specific and dynamic labor market needs.

---

* One benefit of a 401(k) plan is that many employers match a percentage of employees' contributions. In one limited sense, it's free money. Employees who fail to contribute the required minimum amount don't receive it.

- Ireland and New Zealand[51] have enacted family-friendly policies, such as enabling spousal employment. Families that can migrate as a unit are usually happier and more productive.
- Immigration officials in Germany[52] and Sweden[53] understand that cultural integration and support are essential. To this end, they provide language training and community-building to attract and retain top talent.

The economic and societal benefits of immigration are manifold. Still, even in a halcyon political environment, a nation can only realistically accept and acclimate a certain number of ex-patriots every year. Sustained economic growth requires adding new human beings—specifically, babies.

Finally Crossing the Gender Chasm

Unless biology radically changes or scientific advances allow men to make babies sans women, population growth—and, by extension, economic growth—won't happen until societies address the elephant in the room: Women have yet to achieve true political, social, and economic equality.

First Principles

Let's say that your views on gender equality are rooted in the nineteenth century. Maybe they're even, shall we say, *regressive*. In this section, I'll make a purely economic argument for egalitarianism.

The Declining Worldwide Birthrate

The work of Dr. Peter McDonald at the Australian National University and Dr. Jeromey Temple at the University of Melbourne is particularly salient here. The two have extensively studied the factors likely to drive continued economic growth in the new world financial order. Ultimately, prosperity will stem from a combination of population, participation, and productivity—*the three p's*. To be sure, they're all important, but—at least in the case of their home country—overall economic growth lies in productivity and population growth.[54]

This finding is important because birth rates are plummeting worldwide. In March 2024, *The Lancet* reported that "dramatic declines in global fertility rates [are] set to transform global population patterns by 2100."[55] Put bluntly, the world is approaching a "low-fertility future."[56]

Governments have been trying to turn the tide. In response to the current crisis, "Nations are deploying baby bonuses, subsidised childcare and parental leave to try to reverse a rapidly declining fertility rate—largely to no avail."[57]

Boosting Women Is Good Economics

Let's go to Saudi Arabia, a country not known for its tradition of gender equality. The kingdom has recently taken steps to address this issue—and the results have been impressive:

> The economic impact of increased female participation has been substantial, with women's progress alone boosting Saudi Arabia's GDP by approximately 12%. S&P Global predicts that further integration of women into the workforce could add $39 billion to the economy over the next decade.[58]

Policymakers around the world should take note.

Winning the Global War for Talent

Chapter 10 covered how innovation hubs are blooming around the world. If an upwardly mobile individual, couple, or family could move just about anywhere, why wouldn't they go someplace that values child care, paid family leave, and other perks?

Let me put it another way: Country A offers solid employment opportunities, a vibrant culture, and an affordable cost of living. Country B offers everything that Country A does but also takes gender equality far more seriously than its counterpart. Country B's legislature mandates specific policies around family leave, job protection, and the like.

THE CATALYSTS

All things being equal, where will most skilled workers want to live?

Solutions and Recommendations

Here are three specific policy recommendations designed to reap the economic benefits of gender equality.

Normalize Childrearing by Both Genders

COVID-19 normalized remote work, a statistic the data bears out. In the US, 26.2 percent of women worked from home in 2019. That number increased to 49.3 percent in 2020 but dipped to 41 percent in 2022.[59]

Over the past year, Amazon, Chase Bank, other large corporations, and even the federal government have ordered their employees back to the office. Much of the resistance to return-to-office (RTO) mandates stems from the seismic change that working from home afforded to women. In the words of Dr. Liz Allen, a demographer and lecturer at the Australian National Centre for Social Research and Methods:

> Women are asked to have the kids, care for the elderly, participate in the workforce and do the unpaid labour at home. And young people now see through this. ... To be fair, many women in our thirties and forties saw through it as well.[60]

Baby bonuses, subsidized childcare, and improved maternity leave are failing to significantly improve birthrates. They only address one aspect of a complex, multifaceted problem: the *motherhood penalty*.

In 2023, Harvard professor Claudia Goldin conducted an extensive examination of gender-based wage inequality. Before a couple brings a child into the world, a relatively small pay disparity exists. However, after the child's birth, the gap widens, with the mother disproportionately bearing the brunt of its impact. Goldin's groundbreaking work earned her the 2023 Nobel Prize in Economics.[61]

Of course, the motherhood penalty doesn't shock working women, especially those of us without children. One sees its impact every day in the workplace. Women are:

- The first to sacrifice work opportunities when their children need care.
- Frequently the primary caregivers for their children and parents.
- Far more likely to handle childcare duties than their male partners.

This is why part-time work, maternity leave, and baby bonuses don't improve fertility rates. They're predicated on the woman serving as their children's primary caregiver.

What's the solution then?

Policymakers should pass laws that encourage universal day care and reduce men's standard working hours. These policies can begin the process of changing gender norms and encouraging men to care for their offspring beyond bringing home the bacon. Laws that promote sharing childcare costs and responsibilities are "powerfully associated with higher fertility."[62]

Unless and until more countries address the real problem, expect birthrates to remain low.

Call Bullshit on Pinkwashing

Every year, as March 8 approaches, bakeries around the world rejoice. International Women's Day intends to address a real issue. The global holiday celebrates women and, ideally, creates momentum for people to act toward gender equality. In reality, though, related celebrations far too often consist of office parties featuring free cupcakes adorned with pink icing. This is a prime example of *pinkwashing*.

Organizations too often engage in these hollow gestures. They ostensibly call for actions to achieve gender equality without formal commitments. Too many women's organizations share the blame. They take corporate sponsorship dollars and hold events that ostensibly raise awareness. That's fine, but ultimately empty. Neither activity proposes—much less effects—meaningful changes or solutions.

Governments and NGOs can't simply verbally commit to gender equality. They must direct financial and human resources toward actual policy changes. Only then will they truly move the needle.

Lift Women Up With Intentional Inclusion Programs

Let's say I told you that I planned on visiting your town. I then asked you to organize a small dinner. Would you invite four strangers or four people who wouldn't embarrass you? When events matter, we tend to invite whom we know. Our social circles tend not to be terribly diverse.

Intentional inclusion programs seek to broaden our apertures. Examples include mandatory quotas and voluntary awareness initiatives. These programs encourage—or even require—that existing, male-dominated entities and associations consider and include underrepresented groups.

As we've seen throughout this book, forced change tends to irritate established power structures, corporations, and wealthy individuals intent on preserving the status quo. Expect resistance, but know this going in: These inclusion programs work. They present more opportunities for qualified women to succeed. For instance, female quota programs have successfully resulted in making politics less male-driven.[63] There's plenty of evidence that the same holds true with corporate boards.[64]

Key Points

- The idea of principles-based regulations and policies isn't new.
- Once we agree on first principles, the "how" can vary based on cultures and constituents.
- Governments must balance privacy rights with their legitimate need for information. It's high time to implement new technologies.
- Nations that want democracy to survive will no longer be able to rely on America.

PRINCIPLES AND POLICIES

- Defining responsible free speech has always been tricky. Social media exponentially complicates matters. Developing strategies to combat disinformation is essential.
- Social manipulation can serve as a source of good. Policymakers that fail to act now will only see its devastating consequences.
- Countries that fail to address the rising wealth gap risk violent unrest and even collapse.
- Gender equality will increase fertility rates and benefit countries that have adopted progressive policies.

AFTERWORD
A CITIZEN'S CALL TO ACTION

DESPITE BLEAK TIMES, THERE'S REASON FOR OPTIMISM.

> "Be patient and tough; someday,
> this pain will be useful to you."
>
> —*Ovid*

I set out to write a book to help policymakers, regulators, and enforcement officials understand and prepare for the new world financial order. It's critical to remember, though, that each of these people is also a citizen. All citizens—even those who don't make or interpret public policy—possess some degree of agency over their lives and those of others.

It's easy for anyone—policymakers included—to become depressed and defeated when reflecting on the state of their country, let alone that of the world. Just thinking about it is enough for some of us to tear up instantly.

Writing this book taught me more in one year than I've learned in forty-three.

It was easy to feel hopeless. Researching the global erosion of democracy and the simultaneous rise in authoritarian capitalism broke this American's heart. Watching it result from the failure of the left in so many countries to provide sufficient leadership and governance was also soul-sucking.

It was also easy to feel schadenfreude.* The global rise of nationalist, far-right parties in the 2024 elections couldn't have happened if the have-nots didn't vote against their own economic interests and embrace otherism. I'll be the first to admit that my empathy tank depleted quickly afterward as the predicted harms began to unfold. Acknowledging the psychopathy and narcissism in that is easier because I know I'm not alone. The reality of humanity's dark psychology is only upsetting and dangerous when accompanied by a lack of self-awareness.

But one thing consistently gave me hope throughout the process. As a digital nomad, I travel the world. Conferences, events, and business meetings allow me to converse with thousands of people from countless countries and cultures. When I spoke with people about the book to gather opinions or feedback, I heard a few consistent themes.

Knowledge Combats Fear

Whether you're looking at one of the catalysts or all of them, being afraid is a natural response. Many people I spoke with knew about one or even some of them. Some folks were surprised to learn of others. The enormity of what we're facing can be concurrently empowering and daunting. Fear is a rational response, not something we should be ashamed to admit.

---

* *Schadenfreude* is an incredible German word that captures a complex emotion that most humans feel. In simple terms, it's the human experience of taking pleasure in another person's pain or misfortune, often because you feel they did something to deserve it.

You're Not Alone

Ours is a world deeply divided. We even politicize issues of life and death, as the resistance to COVID vaccines amply demonstrated. What would unite us? Perhaps only an alien attack at this point.

Until a terrestrial invasion happens, though, we must unite ourselves. And interestingly, we already have to some extent. Somewhere in the world right now, a person with a vastly different heritage, culture, and background shares the same feelings as you do. Traveling and speaking with so many people gave me a gift: the window to see how many people on this planet are so wonderfully similar. They want the same things for their families and friends as we do. It's trite but true; our commonalities exceed our differences.

Together We Can Act

The Swedish activist Greta Thunberg started a global movement in November 2018 to combat climate change by skipping school. Erin West, a local prosecutor in California, wrote a LinkedIn post asking if anyone else wanted to help victims of pig butchering. In the process, she launched Operation Shamrock, a global initiative to combat it.

We live in an age of worldwide social media, international transportation, and disintermediated finance. As such, a group of well-organized global citizens can effectuate unbounded change. I've seen task forces, groups, and organizations do incredible things with the right intentions and a proclivity for action. They begged for forgiveness; they didn't ask for permission.

In past periods of great wealth inequality, labor protections, progressive taxation, and other political reforms helped mitigate tension and prevent widespread violence. However, today's context—particularly in the US—is different. Blame heightened polarization and the role of social media. Conflict to resolve the wealth gap would be catastrophic. We need both actual solutions and courageous people willing to fight for them.

I'm aware that *The Catalysts* was an intellectual and emotional lift. If you've read this far, I hope you'll join me in turning this book into something that actually makes a difference.

When you're ready, find us at www.thecatalystsmovement.org.

THANK-YOU

For a book this long and expansive, the acknowledgments section could have been as long as the book itself.

First and foremost, I want to thank Phil Simon. He dislikes my lengthy, run-on sentences, so it's only fair that this one goes out to him. Thank you for being my writing partner, ghostwriter, work husband, publisher, project manager, voice of reason, advisor, necessary naysayer, cheerleader, promoter, and friend.

I remember your hesitation in collaborating with me when I told you the book I wanted to write. Given where we started during the ideation phase, I know you and Racket Publishing took a massive leap of faith with this project. We both love movie references. In this instance, you were Harrison Ford in *Indiana Jones and the Last Crusade*. You took a giant step into a ravine, believing my ideas would catch us. I can never thank you enough for your patience and for shaping so many of my thoughts into the words I wanted but couldn't find on my own.

I never understood the relationship between an architect and a general contractor until this project. I could envision the house I wanted, down to every board and nail. But I could never have built it and turned it into something this beautiful without you.

"Thank you" isn't enough, but I'll start there.

The team at Racket Publishing is phenomenal. I'd like to thank Karen Davis, Jessica Angerstein, Marlowe Shaeffer, Vinnie Kinsella, and Johnna

VanHoose Dinse for their patience and commitment to excellence. Thank you for empowering authors and giving us the ability to go our own way.

To my parents, there genuinely aren't enough words. When Warren Buffett talks about "winning the birth lottery," you two are the equivalent of hitting the Mega Millions.

My parents and brother have always been my Orion's Belt; following their light has helped me navigate life. They've always had my back, whether it was support, advice, or faith in me—even when they had no idea where in the world I was.

My mom didn't understand why I wanted to use a hybrid publisher instead of a traditional one. After a lengthy discussion about the state of the publishing industry and the level of control I wanted over the project and my intellectual property, she also took a leap of faith. She and my dad helped me get the project off the ground.

I always knew I was fortunate to have my parents, but this project cemented something in my mind. There was no limit to how high I could fly when I had three people who would always catch me, no matter how far I fell. If you don't grasp the advantage that gives me over those who fly with no net beneath them, I'll refer you to Daniel Markovits's book *The Meritocracy Trap* for a better explanation than I could ever provide.

So, to my incredible family—including Lisa, Beck, and all the rest—for their love and support, I cannot thank you all enough.

Besides my blood family, I've been blessed to have an incredible "framily" (not a typo). These are the friends you choose to be your family; they're often just as good (or better) than those you're born into.

To my best friends, Starr Curry, Lillian Nicole Stewart, Tahira Dosani, and Natalie Loebner, thank you for putting up with me. Starr, you've been with me since high school, Lillian since law school, and Tahira and Natalie, I believe we were sisters in a past life. You've supported me through so many experiences—marriage, divorce, countless moves, jobs, deaths, and disasters. Just the thought of you all brought me peace when book-writing anxiety

THANK-YOU

threatened to swamp me. You are gifts from the universe I don't deserve but will always treasure.

To my entire N-Flux Family—especially Chris Torres, Colleen Daly, Gonzalo Mon, Tahira Dosani, Maicie Jones, Kenneth Gray, Adam Fritz, Alexa Himonas, Jen Ginsburg, and Caty Judkins—you and the gym gave me a home away from home. Finding Krav Maga, jujitsu, and Stoicism was the genesis for this entire book. Phil wouldn't let me include the Stoicism part (too long), but I know some of you will see the virtues throughout. Our work in the gym reshaped my thinking over the past six years. You all reshaped my heart after it had been broken. I'll never be able to repay you for both gifts.

To those with whom I had the honor of working on the House Select Committee to Investigate the January 6th Attack on the US Capitol, it was the privilege of a lifetime.

I came to the committee having just left a startup company, and there was a saying they had there: "The friendships made at a startup are so strong because they are forged through the bonds of trauma." Unsurprisingly, many of us forged lifelong friendships after serving on this committee.

I'll always be grateful to every one of you. Still, I'd like to say a special thanks to Tim Heaphy, Candyce Phoenix, Soumya Dayananda, Sean Tonolli, Temidayo Aganga-Williams, Camisha Johnson, Rebecca Knooihuizen, John Norton, Beth Bisbee, Marc Harris, Lisa Bianco, Barry Pump, Bryan Bonner, Marcus Childress, Jacob Nelson, Robin Peguero, Sandeep Prasanna, Alejandra Apecechea, Jerry Bjeloper, Heather Connelly, Meghan Conroy, Bill Danvers, Stephen DeVine, Kevin Elliker, Margaret Emamzadeh, Katie Abrams, Sadallah Farah, Jacob Glick, Casey Lucier, Damon Marx, Yonatan Moskowitz, Sean Quinn, James Sasso, Samantha Stiles, David A. Weinberg, Dean Jackson, Stephanie Jones, Alex Newhouse, Joshua Roselman, Jamie Fleet, Denver Riggleman, Dan George, and Joe Maher.

Bill Scherer was the committee's chief data scientist and professor and chair of the University of Virginia's Department of Systems and Information Engineering. His contributions to the committee's investigation went far beyond what was included in the report. My heart broke when Bill tragically and unexpectedly passed away in October 2024 while we were collaborating on this book. My thoughts go out to his family and friends. Bill and I didn't always agree, but we had a hell of a time and immeasurable respect for each other. His life and work will never be forgotten.

Thank you to the members of the committee, particularly Representatives Raskin, Lofgren, Aguilar, and Murphy, for the opportunity to serve.

Working on the January 6 Committee was the most taxing job of my life. When I left, my heart and soul were broken. Learning about the horrific state our country had been in for years and then watching the committee's leadership blame it mainly on one man was crushing, even though I knew it was coming.

Starting the Association for Women in Cryptocurrency was a way to heal my heart and give me hope in the world again. I knew it would help; I never could have imagined how much. To Jane Khodarkovsky, Laurel Loomis-Rimon, Jen Farer, and the fifty founding members, thank you for believing in me when all I had was an idea and a plan. That will mean more to me than you'll ever know.

"Thanks" will never be enough to the more than fifty regional ambassadors we now have and the 800 members who have supported me—and, more importantly, each other.

To all of you who let me couch surf while I was in full digital nomad mode—Michelle Gitlitz, Adilah Holivay, Val Harkless, Natalie Loebner, Rollin Badal, Josh Bollar, Bruce Nahan, Rachel Epstein, Michael Wolland, Sarah Zagata Vasani, Alissa Ostrove, Matthew de la Fuente, and others—thank you for opening your hearts and homes to me.

To Liz Sweigart, thank you for giving me the Mount Fuji analogy when I needed it the most. I've repeatedly retold it to so many people, hoping it helps them as much as it did me.

So many of you jumped on a call with me and asked me how I was doing, and I word vomited out my anxiety and imposter syndrome while writing this book. You patiently let me vent and then said exactly what I needed to

THANK-YOU

hear when I needed to hear it. Some people say I'm blessed. Others say it's *amor fati*. Either way, I'm incredibly grateful.

When I started the Association for Women in Cryptocurrency, I contacted many conferences to partner with them, hoping to hold allyship events and inclusive networking breakfasts. Because of my experience and background, many of them invited me to speak.

From October 2022 through the end of 2024, I spoke at over forty conferences and events. I learned so much, especially from the fantastic panels they curated and the speakers they featured. This book culminated from more than a thousand conversations I held with global policymakers, regulators, business leaders, and others who generously shared their thoughts and experiences. We didn't always agree, but there was always respect and a desire to improve the world.

Some of those conversations lasted a few minutes, and some lasted hours. But if you spoke with me in the past two years, you were likely one of the people who inspired this book, and I appreciated every moment.

To the team at GFTN (formerly Elevandi), thank you for supporting me and the association since I first contacted you. You all are amazing.

To Steve Vallas, Jasmin Vallas, and Richelle Cox at Blockchain APAC, thank you for your friendship and for all you've done to support me, the association, and everything that led to this book. You are my favorite tall poppies, and I've treasured growing with you.

To my friends who currently work for governments around the world who asked to remain unnamed (you know who you are), thank you. Your input and feedback gave me a unique, global view into what's really happening in the world, both on stage and behind closed doors.

In addition, I'd like to thank the following individuals for their insights and contributions. Combined, we had hundreds of conversations over the past four years, each of which culminated in this book. I could not have done it without the help of Rich Widmann, Michelle O'Connor, Dante Disparte, Rene Michau, Chris Brummer, Amit Sharma, Juan Zarate, Jennifer Lassiter, Ralph Kubli, John Yaros, Natalie Loebner, Carole House, Samar Senn,

THE CATALYSTS

Chris Tyrell, Gabby Kusz, Kris Klaich, Sandra Ro, ShihYun Chia, Alex Zerden, Jo Ann Barefoot, Aidan Larkin, Dave Birch, Patrick Azzopardi, Matthew Van Buskirk, Sheila Warren, Jonathan Padilla, Ayana Murphy, Jason Brett, Caitlin Long, Tahira Dosani, Alex O'Neill, Arturo Rodriguez, Mike Carter, Jason Allegrante, Joe Schifano, Alex Pelin, Samar Ali, Matthew de la Fuente, and Richard Cayzer.

I must admit, this book resulted from two other books that changed me forever.

The first was Massimo Pigliucci's *How to Be a Stoic: Using Ancient Philosophy to Live a Modern Life.* When my jujitsu coach started a Stoic meetup at our gym in late 2019, none of us knew it would turn into a life-saving support group to cope with lockdowns and a pandemic. We found Stoicism at a time in our lives when nearly everything was out of our control. For me, it provided an essential framework for processing life, love, and decision-making. Our group leader and coach, Chris Torres, chose this book as our textbook, and we dissected every chapter. To Chris, our resident philosopher-warrior, thank you for all the support you've given me over the years.

To David Epstein, author of the book *Range: Why Generalists Triumph in a Specialized World*, thank you for explaining my life so that it made sense. When Chris gave me your book during a Stoic Meetup Group meeting and said, "You should read this," it opened my eyes to how I lived without realizing what I was doing. I'd always wondered why I couldn't do the same thing for too long. Since I was a kid, I've loved learning about so many different things. I could never get one thing to stick long enough to do 10,000 hours and become an expert. And then I read your book and understood why.

For seven years, I was pulling on a common thread among martial arts, Stoicism, geopolitics, and crypto. I'd never have thought to turn it all into a book if you hadn't made the case for why a generalist isn't just okay but even preferable in some situations. You've enabled me to see the value in my expansive thoughts and ignore the judgment I've often received by being

THANK-YOU

"too scattered" and "not focused enough." Your book has been an inspiration on many levels, and I'm grateful. I recommend it to everyone I meet who's struggling on their path and needs your book to be a guidepost.

Finally, there are a few people in my life I must acknowledge because, without them, I wouldn't be where I am now.

I would have been a prosecutor at the Department of Justice (DOJ) forever. I was fortunate to have incredible supervisors and mentors along the way, including Mary Jane Stewart, Jenny Turner, Joyce Vance, Daniel Fortune, Tamarra Matthews Johnson, Jennifer Murnahan, Jim Delworth, Alice Dery, Steve Welk, Stef Cassella, and Ken Blanco.

Being a prosecutor was my dream job, and I never thought of doing anything else until I worked at the Money Laundering and Asset Recovery Section at Main Justice. The thing about *amor fati* and loving fate is that you eventually realize a universal truth: Things must happen how they're meant to happen for us to be where we are now. I was a bird comfortable in the DOJ nest; if I hadn't been shoved out, I never would have been forced to fly. So to Deb Connor, Leo Tsao, Pam Hicks, and Darren McCullough, thank you. I didn't know it then, but I do know it now; but for you, I would likely still be at DOJ. I'm grateful that fate put you in my path.

Last but certainly not least, I'd like to thank anyone who made it this far. Writing a book, especially nonfiction, is terrifying: You display your heart, soul, and beliefs for the world to read. And unlike a social media post that can be deleted, there are no "takebacks."

The greatest compliment in the world is when someone picks up this book and reads it. Maybe you bought it, maybe you received it as a gift, or maybe you found it on a park bench. However it found you, thank you for cracking it open and giving it—and me—a chance. I hope it leaves a positive impact and, if not, at least a lasting one.

BULK PURCHASES

Racket Publishing titles are available at significant quantity discounts when purchased in bulk for client gifts, sales promotions, and premiums. Special editions include books with corporate logos, customized covers, and bespoke letters from the organization or its CEO printed in the front matter. These are available in large quantities for conferences, summits, and other needs. For details and discount information for both print and ebook formats, visit www.racketpublishing.com/connect.

ABOUT THE AUTHOR

Amanda Wick served as a federal prosecutor for the US Department of Justice (DOJ) for nearly a decade, specializing in money laundering and cryptocurrency. She began her career at DOJ working in three US attorneys' offices: Atlanta, Birmingham, and St. Louis. After, she moved to Washington, DC to serve as a trial lawyer in the Money Laundering and Asset Recovery section of DOJ's Criminal Division. As part of a DOJ leadership program, Wick served as a detailee and senior policy advisor at the Financial Crimes Enforcement Network (FinCEN). In 2020, she left the government to serve as the chief of legal affairs at Chainalysis, a blockchain analytics company.

In 2021, Wick returned to government service to serve on the House Select Committee to Investigate the January 6th Attack on the US Capitol. She went on to found and run a global nonprofit organization: the Association for Women in Cryptocurrency. The organization aims to build a global network of women and male allies in the cryptocurrency, blockchain, and web3 industries who will advocate for the equal inclusion of women in the future of digital finance.

Wick serves as a principal with Incite Consulting, where she provides expert and litigation advisory services to law firms and advises a wide range of cryptocurrency-related businesses. She remains a digital nomad living out of a carry-on suitcase and a *National Geographic* backpack. *The Catalysts* is her first book. Learn more at www.amandawick.com.

BIBLIOGRAPHY

Alden, Lyn. *Broken Money: Why Our Financial System Is Failing Us and How We Can Make It Better.* Timestamp Press, 2023.

Arendt, Hannah. *Eichmann in Jerusalem: A Report on the Banality of Evil.* Penguin Classics, 2006.

Ariely, Dan. *Predictably Irrational, Revised and Expanded Edition: The Hidden Forces That Shape Our Decisions.* Harper Perennial, 2010.

Auerbach, David B. *Meganets: How Digital Forces Beyond Our Control Commandeer Our Daily Lives and Inner Realities.* Public Affairs, 2023.

Bernays, Edward. *Propaganda.* Ig Publishing, 2004.

Borowitz, Andy. *Profiles in Ignorance: How America's Politicians Got Dumb and Dumber.* Avid Reader Press, 2022.

Botsman, Rachel. *Who Can You Trust?: How Technology Brought Us Together and Why It Might Drive Us Apart.* PublicAffairs, 2017.

Brody, Paul, and Michael J. Casey. *Ethereum for Business: A Plain-English Guide to the Use Cases that Generate Returns from Asset Management to Payments to Supply Chains.* Epic Books, 2023.

Bullough, Oliver. *Butler to the World: How Britain Helps the World's Worst People Launder Money, Commit Crimes, and Get Away with Anything.* St. Martin's Press, 2022.

Carlisle, David. *The Crypto Launderers: Crime and Cryptocurrencies from the Dark Web to DeFi and Beyond.* Wiley, 2023.

Carr, Nicholas G. *The Big Switch: Rewiring the World, from Edison to Google.* W. W. Norton, 2009.

THE CATALYSTS

Christensen, Clayton M. *The Innovator's Dilemma: The Revolutionary Book That Will Change the Way You Do Business.* HarperBusiness, 2011.

de Tocqueville, Alexis. *Democracy in America.* Translated by Harvey C. Mansfield and Delba Winthrop. University of Chicago Press, 2002.

Dodd, Nigel. *The Social Life of Money.* Princeton University Press, 2014.

Dunn, Geoffrey. *The Lies of Sarah Palin: The Untold Story Behind Her Relentless Quest for Power.* St. Martin's Press, 2011.

Eisinger, Jesse. *The Chickenshit Club: Why the Justice Department Fails to Prosecute Executives.* Simon & Schuster, 2017.

Feld, Brad. *Startup Communities: Building an Entrepreneurial Ecosystem in Your City*, 2nd ed. Wiley, 2020.

Friedman, Milton. *There's No Such Thing as a Free Lunch: Essays on Public Policy.* Open Court Publishing Company, 1975.

Friedman, Thomas L. *The World Is Flat: A Brief History of the Twenty-First Century.* Farrar, Straus and Giroux, 2005.

Galloway, Scott. *Adrift: America in 100 Charts.* Portfolio, 2022.

Garten, Jeffrey E. *Three Days at Camp David: How a Secret Meeting in 1971 Transformed the Global Economy.* Harper, 2021.

Gitlitz, Michelle. *Reimagining Payments: The Business Case for Digital Currencies.* Racket Publishing, 2023.

Goldstein, Jacob. *Money: The True Story of a Made-Up Thing.* Grand Central Publishing, 2020.

Groth, Aimee. *The Kingdom of Happiness: Inside Tony Hsieh's Zapponian Utopia.* Atria Books, 2017.

Hadnagy, Christopher. *Social Engineering: The Science of Human Hacking*, Second Edition. Wiley, 2018.

Herrnstein, Richard J., and Charles Murray. *The Bell Curve: Intelligence and Class Structure in American Life.* Free Press, 1994.

Isaac, Mike. *Super Pumped: The Battle for Uber.* W. W. Norton, 2019.

Leonard, Christopher. *Kochland: The Secret History of Koch Industries and Corporate Power in America.* Simon & Schuster, 2019.

Lewis, Michael. *The Premonition: A Pandemic Story.* W. W. Norton, 2021.

BIBLIOGRAPHY

Locke, John. *Two Treatises of Government*. Cambridge University Press, 1988.

Martin, Felix. *Money: The Unauthorized Biography—From Coinage to Cryptocurrencies*. Vintage, 2014.

Marx, Karl, and Friedrich Engels. *The Communist Manifesto*. Introduction by Gareth Stedman Jones. Penguin Classics, 2002.

Matz, Sandra. *Mindmasters: The Data-Driven Science of Predicting and Changing Human Behavior*. Harvard Business Review Press, 2025.

Mazarr, Michael J., Ryan M. Bauer, Abigail Casey, Sarah A. Heintz, and Luke J. Matthews. *The Emerging Risk of Virtual Societal Warfare: Social Manipulation in a Changing Information Environment*. RAND Corporation, 2019.

Mazzucato, Mariana. *The Entrepreneurial State: Debunking Public vs. Private Sector Myths*. Penguin Books, 2024.

Mill, John Stuart. *Principles of Political Economy: The Complete 5 Books*. CreateSpace Independent Publishing, 2018.

Mullins, Brody, and Luke Mullins. *The Wolves of K Street: The Secret History of How Big Money Took Over Big Government*. Simon & Schuster, 2024.

Nocera, Joe, and Bethany McLean. *The Big Fail: What the Pandemic Revealed About Who America Protects and Who It Leaves Behind*. Penguin Press, 2023.

O'Mara, Margaret. *The Code: Silicon Valley and the Remaking of America*. Penguin Press, 2019.

O'Neil, Cathy. *Weapons of Math Destruction: How Big Data Increases Inequality and Threatens Democracy*. Crown, 2016.

Oreskes, Naomi, and Erik M. Conway. *Merchants of Doubt: How a Handful of Scientists Obscured the Truth on Issues from Tobacco Smoke to Global Warming*. Bloomsbury Press, 2010.

Pahlka, Jennifer. *Recoding America: Why Government Is Failing in the Digital Age and How We Can Do Better*. Metropolitan Books, 2023.

Pariser, Eli. *The Filter Bubble: How the New Personalized Web Is Changing What We Read and How We Think*. Penguin Books 2011.

Plato. *The Republic*. Translated by Benjamin Jowett. Vintage Books, 1991.

Pomerantsev, Peter. *Autocracy, Inc.: The Dictators Who Want to Run the World*. Doubleday, 2024.

Prasad, Rani, and Ranjit Sinha. *BRICS and Resistance in Africa: Contention, Assimilation and Co-optation*. Zed Books, 2019.

Ricardo, David. *On the Principles of Political Economy and Taxation*. London, 1817.

Richardson, Heather Cox. *How the South Won the Civil War: Oligarchy, Democracy, and the Continuing Fight for the Soul of America*. Oxford University Press, 2020.

Sapolsky, Robert M. *Determined: A Science of Life Without Free Will*. Penguin Press, 2023.

Seidman, Dov. *How: Why How We Do Anything Means Everything*. Wiley, 2007.

Simon, Phil. *The Nine: The Tectonic Forces Reshaping the Workplace*. Racket Publishing, 2023.

Smith, Adam. *An Inquiry into the Nature and Causes of the Wealth of Nations*. London, 1776.

Sorkin, Andrew Ross. *Too Big to Fail: The Inside Story of How Wall Street and Washington Fought to Save the Financial System—and Themselves*. Viking, 2009.

Srinivasan, Balaji. *The Network State: How to Start a New Country*. Amazon Kindle, 2022.

Srivastava, Rajiv. *Web3 in Financial Services: How Blockchain, Digital Assets and Crypto Are Disrupting Traditional Finance*. Kogan Page, 2024.

Steil, Benn. *The Battle of Bretton Woods: John Maynard Keynes, Harry Dexter White, and the Making of a New World Order*. Princeton University Press, 2013.

Stone, Brad. *The Upstarts: How Uber, Airbnb, and the Killer Companies of the New Silicon Valley Are Changing the World*. Little, Brown, 2017.

Streitfeld, David. *The Everything War: Amazon's Ruthless Quest to Own the World and Remake Corporate Power*. Little, Brown, 2024.

US Congress. House. Select Committee to Investigate the January 6th Attack on the United States Capitol. *Report on the Activities of the Select Committee to Investigate the January 6th Attack on the United States Capitol of the House of Representatives During the One Hundred Seventeenth Congress*. 117th Cong., 2nd sess., H. Rep. 117-692. https://tinyurl.com/ms6578vb.

Zarate, Juan C. *Treasury's War: The Unleashing of a New Era of Financial Warfare*. PublicAffairs, 2013.

ENDNOTES

Introduction
1. Morgan Chalfant, "Trump: 'The Only Way We're Going to Lose This Election Is If the Election Is Rigged,'" *The Hill*, August 17, 2020, https://tinyurl.com/2cb5j243.
2. Sarah Fortinsky, "One-Third of Adults in New Poll Say Biden's Election Was Illegitimate," *The Hill*, January 2, 2024, https://tinyurl.com/2de3phxw.
3. Gerrit De Vynck and Rachel Lerman, "YouTube Suspends Trump, Days After Twitter and Facebook," *The Washington Post*, January 15, 2021, https://tinyurl.com/yyv9nljs.
4. "Trump Fires Election Security Official Who Contradicted Him," US and Canada, *BBC*, November 18, 2020, https://tinyurl.com/29nqupkj.
5. "Final Report of the Select Committee to Investigate the January 6th Attack on the United States Capitol," GovInfo, December 22, 2022, https://tinyurl.com/2wjwkmyp.
6. Andrew Stanton, "Donald Trump 'Nearly Doubled' Fundraising Record After Verdict: Campaign," *Newsweek*, May 31, 2024, https://tinyurl.com/2osw2x8q.
7. Steve Benen, "Why It Matters That Trump's 'Election Defense Fund' Didn't Exist," MSNBC, June 13, 2022, https://tinyurl.com/2l2b9s4d.
8. Hugo Lowell, "Trump's Raising of $250m for Fund That 'Did Not Exist' Suggests Possible Fraud," *The Guardian*, June 15, 2022, https://tinyurl.com/2atyzdvo.
9. David Enrich et al., "Growing Discomfort at Law Firms Representing Trump in Election Lawsuits," *The New York Times*, November 9, 2020, https://tinyurl.com/y5j8xv6t.
10. "Jan. 6 Committee Shows Video of Protesters Chanting 'Hang Mike Pence,'" NBC News, June 17, 2022, https://tinyurl.com/2akxsu2u.
11. Jack Healy, "These Are the 5 People Who Died in the Capitol Riot," U.S., *The New York Times*, January 11, 2021, https://tinyurl.com/y4b88ulz.
12. Jack Healy.
13. Julia Shumway, "Republicans Running for Oregon Governor Defended the Jan. 6 Capitol Attack. One Was There," *Oregon Capital Chronicle*, April 12, 2022, https://tinyurl.com/25a9ctwn.
14. Jamie Gangel et al., "House Investigators Target the Money Trail Behind January 6 Rally," CNN Politics, October 22, 2021, https://tinyurl.com/2qetpms8.

15 Matthew Yglesias, "America Should Invest in Its Federal Legislature," Slow Boring, November 26, 2021, https://tinyurl.com/4bxtx2cv.
16 "Political Activities," United States Department of Justice, last modified July 8, 2024, https://tinyurl.com/49tdcve7.
17 Mary Clare Jalonick, "Democrats Promote Liz Cheney to Vice Chairwoman of Jan. 6 Panel," PBS NewsHour, September 2, 2021, https://tinyurl.com/24xfy4r5.
18 Brian Fung, "Facebook Bans 'Stop the Steal' Content, 69 Days after the Election," CNN, January 12, 2021, https://tinyurl.com/y42jv8t7.
19 Brittany Bernstein, "Salesforce 'Takes Action' to Keep Trump Campaign Emails from Inciting Violence," Yahoo News, January 14, 2021, https://tinyurl.com/2zqg6wac.
20 House Select Committee to Investigate the January 6th Attack on the US Capitol, 2022, https://tinyurl.com/26sx4gbn.

Chapter 1
1 "Money," The British Museum, December 14, 2019, https://tinyurl.com/29rr3yd8.
2 Joshua McMorrow-Hernandez, "Bahamas to Eliminate the One Cent Coin, but Will the United States Follow?" CoinWeek, September 27, 2019, https://tinyurl.com/2c633hsj.
3 Suomen Pankki, "Historical Finnish Banknotes and Coins," July 10, 2017, https://tinyurl.com/28dwwrgo.
4 Stephen Quinn and William Roberds, "The Evolution of the Check as a Means of Payment: A Historical Survey Economic Review," Federal Reserve Bank of Atlanta, 2008, https://tinyurl.com/5n6askma.
5 Frank Hersey, "Mastercard Launches Retail Biometrics Program with Brazil Pilot," Biometric Update, May 17, 2022, https://tinyurl.com/25lhlm2w.
6 Oyin Adedoyin, "Want to Pay Cash? That'll Cost You Extra," *The Wall Street Journal*, June 6, 2024, https://tinyurl.com/28mma2wo.
7 Diners Club, "History and Legacy," Diners Club International, March 16, 2016, https://tinyurl.com/2zdsearx.
8 "Payment Card Volume Topped $40 Trillion Worldwide in 2022," *The Nilson Report*, GlobeNewswire, May 24, 2023, https://tinyurl.com/2adq8qne.
9 Benedict George, "What Is Bitcoin Pizza Day?," CoinDesk, April 6, 2022, https://tinyurl.com/2pw9ac46.
10 Benedict George.
11 Elizabeth Napolitano, "Chipotle Now Accepting Cryptocurrency Payments at US Locations," CoinDesk, June 2, 2022, https://tinyurl.com/2qrhatto.
12 Adam Smith, *An Inquiry into the Nature and Causes of the Wealth of Nations* (Oxford University Press, 2008).
13 Mary West, "Heart Transplant: How It Works, Cost, Insurance, and More," MedicalNewsToday, August 31, 2022, https://tinyurl.com/2bvq7w67.
14 "Worth Its Weight in Gold," Idioms Online, May 20, 2021, https://tinyurl.com/2nw7kmt9.

ENDNOTES

15 *Oxford English Dictionary*, "Value," accessed June 11, 2024, https://tinyurl.com/29sdlu7c.
16 "Consumer Surplus," *The Economic Times*, accessed March 8, 2025, https://tinyurl.com/4j7ywa9x.
17 "History of the Licensed London Taxi Cab," London Taxi Cabs 0203 00 44 953, April 29, 2015, https://tinyurl.com/2cdjeb4f.
18 Noam Scheiber, "How Uber Uses Psychological Tricks to Push Its Drivers' Buttons," *The New York Times*, June 11, 2024, https://tinyurl.com/m8tts6l.
19 "Uber (UBER)," Companies Market Cap, June 11, 2024, https://tinyurl.com/2a7p37v5.
20 Michelle Chapman, "In a First for Uber Since Becoming a Public Company, an Annual Profit," AP News, February 7, 2024, https://tinyurl.com/248ljxco.
21 Simon Van Zuylen-Wood, "The Struggles of New York City's Taxi King," *Bloomberg*, August 27, 2015, https://tinyurl.com/23v32r4z.
22 Leora Klapper et al., "Financial Literacy Around the World: Insights from the Standard & Poor's Ratings Services Global Financial Literacy Survey," World Bank, November 22, 2015, https://tinyurl.com/2lfge4qe.
23 Corri Hess, "Assembly Reintroduces Bill Requiring Financial Literacy Class as Graduation Requirement for Wisconsin High Schools," Wisconsin Public Radio, April 21, 2023, https://tinyurl.com/2dqc8a9a.
24 Erin El Issa, "2017 American Household Credit Card Debt Study," NerdWallet, December 8, 2017, https://tinyurl.com/2bod944n.
25 Jack Nicas, "He Has 17,700 Bottles of Hand Sanitizer and Nowhere to Sell Them," Technology, *The New York Times*, March 14, 2020, https://tinyurl.com/w3742nn.
26 Khristopher Brooks, "Egg Prices Have Soared 60% in a Year. Here's Why," CBS News, January 17, 2023, https://tinyurl.com/2j6mahcw.
27 Erin Blakemore, "Germany's World War I Debt Was So Crushing It Took 92 Years to Pay Off," History, June 27, 2019, https://tinyurl.com/tw9amtb.
28 "The Weimar Republic 1918–1929—Edexcel," *BBC*, January 3, 2020, https://tinyurl.com/yzl8qx6t.
29 Jacob Goldstein, *Money: The True Story of a Made-Up Thing* (Hachette Books, 2020).
30 Dominique Tassell, "Aussies Warned About Dodgy Detail in Banknotes," 7NEWS, July 18, 2023, https://tinyurl.com/2y7wpnrd.
31 "3 Arrested in Dawn Crackdown of Suspected Counterfeit Notes Production and Circulation in Greater Manchester," Greater Manchester Police, October 4, 2023, https://tinyurl.com/27htgkt2.
32 Tim Sullivan, "Transparency, Trust, and Bitcoin," *Harvard Business Review*, June 1, 2015, https://tinyurl.com/27lq5vvv.

Chapter 2

1 "Lehman Brothers Timeline, Harvard Business School," 2022, https://tinyurl.com/2h6t7ga3.
2 "Lehman Brothers," Corporate Finance Institute, n.d., https://tinyurl.com/248fuvhv.

THE CATALYSTS

3. John Kwaku and Mensah Mawutor, "The Failure of Lehman Brothers: Causes, Preventive Measures and Recommendations," *Research Journal of Finance and Accounting* 5, no. 4 (2014): 2222–2847, https://tinyurl.com/28lor4co.
4. Yassine Bakkar, "Why Did Lehman Brothers Fail?," Economics Observatory, September 28, 2023, https://tinyurl.com/2k24ofup.
5. "Failed Bank List," FDIC, July 28, 2023, https://tinyurl.com/yxhc9ceu.
6. Eric Dash, "U.S. Gives Banks Urgent Warning to Solve Crisis," Business, *The New York Times*, September 13, 2008, https://tinyurl.com/2zfqc3ex.
7. David Kudla, "Morgan Stanley's Future Is Bright for Investors," Market Watch, October 8, 2013, https://tinyurl.com/2phvp3tm.
8. Ben Bernanke, "Troubled Asset Relief Program and the Federal Reserve's Liquidity Facilities," Board of Governors of the Federal Reserve System, November 18, 2008, https://tinyurl.com/2ke2qcb3.
9. "Troubled Asset Relief Program: Lifetime Cost," US Government Accountability Office, December 7, 2023, https://tinyurl.com/2f37jtuh.
10. *Oxford English Dictionary*, "Custodian," accessed July 1, 2024, https://tinyurl.com/2pf4dlkm.
11. Lyn Alden, *Broken Money: Why Our Financial System Is Failing Us and How We Can Make It Better* (Harriman House, 2023).
12. Lyn Alden.
13. Jacob Goldstein, *Money: The True Story of a Made-Up Thing*, 1st ed. (Hachette Books, 2020).
14. Eamon Quinn, "Revealed: Full List of Bank of Ireland Branch Closures," *Irish Examiner*, October 8, 2021, https://tinyurl.com/2oe49xmf.
15. "Ireland: Largest Banks by Assets 2023," Statista, accessed July 1, 2024, https://tinyurl.com/2l367mhc.
16. George J. Benston, "Universal Banking," *Journal of Economic Perspectives* 8, no. 3 (1994): 121–43. https://doi.org/10.1257/jep.8.3.121.
17. Patrick Wolfinbarger, "Custodia Bank Files Appeal over Decision Supporting Fed Denial of Master Account," *Wyoming Tribune Eagle*, June 27, 2024, https://tinyurl.com/2nclg295.
18. Nikhilesh De, "Custodia Bank Loses Lawsuit Challenging Fed Rejection of Master Account Application," CoinDesk, March 29, 2024, https://tinyurl.com/2b6vtdfv.
19. Nicole Willing, "Centralized Finance," Technopedia, October 3, 2023, https://tinyurl.com/2gc4wpo7.
20. Nathan Chandler, "What Is the Butterfly Effect and How Do We Misunderstand It?" HowStuffWorks, August 7, 2020, https://tinyurl.com/yeyb8k75.
21. "The IMF at a Glance," International Monetary Fund, August 28, 2020, https://tinyurl.com/yh8nwscs.
22. "Getting to Know the World Bank," World Bank Group, July 26, 2012, https://tinyurl.com/y52jbnav.
23. "Getting to Know the World Bank."

ENDNOTES

24   "UN Proposes New International Organization to Offer Low-Interest Loans," World Bank Group Timeline, April 12, 1949, https://tinyurl.com/2hrnhp83.
25   Bank for International Settlements, 2019, https://www.bis.org.
26   Giulio Cornelli et al., "Buy Now, Pay Later: A Cross-Country Analysis," Bank for International Settlements, December 4, 2023, https://tinyurl.com/2nc86fyn.
27   Jesse Eisinger, "Why Only One Top Banker Went to Jail for the Financial Crisis," *The New York Times*, April 30, 2014, https://tinyurl.com/zpmn2yc.
28   Kaley Schafer and Peter D. Hardy, "SDNY Sentences Danske Bank in Massive AML Scandal," Money Laundering Watch, January 23, 2023, https://tinyurl.com/2pwfo9a5.
29   Patrick Tibke, "Explained: How These 5 Trade Finance Instruments Can Help Your Business Grow in 2022," Trade Finance Global, January 18, 2022, https://tinyurl.com/2n5o9vq2.
30   "Payments and Transaction Banking," Boston Consulting Group, August 14, 2020, https://tinyurl.com/2z8exfdk.
31   "Cross-Border Payments," Bank of England, January 31, 2023, https://tinyurl.com/2k6ox8hd.
32   "COBOL Blues," *Reuters*, April 11, 2017, https://tinyurl.com/25mpqewc.
33   Anna Irrera, "Banks Scramble to Fix Old Systems as IT 'Cowboys' Ride into Sunset," *Reuters*, April 9, 2017, https://tinyurl.com/2q5y9zuv.
34   "Cross-Border Payments," Financial Stability Board, October 23, 2020, https://tinyurl.com/2ze6gd3z.
35   Harry Newman and Olivier Denecker, "A Vision for the Future of Cross-Border Payments," McKinsey, 2024, https://tinyurl.com/y2ba463l.

Chapter 3

1   Suzanne Maloney, "The Revolutionary Economy," United States Institute of Peace, October 11, 2010, https://tinyurl.com/y34cunzu.
2   Geoffrey Kemp, "The Reagan Administration," United States Institute of Peace, October 5, 2010, https://tinyurl.com/22yk24wr.
3   "Arms Embargoes," Stockholm International Peace Research Institute, September 21, 2010, https://tinyurl.com/2loq3c84.
4   Kali Robinson, "What Is the Iran Nuclear Deal?," Council on Foreign Relations, October 27, 2023, https://tinyurl.com/y47kgw3z.
5   "Iran Deal," The White House, January 20, 2017, https://tinyurl.com/lbk8s52.
6   "President Donald J. Trump Is Ending United States Participation in an Unacceptable Iran Deal," The White House, May 8, 2018, https://tinyurl.com/yfs4ugsp.
7   "Statement from President Joe Biden on Iran Sanctions," The White House, April 18, 2024, https://tinyurl.com/27rwug35.
8   Mohamed Younis, "Iranians Feel Bite of Sanctions, Blame U.S., Not Own Leaders," Gallup, February 7, 2013, https://tinyurl.com/2cre872z.
9   "The Bretton Woods Conference, 1944," US Department of State, 2019, https://tinyurl.com/t24au5u.

10 Benn Steil, *The Battle of Bretton Woods: John Maynard Keynes, Harry Dexter White, and the Making of a New World Order* (Princeton University Press, 2013).
11 "Appendix 1: An Historical Perspective on the Reserve Currency Status of the U.S. Dollar," US Department of the Treasury, 2009, https://tinyurl.com/2lfmd2kh.
12 Anshu Siripurapu and Noah Berman, "The Dollar: The World's Reserve Currency," Council on Foreign Relations, July 19, 2023, https://tinyurl.com/2d2k7lfq.
13 Anshu Siripurapu and Noah Berman.
14 Kristopher Kane, "What Is the Gold Standard?" *Money*, February 26, 2024, https://tinyurl.com/29hm5neu.
15 "Great Depression Facts—Franklin D. Roosevelt," FDR Presidential Library and Museum, 2016, https://tinyurl.com/yh4exjcz.
16 Gary Richardson et al., "Roosevelt's Gold Program," Federal Reserve History, November 22, 2013, https://tinyurl.com/2xott5yw.
17 Gary Richardson et al., "Gold Reserve Act of 1934," Federal Reserve History, November 22, 2013, https://tinyurl.com/3ktjp95a.
18 Gary Richardson et al., "Roosevelt's Gold Program," Federal Reserve History, November 22, 2013, https://tinyurl.com/2xott5yw.
19 "Executive Order 6102—Forbidding the Hoarding of Gold Coin, Gold Bullion and Gold Certificates," The American Presidency Project, April 5, 1933, https://tinyurl.com/29hdkyza.
20 Lawrence W. Reed, "FDR's Other 'Day of Infamy': When the US Seized All Citizens' Gold," Catalyst, April 4, 2023, https://catalyst.independent.org/2023/04/04/us-seized-gold/.
21 Gary Richardson et al., "Gold Reserve Act of 1934," Federal Reserve History, November 22, 2013, https://tinyurl.com/3ktjp95a.
22 Ben Bernanke, "The Dollar's International Role: An 'Exorbitant Privilege'?" Brookings, January 7, 2016, https://tinyurl.com/23vcurwh.
23 Ben Bernanke.
24 Ben Bernanke.
25 Tyler Bartlam, "'Full Faith and Credit' Means Loaning Money to U.S. Is a Safe Bet," NPR, May 12, 2023, https://tinyurl.com/274hz4fn.
26 Kelly Jernigan, "The U.S. Dollar and Its Role in the Global Economy," Commerce Trust, August 28, 2023, https://tinyurl.com/25evdqjc.
27 Johannes Gräb et al., "Quantifying the 'Exorbitant Privilege'—Potential Benefits from a Stronger International Role of the Euro," 2019, https://bit.ly/4eZSG1X.
28 Dante Alighieri Disparte, "De-Dollarization or Re-Dollarization? The Fate of the Dollar in the Internet Age," The Bretton Woods Committee, June 5, 2023, https://tinyurl.com/2292stvj.
29 "Home," Office of Foreign Assets Control, U.S. Department of the Treasury, March 23, 2023, https://ofac.treasury.gov/.
30 "Venezuela: Overview of U.S. Sanctions Policy," Congressional Research Service, February 28, 2019, https://tinyurl.com/3evuraan.

ENDNOTES

31 Rina Rossi, "US Sanctions Are Robbing Venezuelans of Basic Human Rights," Georgetown Public Policy Review, July 4, 2023, https://tinyurl.com/2ya69pzj.
32 "Home," Office of Foreign Assets Control, U.S. Department of the Treasury, March 23, 2023, https://ofac.treasury.gov.

Chapter 4
1   "Raytheon: Number of Employees 2008–2023," Statista, February 21, 2024, https://bit.ly/462R4R2.
2   Nigel Cameron, "The Government Agency That Made Silicon Valley," UnHerd, June 18, 2018, https://bit.ly/4cEH9Ua.
3   "First Soviet Test," PBS, March 22, 2019, https://to.pbs.org/3W5nYf9.
4   Sissi Cao, "Did Jeff Bezos Just Admit to Exploiting USPS as Amazon's 'Delivery Boy'?," Observer, July 16, 2019, https://bit.ly/4d0Cps0.
5   D. V. Cowen, "A Survey of the Law Relating to the Control of Monopoly in South Africa," *South African Journal of Economics*, 18, no. 2 (1950), https://bit.ly/4f35uon.
6   "Restraint of Trade," Cornell Law School, June 17, 2012, https://bit.ly/4bGyVtG.
7   Anu Bradford et al., "Competition Law Gone Global: Introducing the Comparative Competition Law and Enforcement Datasets," *Journal of Empirical Legal Studies* 16, no. 2 (2019): 411.
8   Elizabeth Weber Handwerker and Matthew Dey, "Some Facts About Concentrated Labor Markets in the United States," US Bureau of Labor Statistics, June 2022, https://bit.ly/3XZeBQP.
9   "Gilded Age," History, February 13, 2018, https://bit.ly/3WkIcmx.
10 "Remarks in Providence, Rhode Island," The American Presidency Project, August 21, 2021, https://bit.ly/4fglmUT.
11 "Sherman Anti-Trust Act (1890)," National Archives, September 9, 2021, https://bit.ly/3xLASHr.
12 Julia Maues, "Banking Act of 1933 (Glass-Steagall)," Federal Reserve History, November 22, 2013, https://bit.ly/4f2sfIX.
13 "IADI," International Association of Deposit Insurers, August 15, 2016, https://www.iadi.org/.
14 "The Federal Communications Commission (FCC)," National Telecommunications and Information Administration, July 24, 2023, https://bit.ly/4cHjvq8.
15 Maurice E. Stucke and Ariel Ezrachi, "The Rise, Fall, and Rebirth of the U.S. Antitrust Movement," *Harvard Business Review*, December 15, 2017, https://bit.ly/4cENeAe.
16 Laura Phillips Sawyer, "US Antitrust Law and Policy in Historical Perspective," Working Paper No. 19-110 (Harvard Business School, 2021), https://bit.ly/3Lod7YU.
17 Sara Lebow, "Amazon Will Surpass 40% of US Ecommerce Sales This Year, Despite Competition in Grocery, Home Improvement," Emarketer, April 17, 2024, https://bit.ly/3S5NIHg.
18 Scott Galloway, "Guardrails," *Medium*, April 24, 2023, https://bit.ly/3Ll0i1w.
19 Laura Phillips Sawyer, "US Antitrust Law and Policy in Historical Perspective," Working Paper No. 19-110 (Harvard Business School, 2021), https://bit.ly/3Lod7YU.

THE CATALYSTS

20 "Money, Power and Wall Street," *Frontline*, December 25, 2022.
21 "Department of Justice's Review of Section 230 of the Communications Decency Act of 1996," U.S. Department of Justice, June 3, 2020, https://bit.ly/468DPhJ.
22 "The Breakup of 'Ma Bell,': United States v. AT&T," Federal Judicial Center, February 1, 2022, https://bit.ly/3Y9OBlM.
23 Jennifer Waters, "AT&T Corporation," Britannica Money, April 1, 2024, https://bit.ly/468omhU.
24 Department of Justice, "Department of Justice Filed an Antitrust Suit Charging American Telephone & Telegraph," news release, November 20, 1974, https://bit.ly/4hZyhLt.
25 Bret Swanson, "Lessons from the AT&T Break Up, 30 Years Later," AEI, January 3, 2014, https://bit.ly/3Sv4csT.
26 "Fortune 500: 1969 Archive Full List 1–100," CNN Money, https://cnn.it/4f44oZr.
27 "United States' Memorandum on the 1969 Case," Antitrust Division US Department of Justice, October 5, 1995, https://bit.ly/3Y42QIR.
28 Edward T. Pound, "Why Baxter Dropped the IBM Suit," Business, *The New York Times*, January 9, 1982, https://nyti.ms/4d0TTEt.
29 Steve Lohr and John Markoff, "Microsoft's World: A Special Report.; How Software's Giant Played Hardball Game," Business, *The New York Times*, October 8, 1998, https://nyti.ms/3S6WaWE.
30 Yoni Heisler, "What Ever Became of Microsoft's $150 Million Investment in Apple?" Engadget, May 20, 2014, https://engt.co/3zHeoYB.
31 Michael Liedtke, "Google and Apple Now Threatened by the US Antitrust Laws That Helped Build Their Technology Empires," AP News, May 1, 2024, https://bit.ly/3Y8NGlX.
32 Eric Savitz and Jack Denton, "Alphabet Closes Above $2 Trillion Market Cap for the First Time," Barron's, April 26, 2024, https://bit.ly/3WLVVSi.
33 Eric Savitz and Jack Denton.
34 Dara Kerr, "U.S. v. Google: As Landmark 'Monopoly Power' Trial Closes, Here's What to Look For," NPR, May 2, 2024, https://n.pr/3X0tWzD.
35 David McCabe, "Google Violated Antitrust Laws in Online Search, Judge Rules," Technology, *The New York Times*, August 5, 2024, https://nyti.ms/3SOgxZ3.

Chapter 5
1 "September 11 Attacks: What Happened on 9/11?," US & Canada, *BBC*, January 9, 2025, https://bbc.in/3WG8KOh.
2 "Remember Flight 93: A True Story of American Courage," 9/11 Memorial & Museum, September 11, 2011, https://bit.ly/4dlzHhk.
3 George W. Bush, "Statement by the President in Address to the Nation," The White House, archived September 11, 2001, at https://bit.ly/4cFtPyp.
4 David Moore, "Bush Job Approval Highest in Gallup History," Gallup, September 24, 2001, https://bit.ly/3SJb5XC.
5 "PATRIOT Act," Epic.org, November 7, 2021, https://bit.ly/46OTPpt.

ENDNOTES

6   "Hurricane Katrina: Facts, FAQs, and How to Help," World Vision, November 20, 2023, https://bit.ly/46J3xtw.
7   "George W. Bush in 2005: 'If We Wait for a Pandemic to Appear, It Will Be Too Late to Prepare,'" ABC News, April 5, 2020, https://bit.ly/4aNUrh5.
8   "First Confirmed Case of COVID-19 Found in U.S," History, January 19, 2021, https://bit.ly/46Hpc5n.
9   Lloyd Doggett, "Timeline of Trump's Coronavirus Responses," Congressman Lloyd Doggett, March 2, 2022, https://bit.ly/3SMX5vH.
10 Mary Kay Mallonee and Devan Cole, "Romney Calls Trump's Leadership on Covid-19 'a Great Human Tragedy,'" CNN, December 3, 2020, https://cnn.it/3M5oAgs.
11 Jeffrey Jones, "Majority in U.S. Continues to Favor Stricter Gun Laws," Gallup, October 31, 2023, https://bit.ly/3AmCk3V.
12 "Majority of Public Disapproves of Supreme Court's Decision to Overturn Roe v. Wade," Pew Research Center, July 6, 2022, https://pewrsr.ch/3M5RGfB.
13 "Public Opinion on Abortion," Pew Research Center, May 13, 2024, https://pewrsr.ch/3VP49tf.
14 "Highways and Bridges," AMPP, February 5, 2023, https://bit.ly/4dlFX8Q.
15 Leigh Ann Caldwell, "Democrats Sour on Trump Infrastructure Proposals," NBC News, June 5, 2017, https://nbcnews.to/4cr2Rdx.
16 Peter Weber, "The 13 House Republicans Who Voted for the Bipartisan Infrastructure Bill Are Getting GOP Blowback, Threats," *The Week*, November 10, 2021, https://bit.ly/4cEM1bq.
17 Harlan Ullman, "A Pandemic of Hyper-Hypocrisy Is Infecting American Politics," *The Hill*, October 18, 2021, https://bit.ly/4dJuyz8.
18 "Research Starters: The GI Bill," The National WWII Museum, April 7, 2020, https://bit.ly/3X6gn1X.
19 "The 1950s," History, A&E Television Networks, June 17, 2010, https://bit.ly/3SKY7Zq.
20 Rakesh Kochhar and Stella Sechopoulos, "How the American Middle Class Has Changed in the Past Five Decades," Pew Research Center, April 22, 2022, https://pewrsr.ch/3SNzkE0.
21 Anshu Siripurapu, "The U.S. Inequality Debate," Council on Foreign Relations, April 20, 2022, https://on.cfr.org/4hD8ZCs.
22 "Current US Inflation Rates: 2000–2024," US Inflation Calculator, August 1, 2008, https://bit.ly/4fNxUDa.
23 Jay Shambaugh and Ryan Nunn, "Why Wages Aren't Growing in America," *Harvard Business Review*, October 24, 2017, https://bit.ly/3SMVGoU.
24 "The Productivity–Pay Gap," Economic Policy Institute, October 28, 2022, https://bit.ly/3YLYWVE.
25 Lawrence Mishel et al., "Wage Stagnation in Nine Charts," Economic Policy Institute, January 6, 2015, https://bit.ly/3WJzo8Q.

THE CATALYSTS

26. "Every Job Should Pay a Living Wage," National Employment Law Project, March 11, 2024, https://bit.ly/4dMCP5L.
27. Jeanne Kuang, "Californians Will Vote on a $18 Minimum Wage. Workers Already Want $25 and More," CalMatters, August 14, 2024, https://bit.ly/3AyjeHS.
28. C. A. Bridges, "When Will Minimum Wage Go Up Again in Florida and How Much? What Is Minimum Wage in 2025?" *Tallahassee Democrat*, January 3, 2025, https://bit.ly/40ZuxDS.
29. Noam Levey, "Nineteen Surgeries over Five Years. Then They Lost Their House," KFF Health News, June 17, 2022, https://bit.ly/3SOa00o.
30. "Study: Financial Stress Amongst Employees Has Skyrocketed with 63% of Employees Unable to Cover a $500 Emergency Expense," PRWeb, August 17, 2023, https://bit.ly/4djqoyg.
31. Melissa D. Kalensky, "Death or Debt—This Is Why We Need Health Insurance Guarantees," *The Hill*, September 28, 2017, https://bit.ly/3ytRYKh.
32. Jessica Dickler, "Average Consumer Now Carries $6,329 in Credit Card Debt. 'People Are Stretched,' Expert Says," CNBC, August 8, 2024, https://cnb.cx/4dpg7ki.
33. "Affirm Holdings, Inc. (AFRM)," Yahoo! Finance, https://yhoo.it/3SQcxHG.
34. Hugh Son, "Affirm Buy Now, Pay Later Loans Will Be Embedded into Apple Pay Later This Year," CNBC, June 11, 2024, https://cnb.cx/46Mj1wY.
35. Deidre McPhillips, "US Fertility Rate Dropped to Lowest in a Century as US Births Dipped in 2023," CNN, April 25, 2024, https://cnn.it/4fLFI8w.
36. Claire Cain Miller, "The World 'Has Found a Way to Do This': The U.S. Lags on Paid Leave," The Upshot, *The New York Times*, October 25, 2021, https://nyti.ms/3SQ2en4.
37. David Leonhardt, "The American Dream, Quantified at Last," *The New York Times*, August 14, 2024, https://nyti.ms/4cqijqn.
38. Gabriel Borelli, "Americans Are Split Over the State of the American Dream," Pew Research Center, July 2, 2024, https://pewrsr.ch/4cmUM9K.
39. Solcyré Burga, "U.S Falls Out of Top 20 Happiest Countries for the First Time Ever," *Time*, March 20, 2024, https://bit.ly/3WI2OEp.
40. Paulina Cachero and Claire Ballentine, "Nearly Half of All Young Adults Live With Mom and Dad—and They Like It," *Bloomberg*, 2024, https://bloom.bg/3ytLxXB.
41. "U.S. GDP 1960–2024," Macrotrends, 2024, https://bit.ly/3X4XHiN.
42. "U.S. Debt Credit Rating Downgraded, Only Second Time in Nation's History," Budget Committee, August 4, 2023, https://bit.ly/3yPrvqm.
43. Davide Barbuscia et al., "Moody's Turns Negative on US Credit Rating, Draws Washington Ire," *Reuters*, November 11, 2023, https://reut.rs/4fGMah9.
44. "Real Estate Mogul Leona Helmsley Sentenced to Prison," History, March 8, 2010, https://bit.ly/4fNDdT3.
45. Lauren Aratani, "Wealthiest Americans Pay Just 3.4% of Income in Taxes, Investigation Reveals," *The Guardian*, April 13, 2022, https://bit.ly/46NnUFX.
46. "The Distribution of Household Income in 2020," Congressional Budget Office, November 14, 2023, https://bit.ly/4crU7nx.

ENDNOTES

47 David Floyd, "Trump's Tax Reform Plan Explained," Investopedia, January 23, 2023, https://bit.ly/3M7bNKk.
48 Kathryn Watson, "'You All Just Got a Lot Richer,' Trump Tells Friends, Referencing Tax Overhaul," CBS News, December 24, 2017, https://cbsn.ws/3SOfJU2.
49 "The 2017 Trump Tax Law Was Skewed to the Rich, Expensive, and Failed to Deliver on Its Promises," The Center on Budget and Policy Priorities, April 4, 2024, https://bit.ly/4dppX5z.
50 "The Tax Gap," Internal Revenue Service, September 25, 2017, https://bit.ly/4coOtm7.
51 Laura Davison, "Tax Cheats Are Costing the U.S. $1 Trillion a Year, IRS Estimates," *Bloomberg*, April 13, 2021, https://bloom.bg/4djpKAX.
52 David Shribman, "Lament of the Reagan IRS," Business, *The New York Times*, April 4, 1982, https://nyti.ms/4csjp50.
53 Chye-Ching Huang, "Depletion of IRS Enforcement Is Undermining the Tax Code," Center on Budget and Policy Priorities, February 11, 2020, https://bit.ly/3WNiLck.
54 Kate Dore, "Reconciliation Bill Includes Nearly $80 Billion for IRS Including Enforcement, Audits: What That Means for Taxpayers," CNBC, August 22, 2022, https://cnb.cx/4clSibz.
55 "What Happens If the U.S. Defaults on Its Debt?" Yahoo! Finance, December 2, 2023, https://yhoo.it/4cqUZca.
56 Omkar Godbole, "Soaring U.S. Debt Has Potential to Replay U.K.'s 2022 Market Shock, CBO Warns," CoinDesk, March 26, 2024, https://bit.ly/3yGsyZJ.
57 Jagadeesh Gokhale and Kent Smetters, "When Does Federal Debt Reach Unsustainable Levels?" Penn Wharton Budget Model, October 6, 2023, https://whr.tn/46MgD9o.
58 Mark Memmott, "PolitiFact Awards Obama 'Lie of the Year,'" MPR News, December 13, 2013, https://bit.ly/411TgaQ.
59 Katie Lobosco, "5 Reasons Why the Republican Claim About 87,000 New IRS Agents Is an Exaggeration," CNN, January 11, 2023, https://cnn.it/4dIFYTR.
60 David Wright, "Trump: U.S. Will Never Default 'Because You Print the Money,'" CNN, May 9, 2016, https://cnn.it/3WQBNP4.
61 J. B. Maverick, "What Agencies Oversee U.S. Financial Institutions?" Investopedia, March 14, 2023, https://bit.ly/3YMc0dr.
62 Kevin Frazzini, "Supreme Court Affirms Constitutionality of CFPB Funding," National Conference of State Legislatures, May 22, 2024, https://bit.ly/3SPP6y6.
63 Will Canny, "U.S. CBDC Is Unlikely in the Near Term: Bank of America," CoinDesk, November 15, 2023, https://bit.ly/4crotGS.

Chapter 6

1 Evan Perez and Tim Hume, "Apple Opposes Judge's Order to Hack San Bernardino Shooter's iPhone," CNN, February 17, 2016, https://cnn.it/3zdQrbt.
2 Tim Cook, "A Message to Our Customers," Apple, February 16, 2016, https://apple.co/47lhheb.
3 "Google to Acknowledge Privacy 'Mistakes' to U.S. Senate Committee," CBC Radio-Canada, September 26, 2018, https://bit.ly/3XzdiY9.

THE CATALYSTS

4   David Pierce, "Google Reportedly Pays $18 Billion a Year to Be Apple's Default Search Engine," *The Verge*, October 26, 2023, https://bit.ly/4dVEp5z.
5   "Apple Market Cap," Finance Charts, February 3, 2011, https://bit.ly/3B7wtj1.
6   William Gallagher, "Firm That Unlocked San Bernardino Shooter's iPhone for FBI Is Revealed," AppleInsider, April 14, 2021, https://bit.ly/4cWora7.
7   Ellen Nakashima and Reed Albergotti, "The FBI Wanted to Unlock the San Bernardino Shooter's iPhone. It Turned to a Little-Known Australian Firm," *The Washington Post*, April 14, 2021, https://wapo.st/4dZO1fS.
8   "The Bill of Rights: A Transcription," National Archives, November 4, 2015, https://bit.ly/4dWLliU.
9   William C. Duncan, "The History Behind 'Shouting Fire in a Crowded Theater' and Other Free Speech Phrases," Sutherland Institute, November 17, 2023, https://bit.ly/4gdM8NZ.
10 Rob Wile, "A Timeline of Elon Musk's Takeover of Twitter," NBC News, November 17, 2022, https://nbcnews.to/3TfWOSb.
11 Peter Dizikes, "Study: On Twitter, False News Travels Faster Than True Stories," Massachusetts Institute of Technology, March 8, 2018, https://bit.ly/4dUtPfg.
12 Chantal Da Silva, "Twitter Rebrands to 'X' as Elon Musk Loses Iconic Bird Logo," NBC News, July 24, 2023, https://nbcnews.to/3APL4Q4.
13 Sheila Dang, "Elon Musk Manages Free Speech Versus 'Hellscape' at Twitter," *Reuters*, October 29, 2022, https://reut.rs/3XgBAVC.
14 "Musk Fires Outsourced Content Moderators Who Track Abuse on Twitter," CBS News, November 14, 2022, https://cbsn.ws/47jvnwM.
15 Sheera Frenkel and Kate Conger, "Hate Speech's Rise on Twitter Is Unprecedented, Researchers Find," Technology, *The New York Times*, December 2, 2022, https://nyti.ms/3yZSzUh.
16 "Elon Musk's X Sues Advertisers over Alleged 'Massive Advertiser Boycott' After Twitter Takeover," AP News, August 6, 2024, https://bit.ly/3Xl22gK.
17 Tomás Mier, "All the Celebrities Who've Quit Twitter Because of Elon Musk," *Rolling Stone*, December 20, 2022, https://bit.ly/3Tl4VNF.
18 Jack Nicas and Kate Conger, "Brazil Blocks X After Musk Ignores Court Orders," World, *The New York Times*, August 30, 2024, https://nyti.ms/4d3trd0.
19 "Brazil's Supreme Court Threatens to Suspend X if Musk Doesn't Comply with Court Orders," CNN, August 29, 2024, https://tinyurl.com/BrazilXThreat.
20 Lora Kolodny, "Elon Musk's Starlink Says It Will Block X in Brazil to Keep Satellite Internet Active," CNBC, September 3, 2024, https://cnb.cx/4dQPeWw.
21 "France vs. Telegram: What Does It Mean for Cybercrime?" Intel 471, 2024, https://bit.ly/4aNhUzc.
22 Ingrid Melander and Guy Faulconbridge, "Telegram Messaging App CEO Durov Arrested in France," *Reuters*, August 25, 2024, https://reut.rs/4eb3skO.
23 Ali Abbas Ahmadi, "Telegram CEO Pavel Durov Says His Arrest Is 'Misguided,'" *BBC*, September 6, 2024, https://bbc.in/3MCzwlP.

ENDNOTES

24 "US Copyright Office Fair Use Index," US Copyright Office, November 2023, https://bit.ly/3TprAZ1.
25 Cheyenne DeVon, "On ChatGPT's One-Year Anniversary, It Has More Than 1.7 Billion Users—Here's What It May Do Next," CNBC, November 30, 2023, https://cnb.cx/3AVfq3P.
26 Michael M. Grynbaum and Ryan Mac, "The Times Sues OpenAI and Microsoft over A.I. Use of Copyrighted Work," Business, *The New York Times*, December 27, 2023, https://nyti.ms/47kFfXh.
27 "OpenAI and Journalism," OpenAI, January 24, 2024, https://bit.ly/3MEhOhY.
28 Blake Brittain, "Copyright Intellectual Property Data Privacy Litigation US Newspapers Sue OpenAI for Copyright Infringement over AI Training," *Reuters*, April 30, 2024, https://reut.rs/3AOQb2X.
29 Rachel Reed, "Does ChatGPT Violate *New York Times*' Copyrights?" Harvard Law School, March 22, 2024, https://bit.ly/4giGNFe.
30 Michael J. de la Merced and Cade Metz, "OpenAI in Talks for Deal That Would Value Company at $100 Billion," Technology, *The New York Times*, August 29, 2024, https://nyti.ms/4gkoQpC.
31 Hemant Taneja, "The Era of 'Move Fast and Break Things' Is Over," *Harvard Business Review*, January 22, 2019, https://bit.ly/3zenzzR.
32 "Offshoring," EverythingPolicy, 2024, https://bit.ly/4gaaVS6.
33 "More Than 90% of North American Companies Have Relocated Production and Sourcing Over the Past Five Years," BCG Global, September 21, 2023, https://on.bcg.com/4fXAqGw.
34 Laura Padin, "Prop 22 Was a Failure for California's App-Based Workers. Now, It's Also Unconstitutional," National Employment Law Project, September 16, 2021, https://bit.ly/3XybRJM.
35 Caroline O'Donovan, "Uber and Lyft Spent Hundreds of Millions to Win Their Fight over Workers' Rights. It Worked," BuzzFeed News, https://bit.ly/4gaIS65.
36 Yujie Zhou, "CA Supreme Court Upholds Proposition 22: Gig Drivers Are Independent Contractors," Mission Local, July 25, 2024, https://bit.ly/3XBSgrS.
37 Dhaval Dave et al., "When Do Shelter-In-Place Orders Fight COVID-19 Best? Policy Heterogeneity Across States and Adoption Time," *Economic Inquiry*, August 3, 2020, https://doi.org/10.1111/ecin.12944.
38 Faiz Siddiqui, "Hundreds of Covid Cases Reported at Tesla Plant Following Musk's Defiant Reopening, County Data Shows," *The Washington Post*, March 12, 2021, https://wapo.st/3Tm8WBl.
39 Ron Lieber, "Airbnb Horror Story Points to Need for Precautions," Your Money, *The New York Times*, August 14, 2015, https://nyti.ms/3XlarRk.
40 Marlene Lenthang, "Family Sues Airbnb After 19-Month-Old Dies of Fentanyl Toxicity During Florida Vacation," NBC News, March 6, 2023, https://nbcnews.to/3MFp9xP.
41 "Your Guide to NASA's Budget," The Planetary Society, August 14, 2020, https://bit.ly/3AXaDyK.

THE CATALYSTS

42. "NASA," YouTube, November 16, 2022, https://bit.ly/3TgeA7R.
43. "Amazon's Starlink Rival Completes First Launch of Its Satellite Internet Network," CNET, October 7, 2023, https://cnet.co/4cY85gY.
44. "Space Technology Market Size to Worth USD 916.85 Bn by 2033," Precedence Research, April 4, 2024, https://bit.ly/3Tnby1J.
45. Lydia DePillis, "Amazon's Biggest Customer May Soon Be the US Government," CNN Business, November 15, 2018, https://cnn.it/3XzqEDO.
46. Adrianne Jeffries, "Government Taps Engineers from Google, Red Hat to Fix Healthcare.gov," *The Verge*, October 31, 2013, https://bit.ly/3zn3cQS.
47. Elizabeth Weise, "Amazon HQ2 Timeline: The Winners Are New York City and Arlington, Virginia," *USA Today*, September 12, 2018, https://bit.ly/3XC2lFy.
48. J. David Goodman, "Amazon Pulls Out of Planned New York City Headquarters," *The New York Times*, February 14, 2019, https://nyti.ms/3TiyO11.
49. Matthew Barakat, "Amazon Seeks First Incentive Funds from Virginia HQ2 Project," AP News, April 20, 2023, https://bit.ly/4ed4Ao7.
50. Chuck Grassley, "Klobuchar, Grassley, Colleagues Introduce Bipartisan Legislation to Boost Competition and Rein in Big Tech," June 15, 2023, https://bit.ly/3XmeFIm.
51. Jason Del Rey, "Jeff Bezos's Antitrust Grilling Was a Reminder of Amazon's Power over Its Sellers," *Vox*, July 29, 2020, https://bit.ly/3MYGPop.
52. Mike Tanglis, "New Economy Titans, Old School Tactics," Public Citizen, August 22, 2019, https://bit.ly/3XBF8TO.
53. "Review of Section 230 of the Communications Decency Act of 1996," U.S. Department of Justice, June 3, 2020, https://bit.ly/4eeiFlc.
54. Mike Isaac, "Mark Zuckerberg's Call to Regulate Facebook, Explained," Technology, *The New York Times*, March 30, 2019, https://nyti.ms/3zjWvz2.
55. "Data Protection Under GDPR," Your Europe, 2019, https://bit.ly/4gtIzn4.
56. Dan Simmons, "10 Countries with GDPR-like Data Privacy Laws," *Comforte* (blog), January 13, 2022, https://bit.ly/3Q329KF.
57. "The Digital Markets Act: Ensuring Fair and Open Digital Markets," European Commission, December 8, 2022, https://bit.ly/4cXVwCG.
58. Mark Scott, "E.U. Fines Facebook $122 Million over Disclosures in WhatsApp Deal," *The New York Times*, March 18, 2017, https://nyti.ms/3znxZgt.
59. Kim Lyons, "Ireland's Status as Tax Haven for Tech Firms Like Google, Facebook, and Apple Is Ending," *The Verge*, October 7, 2021, https://bit.ly/4cYGwUT.
60. "Hilton Reigns as Most Valuable Hotel Brand for the Ninth Consecutive Year According to Brand Finance," Stories from Hilton, June 28, 2024, https://bit.ly/3ZcGlSN.
61. "NVIDIA Partners with Foxconn to Build Factories and Systems for the AI Industrial Revolution," NVIDIA Newsroom, October 17, 2023, https://bit.ly/3DaW7V8.
62. David Curry, "Shein Revenue and Usage Statistics (2024)," Business of Apps, October 16, 2024, https://bit.ly/4gzh7Dr.
63. Asad Jung, "Elon Musk Says He'll Move X and SpaceX to Texas," *The Texas Tribune*, July 16, 2024, https://bit.ly/3ARgeGM.

ENDNOTES

64 "About," Tech Diplomacy Network, July 12, 2024, https://bit.ly/40E981L.
65 Amy Zegart, "The Crumbling Foundations of American Strength," *Foreign Affairs*, August 24, 2024, https://bit.ly/3Xl8ggQ.
66 Kevin Roose and Casey Newton, "Can Musk Get Trump Elected? + Steve Ballmer's Quest for the Facts + This Week in A.I," *The New York Times*, August 16, 2024, https://nyti.ms/47qZ2UY.
67 Max Fisher and Amanda Taub, "On YouTube's Digital Playground, an Open Gate for Pedophiles," World, *The New York Times*, June 3, 2019, https://nyti.ms/4dV1i9p.
68 "Facebook Now Linked to Violence in the Philippines, Libya, Germany, Myanmar, and India," *Columbia Journalism Review*, 2021, https://bit.ly/4geNRTb.
69 Lewis Sanders, "Facebook's Cambridge Analytica Data Scandal: What You Need to Know," DW, March 21, 2018, https://bit.ly/4edEdym.
70 Bobbie Johnson, "Privacy No Longer a Social Norm, Says Facebook Founder," *The Guardian*, February 21, 2017, https://bit.ly/4gkpZ0i.
71 "Consoles, Collectibles, Video Games and VR," GameStop, June 28, 1997, https://bit.ly/47iaJgm.
72 James Royal, "What Is a Short Squeeze?" Bankrate, August 4, 2022, https://bit.ly/3Zgy4gw.
73 William White, "Barnes & Noble Education (BNED) Stock Pops 73% in Second Day of Rally," InvestorPlace, May 22, 2024, https://bit.ly/3B7p6In.
74 Elizabeth Lopatto, "OpenAI Searches for an Answer to Its Copyright Problems," *The Verge*, August 30, 2024, https://bit.ly/4eauSao.

Chapter 7

1 Felix Richter, "Infographic: The Rise and Fall of the Compact Disc," Statista, August 17, 2022, https://bit.ly/4el45b3.
2 "RIAA Releases 1997 Year-End Music Sales Statistics," Stereophile, February 24, 1998, https://bit.ly/3Cojbzg.
3 Jimmy Daly, "The Real Reason Colleges Banned Napster," EdTech, December 12, 2012, https://bit.ly/3NRuNNN.
4 Peter Tschmuck, "The Music Industry's Fight Against Napster—Part 3: The Trial," Music Business Research, January 26, 2015, https://bit.ly/3C719By.
5 Michael Brick, "Court Rules Napster Users Infringe on Copyrights," Technology, *The New York Times*, February 12, 2001, https://nyti.ms/4f9Gn33.
6 Andrew Dansby, "Napster Files for Bankruptcy," *Rolling Stone*, June 4, 2002, https://bit.ly/4hBPX0f.
7 John Paul Titlow, "David Bowie Predicted the Future of Music in 2002," *Fast Company*, January 11, 2016, https://bit.ly/3AgIrqP.
8 "Tower Records Files for Bankruptcy," CBS News, February 9, 2004, https://cbsn.ws/4fgUUtS.
9 Matt Ashare, "Breaking the Mainframe Habit: Banks Consider a Cloud Future," CIO Dive, May 13, 2022, https://bit.ly/4fdVLeB.

THE CATALYSTS

10 "Identity Theft Resource Center 2023 Annual Data Breach Report Reveals Record Number of Compromises; 72 Percent Increase over Previous High," Identity Theft Resource Center, January 25, 2024, https://bit.ly/3NQC2FZ.
11 Satoshi Nakamoto, "Bitcoin: A Peer-To-Peer Electronic Cash System," Bitcoin.org, n.d., https://bit.ly/3NTsgCY.
12 "Blockchain," ScienceDirect, January 21, 2018, https://bit.ly/40QvjDJ.
13 Viktor Ihnatiuk, "Review of JPMorgan's Onyx Blockchain Platform," Boosty, August 25, 2024, https://bit.ly/4fv7B3D.
14 "What Is Consensus? A Beginner's Guide," Crypto.com, May 13, 2022, https://bit.ly/3NROftY.
15 "Bitcoin Network Power Demand," Cambridge Bitcoin Electricity Consumption Index, 2023, https://ccaf.io/cbnsi/cbeci.
16 Eliza Gkritsi, "Kazakhstan's President Signs Legislation to Limit Energy Usage of Crypto Mining," CoinDesk, February 7, 2023, https://bit.ly/4fvqxzk.
17 "What Is Proof of Stake (PoS)?" McKinsey, January 23, 2023, https://mck.co/4f7aFDo.
18 Noureddine Lasla et al., "Green-PoW: An Energy-Efficient Blockchain Proof-of-Work Consensus Algorithm," *ScienceDirect* 214 (September 4, 2022), https://bit.ly/4egJlBs.
19 "Cryptocurrency Market Capitalizations," Coin Market Cap, 2024, https://bit.ly/3NX2ei9.
20 Lauren Hendrickson, "What Are Smart Contracts on the Blockchain?" Identity, April 17, 2023, https://bit.ly/4ftZLr9.
21 "What Is DeFi?" Coinbase, January 19, 2021, https://bit.ly/40wku9o.
22 Lawrence Wintermeyer, "Bitcoin Is Catalyzing DeFi's Comeback and Empowering Utilitarian Communities," *Forbes*, May 23, 2024, https://bit.ly/3AAMY7l.
23 Derek Saul, "JPMorgan's Jamie Dimon Says He Won't Talk About Bitcoin Anymore—After Trashing It One Last Time," *Forbes*, January 18, 2024, https://bit.ly/3UFARNo.
24 "Asset Tokenization: What It Is and How It Works," Chainlink, last modified September 5, 2024, https://bit.ly/3YP7PgG.
25 Irina Heaver, "What Crypto Investors Need to Know About Tokenizing Real World Assets," *Forbes*, March 15, 2024, https://bit.ly/4hBbW7f.
26 "Frequently Asked Questions About Exempt Offerings," U.S. Securities and Exchange Commission, 2024, https://bit.ly/3UCe5Wy.
27 Anshika Bhalla, "A Quick Guide to Fungible vs. Non-Fungible Tokens," BlockChain Council, April 22, 2021, https://bit.ly/4f9x96I.
28 Jolene Creighton, "NFT Timeline: The Beginnings and History of NFTs," NFT Now Media, December 15, 2022, https://bit.ly/3Aqm3eA.
29 Chloee Weiner, "Beeple JPG File Sells for $69 Million, Setting Crypto Art Record," NPR, March 11, 2021, https://tinyurl.com/yc6vxdvt.
30 Falon Fatemi, "NFTs Are So Much More Than Just Jpegs, They Are Redefining Access and Ownership in Media and Entertainment," *Forbes*, June 2, 2022, https://bit.ly/3UFkoIR.

ENDNOTES

31. Kevin Samkian, "NFTs: The Future of Real Estate? By Kevin Samkian," Pepperdine, 2023, https://bit.ly/40u17hp.
32. "Fungible vs Non-Fungible Tokens: Explained," Trust, August 8, 2024, https://bit.ly/4elcPOu.
33. Tanaya Macheel, "Ripple's New Stablecoin for Payments Will Be Available to Trade Tuesday," CNBC, December 16, 2024, https://cnb.cx/42EryCb.
34. "UNHCR Wins Award for Innovative Use of Blockchain Solutions to Provide Cash to Forcibly Displaced in Ukraine," UNHCR, 2023, https://bit.ly/40xJE7C.
35. Shobhit Seth, "Central Bank Digital Currency (CBDC)," Investopedia, June 14, 2024, https://bit.ly/4fgBntw.
36. "Central Bank Digital Currency Tracker," Atlantic Council, July 22, 2021, https://bit.ly/3YQHRsZ.
37. "Swift Advances CBDC Innovation as Interlinking Solution Begins Beta Testing," Swift, September 13, 2023, https://bit.ly/3YQ4ldR.

Chapter 8

1. Rachel Botsman, *Who Can You Trust?: How Technology Brought Us Together and Why It Might Drive Us Apart* (New York: PublicAffairs, 2017).
2. Rachel Botsman.
3. Alex Tuckness, "Locke's Political Philosophy," *Stanford Encyclopedia of Philosophy*, October 6, 2020, https://stanford.io/3CEvXd4.
4. Edward White, "The Bloody Family History of the Guillotine," *The Paris Review*, April 6, 2018, https://bit.ly/4eAAJWz.
5. Albert Goodwin and Jeremy Popkin, "Louis XVI | King of France," in *Encyclopedia Britannica*, 2019, https://bit.ly/3CwqeWO.
6. "1947 Indian Independence Act," UK Parliament, 2020, https://bit.ly/40OZZ85.
7. Barack Obama (@Barack Obama), "Democracy is one of the world's boldest experiments," Facebook, September 16, 2024, https://bit.ly/3YYpHES.
8. Staffan Ingemar Lindberg, "Dictatorships Advancing Globally," University of Gothenburg, March 3, 2022, https://bit.ly/40MgAcD.
9. Staffan Ingemar Lindberg.
10. "2024 Edelman Trust Barometer Global Report," Edelman Trust Institute, 2024, https://bit.ly/4ft8Hxr.
11. "Special Report: Trust and Health," Edelman Trust Institute, 2024, https://bit.ly/48Sb621.
12. Robert Sapolsky, "Determined: A Science of Life Without Free Will," Penguin Press, October 17, 2023, https://tinyurl.com/freewillsap.
13. "Motivated Reasoning," *Psychology Today*, 2020, https://bit.ly/4evDok9.
14. Robert Farley, "How Many Died as a Result of Capitol Riot?" FactCheck.org, November 1, 2021, https://bit.ly/3Z8gMSn.
15. Joan E. Solsman, "Ever Get Caught in an Unexpected Hourlong YouTube Binge? Thank YouTube AI for That," CNET, January 10, 2018, https://cnet.co/3YPVfN4.

16 "Investigation: How TikTok's Algorithm Figures Out Your Deepest Desires," *The Wall Street Journal*, July 21, 2021, https://on.wsj.com/4fsVMeZ.

17 Alex Russell, "YouTube Video Recommendations Lead to More Extremist Content for Right-Leaning Users, Researchers Suggest," UC Davis, December 13, 2023, https://bit.ly/4i2xVV8.

18 Timothy Graham and Mark Andrejevic, "A Computational Analysis of Potential Algorithmic Bias on Platform X During the 2024 US Election," 2024, https://tinyurl.com/the-cat-x-2024.

19 Billy Perrigo, "Inside Frances Haugen's Decision to Take on Facebook," *Time*, November 22, 2021, https://bit.ly/3UWe0xb.

20 Jeff Horwitz, "The Facebook Files," *The Wall Street Journal*, September 15, 2021, https://on.wsj.com/4exjIwb.

21 Siva Vaidhyanathan, "Facebook Has Just Suffered Its Most Devastating PR Catastrophe Yet," *The Guardian*, October 8, 2021, https://bit.ly/4hOpmgt.

22 "US Lobbying Expenses of Facebook," Statista, accessed November 16, 2024, https://bit.ly/3Z8UTlN.

23 "Goldman Sachs to Pay Record $550 Million to Settle SEC Charges Related to Subprime Mortgage CDO," U.S. Securities and Exchange Commission, July 15, 2010, https://bit.ly/4fKikIl.

24 "Progress Is Everyone's Business," Goldman Sachs 2010 Annual Report, 2011, https://bit.ly/3UTEGhY.

25 Jesse Eisinger, "Why Only One Top Banker Went to Jail for the Financial Crisis," *The New York Times*, April 30, 2014, https://tinyurl.com/s7kwta4d.

26 "Senator Asks How Facebook Remains Free, Zuckerberg Smirks: 'We Run Ads,'" NBC News, April 10, 2018, https://nbcnews.to/3AW8dAJ.

27 Jonathan Taplin, *Move Fast and Break Things: How Facebook, Google, and Amazon Cornered Culture and Undermined Democracy* (Little, Brown, 2017).

28 Jonathan Lord, "Elon Musk Is Moving X and SpaceX to Texas. The Impact on Staff Culture and Performance Is Likely to Be Big," The Conversation, August 19, 2024, https://bit.ly/4eAEyeh.

29 Louise Story and Eric Dash, "Report Shows Bonuses Paid by Bailed-Out Banks," *The New York Times*, July 30, 2009, https://nyti.ms/3Z9risF.

30 NPR Staff and Wires, "Occupy Wall Street Inspires Worldwide Protests," World, NPR, October 15, 2011, https://n.pr/3OdKnnk.

31 Adam Volle, "Occupy Wall Street," *Encyclopedia Britannica*, November 9, 2022, https://bit.ly/4hK0ypX.

32 James Anderson, "Some Say Occupy Wall Street Did Nothing. It Changed Us More Than We Think," *Time*, November 15, 2021, https://bit.ly/4fvG5U9.

33 "Estimated Advertising and Circulation Revenue of the Newspaper Industry," Pew Research Center, June 29, 2021, https://tinyurl.com/2gpsj8ac.

ENDNOTES

34 David Bauder and David Lieb, "More Than 1,400 Cities and Towns in U.S. Have Lost Newspapers in Past 15 Years," *South Bend Tribune*, March 11, 2019, https://tinyurl.com/2eawg275.
35 Kristen Hare, "More Than 100 Local Newsrooms Closed During the Coronavirus Pandemic," Poynter, December 2, 2021, https://tinyurl.com/2zp42qdu.
36 Scott Galloway, "Fool Me Twice…," No Mercy / No Malice, January 27, 2017, https://bit.ly/40PZElD.
37 Kara Swisher, "Facebook Will Use Facebook Data to Sell Ads on Sites That Aren't Facebook," Recode, September 28, 2014, https://tinyurl.com/2p8vvfxp.
38 Ava Kofman and Ariana Tobin, "Facebook Ads Can Still Discriminate Against Women and Older Workers, Despite a Civil Rights Settlement," ProPublica, 2019, https://bit.ly/3Odaxqc.
39 Ari Levy, "Uber and Lyft Are Pouring Millions of Dollars into Facebook Ads to Protect Their Business in California," CNBC, October 26, 2020, https://cnb.cx/4fvde2r.
40 "US Political Digital Ad Spend by Type 2022," Statista, 2022, https://bit.ly/3CFQw92.
41 Hugo Lowell, "Trump's Raising of $250m for Fund That 'Did Not Exist' Suggests Possible Fraud," US News, *The Guardian*, June 15, 2022, https://bit.ly/3V0gn1Q.
42 "Facebook Says It Sold $100,000 in Ads to Fake Russian Accounts During Presidential Election," ABC News, September 7, 2017, https://bit.ly/4fueqD1.
43 Craig Timberg, "Russian Propaganda Effort Helped Spread 'Fake News' During Election, Experts Say," *The Washington Post*, November 25, 2016, https://wapo.st/3OclYOP.
44 Paul Ratner, "34 Years Ago, a KGB Defector Chillingly Predicted Modern America," Big Think, January 13, 2023, https://bit.ly/4fHuWzy.
45 Jasmine Laws, "Map Shows Countries Where Facebook Is Blocked," *Newsweek*, August 16, 2024, https://bit.ly/3UUGAz4.
46 Olivia Goldhill, "2,400 Years Ago, Plato Saw Democracy Would Give Rise to Tyrannical Leaders," Quartz, June 2, 2018, https://bit.ly/4g7UJ47.
47 Bert Gambini, "Study Explores How QAnon Went from Fringe to Mainstream on Twitter," University of Buffalo, April 4, 2023, https://tinyurl.com/ymac3ccn.
48 "Annual Threat Assessment of the US Intelligence Community," Office of the Director of National Intelligence, February 5, 2024, https://tinyurl.com/mrxnbwhb.
49 Jane Wakefield, "Deepfake Presidents Used in Russia-Ukraine War," Technology, *BBC News*, March 18, 2022, https://bbc.in/40LC7SZ.
50 "How Is the Civil War Taught in School? Depends on Where You Live," *The Florida Times-Union*, August 22, 2017, https://bit.ly/3YTmAhf.
51 Lindsay Richards and Anthony Heath, "'Two Nations'? Brexit, Inequality and Social Cohesion," The British Academy, June 6, 2017, https://bit.ly/3Oio6EA.
52 "As Partisan Hostility Grows, Signs of Frustration with the Two-Party System," Pew Research Center, August 9, 2022, https://pewrsr.ch/4frvKbO.
53 "Bitcoin," CoinMarketCap, February 3, 2025, https://bit.ly/3Z9ghYb.
54 Ofer Lidsky, "The Decline of Human Trust: Blockchain to the Rescue," *Forbes*, May 24, 2023, https://bit.ly/3Ox0fBz.

THE CATALYSTS

Chapter 9

1. Michael Savage, "Fifty Years On, What Is the Legacy of Enoch Powell's 'Rivers of Blood' Speech?," *The Guardian,* April 14, 2018, https://bit.ly/3V79pZ2.
2. "Into Europe," UK Parliament, 2019, https://bit.ly/494HHSy.
3. "EU Referendum: The Result in Maps and Charts," *BBC,* June 24, 2016, https://bbc.in/3Oq6CGu.
4. "Many Rivers Crossed: Britain's Attitudes to Race and Integration 50 Years Since 'Rivers of Blood,'" British Future, April 2018, https://bit.ly/4i5B5Y3.
5. Jonathan Portes, "The Impact of Brexit on the UK Economy: Reviewing the Evidence," CEPR, *Vox* EU, July 7, 2023, https://bit.ly/4fGM34D.
6. "London's Economy After Brexit: Impact and Implications," Cambridge Econometrics, January 2024, https://bit.ly/3Z82Uq8.
7. Yuka Hayashi and Josh Zumbrun, "U.S. Manufacturers Blame Trump-Era Tariffs for Inflation's Rise," MarketWatch, June 1, 2021, https://on.mktw.net/3V88CXY.
8. Kayla Tausche, "Trump Promised Massive Tariffs on Imports but How He'll Pull It Off Is Still Being Figured Out," CNN, November 8, 2024, https://cnn.it/412IrW8.
9. Paul Wiseman and Christopher Rugaber, "Trump's Economic Plans Would Worsen Inflation, Experts Say," The Associated Press, October 15, 2024, https://bit.ly/4g1xg4d.
10. Michelle Lee, "Fact Check: Has Trump Declared Bankruptcy Four or Six Times?" *The Washington Post,* September 26, 2016, https://wapo.st/4992NPu.
11. "In Pictures: Hurricane Helene Destruction," *BBC,* September 27, 2024, https://bbc.in/3ZnMo6B.
12. "The Paris Agreement," United Nations, November 12, 2019, https://bit.ly/495kQWQ.
13. "President Trump Announces Withdrawal from Paris Agreement," Columbia Law School, December 23, 2019, https://bit.ly/40Y9H8k.
14. Antony Blinken, "The United States Officially Rejoins the Paris Agreement," United States Department of State, February 19, 2021, https://bit.ly/3V9LMz7.
15. Matthew Daly and Seth Borenstein, "Trump Says He's Withdrawing the US from the Paris Climate Agreement Again," The Associated Press, January 20, 2025, https://bit.ly/42G3OgT.
16. Rebecca Leffler, "Madonna Removes Swastika from Image of Marine Le Pen," *The Hollywood Reporter,* August 22, 2012, https://bit.ly/3AZgTXa.
17. Eleanor Beardsley, "In France, Politicians Make Halal Meat a Campaign Issue," NPR, March 15, 2012, https://n.pr/3OpMO6k.
18. "France's Le Pen Says Protectionism Can Spur GDP Growth to 2.5 Percent by 2021," *Reuters,* April 13, 2017, https://reut.rs/3VafpQC.
19. Eleanor Beardsley, "Marine Le Pen's 'Brutal' Upbringing Shaped Her Worldview," NPR, April 21, 2017, https://n.pr/412UuCQ.
20. Nicholas Vinocur, "How Marine Le Pen Turned Respectable (and Why You Shouldn't Be Fooled)," *Politico,* February 12, 2024, https://politi.co/49eqENR.
21. "Consequences of the Collapse of the Soviet Union," Norwich University, 2024, https://bit.ly/49ep0vF.

ENDNOTES

22 "Poland," OEC, 2021, https://bit.ly/4108ihp.
23 "Top Wheat Exporter in the World in 2023," TradeImex Info, September 9, 2024, https://bit.ly/4fzaReV.
24 "Comparative Advantage," Corporate Finance Institute, December 1, 2022, https://bit.ly/4eOfAIy.
25 Daniel M. Bernhofen and John C. Brown, "Retrospectives: On the Genius Behind David Ricardo's 1817 Formulation of Comparative Advantage," *Journal of Economic Perspectives* 32, no. 4 (Fall 2018): 227–40, https://doi.org/10.1257/jep.32.4.227.
26 Jim O'Neill, "Is the Emerging World Still Emerging?," International Monetary Fund, Summer 2021, https://bit.ly/4g7BibD.
27 Donald J. Boudreaux and Nita Ghei, "The Benefits of Free Trade: Addressing Key Myths," Mercatus Center, May 23, 2018, https://bit.ly/3ZlXw3L.
28 Patrick J. McDonald, "Peace Through Trade or Free Trade?" *Journal of Conflict Resolution* 48, no. 4 (August 2004): 547–72, https://bit.ly/496x6q1.
29 Ekrame Boubtane, "Immigration: A French Paradox," Le Cercle Des Économistes, January 17, 2024, https://bit.ly/4fZZhJw.
30 Bart Bonikowski et al., *The New Nationalism in America and Beyond: The Deep Roots of Ethnic Nationalism in the Digital Age* (Cambridge University Press, 2024).
31 Kate Berry, "Dave Fishwick of 'Bank of Dave' Has a New Nemesis: Payday Lenders," *American Banker*, May 15, 2024, https://bit.ly/3CEyior.
32 "Exploring Financial Exclusion," *Financial Conduct Authority*, 2024, https://bit.ly/3YZlxfO.
33 Patrick Collinson, "Metro Bank Looks Back to the Future," Money, *The Guardian*, January 30, 2010, https://bit.ly/4i9lMxo.
34 John P. Watkins, "Republicans Exploit People's Biases to Win Elections," *The Salt Lake Tribune*, December 31, 2021, https://bit.ly/3V6GHaE.
35 "Tucker Carlson Promotes the White Supremacist 'Replacement' Theory," Media Matters for America, May 18, 2022, https://bit.ly/4g6BVSI.
36 Ben Quinn, "Social Media Firms Must Tell Users Exposed to Brexit Propaganda, MP Says," *The Guardian*, February 10, 2018, https://bit.ly/3ZrsEzb.
37 Adam Clark Estes, "The Growing Danger of Elon Musk's Misinformation Machine," *Vox*, November 7, 2024, https://bit.ly/4eZigDm.
38 Hindol Sengupta, "BRICS as the 'Voice of the Rest,'" *The Sunday Guardian*, October 26, 2024, https://bit.ly/3ZnmkZl.
39 "Building Better Global Economic BRICS," Goldman Sachs, November 30, 2001, https://bit.ly/3CK9taJ.
40 Spencer Feingold and World Economic Forum, "BRICS: Here's What to Know About the International Bloc," World Economic Forum, November 20, 2024, https://bit.ly/4i7GMon.
41 George Monastiriakos, "The BRICS Is Not a Strategic Threat to the United States," *Geopolitical Monitor*, September 7, 2023, https://bit.ly/3CXaCvy.

42. Federico Fuentes and Patrick Bond, "US Imperial Dominance, BRICS Sub-Imperialism and Unequal Ecological Exchange," CADTM, August 29, 2024, https://bit.ly/3Z8E1dF.
43. Melissa Pistilli, "How Would a New BRICS Currency Affect the US Dollar?" Investing News Network, April 27, 2023, https://bit.ly/415NLYN.
44. Abby Schultz, "The Ranks of Billionaires Is Booming. Tech Stocks Get a Lot of the Credit," *Barron's*, November 22, 2024, https://bit.ly/4eQDd37.
45. "India's Reluctance to Use Chinese Yuan to Buy Russian Oil Holding Up Cargo Payments," *South China Morning Post*, October 16, 2023, https://bit.ly/495gvDb.
46. "BRICS Pushes the IMF to Reform," Observer Research Foundation, 2022, https://bit.ly/496Aod2.
47. Mariel Ferragamo, "What Is the BRICS Group and Why Is It Expanding?," Council on Foreign Relations, October 18, 2024, https://on.cfr.org/4g3Ruuq.
48. Stewart Patrick, "BRICS Expansion, the G20, and the Future of World Order," Carnegie Endowment for International Peace, October 9, 2024, https://bit.ly/42cmTXI.
49. Stewart Patrick.
50. Laurie Chen and Joe Cash, "China Offers Africa $51 Billion in Fresh Funding, Promises a Million Jobs," *Reuters*, September 5, 2024, https://reut.rs/4i4HFOx.
51. Anushka Asthana and Jill Treanor, "Nobel Prize-Winning Economists Warn of Long-Term Damage After Brexit," *The Guardian*, June 19, 2016, https://bit.ly/3CTXcAw.
52. "The Macroeconomy After Tariffs," *The World Bank Economic Review* 36, no. 2 (May 2022): 361–381, https://doi.org/10.1093/wber/lhab016.
53. "The US-China Economic Relationship," The US-China Business Council, January 14, 2021, https://bit.ly/4g7nPk1.
54. Anne Applebaum, "Trump Is Speaking Like Hitler, Stalin, and Mussolini," *The Atlantic*, October 18, 2024, https://bit.ly/4ggF2az.

Chapter 10

1. Ernestine Siu, "This 42-Year-Old Built a $2 Billion a Year Super App Called Grab: I Worked '20 Hour' Days," CNBC, October 7, 2024, https://cnb.cx/3Z3v5Gs.
2. "Grab Celebrates Public Listing Milestone with Employees and Partners in First-Ever NASDAQ Opening Bell Ceremony in Southeast Asia," Grab, December 2, 2021, https://bit.ly/4iaw3JS.
3. "Grab Reports Third Quarter 2024 Results," Grab, November 11, 2024, https://bit.ly/3Zawuv5.
4. Gina Marrs, "Top Unicorns in Singapore," *TechRound*, October 7, 2024, https://bit.ly/4idpPc2.
5. *The Global Startup Ecosystem Report 2023* (Startup Genome, 2023), https://bit.ly/4imlqUy.
6. "List of 117 Unicorn Startups in India (Nov 2024)," Tracxn, February 2, 2024, https://bit.ly/4eVWO1T.
7. "Singapore Population," worldometer, July 16, 2023, https://bit.ly/3ZdqDFj.

ENDNOTES

8. Cameron Davis et al., "A Playbook for Innovation Hubs and Ecosystems, McKinsey, February 28, 2023, https://mck.co/3OzIZv6.
9. "Microsoft Invests $1.5 Billion in Abu Dhabi's G42 to Accelerate AI Development and Global Expansion," Microsoft, April 6, 2024, https://bit.ly/4f0sJhu.
10. David M. Hart et al., "America's Advanced Industries: New Trends," Brookings, August 4, 2016, https://bit.ly/41baByu.
11. "Countries Seeking American Immigrants 2024," World Population Review, February 5, 2024. https://bit.ly/3ZbaQqr.
12. Steven Hubbard, "Fortune 500 Companies with Immigrant Roots Generated More Money Than the GDP of Most Western Nations," Immigration Impact, August 29, 2023, https://bit.ly/3Zu2BHB.
13. "Immigrants Started Nearly 1 in 5 New Businesses in 2023," Gusto, September 6, 2024, https://bit.ly/3B74TTB.
14. Ira Gotliboym, "Small Business Facts," US Small Business Administration, October 2022, https://bit.ly/4182SRw.
15. Julia Gelatt, "Explainer: Immigrants and the U.S. Economy," Migration Policy, October 23, 2024, https://bit.ly/4eZ749r.
16. Mishita Mehra et al., "H1-B Visas Are the Lifeblood of U.S. Tech Innovation—and the Shortcut to Semiconductor Supremacy," *Fortune*, April 23, 2023, https://bit.ly/3V9SqoL.
17. "Ten Actions That Hurt Workers During Trump's First Year: How Trump and Congress Further Rigged the Economy in Favor of the Wealthy," Economic Policy Institute, 2018, https://bit.ly/49dIa4W.
18. "Immigration," Gallup, 2023, https://bit.ly/3CQ8OVk.
19. Gretchen Frazee, "4 Myths About How Immigrants Affect the U.S. Economy," PBS, November 2, 2018, https://to.pbs.org/3ARjHFW.
20. Matt Sheehan, "How Google Took on China—and Lost," *MIT Technology Review*, December 19, 2018, https://bit.ly/4ePcq7b.
21. "Our Approach—How Google Search Works," Google, July 10, 2022, https://bit.ly/49chNMw.
22. Search Engine Market Share China," StatCounter Global Stats, 2019, https://bit.ly/4eOFAn6.
23. Kamala Raghavan, "Impact of Pandemic and Digital Transformation on Global Accounting Profession," *Journal of Global Awareness* 2, no. 1 (2021), https://bit.ly/41d92Qu.
24. "Ukraine Emergency," USA for UNHCR, November 1, 2024, https://bit.ly/4fS5Y0B.
25. "Russians Have Emigrated in Huge Numbers Since the War in Ukraine," *The Economist*, August 23, 2023, https://econ.st/4gbocdf.
26. "Russia's 650,000 Wartime Emigres," *The Bell*, July 19, 2024, https://bit.ly/4iaIzZW.
27. Alexandra Prokopenko, "The Great Russian Brain Drain," George W. Bush Presidential Center, October 9, 2024, https://bit.ly/3B3bZIM.

THE CATALYSTS

28 "Canada's Immigration Website Crashes During US Vote," *BBC*, November 9, 2016, https://bbc.in/3OzD7SO.
29 Lottie McGrath, "'Moving to Canada' Searches Spike After US Election," *Newsweek*, November 6, 2024, https://bit.ly/4fW45Qz.
30 Josh Gerstein and Alexander Ward, "Supreme Court Has Voted to Overturn Abortion Rights, Draft Opinion Shows," *Politico*, May 2, 2022, https://politi.co/3B5r4JK.
31 Jordan Novet, "Salesforce Tells Employees Worried About Abortion Access That It Will Help Them Relocate," CNBC, May 13, 2022, https://cnb.cx/3CQevmd.
32 Emma Goldberg, "These Companies Will Cover Travel Expenses for Employee Abortions," Business, *The New York Times*, August 19, 2022, https://nyti.ms/3ZjUITU.
33 "Innovation & Design," Bain, April 26, 2022, https://bit.ly/4fT0OS4.
34 Lebawit Lily Girma, "The Best Destinations for Remote Workers Are in Europe, Canada and Asia," *Bloomberg*, July 30, 2024, https://bloom.bg/4iaa8Td.
35 "Do Digital Nomads Pay Tax in Portugal in 2024?" Nomads Embassy, January 8, 2024, https://bit.ly/49vVO3D.
36 "Make Tulsa Your New Headquarters and Home," Tulsa Remote, November 15, 2018, https://www.tulsaremote.com.
37 "DTP," Downtown Project DTP Companies, August 5, 2018, https://dtplv.com.
38 Sara Corbett, "How Zappos' CEO Turned Las Vegas into a Startup Fantasyland," *Wired*, April 7, 2014, https://bit.ly/4gbYIwa.
39 Claire Cain Miller and Alicia Parlapiano, "Where Are Young People Most Optimistic? In Poorer Nations," The Upshot, *The New York Times*, November 17, 2021, https://nyti.ms/3OBKzww.
40 Robbie Sequeira, "The US Needs Homes. But First, It Needs the Workers to Build Them," Stateline, January 24, 2024, https://bit.ly/3VdWC7h.
41 Promit Mukherjee, "Canada's Housing Affordability Crisis May Persist for Years Despite Rate Cuts," *Reuters*, September 30, 2024, https://reut.rs/3CQIhHn.
42 "A Brief History of the American Steel Industry," National Material Company, January 24, 2018, https://bit.ly/3B6VfjI.
43 "Mini Mills," Steel Warehouse, August 15, 2023, https://bit.ly/3VhCfWN.
44 Lydia Chavez, "The Rise of Mini-Steel Mills," Business, *The New York Times*, September 23, 1981, https://nyti.ms/3ZdtVZl.
45 "United States Steel Production," Trading Economics, February 19, 2016, https://bit.ly/4gbmJDA.
46 Sarah Burns, "Steel Imports Up in 2024 vs. December 2023," American Iron and Steel Institute, February 26, 2024, https://bit.ly/3OEbUOF.
47 Thomas J. Gibson and Chuck Schmitt, "The Crisis Facing the U.S. Steel Industry," CNN, March 23, 2016, https://cnn.it/49fFjsb.
48 Tim Higgins and Christopher Mims, "Beyond Silicon? The New Materials Charting the Future of Microchips," September 30, 2022, in *Bold Names*, produced by *The Wall Street Journal*, podcast, https://on.wsj.com/3CRvR24.

ENDNOTES

49 Kris Frieswick, "Why Do Smart Appliances Continue to Be So Dumb?" *The Wall Street Journal*, November 21, 2024, https://on.wsj.com/4fP8FAd.
50 Kif Leswing, 2024, "Intel Used to Dominate the U.S. Chip Industry. Now It's Struggling to Stay Relevant," CNBC, April 26, 2024, https://cnb.cx/49gdDDF.
51 "Companies Ranked by Market Cap," CompaniesMarketCap, 2024, https://bit.ly/3B8JR6Z.
52 Clare Duffy and David Goldman, "Intel CEO Resigns After a Disastrous Tenure," CNN, December 2, 2024, https://cnn.it/4eV0Zed.
53 Britney Nguyen, "The Rise of TSMC: How One Chipmaker Started Making Everyone's Chips," Quartz, May 7, 2024, https://tinyurl.com/ycx3btn2.
54 "FACT SHEET: CHIPS and Science Act Will Lower Costs, Create Jobs, Strengthen Supply Chains, and Counter China," The White House, August 9, 2022, https://tinyurl.com/ywptz9dt.
55 "Industrial Policy and International Trade," Congressional Research Service, 2022, https://bit.ly/3ZsJ9Lk.
56 Dylan Butts, "Trump Likely to Uphold CHIPS Act Despite His Campaign Rhetoric, Policy Experts Say," CNBC, November 7, 2024, https://cnb.cx/3ZrEysK.
57 "U.S. Demographic Projections: With and Without Immigration," Penn Wharton Budget Model, March 22, 2024, https://whr.tn/3B1Ns6V.

Chapter 11

1 Pascal Daudin, "The Thirty Years' War: The First Modern War?," *Humanitarian Law & Policy* (blog), February 16, 2018, https://bit.ly/4g121a3.
2 "Peace of Westphalia," in *Encyclopedia Britannica*, edited by the editors of *Encyclopedia Britannica*, last modified January 23, 2025, https://bit.ly/3ZTC3zP.
3 "Switzerland (05/99)," US Department of State, November 26, 2023, https://bit.ly/4g11OUj.
4 "What the Historic Leak of Swiss Banking Records Reveal," *Mail & Guardian*, February 22, 2022, https://bit.ly/49x7GlF.
5 Kalyeena Makortoff, "How Swiss Banking Secrecy Enabled an Unequal Global Financial System," *The Guardian*, February 22, 2022, https://bit.ly/3DeUYMg.
6 Kalyeena Makortoff, "How Swiss Banking Secrecy Shaped the Modern World," *The Guardian*, February 22, 2022, https://tinyurl.com/2p8h9yzm.
7 "History of Tax Havens: Switzerland," Whistleblower Justice Network, accessed March 8, 2025, https://tinyurl.com/42zahv7v.
8 Doug Chayka, "Revealed: Credit Suisse Leak Unmasks Criminals, Fraudsters and Corrupt Politicians," *The Guardian*, February 20, 2022, https://bit.ly/4g5Pz8V.
9 "What the Historic Leak of Swiss Banking Records Reveal," *Mail & Guardian*, February 22, 2022, https://bit.ly/49x7GlF.
10 Matthew Auten, "Money Spending or Money Laundering: The Fine Line Between Legal and Illegal Financial Transactions," *Pace Law Review* 33, no. 3 (Summer 2013), https://bit.ly/49pTjzJ.

THE CATALYSTS

11   "Bank Secrecy Act Requirements," Financial Crimes Enforcement Network, n.d., https://bit.ly/3ZKPrWw.
12   "Bank Secrecy Act (BSA)," Office of the Comptroller of the Currency, n.d., https://bit.ly/3VtT4Og.
13   "Bank Secrecy Act, Anti-Money Laundering, and Office of Foreign Assets Control," FDIC, accessed December 8, 2024, https://bit.ly/3D6LgM0.
14   "Economic Declaration," G7 Research Group, July 16, 1989, https://tinyurl.com/4382txpb.
15   "'Know Your Customer,'" *Bank Secrecy Act Manual*, September 1997, https://bit.ly/41ryHVS.
16   James Chen, "Know Your Client (KYC)," Investopedia, August 6, 2024, https://bit.ly/49tYcrq.
17   "What Is the Difference Between CDD and EDD?," KYC Hub, November 2, 2023, https://bit.ly/49pgvhr.
18   George W. Bush, "President Declares 'Freedom at War with Fear,'" The White House, November 20, 2001, https://bit.ly/3BjdmDf.
19   John Byrne, "9/11 Created the AML Community We Know Today," AML RIGHTSOURCE, 2024, https://bit.ly/4gpBpPF.
20   Kee Malesky, "Follow the Money: On the Trail of Watergate Lore," NPR, June 16, 2012, https://n.pr/4ingheJ.
21   "Bob Woodward and Carl Bernstein: An Inventory of Their Watergate Papers at the Harry Ransom Center," Harry Ransom Center, 2003, https://bit.ly/3ONxLTW.
22   "Revising the Bank Secrecy Act to Protect Privacy and Deter Criminals," The Cato Institute, July 26, 2022, https://bit.ly/3Vp0JNB.
23   Neeraj Agrawal, "It's Time to Have the Conversation: Is the Bank Secrecy Act Unconstitutional?," Coin Center, November 15, 2023, https://bit.ly/4ireYeU.
24   "Tax and Customs Administration to Share Information Automatically to Fight Against International Tax Evasion," Government of the Netherlands, October 29, 2014, https://bit.ly/3ZLZoTX.
25   Usman W. Chohan, "The Cryptocurrency Tumblers: Risks, Legality and Oversight," SSRN, November 30, 2017, https://bit.ly/3Di1QbZ.
26   Brady Dale, "Appeals Court Reverses Sanctions Against Blockchain Privacy App," Axios, November 27, 2024, https://bit.ly/41JNMST.
27   "U.S. Treasury Sanctions Notorious Virtual Currency Mixer Tornado Cash," U.S. Department of the Treasury, August 8, 2022, https://bit.ly/3ZLlPZ6.
28   Liam Frost, "Fifth Circuit Rules OFAC Overstepped Sanctioning Tornado Cash's Immutable Smart Contracts," Decrypt, January 30, 2024, https://tinyurl.com/naa84nvk.
29   Vismaya V., "TORN Jumps 380%, Privacy Coins Railgun, Zcash Surge After Tornado Cash Ruling," Decrypt, November 27, 2024, https://bit.ly/3BcjBc6.
30   US Department of the Treasury, "Tornado Cash Delisting," news release, March 21, 2025, https://tinyurl.com/3vfxcjh3.

ENDNOTES

31 "Five Questions: The Rollback of Bank Regulations in the Dodd-Frank Act," University of Miami, June 18, 2024, https://bit.ly/3D5HBOJ.
32 "10 Most Famous Public Companies That Went Private," Investopedia, November 22, 2024, https://bit.ly/3ZAr3WG.
33 Miranda Fraraccio, "Corporate Transparency Act—What You Need to Know," U.S. Chamber of Commerce, December 18, 2023, https://bit.ly/4g0Km2a.
34 "Beneficial Ownership Information Reporting," Financial Crimes Enforcement Unit, March 24, 2023, https://bit.ly/4gnPld2.
35 Todd Moore, "Protect Your Organization from Cybercrime-as-a-Service Attacks," *Thales* (blog), October 12, 2023, https://bit.ly/3VxUzep.
36 Abigail Reno, "NFIB Prevails in Blocking Burdensome Beneficial Ownership Requirements for Small Businesses," NFIB Small Business Association, December 3, 2024, https://bit.ly/4foWDMK.
37 Brett Wolf, "US Federal Judge Rules Corporate Transparency Act Unconstitutional, Future of Beneficial Ownership Regime in Limbo," *Thomson Reuters*, March 11, 2024, https://tmsnrt.rs/4g5fyNJ.
38 Hayden Field, "OpenAI Disbands Another Safety Team, as Head Advisor for 'AGI Readiness' Resigns," CNBC, October 24, 2024, https://cnb.cx/4f5sp1j.
39 Noor Al-Sibai, "OpenAI's AGI Czar Quits, Saying the Company Isn't Ready for What It's Building," Futurism, October 24, 2024, https://bit.ly/4guYErT.
40 "Economic Crime and Corporate Transparency Act 2023," UK Parliament, 2023, https://bit.ly/4fcqoAv.
41 "Transparency Requirements for Listed Companies," European Commission, September 1, 2022, https://bit.ly/4gsdHlM.
42 Victoria Finkle, "Is There a Better Way to Fight Money Laundering?," American Banker, July 29, 2019, https://bit.ly/49wlTiT.
43 "U.S. Money Laundering Threat Assessment (MLTA)," US Treasury Department, 2005, https://bit.ly/3VwdsOQ.
44 "Combating the Growing Money Laundering Threat," Federal Bureau of Investigation, October 24, 2016, https://bit.ly/3ZL6x6L.
45 Osman Husain, "15 Biggest Compliance Fines ($1Billion and Above)," Enzuzo, September 23, 2024, https://bit.ly/41rR10R.
46 Sheelah Kolhatkar, "Why SAC Capital's Steven Cohen Isn't in Jail," January 2, 2014, https://bloom.bg/4g6leXW.
47 "SAC Capital Fined $1.8 Billion for Insider Trading," PBS News, November 4, 2013, https://to.pbs.org/4fjjv0k.
48 "Cohen Completes $2.4 Billion Purchase of Mets," ESPN, November 6, 2020, https://es.pn/4iwe3JY.
49 "What We Do," Point72, December 11, 2024, https://point72.com/what-we-do.
50 "Binance and CEO Plead Guilty to Federal Charges in $4B Resolution," U.S. Department of Justice, November 21, 2023, https://bit.ly/41yFHQu.
51 "Binance and CEO Plead Guilty to Federal Charges in $4B Resolution."

52. MacKenzie Sigalos and Ryan Browne, "Binance Founder Changpeng Zhao Sentenced to 4 Months in Prison after Plea Deal," CNBC, April 30, 2024, https://cnb.cx/4ivXduM.
53. Marina Mouka, "What Happened to Synapse—Chronicles of a Downfall," Bobsguide, December 2, 2024, https://bit.ly/3ONQ7nV.
54. Patrick Wintour, "Nearly 40% of Dirty Money Is Laundered in London and UK Crown Dependencies," World News, *The Guardian*, May 14, 2024, https://bit.ly/4imDuOl.
55. Mark Bou Mansour, "Tax Haven Ranking: UK Protects Itself While Keeping World Defenceless to British Tax Havens," Tax Justice Network, September 30, 2024, https://bit.ly/4gvLcnz.
56. Casey Michel, "How the US Became the World's Refuge for Dirty Money," *Mother Jones*, January 22, 2024, https://bit.ly/3Zwpxoo.
57. "Dirty Money: How the U.S. Became a Hub for Illicit Funds," *Mother Jones*, January/February 2024, https://tinyurl.com/yc698vhw.
58. James S. Henry, "Taxing Tax Havens," *Foreign Affairs*, January 26, 2022, https://fam.ag/3VysAeB.
59. Kalena Thomhave and Chuck Collins, *Billionaire Enabler States: How U.S. States Captured by the Trust Industry Help the World's Wealthy Hide Their Fortunes* (Institute for Policy Studies, September 28, 2022), 5, https://ips-dc.org/billionaire-enabler-states/.
60. "How to Choose the Best State to Set Up Your Trust," Commonwealth Trust, accessed March 16, 2025, https://tinyurl.com/2p99zxwu.
61. "Insights on Wealth Planning," Northern Trust, accessed March 16, 2025, https://tinyurl.com/mueuhrdp.
62. "Insights on Wealth Planning."
63. "Facts About Trusts and the Wyoming Trust Industry," Wyoming Trust Association, April 27, 2022, https://tinyurl.com/ytky2aay.
64. "IRS Investigating Cases of Sanctioned Russian Assets in SD Trusts," South Dakota Public Broadcasting, September 8, 2023, https://tinyurl.com/2p95y93f.
65. "Global Inequality from 1820 to Now: The Persistence and Mutation of Extreme Inequality," World Inequality Lab, October 20, 2021, https://bit.ly/4goFsfa.
66. "World's Top 1% Own More Wealth Than 95% of Humanity, as 'the Shadow of Global Oligarchy Hangs Over UN General Assembly,' Says Oxfam," Oxfam International, September 23, 2024, https://bit.ly/3BoY2Fc.

Chapter 12
1. "19th Amendment," National Archives Foundation, October 20, 2016, https://bit.ly/3BE0sQq.
2. "2001 Surgeon General's Report Highlights: Marketing Cigarettes to Women," CDC, February 22, 2011, https://bit.ly/4gkhVfH.
3. "Virginia Slims Cashes In on Women's Lib, Declaring: 'You've Come a Long Way, Baby,'" 4As, March 13, 2018, https://bit.ly/3VIzYE8.
4. "Old Tactics, New Products: How Big Tobacco Targets Women in E-Cigarette Marketing," Truth Initiative, March 28, 2023, https://bit.ly/4fp17De.

ENDNOTES

5   "Collection: Marlboro Men," Stanford University, September 27, 2022, https://stanford.io/404ROCT.
6   Corbin Hiar, "Lawmakers Study Big Tobacco Perjury Before Big Oil Showdown," Congressman Ro Khanna, October 27, 2021, https://bit.ly/3VPVcjp.
7   "Surveillance for Selected Tobacco-Use Behaviors—United States, 1900–1994," CDC, November 18, 1994, https://bit.ly/4ftiJxH.
8   Andrew Glass, "Congress Bans Airing Cigarette Ads, April 1, 1970," *Politico*, April 1, 2018, https://politi.co/49J197H.
9   "Cigarette Labeling and Health Warning Requirements," FDA, March 26, 2020, https://bit.ly/49M1xlR.
10 "Current Cigarette Smoking Among Adults in the United States," U.S. Centers for Disease Control and Prevention, September 17, 2024, https://bit.ly/4gIKTWA.
11 Michael Sauter, "Price of a Pack of Cigarettes Through the Decades," 24/7 Wall Street, June 19, 2019, https://bit.ly/3Bof0Uk.
12 "Federal Trade Commission Cigarette Report for 2022," Federal Trade Commission, 2023, https://bit.ly/4gF237W.
13 "Growing," The Tobacco Atlas, November 3, 2023, https://bit.ly/3BNokB3.
14 "Biography," European Route of Industrial Heritage, June 25, 2022, https://bit.ly/4iKjdCA.
15 "Biography About Founder of the Gist and Spiritus Factory," Biotech Campus Delft, April 1, 2019, https://bit.ly/4fqsZ9K.
16 Tim Eisenhauer, "Social Engineering and Employee Engagement," Axero Solutions, August 15, 2019, https://bit.ly/4gnDITK.
17 "What Is Social Engineering—The Human Element in the Technology Scam," CompTIA, October 20, 2020. https://bit.ly/3VNfYAa.
18 Ward Cromer and Paula Anderson, "Freud's Visit to America: Newspaper Coverage," *Journal of the History of the Behavioral Sciences* 6, no. 4 (October 6, 1970): 349–53, https://bit.ly/49LMbh.
19 "The Interpretation of Dreams," Freud Museum London, October 26, 2020, https://bit.ly/3BEOpSX.
20 Benjamin Plackett, "Was Freud Right About Anything?" Live Science, 2020, https://bit.ly/4iLIMTu.
21 Iris Mostegel, "The Original Influencer," *History Today*, February 6, 2019, https://bit.ly/3VNksqD.
22 Richard Gunderman, "The Manipulation of the American Mind: Edward Bernays and the Birth of Public Relations," ScholarWorks, July 9, 2015, https://bit.ly/402hd19.
23 "What Is Social Engineering in Cybersecurity?," Cisco, August 13, 2021, https://bit.ly/4fpA9LK.
24 Parsa Erfani and Margaret Bourdeaux, "Can Vaccine Incentive Reward Programs Increase COVID-19 Vaccine Uptake?," n.d., https://bit.ly/4fm1QVL.
25 Gregory Wheeler, "Bounded Rationality (Stanford Encyclopedia of Philosophy)," Stanford, November 30, 2018, https://stanford.io/3DniuHj.

26 Max Witynski, "What Is Behavioral Economics?" University of Chicago News, August 11, 2021, https://bit.ly/3DyFrqM.
27 R. D. Tuddenham, "Soldier Intelligence in World Wars I and II," *The American Psychologist* 3, no. 2 (1948): 54–56. https://doi.org/10.1037/h0054962.
28 "Flynn Effect," ScienceDirect, November 1, 2020, https://bit.ly/4fAB0sS.
29 Lisa H. Trahan et al., "The Flynn Effect: A Meta-Analysis," *Psychological Bulletin* 140, no. 5 (2014): 1332–60, https://doi.org/10.1037/a0037173.
30 Franck Ramus, "Declining Global IQ: Reality or Moral Panic?" *Polytechnique Insights*, November 2, 2023, https://bit.ly/4iHCB37.
31 Yan-Yi Lee, "The Flynn Effect: Has Human Intelligence Reached Its Peak?" *Varsity*, January 25, 2022, https://bit.ly/404VuFO.
32 Yan-Yi Lee.
33 Lawrence Hamilton, "Conspiracy vs. Science: A Survey of U.S. Public Beliefs," Carsey School of Public Policy, April 21, 2022, https://bit.ly/3VQuMOK.
34 Taylor Orth, "From Millionaires to Muslims, Small Subgroups of the Population Seem Much Larger to Many Americans," YouGov, March 15, 2022, https://bit.ly/3ZZMPo3.
35 Yuval Noah Harari, "We Should Never Underestimate Human Stupidity," CNBC, July 12, 2018, https://bit.ly/41Pe9GG.
36 Craig Fehrman, "The Incredible Shrinking Sound Bite," Boston, January 2, 2011, https://tinyurl.com/uzzsf7z9.
37 Craig Fehrman.
38 "Average Human Attention Span Statistics & Facts," Social Recovery Center, June 18, 2024, https://bit.ly/3ZOGQRw.
39 Scott Galloway, "Think Slow," No Mercy / No Malice, December 19, 2024, https://bit.ly/41OvgZz.
40 George Duke, "Sophists," *Internet Encyclopedia of Philosophy*, May 28, 2010, https://bit.ly/4fCfuEd.
41 "Bullshit Asymmetry Principle," ModelThinkers, November 7, 2022, https://bit.ly/4gJVwrU.
42 "Fact-Checking U.S. Politics," PolitiFact, September 9, 2007, https://www.politifact.com/.
43 Bill Adair, "What I Didn't Understand About Political Lying," *The Atlantic*, October 9, 2024, https://bit.ly/3BPMWcm.
44 "Social Media Manipulation by Political Actors an Industrial-Scale Problem, Report Finds," Phys.org, January 13, 2021, https://bit.ly/3BEF1i2.
45 Samantha Bradshaw et al., "Industrialized Disinformation: 2020 Global Inventory of Organized Social Media Manipulation," Oxford Internet Institute, January 13, 2021, demtech.oii.ox.ac.uk.
46 Hannah Arendt, "Eichmann in Jerusalem," *The New Yorker*, February 8, 1963, https://bit.ly/4gHla0H.
47 "Adolf Eichmann," United States Holocaust Memorial Museum, August 30, 2018, https://bit.ly/3ZOth4u.

ENDNOTES

48. Stanley Milgram, "Behavioral Study of Obedience," *The Journal of Abnormal and Social Psychology* 67, no. 4 (1963), 371–378, APA PsycNet, https://bit.ly/4fqjrvv.
49. Kim Mills, "Most Will Administer Shocks to Others When Prodded by 'Authority Figure,'" American Psychological Association, 2008, https://bit.ly/49IYCu9.
50. Kim Mills.
51. "Tobacco-Related Mortality," Centers for Disease Control and Prevention, August 22, 2022, https://bit.ly/4grckEr.
52. Wayne Hall and Chris Doran, "How Much Can the USA Reduce Health Care Costs by Reducing Smoking?," *PLOS Medicine* 13, no. 5 (2016), https://doi.org/10.1371/journal.pmed.1002021.
53. Barbara L. Zabawa, "What Is a Tobacco Surcharge and How Does My Company Offer One?," EX Program, November 9, 2021, https://bit.ly/3ZQjKdn.
54. Michael C. Horowitz, "Battles of Precise Mass," *Foreign Affairs*, October 22, 2024, https://fam.ag/3VUhjFp.
55. Joshua Hallenbeck, "Data of 3 Billion People Exposed in One of the Largest Data Breaches in History. Here's What You Need to Know," Yahoo! News, August 11, 2024, https://yhoo.it/4fqcgU9.
56. Altaba, Formerly Known as Yahoo!, Charged with Failing to Disclose Massive Cybersecurity Breach; Agrees to Pay $35 Million," U.S. Securities and Exchange Commission, April 24, 2018, https://bit.ly/402UGRP.
57. "Equifax Data Breach," Epic.org, November 5, 2021, https://bit.ly/4glgzS3.
58. Brian Krebs, "The Global Surveillance Free-For-All in Mobile Ad Data," Krebs on Security, October 27, 2024, https://bit.ly/4gov3Rc.
59. "Which States Produce the Most Coal?," US Energy Information Administration, October 20, 2023, https://bit.ly/3ZNRCri.
60. Lee Rainey, *Coal Mining Equipment at Work: Featuring the World Famous Mines and Mining Companies of Western Kentucky* (Enthusiast Books, 2011).
61. "Causes and Effects of Climate Change," United Nations, March 17, 2024, https://bit.ly/3BDyxQH.
62. "Kentucky's Coal-Colored Climate Change Denial," WKU Journalism, August 11, 2021, https://bit.ly/3Dwq8z1.
63. Elliot Smith, "'Bregret'? Many Brits Are Suffering from Brexit Regret," CNBC, March 3, 2023, https://cnb.cx/4iMa9gm.
64. Frances Moore Lappé, "Beyond Shame and Blame: Why Do Republicans Vote Against Their Self-Interest?," *Common Dreams*, August 2, 2024, https://bit.ly/4gmXSxq.
65. "Bannon on Trump Era Technique: 'Flood the Zone with Sh*T,'" CNN, November 2, 2020, https://cnn.it/4iObLGe.
66. Ali Swenson and Kelvin Chan, "Election Disinformation Takes a Big Leap with AI Being Used to Deceive Worldwide," The Associated Press, March 14, 2024, https://bit.ly/3DAj7wV.

67 Heather Chen and Kathleen Magramo, "Finance Worker Pays Out $25 Million After Video Call with Deepfake 'Chief Financial Officer,'" CNN, February 4, 2024, https://cnn.it/4iEyK6V.
68 Zeke Faux, "$75 Billion Lost to Pig-Butchering Scam, New Study Estimates," *Time*, March 1, 2024, https://bit.ly/4gr9OxY.
69 Zeke Faux.
70 "Home," Gloo, June 21, 2023, https://gloo.us/.
71 "Home."
72 Rob Mudge, "US: Religious Data Platform 'Targets Mentally Ill, Vulnerable People,'" Deutsche Welle, September 27, 2020, https://bit.ly/4230JHB.
73 Liv McMahon, "Hawk Tuah Girl: Online Star Faces Crypto Coin Criticism," *BBC*, December 6, 2024, https://bbc.in/3ZKbM5E.
74 "Investors Sue Creators of Hawk Tuah Meme Coin for Alleged Securities Violations After 90% Price Drop," Yahoo! Finance, December 20, 2024, https://yhoo.it/4fC3Zwl.
75 Michael J. Mazarr et al., *The Emerging Risk of Virtual Societal Warfare: Social Manipulation in a Changing Information Environment* (RAND Corporation, 2019).

Chapter 13

1 Christian Fuchs, "The Rise of Authoritarian Capitalism," Global Dialogue, December 4, 2018, https://bit.ly/3W5Wt64.
2 Kevin Rudd, "The Rise of Authoritarian Capitalism," Opinion, *The New York Times*, September 16, 2018, https://nyti.ms/40loltf.
3 Christian Fuchs, "The Rise of Authoritarian Capitalism," Global Dialogue, December 4, 2018, https://bit.ly/3W5Wt64.
4 Gábor Scheiring, "From Democracy to Authoritarian Capitalism," *Review of Democracy*, June 16, 2023, https://bit.ly/4047Pcb.
5 Ben Raderstorf, "The Authoritarian Playbook," Protect Democracy, June 15, 2022, https://bit.ly/3C94EaW.
6 "Brazil's Bolsonaro Has Been Barred from Running for Office Until 2030," NBC News, July 1, 2023, https://nbcnews.to/4a4fw6A.
7 "Dark Money Reform Bill Blocked in U.S. Senate; Brennan Center Responds," Brennan Center for Justice, September 22, 2022, https://bit.ly/4216pS4.
8 Mike Dolan, "Column: Will Biden Have a 'Strong Dollar' Mantra?" *Reuters*, November 13, 2020, https://reut.rs/421N0QX.
9 Vikrant Singh, "Russia, China Completely Abandon US Dollar in Bilateral Trade, Says Russian PM," Wion, December 20, 2023, https://tinyurl.com/2mv48r67.
10 "Maas Wants End to US Dominance," Deutsche Welle, August 27, 2018, https://bit.ly/407EZHA.
11 Mohammed Saaida, "BRICS Plus: De-Dollarization and Global Power Shifts in New Economic Landscape," *BRICS Journal of Economics* 5, no. 1 (2024): 13–33, https://doi.org/10.3897/BRICS-econ.5.e117828.
12 Matthew Burgess, "De-Dollarization Is Happening at a 'Stunning' Pace, Jen Says," *Bloomberg*, April 18, 2023, https://bloom.bg/4h5dhCg.

ENDNOTES

13 "Gold Price History," GoldPrice, January 14, 2004, https://bit.ly/423ZsQm.
14 "2024 Central Bank Gold Reserves Survey," World Gold Council, June 18, 2024, https://bit.ly/4gHP45p.
15 "Bitcoin Storms Above $100,000 as Trump 2.0 Fuels Crypto Euphoria," *Reuters*, December 5, 2024, https://tinyurl.com/4rc2aej4.
16 Steven Stradbrooke, "Binance/Circle USDC Tie Up Targets Tether's Stablecoin Dominance," CoinGeek, December 12, 2024, https://bit.ly/3DRbz9m.
17 David Henderson, "Jeff Hummel on Tether," Econlib, December 6, 2024, https://bit.ly/42XwZML.
18 Joseph Jasperse and Sarah Hammer, "The State of Stablecoin Regulation and Emergence of Global Principles," American Bar Association, September 24, 2024, https://bit.ly/3W6XURK.
19 Santiago Bedoya Pardo, "CBDC Searches Soar by 769%," *International Accounting Bulletin*, January 4, 2023, https://bit.ly/4a2Pq45.
20 Hung Tran and Barbara Matthews, "CBDCs Will Further Fragment the Global Economy—and Could Threaten the Dollar," Atlantic Council, November 16, 2023, https://bit.ly/4h4bdus.
21 Robert Wade, "Long Read: The Beginning of the End for the US Dollar's Global Dominance," LSE International Development, February 29, 2024, https://bit.ly/40mMImM.
22 Huileng Tan, "De-Dollarization: Rich Countries Plan to Buy More Gold," *Business Insider*, June 20, 2024, https://bit.ly/4h4JWb6.
23 Matt Peterson, "The U.S. Dollar Is Riding High. Trump Could Put an End to All That," Yahoo! News, January 2, 2025, https://yhoo.it/3WaGST0.
24 Stefan Ellerbeck, "What Is 'Friendshoring'? This and Other Global Trade Buzzwords Explained," World Economic Forum, February 17, 2023, https://bit.ly/3CaiSbA.
25 "China's Growing Global Influence: What's at Stake?," US Global Leadership Coalition, April 2021, https://bit.ly/3DNowkI.
26 "China's Growing Global Influence: What's at Stake?"
27 Jake Sullivan and Hal Brands, "China Has Two Paths to Global Domination," Carnegie Endowment, May 22, 2020, https://bit.ly/4252ggb.
28 Christopher Chivvis, "Why Brazil's Relationship with the United States Isn't Taking Off," Carnegie Endowment for International Peace, 2023, https://bit.ly/4j7tVTy.
29 "Brazil Leads the World in Exports of Seven Food Commodities," Merco Press, March 9, 2024, https://bit.ly/4fN2kUM.
30 Mariana Durao and Beatriz Amat, "Oil Tops Brazil Exports, Bolstering COP30 Host's Challenge," *BNN Bloomberg*, January 6, 2025, https://tinyurl.com/4t9y6bdm.
31 Ashley Capoot, "Apple Doubles India iPhone Production to $14 Billion as It Shifts from China: Report," CNBC, April 10, 2024, https://cnb.cx/4h1J4Ej.
32 Chirag Chopra and Piyush Gupta, "India's Unified Payment Interface's Impact on the Financial Landscape," World Economic Forum, June 26, 2023, https://bit.ly/4fO7H6c.

33 Rohit Bansal, "Decoding India's UPI Phenomenon: A Digital Revolution with Global Implications," Observer Research Foundation, September 5, 2024, https://bit.ly/3PtXvFa.
34 Tessa Stuart, "The Crypto Industry Emerged as a 'Political Money Death Star' in 2024," *Rolling Stone*, November 17, 2024, https://bit.ly/4gZjSy0.
35 Tim Lau, "Citizens United Explained," Brennan Center for Justice, December 12, 2019, https://bit.ly/4h6jGx0.
36 Rick Claypool, "Big Crypto, Big Spending: Crypto Corporations Spend an Unprecedented $119 Million Influencing Elections," Public Citizen, August 21, 2024, https://bit.ly/4Oot1uT.
37 Dan Milmo and Kari Paul, "Facebook Disputes Its Own Research Showing Harmful Effects of Instagram on Teens' Mental Health," *The Guardian*, September 30, 2021, https://bit.ly/409BIrx.
38 Emily Young et al., "Frequent Social Media Use and Experiences with Bullying Victimization, Persistent Feelings of Sadness or Hopelessness, and Suicide Risk Among High School Students—Youth Risk Behavior Survey, United States, 2023," *Morbidity and Mortality Weekly Report*, 73 no. 4 (2024): 23–30, https://doi.org/10.15585/mmwr.su7304a3.
39 "S.1409—Kids Online Safety Act," Congress.gov, 2023, https://bit.ly/4h5BKHO.
40 Barbara Ortutay, "What to Know About the Kids Online Safety Act and Its Chances of Passing," The Associated Press, July 21, 2024, https://bit.ly/4h2lW8H.
41 "Meta Selects Northeast Louisiana as Site of $10 Billion Artificial Intelligence Optimized Data Center; Governor Jeff Landry Calls Investment 'a New Chapter' for State," Louisiana Economic Development, December 4, 2024, https://bit.ly/3BWdVDo.
42 Greg LaRose, "Stalled Kids Online Safety Act Pits Speaker Mike Johnson Against Powerful Republicans," *Louisiana Illuminator*, December 19, 2024, https://bit.ly/3PuCs5m.
43 Carrie Johnson, "Justice Department Changes Rattle Current and Former Agency Veterans," NPR, January 31, 2025, https://n.pr/3WFpkPa.
44 Juan C. Zarate, *Treasury's War: The Unleashing of a New Era of Financial Warfare* (PublicAffairs, 2013).
45 Michelle Celarier, "Ray Dalio Makes His Exit from Bridgewater," Institutional Investor, October 4, 2022, https://bit.ly/409BXTi.
46 Ben Bartenstein, "Dalio, Abu Dhabi Royal's G42 Said to Shelve Investment Venture," July 22, 2024, https://bloom.bg/425yzM6.
47 Mercedes Ruehl, "Bridgewater Founder Ray Dalio Joins Billionaires Snapping Up Singapore 'Shophouses,'" *Financial Times*, May 23, 2024, https://on.ft.com/405wA7B.
48 "Safe Cities Index 2021," The Economist Safe Cities, April 15, 2024, https://bit.ly/4Oo3GRx.

Chapter 14

1 "Social Contract," in *Encyclopedia Britannica*, edited by the editors of *Encyclopedia Britannica*, last modified February 13, 2025, https://bit.ly/4gjY3c5.

ENDNOTES

2 "Our Work," United Nations, March 3, 2021, https://bit.ly/3PDkVrU.
3 Julia Black, "Forms and Paradoxes of Principles Based Regulation," *SSRN*, October 6, 2008, https://doi.org/10.2139/ssrn.1267722.
4 "Rules Versus Principles Based Regulation," CFA Society United Kingdom, February 7, 2023, https://bit.ly/3DXg16x.
5 John Geddes, "Is Canada's Charter Better Than the US Constitution?," The World from PRX, July 31, 2016, https://bit.ly/4gFuO3D.
6 Trevor Timm, "Elon Musk Has Become the World's Biggest Hypocrite on Free Speech," Opinion, *The Guardian*, January 15, 2024, https://bit.ly/4g2nvCI.
7 Cameron Joseph, "Fox News Paid $787M to Avoid Saying 'Sorry' for Lying About the 2020 Election," Vice, April 19, 2023, https://bit.ly/4g2Cqg0.
8 "Voting Technology Company Settles Lawsuit Against OAN Over 2020 Election Claims," NPR, April 16, 2024, https://n.pr/3WpWj9Y.
9 Aitor Hernández-Morales, "Zuckerberg Urges Trump to Stop the EU from Fining US Tech Companies," *Politico*, January 11, 2025, https://tinyurl.com/47zacnp3.
10 "Cause of Action," Cornell Law School, last reviewed July 2022, https://bit.ly/3PEkDAW.
11 "Litigation, Overview—Truth: Tort Defense," *Bloomberg Law*, June 1, 2024, https://bit.ly/40kVW1x.
12 "Wisconsin Journalists Vulnerable to Frivolous Lawsuits," *O'Clock Buzz*, WORT, January 6, 2025, https://bit.ly/3Wpo96b.
13 Jay Adkisson, "The European Union Adopts Anti-SLAPP Directive," *Forbes*, June 6, 2024, https://bit.ly/3Ww6REw.
14 "How It Started, How It Is Going: Media Literacy Index 2022," Open Society Institute Sofia, October 12, 2022, https://bit.ly/4alTDzW.
15 Jenny Gross, "How Finland Is Teaching a Generation to Spot Misinformation," World, *The New York Times*, January 10, 2023, https://nyti.ms/4jonCew.
16 Elizabeth Wallace, "Enabling Digital Privacy with Zero-Knowledge Proofs," RTInsights, October 5, 2023, https://bit.ly/4h7vVdb.
17 Paul Pelletier, "Trial and Error," *The Baffler*, March 19, 2019, https://bit.ly/4gZBOce.
18 Katelyn Polantz, "Paul Manafort Sentenced to 47 Months in Prison, Far Short of Expectations," CNN Politics, March 7, 2019, https://cnn.it/4h0r5yf.
19 Amita Kelly et al., "Trump Pardons Roger Stone, Paul Manafort, and Charles Kushner," NPR, December 23, 2020, https://n.pr/4g3ZMSB.
20 Cheyenne Ligon, "Tigran Gambaryan: The Star Crypto Investigator Kidnapped by Nigeria," CoinDesk, December 10, 2024, https://bit.ly/4jlJ9Ve.
21 Hardy Merriman et al., "Fostering a Fourth Democratic Wave: A Playbook for Countering the Authoritarian Threat," International Center on Nonviolent Conflict, 2023, https://bit.ly/4jBALkP.
22 Julian Barraza, "The 5 Richest Current U.S. Governors," AOL, September 16, 2022, https://aol.it/40C2Cto.
23 "Worldwide NGO Directory," WANGO, January 4, 2007, https://bit.ly/4hlQ8vt.

THE CATALYSTS

24 "Financial Regulators' Dilemma: Administrative and Regulatory Hurdles to Innovation," Alliance for Innovative Regulation, January 1, 2020, https://bit.ly/40lwNny.
25 Camille Walsh, "Everything You Need to Know About Regulatory Sandboxes," State Policy Network, October 12, 2021, https://bit.ly/40hfGTI.
26 "Regulatory Sandboxes—Testing Environments for Innovation and Regulation," Federal Ministry for Economics Affairs and Climate, May 19, 2022, https://bit.ly/40E4HF9.
27 Kiara Alfonseca, "What Does the Civil Rights Statute in Trump's Potential Jan. 6 Indictment Letter Mean?," ABC News, July 28, 2023, https://bit.ly/3Cj4uhp.
28 *Minority Report*, IMDb, June 20, 2002, https://imdb.to/3Wpr52M.
29 "Leeching | Medical Procedure," in *Encyclopedia Britannica*, edited by the editors of *Encyclopedia Britannica* (2019), https://bit.ly/3EbPeDr.
30 "Application of the Securities and Mutual Fund Exemptions to Cryptocurrency, Stablecoins, and Related Investments," United States Office of Government Ethics, July 5, 2022, https://bit.ly/4h5VtYe.
31 Dominic Barton, "The Rise of the Middle Class in China and Its Impact on the Chinese and World Economies," 2022, https://bit.ly/4jwLZXJ.
32 Christine Godt and Markus Burchardi, "Immigration, Innovation, and Growth," *National Bureau of Economic Research* 33, no. 1 (2020): 25, https://doi.org/10.14512/oew350128.
33 "Billionaire Wealth Surges by $2 Trillion in 2024, Three Times Faster Than the Year Before, While the Number of People Living in Poverty Has Barely Changed Since 1990," Oxfam International, January 20, 2025, https://bit.ly/3PRLhX6.
34 "Billionaire Wealth Surges by $2 Trillion in 2024, Three Times Faster Than the Year Before, While the Number of People Living in Poverty Has Barely Changed Since 1990."
35 Kristofer Hamel, "Look East Instead of West for the Future Global Middle Class," Development Matters, May 7, 2019, https://bit.ly/3Ch0cXM.
36 David Madland and Nick Bunker, "The Middle Class Is Key to a Better-Educated Nation," American Progress Action, 2011, https://bit.ly/42qrxlf.
37 Xiaoyong Hu et al., "Impact of Social Class on Health: The Mediating Role of Health Self-Management," edited by Filipe Prazeres, *PloS One* 16, no. 7 (2021), https://doi.org/10.1371/journal.pone.0254692.
38 Michael Strain, "The Link Between Wages and Productivity Is Strong," American Enterprise Institute (AEI) and Institute for the Study of Labor (IZA), 2019, https://bit.ly/42k3mog.
39 Josephine Franks, "Universal Basic Income: What It Is and Why People Will Be Given Free Money for Doing Nothing," Sky News, June 6, 2023, https://bit.ly/3E36w5O.
40 "History of Federal Minimum Wage Rates Under the Fair Labor Standards Act, 1938–2009," U.S. Department of Labor, 2009, https://bit.ly/4hpvomR.
41 Barclay Butler, "The Global Housing Market Crisis of 2023," IntaCapitalSwiss SA, December 7, 2023, https://bit.ly/3WlyS1x.

ENDNOTES

42 "The State of the Nation's Housing," Joint Center for Housing Studies of Harvard University, 2024, https://bit.ly/40lZWi8.
43 Gretchen Morgenson, "Senators Take Aim at Big Private Equity Landlords as Rents Soar," NBC News, October 24, 2024, https://nbcnews.to/4gcQpjG.
44 "Government Announces Two-Year Extension to Ban on Foreign Ownership of Canadian Housing," Department of Finance Canada, February 4, 2024, https://bit.ly/3WqwEy1.
45 "Government Announces Two-Year Extension to Ban on Foreign Ownership of Canadian Housing."
46 "New Zealand Tourism Revenue," CEIC Data, June 21, 2019, https://bit.ly/4gaCOJz.
47 "S&P Global FinLit Survey," Global Financial Literacy Excellence Center (GFLEC), January 11, 2023, https://bit.ly/40kZOQ8.
48 "Denmark Green Card," ISA Global, August 10, 2014, https://bit.ly/4g5hJjH.
49 "Federal Skilled Worker Program," Government of Canada, 2024, https://bit.ly/4joHzBT.
50 "Points Table for Skilled Independent Visa (Subclass 189)," Australian Government, January 22, 2019, https://bit.ly/4gZn0dX.
51 "Working Here If Your Partner Is in NZ," New Zealand Government, August 19, 2024, https://bit.ly/40jZjG5.
52 "State of Immigrant Integration," OECD, 2024, https://bit.ly/3WtKcIM.
53 "Governance of Migrant Integration in Sweden," European Commission, June 2024, https://bit.ly/4artsb7'.
54 "Australia's Overall Economic Growth Lies in 'Productivity and Population Growth,'" Sky News Australia, December 29, 2020, https://bit.ly/40r8OTV.
55 "The Lancet: Dramatic Declines in Global Fertility Rates Set to Transform Global Population Patterns by 2100," Institute for Health Metrics and Evaluation, March 20, 2024, https://bit.ly/40Dfm2R.
56 Tory Shepherd, "Birthrates Are Plummeting Worldwide. Can Governments Turn the Tide?," *The Guardian*, August 10, 2024, https://bit.ly/40GknYs.
57 Tory Shepherd.
58 Christine Burke, "Saudi Arabia's Female Leaders Show Narrowing Gender Gap Brings Economic Benefits," *Bloomberg*, November 24, 2024, https://bloom.bg/3E38Vxm.
59 Caitlin Gilbert et al., "Remote Work Appears to Be Here to Stay, Especially for Women," *The Washington Post*, June 22, 2023, https://wapo.st/4hmPmhP.
60 Tory Shepherd, "Birthrates Are Plummeting Worldwide. Can Governments Turn the Tide?," *The Guardian*, August 10, 2024, https://bit.ly/40GknYs.
61 Phillip Inman, "Claudia Goldin Wins Nobel Economics Prize for Work on Gender Pay Gap," World, *The Guardian*, October 9, 2023, https://bit.ly/42pWnuf.
62 Pau Baizan et al., "The Effect of Gender Policies on Fertility: The Moderating Role of Education and Normative Context." *European Journal of Population* 32, no. 1 (2016): 1–30. https://doi.org/10.1007/s10680-015-9356-y.

63 Jaya Nayar, "Equal Representation? The Debate Over Gender Quotas (Part 1)," *Harvard International Review*, November 29, 2021, https://bit.ly/4awSXYk.
64 Alina Dizik, "Do Quotas for Corporate Boards Help Women Advance?" The University of Chicago Booth School of Business, June 15, 2015, https://bit.ly/3WursJg.

INDEX

A

ACLU (American Civil Liberties Union), 322-325
Adair, Bill, 272
Affordable Care Act, 116
AI deepfakes, 189, 280
Airbnb, 131-132, 336-337
Airline Deregulation Act, 88
Alphabet, 183-186, 219
Altman, Sam, 129
American dream, 110-111
AML (anti-money laundering), 239
  CZ (Binance) and, 254-255
  September 11 attacks and, 241-242
  tools, 157
antitrust law, 80-89
  courts and, 89-94
  key cases, 90-93
  neoliberalism, 88-89
Arendt, Hannah, 274-275
ARPA (Advanced Research Projects Agency), 78
ARPANET, 78
asset tokenization, 163-167
The Association for Women in Cryptocurrency, 14-15
AT&T antitrust case, 90
authoritarian capitalism, 290-291
authoritarianism, 169-170
  liberal democracy and, 290
  opportunism and, 292
  tactics, 292
  trust and, 172-174
    data weaponization and, 183-186
    government regulations, 177-180
    journalism and, 182-183
    network usage, 187
    social media, 176-177, 188
Azimuth, 125

B

balance-of-payments deficit, 66
banking
  accredited investors, 202-203
  banks as custodians, 41-42
  BSA (Bank Secrecy Act), 239
  CDD (customer due diligence), 240
  central banks, 44-46
  centralization, 45-46
  commercial banks, 43
  EDD (enhanced due diligence), 240
  fractional reserve banking, 42-43
  full-reserve banking, 42
  investment banks, 44

liquidity, 50-51
M&A (mergers and acquisitions), 44
regulatory bodies, 119-121
Switzerland, 237
universal banks, 44
World Bank, 48-49
behavioral economics, 268
Bernanke, Ben, 40, 66
Bernays, Edward, 265-266
Bezos, Jeff, 79, 132-134
Big Tech
  business portability, 138-139
  corporate profits, 144-145
  data weaponization, 142-143, 183-186
  defamation laws, 320
  digital technologies, 138-139
  effects of, 139-145
  financial chaos, 143-144
  free speech and, 126-127
  innovation hubs, 221-222
  misinformation/disinformation, 140-141, 320
  monopolies, 179-180
  privatization, 133
  regulators, 178-179
  social media algorithms, 141
  trust, government regulation and, 177-180
  US *versus* EU, 136-137
Binance, 254-255
birthrate decline, 340-341
BIS (Bank for International Settlements), 49-50
bitcoin
  bitcointalk.org, 24
  Cheney, Liz, 117-119
  PoS (proof of stake), 154
  PoW (proof of work), 154
  terminology, 24n
Bitcoin, 152, 158-159
  Bitcoin Pizza Day, 25
  DeFi and, 159-160
  Nakamoto, Satoshi, 151-152
  pizza purchase, 24-25
  terminology, 24n
blockchain, 150-158
  The Association for Women in Cryptocurrency, 14-15
  crypto mining, 154
Blockchain Ireland, 15
Blue Origin, 132
BNPL (buy now, pay later), 49
Bolsonaro, Jair Messias, 291-292
BOR (Beneficial Ownership Registration), 249-250
Brand, Stewart, 221-222
Brandolini, Alberto, 271
Brazil, 291-292, 301-302
Bretton Woods, 61-63, 298
  gold standard and, 66
  system collapse, 68
Brexit, 115, 192
BRI (Belt and Road Initiative), 301
BRIC/BRICS/BRICS+, 205-208, 294, 301-304
Bridgewater Associates, 309
BSA (Bank Secrecy Act), 239
  digital currencies, 244-245
  legal challenges, 249-251
  Watergate, 242-243
bullshit asymmetry principle, 271
Burger, Jerry, 275-276
Bush, George W., 100-102
Bush, Vannevar, 77-78
but-for cause, 12n

C

Cambridge Analytica, 142-143
Canada's Charter, 317
capital, definition, 41n
capitalism
  antitrust law, 80-82
  authoritarian, 290-291

INDEX

Occupy Wall Street, 181-182
  state, 290-291
  wealth gap, 333
cause of action (defamation case), 320-321
CBDCs (central bank digital currencies), 121, 166-167, 298
CBO (Congressional Budget Office), income inequality, 114
CBPs (cross-border payments), 52
CDA (Communications Decency Act), 88-89
CDD (customer due diligence), 240
CeFi (centralized finance), 45-46, 150-151
central banks, 44-46
centralized finance (CeFi). *See* CeFi (centralized finance)
CFPB (Consumer Financial Protection Bureau), 120
CFT (countering the financing of terrorism), 157, 239, 241-242
CFTC (Commodity Futures Trading Commission), 50, 120
CFTRA (Currency and Foreign Transactions Reporting Act), 238-239
Chainanalysis, 156
ChatGPT, 128
Cheney, Liz, 9-12, 117-119
China, BRICS+, 301-302
chips (computers). *See* semiconductors, innovation and
CHIPS and Science Act, 231
Christian nationalism, 10
cigarette smoking, 262-263
Circle, stablecoin and, 166
Civil Rights Act of 1964, 86
Clayton Antitrust Act, 84
climate change, 194-195
coal in Kentucky, 279-280

COBOL (Common Business-Oriented Language) programming language, 53-54
Coby, Gary, 273
cognitive bias
  social engineering and, 266-276
  trust and, 175
  voting and, 203
Cohen, Steve A., 254, 324
CoinDesk, 24
collaboration tools, 222-224
command economy, 197
commercial liberalism, 200
Communitech, 227
constitutional monarchy, 172
Consumer Protection Act, 158
consumer surplus, 27-28
corporate contribution to elections, 305-307
corporate profits, 144-145
corporate taxes, 133-134
correspondent banking, 51-52
Costco, immigration and, 219
COVID-19
  collaboration tools, 222-224
  employment safety restrictions, 131-132
  inflation and, 32
  Trump reaction, 102-103
  WFH (work from home), 222-224
credit cards, 23-24
CRP (Committee to Reelect the President), Watergate and, 242-243
CRS (common reporting standards), 243
cryptocurrency, 296-297. *See also* bitcoin; Bitcoin
  The Association for Women in Cryptocurrency, 14-15
  Binance, 254-255
  BSA (Bank Secrecy Act), 244-245

CBDCs, 298
Cheney, Liz, 117-119
corporate elections, 305-307
Ethereum, 152, 155
  HAWK, 283
  mainstream, 158-161
  P2P example, 159
  Stablecoins, 166, 297
  Tornado Cash, 244
  transfer of funds, 244-245
crypto mining, 154
CTA (Corporate Transparency Act), 249
Cuban Missile Crisis, 69
currency, 121
  fiat currencies, 68
  floating exchange rates, 68
  foreign exchange reserves, 70
  gold, US dollar and, 63-64
  versus money, 31-32
  reserve currency, 63
  SDNs (specially designated nationals), 73
  US weaponization, 71-73
  world, 63
Custodia, 45-46
cybercrime
  BOR and, 249-250
  social engineering, 266
CZ (Changpeng Zhao), 254-255

D

DACOM (Digital Asset Compliance & Market Integrity Summit), 255
Dalio, Ray, 309
dark money, 293n, 330
DARPA (Defense Advanced Research Projects Agency), 78
data weaponization, 142-143, 183-186
debt crisis, projection, 111-113
decentralized finance. *See* DeFi (decentralized finance)

decision-making, 267-268
deepfakes, 280
defamation laws, 319-321
DeFi (decentralized finance), 149, 155-157, 197-198
  Bitcoin, 159-160
  crypto and, 296-297
  libertarianism and, 247
  Rand, Ayn, 247
  transfer of funds, 244-245
democracy
  monarchies and, 171-172
  protecting, 326-444
  trust and, 170-173
democratic socialist, 172
deregulation, 88-89
diamond-water paradox, 26
digital currencies. *See* cryptocurrency
digital nomads, 223-224, 226-229
Digital Silk Road initiative, 302
digital technologies, 138-139
  digital nomads, 223-224
  digital transformation, 222
  international work, 224
Dimon, Jamie, 160-161
Direct Persuasion, 273
disaster preparedness, 101-102
disinformation. *See* misinformation/disinformation
DLTs (distributed ledger technologies), 152-153
DMA (Digital Markets Act), 136-137
Dodd, Nigel, 33-34
Dodd-Frank Wall Street Reform, 158, 246
DOJ (US Department of Justice), 6-7
dollarization, 69-71
dollar smile theory, 295
double spend, 151-152
Durov, Pavel, 127
duty of care, 307
DVS (Dominion Voting Systems), 319

INDEX

E

economic dysfunction, middle class and, 106-114
economic interdependence, 198-200
Economic Policy Institute, wage stagnation, 108
economic sanctions, 58-60, 72-74, 307-309
economy
  command economy, 197
  global economy withdrawal, 209-210
  health, middle class and, 333
  immigration and, 334 (*See* immigration)
  population growth and, 232
  socioeconomic mobility, 334-335
  UBI (universal basic income), 336
  women and, 341
EDD (enhanced due diligence), 240
Edelman Trust Institute Trust Barometer, 173, 179
EFF (Electronic Frontier Foundation), 322-325
Eichmann, Adolf, 274-275
election contribution, corporations, 305-307
Emergency Economic Stabilization Act, 40
employment law
  privatization and, 129
  Proposition 22 (California), 130-131
  safety precautions, 131-132
Equifax attack, 277-278
Ethereum, 152, 155
ethics, perceptions of competency and, 174
EU (European Union), 192
  6AMLD (6th AML Directive), 325
  Daphne's Law, 321
  DMA (Digital Markets Act), 136-137
  GDPR (General Data Protection Regulation), 136
  US Dollar, 294-295
Europe
  Big Tech and, 136-137
  innovation hubs, 227
European Economic Community, 192
exchange, value and, 26
extremism, right-wing, 10

F

Facebook, 177, 184
fair use doctrine, 128-129
Farook, Syed, 123
FATF (Financial Action Task Force), 239
FCA (Financial Conduct Authority), 50
FCC (Federal Communications Commission), 85-86
FDIC (Federal Deposit Insurance Corporation), 119
Federal Reserve System, 119
fertility rates, 109, 340-341
fiat currencies, 68
financial hubs, 214-215
financial institutions
  BIS (Bank for International Settlements), 49-50
  regulatory bodies, 47-51
  World Bank, 48-49
financial literacy, 30-31, 338-339
financial warfare, 72
FinCEN (Financial Crimes Enforcement Network), 50, 118, 120
FINRA (Financial Industry Regulatory Authority), 120
fintech, 157-158
  regulatory gaps, 256
First Amendment rights, 125-126. See *also* freedom of speech

Fishwick, David, 201-202
The Flynn Effect, 268
fractional reserve banking, 42-43
freedom of speech
  absolute, 318
  defamation laws and, 319-321
  fair use, 128-129
  misinformation/disinformation, 319
  Telegram app, 127
  Twitter/X and, 126-127
  unelected officials and, 318
free trade, 198, 200
FSA (Financial Services Agency), 50
FTC (Federal Trade Commissions) Act, 84
full-reserve banking, 42
fungible tokens, 165-167

G

Gambarayan, Tigran, 325
GameStop, 143-144
GDP (gross domestic product), 112
GDPR (General Data Protection Regulation), 136
Geithner, Timothy, 39-40
Generative AI, 142, 189
geopolitics, Big Tech and, 139-140
GI Bill, 106
gig economy, 130
Gilded Age, antitrust law and, 82-83
Glass-Steagall Act, 85-86
globalism, 197-200
  failures by elected officials, 201-202
  GDP (gross domestic product) and, 198-199
  global economy withdrawal, 209-210
  inequality and, 292
  pandemics, 199-200
  trade blocks, 300-301
Gloo app, 282-283

gold, 296
  US dollar, 63-64
gold standard, 64
  FDR and, 65-66
Google
  antitrust case, 93
  China and, 222
  immigration and, 219
Grab couriers, 212
Gramm-Leach-Bliley Act, 88
Great Depression, 65
GSER (Global Startup Ecosystem Report), 214, 216

H

Haugen, Frances, 177
HAWK digital coin, 283
healthcare costs, 109
Heaphy, Tim, 6
history of money, 19-21
home mortgages. *See* mortgages, subprime lending crisis
hotelization, 336-337
House Select Committee Investigating the January 6th Attack, 6-13
housing costs, 109, 336
  digital nomads and, 228-229
  labor shortage and, 337
Hsieh, Tony, 228

I

IBM, antitrust case, 91
Identity Theft Resource Center, 150
IMF (International Monetary Fund), 48, 61
immigration
  anti-immigration rhetoric, 339
  economic growth and, 334
  housing costs, 228-229
  innovation hubs, 218-221
  policy innovations, 339-340
  population growth, 232

INDEX

refugees, 224-226
  USA for UNHCR, 224
imperialism, 210
inclusion, intentional, 344
income inequality, 107
  gender-based, 342
  globalization and, 292
  Tax Cuts and Jobs Act, 114
  taxes, 113-114
  wealth gap, 258
inflation
  COVID-19 and, 32
  neo-nationalism, 209
  post-WWI Germany, 32-33
  wages and, 33
information availability, 175-176, 270-272
Infrastructure Investment and Jobs Act, 104-105
innovation, 212
  CHIPS and Science Act, 231
  collaboration tools, 222-224
  digital nomads, 223-227
  digital transformation, 222
  helping other countries, 226
  international work, 224
  irresponsible, 251-252
  mobile payments, 229
  responsible, 333-334
  semiconductors, 231-232
  Startup Genome, 213-214
  startups, 213-214
  unicorns, 217
  venture capital and, 213
  WFH (work from home), 222-224
innovation hubs, 217-222
  Big Tech and, 221-222
  Canada, 227
  Communitech, 227
  Europe, 227
  immigration and, 218-221
  Las Vegas, 228

Tulsa, Oklahoma, 227
  US vulnerability, 229-232
intelligence, collective, 268-269
International Bank for Reconstruction and Development, 61
international financial institutions, 47-49
international trade, 51-53
international work, 224
investment banks, 44
IQ (Intelligence Quotient) averages, 268-269
irresponsible innovation, 251-252
IRS (Internal Revenue Service) underfunding issues, 114-115

J

January 6th Attack on US Capitol, 3-5
  Official Election Defense Fund, 272-273
  online rhetoric, 10-11
  social media information, 10
Jones, Alex, 319
journalism, trust and, 182-183
JPMorgan, Kinexys, 152
jurisdictional arbitrage, 304

K

Kentucky coal, 279-280
Keynes, John Maynard, 61
Kinexys, 152
KOSA (Kids Online Safety Act), 306-307
KYC (Know Your Customer) rules, 240

L

law of comparative advantage, 198
lead prosecutor, 6n
Lehman Brothers, 37-38, 40
Le Pen, Marine, 195-196
leverage ratio, 38

lex Julia, 80
liberal democracy, 290
lies by politicians, 116-117, 272-273
line prosecutor, 6n
Ling, Tan Hooi, 211-212
liquidity, 40
liquidity ratio, 50-51
loans, commercial banks, 43
Locke, John, 172

M

M&A (mergers and acquisitions), 44
Maastricht Treaty of 1992, 192
Macron, Emmanuel, 196
Malik, Tashfeen, 123
Manafort, Paul, 324
Marshall, Laurence, 77
McCarthy, Kevin, 116-117
meritocracy, 274
Meta, data weaponization and, 183-186
Microsoft antitrust case, 91-93
middle class
　American dream, 110-111
　economic health, 333
　fertility rate, 109
　GI Bill, 106
　healthcare costs, 109
　housing costs, 109
　income inequality, 107
　meritocracy and, 274
　taxes, 113-114
　wage stagnation, 107-108
Milgram, Stanley, 275
Mill, John Stuart, 26
misinformation/
　disinformation, 319
　AI deepfakes, 189
　Big Tech spread, 140-141
　education, 321-322
　social media amplification, 188
　trust and, 175-176

monarchies, 171-172
money
　as construct, 20, 33-34
　versus currency, 31-32
　as form of payment, 23-25
　history, 19-20
　social elements, 33-34
　as store of value, 21-22
　as unit of account, 22
money laundering, 239-240, 253
　UK and, 256-257
　US and, 256-257
mortgages, subprime lending crisis, 38-40
Musk, Elon
　COVID-19 safety, 131-132
　free speech and, 126-127
　SpaceX, 132
　Starlink, 132
　US election, 140
MyTeks couriers, 212

N

Nakamoto, Satoshi, 151-152
Napster, 148
narrative fallacy, 271-272
NASA (National Aeronautics and Space Administration), 132-133
nationalism, 189-192
　nationalists on issues, 203
　racism, 203-204
　reemergence, 200-204
　white supremacy and, 203-204
National Science Foundation, 78
naval blockade, 69
neoliberalism, 88-89
neo-nationalism
　BRIC/BRICS/BRICS+, 206-208
　climate change, 194-195
　consequences, 209-210
　France, 195-197
　social media and, 204

INDEX

trade wars, 193-194
world order, changing, 205
New Deal, 84-85
NFTs (non-fungible tokens), 29, 163-165
Nineteenth Amendment to US Constitution, 261-262
Nixon, Richard M., 67-68, 242-243

O

Obama, Barack, 116
OCC (Office the Comptroller of the Currency), 119
Occupy Wall Street (OWS), 181-182
OECD (Organisation for Economic Co-operation and Development), 256-257
OFAC (Office of Foreign Assets Control), 72-73
Official Election Defense Fund, 272-273
offshoring work, 129
oligarchs, 202-204
Onyx, 152
opacity in finance, 237-245
OpenAI
  AGI Readiness, 251-252
  fair use and, 128
Opn Sesame, 273
opportunism, authoritarianism and, 292
OSRD (Office of Scientific Research and Development), 78

P

PACs (political action committees), 177
  data weaponization and, 184-185
  Meta, 177
  Musk, Elon, 276n
  Save America, 273n
Pahlka, Jennifer, 120

pandemics
  Bush, George W., 101-102
  globalism and, 199-200
  team disbanding by Donald Trump, 102-103
Paris Agreement, 194
partisanship
  abortion, 104
  COVID-19, 101-103
  gun laws, 104
  Infrastructure Investment and Jobs Act, 104-105
  September 11 attacks, 100
  toxicity, 104-105
Patriot Act, 100, 241
payment
  methods, evolution, 23-24
  Swift, 54-55
Perlman, Noah, 255
pinkwashing, 343-344
political dysfunction, 104. *See also* partisanship
  privatization, 134-136
political partisanship, 7-8
  privatization and, 134-136
politicians, corporation contributions, 305-307
PolitiFact, 272
population growth, economic growth and, 232
portability of business, 138-139
PoS (proof of stake), 154
post-democracy world, 292-293
PoW (proof of work), 154
Powell, Enoch, 189-192
PR (public relations), social engineering and, 266
PRA (Prudential Regulation Authority), 50
privacy
  erosion, social media and, 142-143
  Identity Theft Resource Center, 150

law enforcement, 324-325
rights, 322-325
ZKPs (zero-knowledge proofs), 324
private equity, transparency and, 247-248
privatization
corporate taxes, 133-134
employment law, 129-131
fair use, 128-129
free speech and, 125-126
infrastructure, 133
political partisanship, 134-136
safety protection, 131-132
space exploration, 132-133
tech companies, 133
utilities, 133
Project Kuiper, 132
public relations. *See* PR (public relations)
PWBM (Penn Wharton Budget Model), 115-116

Q-R

QAnon, 188

racism, nationalism and, 203-204
Rand, Ayn, 247
Raskin, Jamie, 8-14
Raytheon, 77
RCEP (Regional Comprehensive Economic Partnership), 302
real estate, NFTs and, 165
refugee movement, 224-226
regulatory frameworks
awareness of industries, 178-179
banking, 119-121
democracy preservation, 329
domestic, 50-51
Facebook targeted ads, 184
gaps, fintech and, 256

IMF (International Monetary Fund), 48
international, 47-50
national, 50
principle-based policies, 316-317
transparency and, 252-253
unelected officials, 318
reserve currency, 63
reserve diversification, 296
reshoring work, 129
RIAA (Recording Industry Association of America), 148
Ricardo, David, 198
Richardson, Heather Cox, 204
right-wing extremism, 10
Rivers of Blood speech (Powell), 191-192
robber barons, 82-83
Roosevelt, Franklin Delano
Bretton Woods Conference, 61
GI Bill, 106
gold standard and, 65-66
Roosevelt, Theodore, 83
RTX Corporation, 77
RWA (right-wing authoritarianism), 290-291
RWAs (real-world assets), 161-162

S

SAC Capital, 254
Salesforce messages, January 6th attack, 10
sanctions, 58-60, 72-74, 307-309
Sandy Hook shooting, 319
Save America PAC, 273n
SDNs (specially designated nationals), 73
SEC (Securities and Exchange Commission), 50, 85, 120
semiconductors, innovation and, 231-232

INDEX

September 11 attacks, 99-100
   financial services industry, 241-242
Serviceman's Readjustment Act, 106
Sherman, John, 84
Sherman Antitrust Act, 83-84
Simmel, Georg, 33-34
Singapore as financial hub, 214-216
SIPC (Securities Investor Protection Corporation), 120
SLAPP (strategic lawsuit against public participation), 321
Smartmatic, 319
Smith, Adam, 25-26, 81
Smith, Charles, 77
social contract, 314-316
social elements of money, 33-34
social engineering
   Arendt, Hannah, 274-275
   attention spans, 270
   Bernays, Edward, 265-266
   bullshit asymmetry principle, 271
   collective intelligence and, 268-269
   decision-making and, 267-268
   democracy and, 327-328
   democracy preservation, 330-332
   discernment regarding information, 270-271
   Freud, Sigmund, 265
   Gloo app, 282-283
   Kentucky coal, 279-280
   lying politicians, 272
   meritocracy, 274
   Milgram, Stanley, 275
   Official Election Defense Fund, 272-273
   PR (public relations), 266
   scams, 280-282
   tobacco companies and smoking, 262-263
   Van Marken, Jacob Cornelis, 264
   virtual societal warfare, 284
socialism, 172

social media
   Annual Threat Assessment, 188
   data weaponization, 142-143
   misinformation and algorithms, 140-141
   neo-nationalism and, 204
   privacy, erosion of, 142-143
   QAnon, 188
   US Capitol attack and, 10
socioeconomic mobility, 334-335
Soviet Union fall, USD and, 70-71
SpaceX, 132
Sputnik, 78
stablecoins, 166, 297
Starlink, 132, 140
Startup Genome, 213-214
state capitalism, 290-291
steel mills of the US, 230-231
subprime mortgage lending crisis, 38-40
Swift (Society for Worldwide Interbank Financial Telecommunications), 54-55, 71-72, 295
Switzerland's neutrality, 236-237
Synapse Financial Technologies, 256

T

Tan, Anthony, 211-212
tariffs, neo-nationalism and, 193-194
TARP (Troubled Asset Relief Program), 40
Tax Cuts and Jobs Act, 114
taxes, 113-115, 133-134
tax havens in US, 257-258
tech companies. *See* Big Tech
Tech Diplomacy Network, 139
technological diplomacy, 303-304
technology
   banking, 53-55
   data privacy preservation, 323-324
   Digital Silk Road initiative, 302

fintech, 157-158
gig economy, 130
intelligence and, 269
security, 124-125
tech-savvy policymakers, 332
trust and, 170-171
user privacy, 124-125
Telecommunications Act of 1996, 88
Telegram app, 127
Tether, 166, 297
Thirty Years' War, 235-236
Thompson, Bennie G., 12
tobacco company advertising, 262-263, 276
Tornado Cash, 244
trade blocks, 300-301
trade finance, 52
trade wars, neo-nationalism and, 193-194
transparency in finance, 237
  AML (anti-money laundering), 239
  BSA (Bank Secrecy Act), 239, 249-251
  CFT (countering the financing of terrorism), 239
  CFTRA (Currency and Foreign Transactions Reporting Act), 238-239
  compliance, 253-256
  CRS (common reporting standards), 243
  crypto, 244-245
  CTA (Corporate Transparency Act), 249
  DeFi, 244-245
  FATF (Financial Action Task Force), 239
  hidden assets, 257-258
  KYC (Know Your Customer) rules, 240
  money laundering, 239-240, 253
  opposition to, 245-252

  Patriot Act, 241-242
  private equity and, 247-248
  regulatory frameworks and, 252-253
  US tax havens, 257-258
  wealth gap, 258
Treaty of Versailles, 32-33
Trump, Donald
  climate change, 194-195
  COVID-19, 102-103
  tariffs, 193-194
trust
  AI deepfakes, 189
  Big Tech, 177-180
  cognitive bias and, 175
  data weaponization and, 183-186
  deepfakes, 280
  Edelman Trust Institute Trust Barometer, 173, 179
  human nature and, 175
  information availability, 175-176
  institutional, erosion of, 280-282
  journalism and, 182-183
  social media
    algorithms, 176-177
    misinformation, 188
  technology and, 170-171
TSMC (Taiwan Semiconductor Manufacturing Company), 231
Twitter/X, 126-127, 183-186

U

Uber, 28-29, 130
UBI (universal basic income), 336
Ukraine
  Starlink and, 140
  Zelenskyy deepfake, 189
unemployment, 209
unicorns
  innovation and, 217
  Silicon Valley, 78
  Singapore, 216

INDEX

United Nations Monetary and Financial Conference. *See* Bretton Woods
universal banks, 44
USA for UNHCR (United States Association for the United Nations High Commissioner for Refugees), 224
US Capitol attack. *See* January 6th Attack on the US Capitol
US Constitution, Nineteenth Amendment, 261-262
USD (US dollar)
   Bretton Woods Conference, 61-64
   BRICS+ countries, 294
   China, 294
   cryptocurrency and, 296-298
   de-dollarization, 294-296, 299
   dominance, 69-71
   EU, 294-295
   exorbitant privilege, 64
   gold and, 63
   national currencies, 67
   Nixon shock, 67-68
   Russia, 294
US debt crisis, 310
US Department of Justice. *See* DOJ (US Department of Justice)
US national debt, 111-116

V

Value, 25-29
Van Marken, Jacob Cornelis, 264
VC (venture capital), 213
virtual societal warfare, 284
voting rights, women's suffrage, 261-262
Voting Rights Act of 1965, 86

W

wages
   American dream, 110-111
   Economic Policy Institute, 108
   federal minimum wage, 108-109
   healthcare costs, 109
   housing costs, 109
   inflation and, 33
   stagnation, 107-108
war on terror, 100
Watergate, 242-243
wealth gap
   capitalism and, 333
   transparency in finance, 258
WFA (work from anywhere), 222-224
WFH (work from home), 222-224
White, Harry Dexter, 61
white supremacy, 203-204
women's rights
   economy and, 341
   income inequality, 342
   motherhood penalty, 342
   pinkwashing, 343-344
   suffrage, 261-262
women's suffrage, 261-262
World Bank, 48-49
   International Bank for Reconstruction and Development, 61
world financial order
   Bretton Woods Conference, 61-64
   emerging, 311-312
   gold standard, 64
   post-war, 61-62
   summary of previous, 94-95
World Trade Center attacks, 99-100

X-Y-Z

Zappos, 228
ZKPs (zero-knowledge proofs), 324

www.ingramcontent.com/pod-product-compliance
Lightning Source LLC
Chambersburg PA
CBHW020530030426
42337CB00013B/792